# Practical Sports Coaching

*Practical Sports Coaching* is a thorough and engaging guide for all sports coaching students and practitioners. Drawing on real-life case studies and examples, the book is designed to develop practical coaching skills and provide readers with the methods and tools they need to become an expert coach. Structured around all facets of the coaching process, the text comprehensively covers topics such as:

- preparation for coaching
- mentoring
- the philosophy of coaching
- direct intervention
- coaching methods
- the use of modern technology.

The book's practical approach allows the reader to consider common challenges faced by coaches, suggesting solutions to performance concerns and preparing students for the realities of professional sports coaching. Online materials including presentation slides and useful weblinks make the book a complete resource for students and lecturers alike.

*Practical Sports Coaching* helps to bridge the gap between theory and practical coaching skills, and is an essential text for coaching students looking to deepen their understanding of sports coaching and experienced coaches developing their own practical skills.

**Christine Nash** is currently Deputy Head of the Institute for Sport, Physical Education and Health Sciences at the University of Edinburgh in Scotland, UK, and also Programme Director for the new online MSc in Sport Coaching and Performance. She was a national swimming coach in the UK and has coached in the USA. She is currently involved in supporting coach education with a variety of sports. She is a member of the Coaching Standards Group, the committee that endorses coach education courses in the UK. She also sits on the research committee of the International Council for Coaching Excellence.

www.routledge.com/9780415702485

# Practical Sports Coaching

Edited by
Christine Nash

Routledge
Taylor & Francis Group

LONDON AND NEW YORK

First published 2015
by Routledge
2 Park Square, Milton Park, Abingdon, Oxon OX14 4RN

and by Routledge
711 Third Avenue, New York, NY 10017

*Routledge is an imprint of the Taylor & Francis Group, an informa business*

*British Library Cataloguing in Publication Data*
A catalogue record for this book is available from the British Library

*Library of Congress Cataloging-in-Publication Data*

Practical sports coaching / edited by Christine Nash.
    pages cm
  Includes bibliographical references and index.
 1. Coaching (Athletics)   I. Nash, Christine.
  GV711.P73 2014
  796.07'7—dc23
  2014021403

ISBN: 978-0-415-70248-5 (hbk)
ISBN: 978-1-4441-7670-4 (pbk)
ISBN: 978-0-203-76756-6 (ebk)

Typeset in Perpetua & Bell Gothic
by Apex CoVantage, LLC

# Contents

# Figures

# Tables

# Templates

# Examples

# Contributors

**Christine Nash (Editor)** is currently Deputy Head of the Institute for Sport, Physical Education and Health Sciences at the University of Edinburgh in Scotland, UK, and also Programme Director for the new online MSc in Sport Coaching and Performance. She was a national swimming coach in the UK and has coached in the USA. She is currently involved in supporting coach education with a variety of sports. She is a member of the Coaching Standards Group, the committee that endorses coach education courses in the UK. She also sits on the research committee of the International Council for Coaching Excellence.

**Andy Abraham** is Principal Lecturer in and Academic Group Lead for sport coaching at Leeds Metropolitan University, UK. He has been engaged in research and teaching in sport coaching since 1997. His principal interests are in coach and coach educator practice, expertise and development. He is a voluntary coach in youth rugby union.

**Jill Clark** is a freelance consultant and technical author. She has worked in the geospatial industry for more than 20 years in software and application development, both in the UK and USA, and in consultancy. She recently co-authored *The GIS Guide to Public Domain Data* with Joseph Kerski, and is a Chartered Land Surveyor and owner of BoldPrint Ltd., a technical writing services company.

**Dave Collins** is Chair and Director of the Institute of Coaching and Performance (ICaP) within the University of Central Lancashire, UK, which focuses on a broad spectrum of human challenge. The majority of his work is in high-level sport, encompassing training and preparation, expertise in coaching and support science disciplines, skill development and refinement, and talent development. Dave is also Director of Grey Matters Consultants and a former Performance Director of UK Athletics. He has worked with more than 60 World or Olympic medallists, as well as professional sports teams, dancers, musicians and executives in business and public service.

**Penny Crisfield** was inducted into the Coaching Hall of Fame in 2005, winning the Dyson Award for coach education. She has an international reputation in coaching and coach education. She works closely with the International Council in Coach Education and has led master classes in Canada and China. Recently Penny launched Version 1.1 of the International Coach Developer Framework at the Global Coaches House in Glasgow during the Commonwealth Games.

**Cedric English** is Lecturer of Sports Coaching at Edinburgh Napier University, Edinburgh, UK. Following a career as a professional cricketer in South Africa between 1992 and 2000, he moved to Scotland where he continued to play and coach, representing Scotland between 2004 and 2005. Over this period he built up experience in coaching and talent development pathways in England, Scotland, South Africa and New Zealand. He is currently completing his PhD in the area of Talent Development and Coach Learning in South Africa cricket.

**Shirley Gray** is Lecturer in Physical Education at the University of Edinburgh, UK. Her background is in both sports coaching and physical education teaching. Her main research interests are coaching/teaching pedagogy, more specifically in relation to teaching decision-making skills in team games.

**Edward Hall** is a PhD student at the University of Edinburgh, UK, examining the coaching process within women's rugby. Following roles in community rugby development, he moved into adult performance sports coaching in 2006. Edward has coached in university, premiership, county, regional and national development domains across a spectrum of performers from novice athletes to World Cup winners, males and females.

**Mohamad Faithal Haji Hassan** obtained his Bachelor of Sport Science (Hons) degree with a major in Sport Psychology and Coaching from the University of Malaya, Malaysia. He also has a Diploma in Physical Education (PE) from Malaysian Ministry of Education. He was a secondary school PE teacher between 1989 and 2000. In 2001 he joined the University of Malaya, Malaysia, as a tutor and pursued his Master of Applied (Sport Coaching) in the University of Queensland, Australia. Upon his return, he was appointed as a lecturer in Science of Coaching. His interest in motivational climate has motivated him to pursue his research in this area for his PhD thesis. He gained his Doctor of Philosophy in Coaching Science from UWIC (now Cardiff Metropolitan University) in 2011. Now, Faithal is the Deputy Director in the Sport Centre, University of Malaya, and he works very closely with high-performance athletes and coaches.

**Peter Horton** is a Senior Lecturer in the School of Education at James Cook University, Australia, and Fellow of the Cairns Institute. He is a member of two regional boards of the *International Journal of the History of Sport* and is on the Editorial Board of *International Sport Studies*. He has a range of research interests looking at the sociocultural analysis of historical and contemporary dimensions of sport, Olympic studies, coach education and physical education and health. Historical, sociological and cultural studies of sport in Australia, China, the Asia Pacific region, southeast Asia and Brazil are significant features of his recently published work. An elite athlete and coach himself, he is a confessed sport tragic.

**Joseph Kerski** is a geographer who believes that spatial analysis through digital mapping can transform education and society through better decision making using the geographic perspective. He holds three degrees in geography and has served as geographer and cartographer at NOAA, the US Census Bureau, and the US Geological Survey. He teaches online and face-to-face courses at primary and secondary schools, through MOOCs, and universities such as the University of Denver, USA. Since 2006 he has served as Education Manager for Esri, focused on thought leadership in geospatial technology education. This includes GIS-based curriculum development, research in the effectiveness of GIS in education, professional development for educators and fostering partnerships to support GIS in formal and informal education at all levels, internationally. He has written such books as *Spatial Mathematics* and *The Essentials of the Environment*, and co-authored *The GIS Guide to Public Domain Data* with Jill Clark.

**John Kiely** is Senior Lecturer in Elite Performance at the University of Central Lancashire, UK, having previously experienced life as an international competitor, coach, sports scientist and strength and conditioning specialist. During this time John worked directly with the coaches of Olympic and World Champions in three major sports. He has coached a Paralympic track medallist and European champion, numerous combat-sport athletes and lots (and lots!) of kids.

**Áine MacNamara** is Senior Lecturer in Elite Performance in the Institute of Coaching and Performance at the University of Central Lancashire, UK. Her research is focused on talent development across performance domains and she is particularly interested in the role that psychological characteristics play in the realisation of potential. In collaboration with colleagues, this research has been published in peer-reviewed journals as well as applied applications within different performance systems (e.g., education, sport). Other research interests include the development of expertise, performance enhancement and coaching.

**Amanda Martindale** is Lecturer in Sport and Performance Psychology at the University of Edinburgh, UK. She is a Chartered Psychologist (BPS Division of Sport and Exercise) and has provided psychology support to numerous elite-level athletes across a range of sports. Her research interests include accessing expert cognition, developing professional expertise and mindfulness approaches to performance enhancement. She is particularly interested in the development of professional judgement and decision-making expertise and is fascinated by how professionals make difficult decisions in complex, high-stakes and time-pressured environments.

**Russell Martindale** is a Chartered Sport and Exercise Psychologist and has been researching and working in the area of talent identification and development since 2000. He has been a professional youth sport coach in the UK, USA and Australia and now works exclusively as a sport psychologist. He has worked with athletes across a variety of different sports, ranging from development level to Olympic/World medallists. Russell has also worked with coaches and National Governing Bodies to help facilitate effective talent development environments.

**Steve Mckeown** is Senior Lecturer on the BSc Sports Coaching course at Leeds Metropolitan University, UK. Over the past 25 years Stephen has worked in a Zimbabwean rural school, as Sports Development Officer for Sheffield City Council and as Assistant Headteacher and Director of PE and Sport at a Specialist Sports College in Sheffield, UK. Stephen is a staff tutor and under-16 performance coach for Volleyball England. Stephen has particular interest in children's acquisition and development of Fundamental Movement and Behavioural Skills

(FMBS). He is currently undertaking action research on how key principles of functional stability can enhance children's learning of FMBS and sports-specific skills.

**Terry McMorris** initially trained as a schoolteacher and taught for 17 years before undertaking a Master of Physical Education degree in coaching science at the University of New Brunswick, Canada. Terry also played semi-professional football and cricket and became a Fully Qualified Football Association Coach (equivalent of the modern-day UEFA A license). After returning from Canada he was Director of the Centre of Excellence (forerunners of the Academy system) at Middlesbrough FC and, later, as youth team coach at Hartlepool United FC. Terry became Professor of Motor Behaviour at the University of Chichester in 2005, Emeritus Professor in 2009 and was Visiting Professor at Edinburgh University from 2009 to 2012. He has written two books on coaching/motor learning and over 70 papers in peer-reviewed journals, and he has given presentations in more than 10 countries.

**Sarah McQuade** is Director of E.T.C. Consultants, a coach development consultancy practice. Her career has included teaching physical education and lecturing and coaching in the UK, Australia and the USA before working as an education consultant at sportscoachUK. She has worked with various UK and international governing bodies and sports organisations specialising in coach education and coach development. She now splits her time between the UK and the USA, working as an adjunct professor at Westfield State University, USA.

**Gareth Morgan** is Senior Lecturer and MSc Sport Coaching programme leader at Leeds Metropolitan University, UK. His research and teaching interests include the areas of talent development, annual/longer-term planning, and the development of players' psychobehavioural skills through coaching. He has been an Academy Football Coach since 2001.

**Kevin Morgan** gained a BA (hons) degree in human movement studies and a PGCE in physical education (PE) from South Glamorgan Institute of Higher Education, UK, and began his career as a secondary school PE teacher. In 1993 he moved into higher education as a teacher trainer at De Montfort University (DMU), Bedford, and in 2000 he joined Cardiff Metropolitan University (formerly, UWIC) as a senior lecturer in sport and physical education. In 2006 he became Programme Leader for the MSc Coaching Science programme at UWIC. His particular research interests are in motivational climate and teaching and learning methods. Kevin gained an MPhil in 2000 at DMU and a PhD from UWIC in 2006 focusing on the teaching approaches that promote an effective motivational climate in PE lessons.

**Bob Muir** is Senior Lecturer in Sport Coaching at Leeds Metropolitan University, UK. His teaching, research and consultancy interests focus on coaching pedagogy and practice, coach education, learning and professional development. Bob is also a highly experienced basketball coach, working predominantly with senior national league teams.

**Julian North** is Senior Research Fellow at Leeds Metropolitan University, UK. His research interests include the components and processes underpinning participant and performer development and coaching and how social scientific research ideas help or (or otherwise) to inform practitioners. He has worked for a range of private, public and higher-education organisations in a variety of social and sport research roles in both the UK and Australia.

**Sergio Lorenzo Jiménez Sáiz** is Lecturer and Head of MSc Sport Science and Nutrition at the European University of Madrid, Spain. His main areas of interest are in talent development, coach education and notational analysis in team sports. He has published more than 20 papers in these areas. Also, Sergio is a Professional Basketball Coach in Estudiantes (Spanish Club) and he was Spanish Championship U20 winner in 2006.

**John Sproule** is Senior Lecturer within the Institute of Sport, Physical Education and Health Sciences at the University of Edinburgh, UK. Examples of his consultancy activity include work in coach education for the International Division of the English Sports Council in the West Indies; evaluation research for the Australian Sports Commission in Australia; World Cup acclimation for the Scottish rugby squad; acclimation consultant for Commonwealth Games athletes and elite ultra-distance athletes participating in the Marathon Des Sables. He has a lead role within international education through the International Baccalaureate Organisation.

**John Stoszkowski** is Lecturer in Sports Development and Coaching in the Institute of Coaching and Performance at the University of Central Lancashire (UCLan), UK. His research is focused on the psychosocial aspects of coach development and he is also actively researching the field of talent development. Prior to joining UCLan, John was a Regional Coaching Development Manager at the Professional Golfers' Association and also worked in sports development at The English Golf Union. He has also been involved in the development and management of school coaching programmes and teacher training, as well as coaching football, for a number of years.

**Kevin Till** is currently a lecturer on the BSc Sports Coaching course at Leeds Metropolitan University, UK. His main areas of research are paediatric physiology, strength and conditioning, talent identification and development with a specific focus on youth sport. Kevin has approximately 10 years experience of working as a strength and conditioning coach within rugby league, football and cricket.

# Chapter summaries

## CHAPTER 1: THE ROLE OF THE COACH

In this chapter the scope, nature, importance and complexity of the role of a sports coach is reviewed and interrogated. It not only delves into the vast range of associated roles and functions, but also outlines the responsibilities associated with the undertaking at all levels. However, no attempt is made to 'define' the role as no consensus exists as to the definition of the term 'coach' or the roles coaches are required to assume. The key message is that every coaching context is different, every athlete or team is different *and* so too is every coach. This chapter deliberately problematises the role of the coach and in doing so prepares the reader for the scope and intensity of the subsequent sections of this text. Coaching, is after all, the 'serious' side of the fun and joy sport proffers!

## CHAPTER 2: PLANNING YOUR COACHING: A FOCUS ON YOUTH PARTICIPANT DEVELOPMENT

This chapter provides a broad overview of the planning process in sport coaching, particularly aimed at the youth participant, although the principles are valid in every coaching context. The benefits of pre-planning can be seen at all levels of a sport, whether it is short term or long term. The different elements that are involved in a coaching programme all require careful consideration and planning which, traditionally, coaches do not consider as important as the delivery aspects of coaching. There is a saying in sport, 'fail to prepare, prepare to fail'. To this end a coach needs to be organised and prepared, both in the short and long term. The largely sequential view of coaching suggests that improved performance can be attained through a planned, coordinated and progressive process.

## CHAPTER 3: THE IMPORTANCE OF A COACHING PHILOSOPHY

This chapter discusses the importance of a coaching philosophy to practicing sport coaches. Globally, many coach education programmes include aspects examining coaching philosophy and the subsequent development of a personal coaching philosophy. According to researchers in sport coaching, the development of a coaching philosophy should be grounded in developmental psychology, particularly for coaches involved in youth sport.

Philosophy underpins all aspects of coaching, and by creating a formal philosophy coaches may improve their coaching effectiveness and subsequently develop their practice. The role that coaches fulfil is based on their experience, knowledge, values, opinions and beliefs, but how coaches frame their role and form their philosophy is still unclear. A philosophy is based upon beliefs, those formed through sport as a participant and coach, and based upon educational background and life experiences. A personal coaching philosophy can be viewed as a tool to enable coaches to question their practice and develop their own understanding and knowledge, as well as their performers.

## CHAPTER 4: THE COMPETITION ENVIRONMENT

Today's athletes, whether recreational or elite, run and swim faster, throw farther and jump higher than their competitors from the past. The coach must create a healthy competitive environment that allows the athletes to succeed, breeding confidence and further success. But how does the coach manage all the factors that contribute to successful competitive performance? This chapter examines how the coach manages the competition environment in the lead up to competition, during the actual event and the aftermath. Competition can cause performers to react negatively to the pressure and the sport coach needs to understand how to integrate all these pressures into practice in a manner that allows athletes to perform at their best during competition.

## CHAPTER 5: THE PRACTICE SESSION: CREATING A LEARNING ENVIRONMENT

Practice results in learning which means a relatively permanent change in performance. Learning can be explicit or implicit. Schmidt's Schema Theory suggests that, during practice, we develop recall and recognition schemas. The recall schema is responsible for the choice and imitation of action, while the recognition schema evaluates ongoing activity and makes appropriate changes to the action. According to Dynamical Systems theorists, practice allows us to become attuned to affordances. To cognitivists, quality instruction, verbal or visual or both, is necessary, whereas Dynamical Systems theorists believe that all the coach needs to do is set the goals.

Practice can be whole, part or part-progressive. The success of practice can be affected by scheduling, with blocked practice producing superior immediate, post-practice performance, but random and serial practice resulting in better learning following a period of no practice. Similarly, variability of practice aids error labelling and so better quality learning. Quality of learning during and after practice can also be aided by the coach providing good quality feedback. Feedback should be intelligible to the learner and of the appropriate precision. Beginners require a lot of prescriptive feedback, while experienced performers benefit better from descriptive feedback and less of it.

In order to ensure commitment from the athletes, coaches can use performance profiling and regularly provide their athletes with updates concerning development by using some form of testing and feedback in such forms as learning curves.

## CHAPTER 6: THE PRACTICE SESSION: CREATING A MOTIVATIONAL CLIMATE

This chapter has outlined achievement goal theory (AGT) and the different types of motivational climate that can be fostered by coaches, parents and peers, particularly in practice sessions. The primary focus has been on providing practical strategies for coaches on how to foster an effective learning environment by manipulating the TARGET structures (Ames 1992; Epstein 1989) to be 'mastery' involving. Such a motivational climate is focused on individual effort, improvement and learning and provides equal opportunity for all participants to achieve their full potential in sport and to enjoy their sporting experiences. Social factors in coaching are also considered to be crucial in fostering a positive motivational climate. Theory and research has been presented throughout the chapter to justify the practical and social strategies suggested for sports coaches. It is hoped that this chapter will enhance the quality of the motivational climate created by coaches and help to foster a learning environment that encourages long-term involvement and motivation in sport for all ages and all levels of participation.

## CHAPTER 7: THE PRACTICE SESSION: TALENT DEVELOPMENT

Talent identification and development is an important part of youth sports coaching and it is clear that coaches and significant others play an important role at every stage. This chapter provides an understanding of how young people develop from novice to elite level. It also outlines common pitfalls and misconceptions about the necessary requirements and characteristics of talented youngsters (such as early selection, specialisation and win focus). Implications for effective talent development are provided, with practical examples of what coaches can do to facilitate the process and help to develop the potential of all young people within their influence.

## CHAPTER 8: COACHING TACTICS

The purpose of this chapter is to develop the readers' knowledge and understanding of coaching tactics in games. This is an important issue in coach development because tactical knowledge is a critical component of coaching expertise. In doing so, it has identified tactics from team invasion games, central net and wall games as well as striking and fielding games. Moreover, it suggests that the development of players' tactical understanding can impact positively on their decision-making performance during games play. This chapter has also introduced the reader to the game-focused, player-centred approaches to coaching to demonstrate the ways in which coaches can enhance player tactical knowledge and decision-making skill. It has stressed the need for coaches to simplify, or complicate, game tactics to provide their players with developmentally appropriate game forms that continue to make authentic decision-making demands on their players, even players at an early stage of the learning process. To further develop the readers' knowledge and understanding of the issues described, the theories of learning that attempt to explain how players develop decision-making skills were also presented. It is hoped that this chapter encourages coaches to continue to develop their knowledge of tactics, coaching tactics and player learning so that they have the knowledge and skills to improve their players' game performance, thus providing them with success, confidence and enjoyment in games participation and learning.

## CHAPTER 9: HOW COACHES LEARN AND DEVELOP

Learning is a complex area and there is no all-embracing theory of learning that is best for educating coaches. As well as formal learning, such as organised coach education courses, coaches can also learn in a more *ad hoc* manner, informally, non-formally and self-directed. Coaching has a long history, which can be traced back to Socrates, who believed that individuals learn best when they have ownership of a situation and take some form of personal responsibility for the outcome. This chapter gives sport coaches the necessary tools to understand the best methods for their development, given their experience and particular coaching context.

## CHAPTER 10: EMOTIONAL INTELLIGENCE

This chapter examines emotional intelligence and its use in sports coaching. Developing more emotionally intelligent coaches means they remain in post longer, are more effective and feel better about their jobs. It has been found that Olympic athletes, world class musicians and chess grand masters all have one specific attribute in common: all participate in consistent and repetitive training over a prolonged period of time. This implies they have an emotional strength in the area of self-discipline. Coaches with a high level of emotional intelligence will be more effective, will be better able to motivate and relate to players and support staff, will have improved problem-solving and decision-making capabilities and will be better prepared to resolve conflicts in the workplace. An important aspect of emotional intelligence is the notion that it is trainable and, therefore, coaches could seek to enhance it. The ability of coaches to recognise their own or their players' emotions or moods plays an important role in the process of leadership, so including emotional intelligence training and support builds abilities such as self-awareness, self-management, self-motivation, empathy and social skills.

## CHAPTER 11: MENTORING AS A COACH DEVELOPMENT TOOL

Mentoring is acknowledged to be a dynamic, reciprocal relationship within a working environment, generally involving an individual with more experience in a specific field (the mentor) and a less experienced individual, often a beginner in that field. Within the practical coaching situation, mentoring can be a valuable tool for coaches, enabling them to learn by relating theory into actual coaching environments. The mentor can be instrumental in helping to develop many skills necessary for self-development, such as decision making, self-reflection and critical thinking.

This chapter examines models of mentoring, the impact of mentoring and the evaluation of mentoring programmes. Many sports organisations endorse mentoring and promote mentoring programmes, but there are great differences in approach, support, organisational importance and depth.

# CHAPTER 12: REFLECTIVE PRACTICE

- Reflection tends to focus interactively on the outcomes of the action, the action itself and the intuitive knowing implicit in the action (Schön 1991).
- It is this entire process of reflection which Schön (1991) describes as being central to the ways in which practitioners can deal well with situations of uncertainty, instability, uniqueness and conflict that are so apparent in sports coaching practice.
- If carried out effectively, reflective practice can help sports coaches develop a better understanding of their own coaching practice and chart the progress of their professional development.
- Reflective practice has the potential to significantly influence the effectiveness of your coaching practice and, as such, is worthy of due care and consideration in the set-up, conduct and evaluation of your coaching.
- It is certainly worth clarifying exactly 'what' we should reflect on as this will almost certainly have extensive ramifications for the quality of the process and indeed whether or not it is worthwhile. Objects of reflection may include intuitive judgement, knowledge, decision making, coaching philosophy and the role of the coach.
- It helps if the criteria against which the reflection will be made are stated up front. These can be a combination of planned for/predicted outcomes, theoretically informed methods (e.g. on pedagogy) or sport-relevant developmental pathways.
- Reflection-in-action may be like a 'sketchpad' for the sports coach to try out various solutions to difficult problems (Schön 1991).
- It is certainly worth reviewing your current reflective practice techniques to ensure you are getting as much as possible from the process (e.g. by considering the content of your reflection or 'what' you are reflecting on and how much you get out of this).
- It is worth establishing trusting relationships with colleagues whom you can contact to 'check your thinking' or act as a 'sounding board' for your framing, intentions and actions.
- It is also possible to develop the skill of self-reflective awareness (e.g. using mindfulness training) and it may be that additional practice such as this can provide the scaffolding to support the further development of this skill within a coaching context.

# CHAPTER 13: LEARNING THROUGH COMMUNITIES OF PRACTICE IN SPORT COACHING

Coaches will benefit from being part of a larger community to construct solutions to coaching problems that they face and this can be done on an informal basis. These can be considered as communities of practice (CoP). Coaching can be a lonely activity, and by using social interaction, authentic activity and participation within communities of practice, coaches are better able to construct meaning in practical ways. This enables knowledge to be applied outside of formal learning settings. Within some sports organisations and club environments there are sufficient coaches for this to occur organically, however Culver and Trudel (2006) advocated the importance of a facilitator in the process, to ensure a positive learning outcome. This chapter reviews the concept and development of communities of practice within sports organisations. It stresses the importance of the organisational culture and, using a real-life example of cricket in South Africa, shows the impact of administrative shortfalls on coaching effectiveness.

## CHAPTER 14: TECHNOLOGY IN SPORTS COACHING

This chapter focuses on the use of digital technologies in sports coaching for recording, analysing and reporting sports-related data. Although using technology in sport in nothing new, the last few years have seen the emergence of some innovative tools and techniques that have revolutionised both the amount and type of information that's available to a coach. Video cameras, laser timing and tracking applications, the latest wearable technology and a host of increasingly miniaturised sensors are now everyday items in the coach's toolkit. However, with increasing choice and sophistication of available technologies also come additional challenges to choose the technology that is most appropriate for a particular coaching application and to acquire the necessary skills to use the technology effectively.

## CHAPTER 15: USING GEOTECHNOLOGY TOOLS IN SPORTS COACHING

This chapter focuses on the use of geotechnologies in sports coaching for the display, analysis and reporting of sports-related spatial data, the management and planning of coaching programmes and the implementation of various policies relating to sports coaching. Although the use of GPS devices to track athletes and activities is now widespread, the adoption of analytical tools to interpret and present that data is still relatively uncommon. Given the inherently spatial nature of sport, these new techniques for data collection and data analysis are set to have a significant impact on sports coaching.

## REFERENCES

Ames, C. (1992) Achievement goals, motivational climate and motivational processes. In *Motivation in Sport and Exercise*. Roberts, G. C. (ed.) (Champaign, IL: Human Kinetics): 161–176.

Culver, D. and Trudel, P. (2006) Cultivating coaches' communities of practice: Developing the potential for learning through interactions. In *The Sports Coach as Educator: Re-conceptualising Sports Coaching*. Jones, R. (ed.) (London: Routledge): 97–112.

Epstein, J. (1989) Family structures and student motivation: A developmental perspective. In *Research on Motivation in Education*. Ames, C. and Ames, R. (eds.) (New York: Academic Press) 3: 259–295.

Schön, D. (1991) *The reflective practitioner: How professionals think in action*. (Aldershot: Ashgate).

# Preface

Sport coaches play a major role in enabling successful sport experiences for various groups whether their interest is coaching for participation or performance. This book synthesises the current state of sport coaching and provides an update on sports coaching best practice. The problems and issues faced by sports coaches on a daily basis are highlighted in a number of statements from practicing coaches at varying levels of qualification and experiences, with supporting case studies based on real coaching scenarios.

*Practical Sports Coaching* is aimed at experienced coaches who wish to extend their capacity by engaging in learning that promotes analysis and critical reflection of their coaching practice. The book is divided into five sections:

> Section 1 covers the non-intervention coaching elements, such as planning, philosophy and the role of the coach.
> Section 2 examines the many environments that coaches have to consider, for example competition, learning and talent development.
> Section 3 considers how coaches learn and develop to meet the needs of the differing populations they are coaching.
> Section 4 investigates the use of technology, in particular digital technology, which is now becoming available to coaches at all levels to incorporate into their coaching practice.
> Section 5 pulls together all the elements in the book that contribute to expert coaching.

Sport coaching is emerging as a subject that can be studied at university at both undergraduate and postgraduate level. However, the process of professionalisation in sport coaching is not linear. Generally, a profession is expected to have a scholarly grounding in an academic discipline with a body of knowledge, skills and research in that domain, yet Eraut defines the concept of a profession as 'the social control of expertise' (2002, p. 2). The apparent lack of a defined career pathway and professional recognition could affect the selection, employment and deployment of potential coaches. This has obvious implications for coach learning and development. 'Coaching is a complex mix of behaviours, characteristics, knowledge and effectiveness, yet coaches often have not had or not taken the opportunity to be trained' (Kidman 2001, p. 15).

## REFERENCES

Eraut, M. (2002) *Developing professional knowledge and competence.* (London: Routledge Falmer).

Kidman, L. (2001) *Developing decision-makers: An empowerment approach to coaching.* (Christchurch, New Zealand: Innovative).

# Acknowledgements

This book has been a labour of love – at times rewarding, other times frustrating but generally enjoyable. I have really enjoyed the debates, discussions and collaborations with the other authors that have culminated in this book. These authors need to be congratulated for their professional contributions and the high quality of their work. I would also like to thank the anonymous coaches who allowed us to include their thoughts, opinions and reflections to make this book as authentic and practical as possible. Any quotes from such coaches and administrators appearing within this text were taken from interviews with coaches and administrators in South Africa, Scotland, USA, Canada, Ireland, Australia, Wales and England between 2011 and 2014. Names were kept anonymous to protect the interviewees' identities.

# Foreword

*Penny Crisfield*

Coaches are playing an increasingly important and diverse role in sport and the community in the UK and globally. Coaches are also engaging with a broader range of participants who place significantly greater demands on them. They are not only expected to coach the sport technically and tactically but to coach and develop the person physically, emotionally, socially and cognitively as well.

The International Council for Coaching Excellence (ICCE) has defined sports coaching as '*the guided improvement of sports participants in a single sport at identifiable stages of partici-pant development*' (ICCE Coaching Framework, 1.2, 2013, p. 14) and claim that '*coaching is in its most dynamic era in history*' (ICCE Coaching Framework, 1.2, 2013, p. 7). The ICCE has responded to this challenge by harnessing and coordinating the skills and expertise of coaching experts across the globe to produce an international coaching framework. This provides a research-based, authoritative and flexible reference document to provide sports federations, coaching organisations, international federations and educational institutions with good practice guidelines to support the design, benchmarking and refinement of their coach education and development programmes. It emphasises that this is not a '*set of proposed mandates*' but stresses the need for '*multiple effective approaches . . . tailored to sport- and country-specific circumstances*'. In *Practical Sports Coaching*, Chapter 1 focuses on the role of the coach, Chapter 2 on planning and Chapter 3 on coaching philosophy. Other chapters explore the growing range of skills and knowledge required of coaches today (for example talent iden-tification is discussed in Chapter 7, tactical coaching and decision training in Chapter 8, emotional intelligence in Chapter 10, digital technology in Chapter 14 and geotechnologies in sport coaching in Chapter 15).

Coaches, alongside coach developers, sport scientists and sports organisations, have a responsibility to improve and expand their capabilities and expertise to support the athletes and communities they serve. Coaching expertise has been defined as '. . . *the consistent applica-tion of integrated professional, interpersonal and intrapersonal knowledge to improve athletes' competence, confidence, connection and character in specific coaching contexts*' (Côté and Gilbert 2009). Chapter 12 deals with the all-important skill of self-reflection while Chapter 16 discusses how coaches become experts.

Coaches develop their skills and knowledge in a range of ways. Much is unmediated learn-ing (without the guidance or input of someone else) and often comes through hands-on expe-rience, informally: 'the lifelong process by which every person acquires and accumulates knowledge, skills, attitudes and insights from daily experiences and exposure to the environ-ment' (Combs and Ahmed 1974, p. 8).

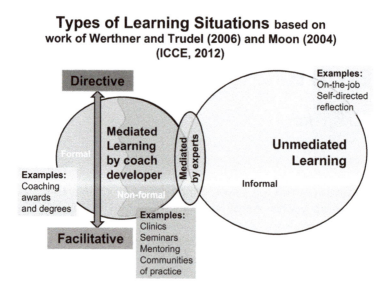

**Types of Learning Situations** based on
work of Werthner and Trudel (2006) and Moon (2004)
(ICCE, 2012)

*Figure F1* Types of learning situations.

Some learning is mediated by someone else, often a more experienced coach or a coach developer. The term 'coach developer' has been coined by the ICCE to describe those '*trained to develop, support and challenge coaches to go on honing and improving their knowledge and skills in order to provide positive and effective sport experiences for all participants*' (Crisfield *et al.* 2012). Coach developers include all those who have undergone training to fulfil one or more of the following roles: coach educators, learning facilitators, presenters, mentors and assessors. They need to be experts in learning as well as experts in coaching and in the context of the coaches with whom they will work.

Coach developers respond to coaches' needs and the context in which they operate by providing and facilitating a range of formal and non-formal learning opportunities. They are able to synthesise the input of more experienced coaches and experts, assess coaches and encourage them to take responsibility for their ongoing development. They act as role models of best practice, portraying a growth mind set, critical reflective skills and a hunger for personal improvement. Coach developers are able to help coaches to become 'learning coaches' (Armour 2010) by teaching them how to learn and reflect, as covered in Chapter 9.

It appears from the research that all types of learning situations are important to coaches. Learning will be most beneficial if it is appropriate for the context, if it is delivered over a short time frame and where cost is not an obstacle (Kathy Brook 2011, unpublished paper). It should mirror the complex and changing environment in which coaches operate. Effective coach development should therefore offer a blended learning package comprising all types of learning opportunities and must be based on sound learning theories and adult learning principles. This promotes learning and behavioural change and encourages coaches to take responsibility for additional self-directed learning. In *Practical Sports Coaching*, Chapter 4 discusses the competitive environment and Chapter 6 examines how to create the learning environment.

Traditionally coach developers have focused their role on mediated 'formal' education (coaching awards and degree programmes) and to a lesser extent on 'informal' opportunities (for example through clinics, seminars, mentoring and communities of practice). Mediated coach education (especially in formal learning situations) is often classroom-based, assessment focused and qualification based. However, research suggests that coaches learn more from practical experience and interaction with other coaches (Carter and Bloom 2009), so there is a need to take formal coach education out of the classroom and onto the track, gym, pool or court. Simulated micro-coaching in formal mediated situations, mentorships and clinics in non-formal mediated situations would therefore be advocated.

The all-important unmediated learning situations have largely been left to chance. Yet there is considerable evidence to support the contention that unmediated learning contributes significantly to a coach's learning (Fraser-Thomas and Cote 2009). '*Unmediated learning situations should be considered an important way to learn because the meaningfulness of the material of learning is probably high*' (Werthner and Trudel 2006, p. 204). However, they noted that the effectiveness of unmediated learning may depend on '*coaches' ability to learn by themselves, their openness and eagerness to create new learning opportunities and the fact that coaches cannot look for information on a topic if they do not know it exists*'. While coach developers can have no direct impact here, the very best coach developers can and do encourage this type of learning by teaching coaches self-reflective skills, encouraging critical thinking, signposting new learning and creating a learning environment that encourages and fosters coaches to become 'learning coaches', self-motivated, with a passion for further development and learning and a willingness to take responsibility for their own development and learning. Similarly coach developers may impact positively on the likelihood of incidental learning and unconscious self-reflection (internal learning). If unmediated learning is be encouraged, there may be a need to find ways to recognise evidence from this source as an acceptable contribution towards professional development, accreditation, qualification and licensing. The ability to stimulate and trigger unmediated learning may well be an important challenge for coach developers and researchers to establish how this may be most effectively achieved. Chapter 9 in *Practical Sports Coaching* examines the importance of coach educators in the learning process, Chapter 10 advocates the importance of emotional intelligence training, Chapter 11 explores the potential impact of mentors on coach development while Chapter 13 reviews communities of practice.

Most sports organisations now offer formal and non-formal competence-based coach education programmes, and there is anecdotal evidence about the impact of this training on increased competence and on coaching practice. However, there has been little systematic research or longitudinal studies to show the effects of coach learning on improvements in coaching practice or on athlete outcomes. Cushion *et al.* (2010) go as far as saying that current 'approaches to coach learning remain largely uninformed explicitly by learning theory'. Sergio Lara-Bercial and Pat Duffy (2012) conclude their literature review by saying that '*while coaches acknowledge that a big part of learning happens "on the job" they would like to experience the complementary benefit of perhaps a guiding hand while they are doing so, be it in the shape of formal learning, or via interaction with a mentor or critical friend. . . . If coaching is contingent and at times unpredictable, it follows that a good dose of on-the-job experience, coupled with fair amounts of declarative knowledge and adequate support which can accelerate learning and provide guidance through turbulent waters is paramount to the development of coaching expertise*' (unpublished paper, 2012).

The importance of knowledgeable and experienced coaches is essential in the development of sport and people at all participation and performance levels. As Liam Moggan, a well respected coach developer from Ireland says, '*we can't learn for them*' and Frank Dick (former director of coaching for UK Athletics, coach of Daley Thompson and team manager during four Olympics 1979–1994) adds that '*some things can be taught, some you can only learn, the art of coaching is one*' (Dick 2013, in ICCE 2013). Frank goes on to talk of coaches as rough diamonds and advises that it is best to avoid rubbing off the edges because coaches need this to be successful. However, coaches at all times need to be open to learning and to acquiring new knowledge. They need to engage in deliberate purposeful practice; if they don't focus on what they want to develop or improve or do more, less or differently, any improvement is haphazard and a matter of luck. Coach developers therefore have a responsibility not just to be experienced coaches or transmitters of coaching knowledge but to be able to help coaches become reflective practitioners and lifelong learners. As Kathy Armour suggests, '*coach educators need new forms of learning support to enable them to model the learning approach that will inform the development of the learning coach*' (Armour 2010). *Practical Sports Coaching* goes some considerable way to help both coaches and coach developers to do just that.

## REFERENCES

Armour, K. M. (2010) The learning coach . . . the learning approach: Professional development for sports coach professionals. In *Sports Coaching: Professionalisation and Practice*. Lyle, J. and Cushion, C. (eds.) (Edinburgh).

Carter, A. D. and Bloom, G. A. (2009) Coaching knowledge and success: Going beyond athletic experiences. *Journal of Sport Behaviour,* 32(4), 419–437.

Combs, P. H. and Ahmed, M. (1974) Attacking rural poverty: How non-formal education can help P8. (Baltimore: The John Hopkins University Press).

Côté, J. and Gilbert, W. (2009) An integrative definition of coaching effectiveness and expertise. *International Journal of Sports Science and Coaching,* 4(3), 307–323.

Crisfield, P. and Brook, K. (2012) The importance of coach developers within the global coaching framework: A position statement (unpublished).

Cushion, C., Nelson, L., Armour, K. M., Lyle, J., Jones, R. L., Sandford, R., O'Callaghan, C. (2010) *Coach learning and development: A review of literature.* (Research Report for Sport Coach UK).

Fraser-Thomas, J. and Cote, J. (2009) Understanding adolescents' positive and negative developmental experiences in sport. *The Sport Psychologist,* 23, 3–23.

ICCE (2012) *International sport coaching framework.* (Champaign, IL: Human Kinetics).

ICCE (2013) *International sport coaching framework.* (Champaign, IL: Human Kinetics).

Lara-Bercial, S. and Duffy, P. (2012) Coaching 4 performance programme: Sports coaching literature review (unpublished).

Moon, J. A. (2004) *A handbook of reflective and experiential learning: Theory and practice.* (London: Routledge Falmer).

Werthner, P. and Trudel, P. (2006) A new theoretical perspective for how coaches learn to coach. *The Sport Psychologist,* 20(2), 198–212.

# Section 1

The book structure is designed to help sport coaches develop their practical sport coaching. Chapters in Section 1 are intended to address issues that coaches may face in the non-intervention phase of coaching.

- Chapter 1 examines the many roles of the coach and highlights the multi-faceted nature of coaching. The United Kingdom Coaching Strategy describes the role of the sports coach as one that '*enables the athlete to achieve levels of performance to a degree that may not have been possible if left to his/her own endeavours*'. The role of the coach varies according to the level and context of the coaching programme. It is essential that coaches recognise that roles will change and understand the contextual factors that contribute to these changes.
- Chapter 2 discusses the planning process and the various approaches to planning a coaching programme specifically designed for the youth performer. Many of these principles will hold true for other performers as planning, like coaching, is a process that can be both short and long term. Some coaches plan on a session by session basis whereas others can work on a four year programme.
- Chapter 3 assesses the importance of a coaching philosophy and the subsequent impact upon coaching practice. Philosophy underpins all aspects of coaching, and by creating a formal philosophy coaches may improve their coaching effectiveness and subsequently develop expertise. Although the role that coaches fulfil is based on their experience, knowledge, values, opinions and beliefs, how coaches frame their role and form their philosophy is still unclear.

The authors believe that these are the most important chapters to consider as part of the pre-coaching process. Coaches at every level and sport should consider aspects of planning and philosophy and how that relates to their role as a coach. The benefits of a coaching philosophy can be evaluated by long-term coaching effectiveness. Understanding how your team or individuals need to compete provides a clearer picture of how to structure sessions and the content to include in a season. This demonstrates the necessity for planning, allowing for flexibility depending on the immediate needs of performers. As a result, the role of the coach in this process becomes clearer as do the goals pursued by teams and individuals.

# Chapter 1

# The role of the coach

*Peter Horton*

This chapter will investigate the role of the coach and provide some discussion as to what being a coach involves, and in what contexts coaches operate. This initial review will provide some philosophical and academic foundations for a more thorough assessment of the role of the coach than is generally available.

Although all levels of official coaching policy, mandate, strategic plan, advertisements and manuals are required to outline a coach job description for the position they refer to, it is difficult to provide a definitive outline of what the eventual role and responsibilities of a coach will entail. Many of the current descriptions are often inadequate, minimalistic, expansive and, in some cases, legally questionable. This is particularly significant considering that in most situations, even in the most developed sporting nations such as the United Kingdom (UK), the United States (USA), New Zealand and Australia, the vast majority of coaches are volunteers. In the UK for example, approximately 70% of coaches are volunteers (sportscoachUK 2011).

The available literature contains many previous attempts at defining the role of the coach. The forms of, and motivations behind, those definitions are as diverse as the sports and the contexts in which coaches work. Similarly, the definition of the term 'coach' is also varied. For example, in elite rugby football it is the coach who leads the overall programme, while in elite football (soccer) in Europe the coach is the manager, a distinction that is sometimes subtle. To add to the complexity in defining the term 'coach' there are many different categories of coach, such as Head Coach, Director of Coaching, Assistant Coach and so on. There are also many specialist coaching roles, particularly in professional team sports such as rugby football. Those specialist roles may include Defense Coach, Offense Coach, Re-start Coach, Kicking Coach, Forwards Coach, Backs Coach, Scrum Coach and probably Coaching Coach!

This chapter will avoid providing a rigid interpretation of the role of a coach, primarily because it is impossible to predict what the role will initially involve or eventually become. This precludes any simple, meaningful definition of the role of a coach, because in many countries anyone can call himself or herself 'coach' but have no qualifications at all. Perhaps the only thing that can be stated clearly is that it would be naïve to believe that a single description of the role of a coach could suffice – one size does not fit all.

However, this lack of consensus as to the definition of a coach does not mean that attempts should not be made to establish what the position of coach should entail within each sporting context, at least on an operational level. Most coaching positions have a primary set of responsibilities that go with the role. The complexity of the coach-athlete/team relationship can be illustrated with a discussion of the impact of national coaches and their teams' performances in a World Cup or at an Olympic Games. The topics under review are likely to be based around performance outcomes; which athletes met their targets and more likely which athletes did not. However, in the context of junior teams and individual athletes, the impact of the coaches and their interactions with individuals and the teams as a whole may be more complex than that of a national coach – elite coaches are usually better resourced and supported than the volunteer coaches of junior teams. Junior coaches tend to have a widening participation, retention and fun remit. This comparison simply re-emphasises the point that all coaching roles carry varying contextual responsibilities and *all* require that the coaches, and other related staff or volunteer office holders, should have the appropriate training to perform these responsibilities effectively. As Lyle (2013, p. 25) recently proposed, 'Increasing participation and maximising the impact of sporting success are often adduced as ancillary elements of the coach's role'.

As mentioned earlier, this chapter will review selected work from the academic literature on the topic, and illustrate what the two major pillars of the coaching industry – the administrative and controlling bodies of sports and of sports coaching and the coaches themselves – believe the role of the coach to be and what the implicit responsibilities of this role are.

## COACHING PROGRAMMES: THE DOGMA

What does the industry say the role of the coach is? Not surprisingly, most descriptions drawn from current coaching material now describe the responsibilities of the coach as many and varied; coaching is now widely accepted as a multifaceted undertaking that requires those who wish to engage with/in it to have both a 'calling' and a qualification to coach. Although the majority of coaches are still volunteers, it is now a 'profession' that requires training and a range of competences, backed by an equally extensive collection of qualifications and professional standards. The accreditation process and the implementation of professional standards are established in all major sporting nations, and are administered either directly by government or adjunct national bodies. For example, in the UK sportscoachUK oversees and manages the UK Coaching Certificate system, in Australia the responsibility lies with the Australian Sports Commission and in the USA the National Coaching Accreditation Program oversees the National Coaching Registry of Coaches and the structure of all major sport coaching education programmes.

The concept of the coaching role is generally covered in many coach education courses, often at an initial level (Roetert and Lubbers 2011). Many coaches undertaking these early coaching qualifications are involved with coaching either beginner or youth participants. Young sportspeople often characterise their involvement in sport as enjoyable, challenging, for social reasons and for fitness (Weiss 2003). The role of the youth sports coach is traditionally male dominated, contributing to a stereotypical view of sport. For youth sport to overcome this perception, the number of female coaches in youth sport must increase to levels equal to their male counterparts (Leberman and LaVoi 2011; Norman 2013). This is considered important in a number of countries: the Canadian 'We are Coaches' programme was specifically designed to attract mothers into coaching at the community level (Demers 2009) and the Scottish 'Women in Coaching' programme was aimed at retaining and increasing the quality of female coaches (sportscotland 2012).

In the National Coaching Plan of Rugby Union Football in Australia in 1977, the National Director of Coaching, R.J.P. (Dickie) Marks, outlined the requirements of the job of a coach for a rugby team. He suggested that the fundamental purpose of coaching was, 'to a large extent a question of resolving complexities into simplicities' (Marks 1977, p. 3). Marks suggested that in line with 'concept coaching' the role of the coach involves three main areas of responsibility – Power, Skill and Motivation. Due to his national role, Marks' attention was centred on a team's performance and he maintained that a weakness in any one of these elements would result in the team performing poorly. He went on to briefly outline each and added a consideration of three related coaching concepts: Pressure Training, Key Factor Analysis and Environmental Prompting. As limited as this schema seems by today's standards and expectations, this represented best practice at the time. Over the next three decades his mantra has been inverted; we now strive towards turning simplicities into complexities. This will become apparent as we investigate the demands currently placed upon coaches by sporting and coaching bodies.

Three decades later, in 2007, the Level 1 Coaching Manual of the International Ice Hockey Federation (IIHF) also discusses the role of the coach in the context of three different roles – a Leader, a Teacher and an Organizer. The specific responsibilities for each role can be viewed at the IIHF website. The roles defined for an IIHF level 1 coach are clearly more demanding than that of the ARU National Coaching Plan circa 1970, as the three aspects of the coach's responsibilities are extended to incorporate fifteen specific skills. The introduction to this section in the IIHF manual provides a few words of caution for those who are just entering the fray:

> To have a positive and lasting impact on the athletes you coach, you need to be effective as a leader, teacher, and organiser; encourage and support your players; coach enthusiastically, and express genuine concern for the athletes' total well-being.
>
> Your athletes' decisions about long-term participation in hockey are largely determined by the type of impact you have on them. Your role becomes more important when you consider that the influence you have on your players extends well beyond the contact you have with them in the hockey environment.
>
> (International Ice Hockey Federation 2007)

There are many reasons why the full range of responsibilities at all levels of coaching must be documented. One of the most significant motivations for this is the increasingly litigious nature of society in the developed world and the subsequent requirements to ensure that a duty of care is at all times, and in all circumstances, not only assumed but also seen to be assumed by all qualified and ratified coaches of sport squads, teams and individual athletes. Their roles and responsibilities must be explicitly defined and published to protect all stakeholders, including the coaches.

This has a number of significant implications. First, it would be good to think that the rationale behind this documentation would be to ensure that coaches are inducted into the 'profession' and the appropriate practice of sports coaching. Second, it would be useful to ensure that coaches are continuously developing skills and professional qualifications so that they are able to assume and perform the complex array of activities coaches in all sports and at all levels are now expected to undertake. The sporting organisations and the government or government-sanctioned coaching bodies are also required, in the best interests of the coaches, to monitor the work of all their coaches, both professionals and volunteers. These coaching authorities should also, without exception, institute continuous professional development (CPD) programmes, not only to advance the skills and practices of their charges but also to make sure that the integrity and standard of their work does not decline. Having said that, as an advocate of the benefits, CPD is all about establishing a 'productive' experience for individuals and teams and for all the stakeholders, from parents to an entire nation. The critical point here is that each coaching context has different aims, objectives and demands, and no two are the same. Additionally, high-level positions carry enormous levels of pressure and responsibility for the consequences.

Putting this simply, Martens stated that, 'Sports coaches help people participating in sports to work towards achieving their full potential working with them closely to improve performance' (Martens 2012, p. 54). Martens maintained that the role of coaches embraces:

- the identification of 'needs'
- the understanding of 'context'
- an awareness of physical *and* psychological fitness and the maximisation of performance.

However, reflecting upon Martens' long-established position on the role and work of coaches, it is suggested that 'satisfaction' and 'enjoyment' would also be central features of his coaching philosophy and certainly of his own coaching practice (Martens 2012).

In competitive sport, the prioritisation of each of the four central elements of sports coaching – the sporting context, the athletes, the coach and the stakeholders – will, in many ways, characterise the nature of the entire process. The analysis of complex human activity, such as competitive sport at all levels, whether professional or not, must be subject to critical review. No matter how many roles are listed, there will always be exceptions, extensions and the need for idiosyncratic roles to be included.

All attempts to define the role of a coach must first establish the uniqueness of every situation and to consider the characteristics, needs, desires and motivations of those involved in a particular situation. This will allow specific 'jobs' to be identified and the responsibilities associated with each will be outlined in the 'contract' assumed by the person who takes up the role. This could be completed after a specific coach has been appointed. This can, and perhaps should, happen at all levels, considering some of the 'catch-all' lists that have been presented as job descriptions for coaches. It would often seem that the younger the athletes, the more diverse and certainly, in terms of the individual athlete, the more onerous the responsibilities become. This more humanistic approach would be a better fit in response to a growing awareness of responsibilities. Again, as argued earlier, this relates to sport at all levels.

Think about:

- When did you first hear about the role of the coach?
- Do you have a 'job description' that adequately covers your role?

Having argued that no definitive description of the role of the coach can be written, it would also be consistent to maintain that no definitive characterisation can be made of a squad, team or an athlete, or of the context in which a sport is coached or competitively engaged in. The following descriptions illustrate the difficulties associated with defining the boundaries and parameters of the coaching domain including the context, the athletes, the coach and the stakeholders. Before embarking on this, it must be stated that there will be an almost unlimited scope for different interpretation with respect to all descriptions, categories, characterisations and classifications.

## THE CONTEXT

The context represents the environment in which the sport and the associated coaching evolved from, is conducted in and is supported by. An analysis of the context involves a consideration of dimensions that go well beyond the literal aspects of location, geography and climate, though these are important and of significance. What *is* the sport and what is the nature of the sport: its tradition, culture, administrative status (school, club, representative, amateur, semi-professional or professional), competitive-level and age-level and, of course, is it a team or an individual sport?

The coaching context depends on the sport or activity being played and the level of participation. It also depends on the level of competitive ambitions and motivations the athlete, team, club, sport academy, franchise or representative body (region, state, county or nation) and the supporters and other stakeholders have. The nature of sport is now such that it will inevitably also be influenced by financial and economic factors. Related to this will be demographic elements of socio-economics, ethnicity and educational and occupational backgrounds of the athletes, the team or squad and their families, officials and, equally as important, the supporters.

The context, and the resolution of the associated factors, will in many ways define the challenges facing coaches. In addition, the primary consideration for the coaches will be their athletes and how they can reconcile the multitude of physical, psychological, emotional, social, cultural, ethnic, spiritual and, not least of all, athletic differences among their players.

## THE ATHLETES

Just as all coaching contexts are different, so too is every individual athlete in every single coaching situation. Adapting to change is a fundamental function of a sports coach and a primary challenge for a coach is to respond to the many challenges presented by their athletes. The response to deep-rooted personal differences including gender, age, physical development, psychology, health, culture, ethnicity, religion, family background, personality, learning type and intelligence is often combined with an equally extensive array of sport-related factors including strength, fitness, skills, strategic understanding, motivation, teamwork, group dynamics and micro-politics.

Naturally, the level of sports participation and the consequences and impact of the performance will also add to the complexity of the interplay between the coach and the athletes. The coach has to deal with an almost unimaginable number and variety of contexts, groups of players or individual athletes, each of whom is unique in terms of personality, physique, skills, experience and motivation. In addition, each coach is as unique as each athlete and, just as the athletes must be coached appropriately, so too must every 'context' be supported by an 'appropriate' coach.

## THE COACH

Every variable outlined for the context and the athletes is as relevant and significant in any discussion of the coach. As an individual, the coach is, like the athletes, the product of genetics, family environment, culture and experiences. However, the professionalism of coaches and their appropriateness for specific coaching contexts derives from both personal qualities and a range of skills, for although coaching *is* now a profession, for most it remains a voluntary community service. The paradox that this predicates was discussed over a decade ago when Nash (2001) highlighted a raft of contradictions in the UK government's policies aimed at sports coaching, which on one hand acclaimed the contribution of volunteers to the communities but on the other hand demanded that the industry move to establish higher standards of coach accreditation and closer scrutiny of the practice of coaches – in other words, become more professional. The articulation of how coaching is to become professionalised and what, in fact, the expression 'being professional' actually means remains unclear. However, it is suggested that coaches can, and should, be more 'professional' in their practice, whether they are paid or not.

How then can the suitability or appropriateness of a coach in respect to a specific context be assessed? In many real situations this exercise would be considered a luxury because in many instances there is no one else who could, or even wants, to do it. People wishing to coach, or those merely answering the pleas for a coach from desperate parents, are required to gain clearance in the first instance as to their moral and/or ethical suitability as a part of their application to become coaches. Appointing an appropriate coach for a specific post will then be, or should be, decided by matching the candidate with the position against an established set of criteria, or a role descriptor. It is now mandatory in most countries that candidates should have an appropriate coaching qualification and that their experience should be consistent with the demands of the context. It is vital that their approach and coaching philosophy (see Chapter 3) matches the level and expectations of the position, and that they are able to communicate these to their athletes and all other stakeholders.

These initial requirements are to a degree immutable, but perhaps the consideration of a person's psycho-social profile, his or her motivation and passion for the activity along with such intangible dimensions as personal demeanour, style and 'humanity' will in the end be the most significant factors in determining a candidate's appropriateness. Unfortunately this cannot be truly assessed until he or she has engaged fully in the work the position demands.

## THE STAKEHOLDERS, *ET AL.*

The complexity and variation in the role and the responsibilities of a coach have always extended well beyond the playing and coaching environments. The often repeated tales of 'pushy' parents, rabid spectators and violent clashes between supporters at junior football fixtures are legendary. There have always been committed stakeholders, the extrinsic forces that must be recognised as a part of the world of the coached sports teams. For example, football teams have become symbols of the collective identity of a community, village, town, school or university, even an ethnic group and, of course, a nation. Professional sport has become the most visible and dominant form of sport internationally. As the relationship between sport and television is now inseparable, the interface between vested interests and corporate stakeholders, the performances of athletes, teams and even entire sporting competitions and the resulting economic consequences become major considerations for the role and the performance of coaches.

The elite levels of the major team sports such as football (soccer), basketball, baseball, cricket, American and Australian Rules football, rugby union and such individual sports as golf, tennis, swimming and skiing are commercially attractive to the media and are now an integral component in the world of broadcasting, advertising, sponsorship, finance and investment. All of this is now part of the world of the elite coach. However, this has produced a natural trickle-down effect into junior sport, school sport, sports academies and the college and university sport programmes in the USA, Canada and, to a lesser extent, in the UK and Australia. The prospect of sport scholarships to top schools, or to schools of excellence or sports academies, regardless of whether they are club-based, state academies or national coaching programmes such as the Australian Institute of Sport (AIS), has increased the level of expectation of aspirational athletes and ambitious parents. The consequences are obvious for junior and even school coaches who are now under a different level and form of pressure to produce what are considered to be the right results – now it is all about contracts and scholarships.

The primary stakeholders, particularly in regards to junior and school sport – the parents, family and friends of the athletes – have always been and will remain important and influential in coaching. However, once sport came under the wider influence of sponsors, the media and geopolitical forces, the place and importance of stakeholders increased, as too have their demands. Such demands place a direct burden on club administrators, coaches and athletes alike and their performances now have consequences that go well beyond any individual competition and the sporting arena.

The revolving-door sacking dramas of football managers in the English Premier League are certainly indicative of the idiom that, 'he who pays the piper calls the tune'. At the elite level, that of a nation's Olympic coach, the responsibilities are onerous. The quality of a nation's Olympic team's performances is directly attributed to the coaches and in particular the head coach. The sacking of Leigh Nugent, Australia's head swimming coach at the London Olympic Games, following Australia's indifferent performance in the pool and, after what was essentially a judicial inquiry, is indicative of the pressure that accompanies such roles.

Think about:

- Can you highlight the major factors influencing your particular coaching context?
- How would you describe your athletes?
- What is your background and motivation as a coach?
- Who are your stakeholders and how influential/important are they to you in your role as the coach?

The key to succeeding in the role of a sport coach at all levels is the ability to respond to the multitude of demands that each specific endeavour presents. Each context is multilayered

**9**

and varied, just as the athletes involved are, and the impact of stakeholders and external forces upon sport is immense. It is essential that the right people are doing the right jobs, for the right reasons. However, this does not mean that there is no room for change, as coaches also have to be agents of change. Many of the descriptions, mandates, opinions and anecdotes associated with the role of a coach are fairly typical. Some, however, offer a sense of change and a different interpretation, and it will hopefully be those that will precipitate a change in the way readers think about the 'art of coaching'. The next section provides some opinions from the 'real' world of coaching. However, there is no guarantee that this will clarify the matter entirely; individuals must satisfy their own curiosity as to what being a coach means to them.

## VOICES FROM THE 'FIELD'

This national level basketball coach reflected upon his role as a coach and how this role had changed throughout the various coaching contexts that he experienced.

> I have a feeling that the role of the coach depends what level you want to talk about. I think it's fair to say if one was to open my little textbook, my diary over the years, I've been involved at all levels. When I first came to this country I got very heavily involved with the juniors international team, which was then under 19, now under 18, and I think what you're looking for in terms of coaching is nurturing, more of a maternal/paternal viewpoint where you are trying to seek out the talent and to sort of put it in a space, in a place where it can grow and emerge. That then takes us into the kind of heady world of talent identification there but I think it's that nurturing, that helping kids find themselves at that level. Dealing with young players at international level is in itself is quite a task because kids can get dramatically insulted at international level in basketball.
>
> As players get a greater sense of expectation, for example, I worked with some players at a semi-professional level, which involved working with a club which recruited Americans, you change the agenda slightly, you're much more results orientated and you're much more concerned with person-management. If you then go on from that to senior international level, say GB, I was involved with 5 teams at GB level, it's man-management and possibly massaging egos as well.
>
> At all levels, junior, semi-professional and through to GB international level I think a coach has to turn the dial and re-tune, re-organise their agendas and work out what you've got in front of you. If you're giving me a paragraph or two on what the role of the coach is, I think it's somewhere along those lines. I don't think it's necessary for coaches to think that they can move with the transition I just described. It might well be that some coaches' skills are at a level that they can't switch back or switch up. In appointing coaches, you have to make a pretty measured judgement about a successful junior coach who wants to be a senior international coach and sometimes it just doesn't configure.
>
> A case in point might be, as a coach you might be pretty good at nurturing with young players and you've got a kind of style about you that seems to fit that clientele. If you then step into another world, which I call the massaging of egos and person management, it might not be as easy for that person to make the transition. A guy brings his junior methods to a senior men's team and you're thinking 'Oh come on, you're going to have to

back down from this' because it's just not quite the language, not quite the feel of things. I think experience is important but that doesn't mean you need to have 20 years experience before you can do something – the experience may be very immediate. An example could be in the States, a lot of players who are at college, who have their 4-year scholarship, they'll often go into high school coaching fairly quickly because they can't continue their playing career. So they'll go into high school coaching fairly quickly and from there they may get back into the actual college system as an assistant coach during recruiting. So their experience, alright they've played in high school, they've gone to college, they coach for maybe 2 to 3 years, then they're back in the college system. Their experience, on the face of it, is very short but it may be incredibly impactful and can impact on the players they're working with. I think the critique of your playing background also applies in the UK, most probably notoriously in the past, in Association Football.

This considered view of both his role and how it has developed during his years in coaching reinforces the importance of the context, the athletes and the coach in this mix. Perhaps the mainly non-professional environment of basketball in the UK meant that this coach did not consider, or have to consider, the stakeholders. Ewan McKenzie, current coach of 'The Reds', the Super 15 Rugby team based in Brisbane, in his article unambiguously entitled, 'Joys of turning poison chalice into silverware', opened with this statement: 'Coaching is a constant roller-coaster ride' (McKenzie 2013). Given the complex nature of the role of the coach, this may be an underestimation. From the following comments and descriptions from practicing coaches, the joy-ride analogy may be inaccurate. Perhaps the role would be better described as a 'fun-fair' full of rides – some scary, some exciting and many rather ordinary. McKenzie also shrewdly pointed out that in coaching:

> it's just as important to convince those around you that success will come. But it's just as important to manage winning on the field with results off it. You must appreciate the off-field dynamics, including commercial, marketing, political and, media commitments, because you can have great ideas but without the ability to get your message across, you will always fall short.
>
> (McKenzie 2013)

Professional rugby union in the Southern Hemisphere is a very prominent feature of mediasport, and McKenzie is clearly very mindful of the importance of his role and his relationship with the sport's major stakeholder, Foxtel, and its global affiliates including, obviously, those in New Zealand and South Africa. The Super 15 competition would be bereft of capital without the lucrative funding generated by broadcasting rights.

McKenzie also reflects on the nature of his own style and form as a coach, which is very much a 'hands-on' approach rather than that of a manager-coach surrounded by a coterie of specialist coaches and a fleet of support staff who oversee and monitor everything from core strength and conditioning to the players' spiritual needs. McKenzie favours a team of three, himself and two assistants, as he suggests with any more there is 'nothing juicy' left for the head coach to do. The manager-coach misses out on the 'challenge and credibility of delivering a piece of the technical and tactical coaching action'. His preferred coaching style is to be in the 'trenches'; his philosophy is the more coaches you have, the more you manage and the less you actually coach (McKenzie 2013).

Despite his obvious preoccupation with the 'technical and tactical coaching action', McKenzie also believes that at this level of sport coaches should also focus on making the ever-present team dynamics their domain as well. He also reflects on the need to be in tune with the 'culture' of the team, noting it is in a 'constant state of flux'. Individual players are, according to McKenzie, all different and all have exigencies and pressures that stem from their lives outside of the game – family, education, financial matters and social media – that have an impact on their contribution to the team. Knowledge of this cultural and social setting is vital for a coach working in such a context, McKenzie maintains: 'It's critical to be abreast of these dynamics and to be able to coach in this space has been the difference. . . . Customising your methods, not a blanket approach, gets you the best outcome. This is complicated' (McKenzie 2013).

The complexity of the role of a coach emerges in both of these observations from elite coaches. The UK basketball coach reaffirms the view that 'one style' does not fit all contexts, and what works with U/19s international players will not work with senior internationals, who the basketball coach suggests need to be 'person managed' with their egos requiring constant massaging. He makes an astute comment about coach advancement; some coaches should, he suggests, not make the transition to the next level: 'you have to make a pretty measured judgment about a successful junior coach who wants to be a senior international coach, sometimes it just doesn't configure.' The rugby coach does consider the input of the media to impinge upon his role as well as the money and prestige that brings to his organisation.

Think about:

- What is your role in your present coaching position?
- Have you noticed changes within your role as you progress through your coaching career?
- Can you highlight the key points made by the elite basketball and rugby coaches above?
- Do you think that these reflections are only pertinent to team sport coaching?

## IN THE 'FIELD' EMBEDDED

The characterisation of the coaching role at varying levels emerged as a central theme in a review of the perceived role frames and philosophies of a cohort of coaches undertaken by Nash, Sproule and Horton in 2008. It became apparent that early career coaches, possibly by necessity and/ or a lack of confidence, were preoccupied with behaviour management and safety, illustrated in this comment from an inexperienced football coach, made when asked what his role was as a coach: 'to make sure everything is safe and to deliver fun sessions where they're getting a chance to improve their skills, even just learn different sports'. More senior coaches, particularly those 'working' at an elite level, were more engaged in managerial and strategic roles. An elite track and field coach, who coaches a stable of middle-distance runners, commented:

> I suppose it's management of the training, the planning of, the management and co-ordination of training and competition plan. With the athletes that I've got, they're fairly committed, fairly good – the planning bit is the easy aspect – then we've got to start linking in strength and conditioning, getting the massage at the correct time, getting the

aqua-running suite sorted, so there's actually a bit of lifestyle planning in there as well because I try to ease the burden.

(Nash et al. 2008, p. 544)

As the coach of a squad of elite, individual athletes, his role is very different from that of a coach of a team sport. However, this comparatively young coach is, just as is the vastly more experienced rugby coach, Ewan McKenzie, concerned with the 'whole athlete'. He feels that he needs to be aware of, and in touch with, his athletes' 'holistic development' including and beyond the track.

The study by Nash *et al.* demonstrated that the higher the level at which the coaches in their sample performed, not only did their role become more complex and, concomitantly, more onerous, some had begun to see themselves as part of an 'industry' turning young athletes (players) into commodities to feed the demands of the 'professional game'. A coach from a professional football club believed that his role had changed from 'coach' to 'stakeholder':

My view is that the coach represents effectively a shareholder, and given the professional game, we're speaking about shareholders, we're speaking about a game that's developing furiously in a business context. I think the coach is seen as a part of that whole mechanism. So as you're actually working with youngsters, very aware that the youngsters you're working with have got to serve a purpose for the club and that it is eventually to play for the first team. Because of that, the whole process of learning isn't something the coach is aware of, it's almost sort of a bully boy tactic is used, but it's as much because the manager and subsequently the chairman, are looking for something tomorrow and little attention is paid to the maturation process.

(Nash et al. 2008, p. 545)

It is evident that this highly regarded senior football coach views his players as 'apprentices' who must be developed to produce a return on investment and, literally, in the context of the professional club, a profit. Those who adopt such methods for financial returns show little real concern for, or nurturing of, their players and, it would appear, have no real concern or consideration of their needs. From his rather disturbing comments, his perception illustrates the complex range of functions that comprise the role of a coach in professional football.

This female swimming coach also viewed her role from a different perspective, saying:

I am the first female to hold this position and it is very stressful. I feel I am constantly looking over my shoulder, asking myself if I am making the correct decisions. I think that there are a number of other coaches who want me to fail and in this role it is very important, for the swimmers, that I don't. I also coach in one of these sports where there are female coaches but I don't know how other females manage in other sports like football.

This observation demonstrates another pressure placed upon coaches in positions of responsibility. Being the 'first' in any coaching role brings a raft of additional anxieties over and above the coaching remit as well as the added difficulty of being in the minority within the coaching community.

**13**

Many elite coaches are driven to succeed with much of this drive coming from the established and dominant culture of the sport they are working in (see Chapter 13). However, a top junior tennis coach considered his junior players in a completely different manner, 'the main role for me', he said, 'was to make sure that if they are 8, 9, 10 years old, they are still playing in their twenties. If I have done that, then I think I've succeeded'. He is driven by the 'context', which he characterised as a 'nurturing environment'.

One may well ask, should the role of a coach begin and end with the long-term interest of the athletes? The role of a coach is driven by the context, but it is equally important that it should be about the long-term development of the athletes, not just in their sport but in the whole of their lives. The following quote from this coach summed up his view of his role:

> In my case, my role as a coach was nourished and supported by my positive relationships with my players, their parents and other coaches; consequently I sought to replicate those qualities in other aspects of my life, particularly at work. Coaching then is not just something I *do*, it is something I *am*.
>
> (Peel *et al.* 2013, p. 738)

Think about:

- Are you more concerned with session issues (behaviour management) or strategic issues (how to manage the group or team)?
- Is the role of a coach to nurture and develop talent?
- Is the role of a coach more important within the professional environment of sport coaching?
- How answerable are coaches to athletes, parents, organisations and stakeholders?

One theme common to all discussions of the role a coach is that the role actually involves many different aspects. Considering the previous analyses of the context, athletes, coach and the stakeholders, it should come as no surprise that the lists of coach activities and job descriptions from sports bodies, coaching organisations and private companies are so extensive.

Although it would be unlikely any one person could achieve this collective undertaking on his or her own, a coach, working together with parents and teachers to assist, could perform the majority of the roles. As to whether or not the coach could ever attain all the roles remains a matter of conjecture.

## REFERENCES

Demers, G. (2009). 'We Are Coaches': Program Tackles the Under-Representation of Female Coaches. *Canadian Journal for Women in Coaching* 9: pp. 1–9.

International Ice Hockey Federation (2007). Role of the Coach. *Level 1 Coaching Manual*. Retrieved: 11 April 2014. www.iihf.com/fileadmin/user_upload/PDF/Sport/Coaching_manuals/2_Level_I_Role_of_the_Coach.pdf

Leberman, S. I. and LaVoi, N. M. (2011). Juggling Balls and Roles, Working Mother-Coaches in Youth Sport: Beyond the Dualistic Worker-Mother Identity. *Journal of Sport Management* 25(5): pp. 474–488.

Lyle, J. (2013). Role Models, Sporting Success and Participation: A Review of Sports Coaching's Ancillary Roles. *International Journal of Coaching Science* 7(2): pp. 25–40.

Marks, R.J.P. (1977). *The Rugby Coaching Manual*. (Queensland: National Coaching Plan, Rothmans' National Sports Foundation): p. 5.

Martens, R. (2012). *Successful Coaching* (4th Ed.). (Champaign, IL: Human Kinetics).

McKenzie, E. (2013). Joys of Turning Poison Chalice into Silverware. Retrieved: 28 March 2013. www.brisbanetimes.com.au/rugby-union/union-news/joys-of-turning-poison-chalice-into-silverware-20130327–2gup2.html#ixzz2OmsGSlRl

Nash, C. (2001). Volunteerism in Sports Coaching – A Tayside Study. In *Leisure Volunteering: Marginal or Inclusive*. Graham, M. and Foley, M. (Eds.). (University of Brighton: Leisure Studies Association Publication).

Nash, C. S., Sproule J. and Horton, P. (2008). Sport Coaches' Perceived Role Frames and Philosophies. *International Journal of Sports Science and Coaching* 3(4): pp. 535–550.

Norman, L. (2013). The Challenges Facing Women Coaches and the Contributions They Can Make to the Profession. *International Journal of Coaching Science* 7(2): pp. 3–23.

Peel, J., Cropley, B., Hanton, S. and Fleming, S. (2013). Learning Through Reflection: Values, Conflicts, and Role Interactions of a Youth Sport Coach. *Reflective Practice* 14(6): pp. 729–742.

Roetert, E. and Lubbers, P. (2011). The Role of Sport Science in Coaching Education. *Coaching and Sport Science Review* 19(54): pp. 5–6.

sportscoachUK (2011). *Sports Coaching in the UK III – A Statistical Analysis of Coaches and Coaching in the UK*. Retrieved: 11 April 2014. www.sportscoachuk.org/sites/default/files/Sports-Coaching-in-the-UK-III.pdf

sportscotland (2012). *Women in Coaching Programme Evaluation Report*. (sportscotland).

Weiss, M. (2003). *Developmental Sport and Exercise Psychology : A Lifespan Perspective*. (Fitness Information Technology).

Chapter 2

# Planning your coaching
## A focus on youth participant development

*Andy Abraham, Sergio Lorenzo Jiménez Sáiz,
Steve Mckeown, Gareth Morgan, Bob Muir,
Julian North and Kevin Till*

There is very little in life that doesn't need some sort of plan to facilitate the achievement of a goal, be it writing a shopping list, looking at a map to plan a route, or even putting a postcode into a satellite navigation system. In essence, planning is our attempt to predict the future so that when the future arrives we are prepared for it. At its simplest planning is waking up and deciding what to have for breakfast; at its most complex planning is preparing the allocation of resources to look after an aging population in 30 years time. Planning in coaching sits somewhere between these two time frames, but even in coaching time frames vary. The plan could be for a single coaching session, it could be for a 10-week programme or it could be a 4- to 8-year talent development programme. However, what is known is the planning becomes more complex based on two factors: the number of variables that have to be accounted for and how far into the future that planning is required to predict.

Unfortunately, experience and research tells us that planning is something that people either don't readily engage in or, if they do, they don't do it particularly well. This lack of planning is not altogether surprising for two reasons. First, evidence examining human learning and development suggests that humans have a preference to 'do' first and 'think' later, if at all (Kahneman and Klein 2009). Second, planning is difficult, time consuming, inefficient (at least in the short term) and often unrewarded/unrecognised in the allocation of time and effort for either paid or unpaid coaches. For both reasons planning often has little cultural value. Yet, despite this lack of value, research has consistently shown that the capacity to plan and rationalise through coaching practice is a determining factor of coaching expertise and effectiveness (Abraham, Collins and Martindale 2006; Jones, Housner and Kornspan 1995; Lyle 2010; Martindale and Collins 2005; Schempp, McCullick and Sannen Mason 2006). Indeed, engaging in planning is crucial in the development of a coach since it encourages deep thinking, raises expectations of both coach and player and provides a template from which thoughtful reflection can occur post-delivery (Abraham and Collins 2011a). Given such importance the goal for this chapter is to offer ideas as to why coaches should engage in planning and (given the comment about doing first, thinking later) perhaps more importantly what they can plan for and how they can do it.

Because planning is so complex, however, one chapter cannot do the whole process justice. To overcome this issue, at least to some extent, the focus of the chapter will be planning for the development of young people. Although coaches generally work with young people, this aspect of their work has received little attention in academic literature. Furthermore, the term 'participant' will be used as the catch all term that might otherwise be referred to as athlete, child, player and so on.

## THE JARGON OF PLANNING AND ITS RELEVANCE

The importance of planning has been acknowledged for a number of years. Much of this work has been completed in the area of the physical preparation of athletes, particularly in physical sports such as athletics (see Bompa and Haff 2009). This work introduced many ideas and jargon into the realm of planning, some of which will be used in this chapter. To help clarify some of the jargon, Table 2.1 and Figure 2.1 explain some commonly used terms and expressions.

As this chapter focuses on the development of young participants, particular attention will be placed on the use of macro, meso and micro and not the different 'phases' or 'training loads' identified. This is not to downplay the importance of these phases and loads; they have been used with good effect in planning for Olympic athletes. However, given the focus of this chapter the 'phase' and 'training' terminology and aligned methodology lack relevance for the majority of young participants for two reasons. First, consideration of training load becomes a major issue when participants are engaged in large amounts of training (20 hours plus) each week. Most young participants, even those engaged in talent programmes, are unlikely to be

*Table 2.1* A glossary of common planning jargon

| Term | Meaning |
|------|---------|
| Stress response cycle | A conceptual basis to physical and psychological system development dependent on placing the 'system' under stress. The key idea is that stress will unbalance the 'system' but that the system will then compensate and super-compensate; however, if this super-compensation isn't built on, then the system will return to its old state. See Figure 2.1 |
| Macro cycle | Planning ideas for the achievement of goals are put in place for extended periods of time. The longest time frame is known as the macro cycle. The length of a macro cycle is often dependent on the sport, the frequency and importance of competition goals or stage of athlete development. Olympic sports will often have 4-year cycles (or even longer). Elite sport teams may only have annual or biannual cycles. Talent development programmes may have up to 6-year plans. |
| Meso cycle | Macro cycles are often broken into meso cycles. These cycles will represent meaningful planning stages (or phases – see below) with aligned goals in the achievement of the overall goal of the macro cycle. |
| Micro cycle | In a similar fashion, meso cycles are broken into micro cycles. |
| General preparatory phase | This phase provides balanced, all round physical conditioning incorporating strength, endurance, speed, flexibility and other factors of fitness. |

*(Continued)*

**17**

*Table 2.1* (Continued)

| Term | Meaning | |
|------|---------|---|
| Specific preparatory phase | This phase concentrates on sport specific fitness and exercises, which are more specific to the demands of the sport. | |
| Competition phase | This phase may contain one, a few or a season worth of competitions. The main aim is to prepare for competition and maintain fitness. | |
| Transition phase | This phase is used to facilitate biological regeneration, psychological rest and relaxation as well as to maintain an acceptable level of general physical preparation. | |
| Volume of training | The amount of time devoted to training on a certain aspect of performance. A term that is derived from physical conditioning literature but can be applied to all types of training. | These three terms are often employed within the same planning literature as they are seen as being co-varying, i.e. a certain part of a plan may have high volume, intensity and frequency. However, this training may be too much 'stress' over an extended period and one or more of them may drop, i.e. high volume, medium intensity, low frequency. Decisions as to which is done and when are based on knowing the participant and the goals being worked towards. |
| Intensity of training | The amount of effort applied to training a certain aspect of performance. Again a term that is derived from physical conditioning but can be applied to all types of training. | |
| Frequency of training | How often training on a certain aspect of performance occurs. Also a term that is derived from physical conditioning but can be applied to all types of training. | |

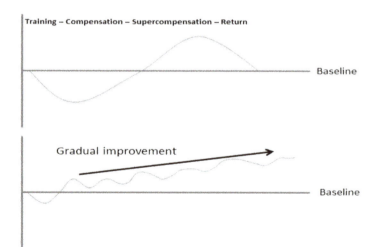

*Figure 2.1* Stress response model. The top figure represents a single stress response cycle. The lower figure represents the 'ideal' outcome of continuous stress response cycles over a longer period of time. Over time, as stress responses build on top of progress made from previous responses, performance should show an improvement – especially if the stressor is (as it should be) linked to the performance improvement required.

engaged in this level of training. (Although there are exceptions, including young swimmers.) Second, competition often has different priorities at youth level as opposed to elite level. Although the role of competition is discussed later on in this chapter, when planning for young participants the overriding philosophy is one of using competition for the sake of development and not for winning.[1] The methodology of phases is aligned with 'peaking' for competition (Bompa and Haff 2009) and has more to do with elite and emerging elite athletes than it does with young developing participants. Such a 'philosophy' could be classed in the 'that's okay in principle but doesn't happen in practice' bracket. Culturally, youth sport is often strongly judged through who has the most successful team or athlete. However, and as is suggested later, to have the impact that they desire coaches must develop the culture that they believe is required to achieve their goals. Planning for changing mindsets is often as important as planning for performance change.

A disclaimer here is that winning does become important for some during the early stages of their athletic careers. Coaches who find themselves in these situations should therefore extend their knowledge to account for this. Furthermore, young participants do have additional mental and physical loads through school, social life and playing other sports. Peak loads in these other areas of life should be considered in planning.

Further terminology will be introduced in the rest of this chapter; this is inevitable simply because jargon is developed to summarise complex ideas, and planning is complex. However, this terminology will always be accompanied with explanatory notes.

## THINKING, THINKING TOOLS AND PLANNING

It was mentioned earlier that people have a preference to do first and (maybe) think later. There are actually sound biological/evolutionary reasons for this phenomenon. Much of life requires people to make quick decisions to the extent that slow thoughtful decisions may not be useful in achieving immediate moment-to-moment goals. In effect, quick and intuitive decisions are useful because they are efficient in getting on with life. Myers (2010) and Halpern (2014) note that issues arise, however, when people continue to make intuitive decisions when in fact slower, more deliberative decisions should have been made:

> Intuition is adaptive. It enables us to drive on automatic. It feeds our creativity. But sometimes it leads us into ill-fated investments, fuels overconfident predictions, and even takes us into war. Awareness that intuition's vision could use some correction in realms from sports to business, commends disciplined training of the mind.
>
> (Myers 2010, p. 376)

> Planning seems to be an important component for changing many behaviours. . . . it is useful to plan how you will think and act. Plans are prescriptive descriptions about what to do and they prevent habitual responses that may not work.
>
> (Halpern 2014, p. 21)

The coaching connection is that coaching sessions often require coaches to be intuitive in their practice; the question is what is driving this intuitive practice? Although coaches will often refer to the importance of experience in being able to make good decisions, this statement lacks some crucial definition. Lots of people can have experience, but only some seem to have expertise (Nash, Martindale, Collins and Martindale 2012). One defining factor is the deliberateness of that experience, 'the disciplined training of the mind', and it is this deliberateness that planning (and reflecting for that matter) can offer.

However, saying deliberate planning is important is one thing, engaging in deliberate planning is another. Deliberate planning requires coaches to think, but think about what? Schempp *et al.* (2006) found that novice coaches plan around simple heuristics such as maintaining control and filling time. Alternatively, more expert coaches plan around thoroughly understanding the nature of the performance and development problems facing them before progressing into developing a plan of action to solve the problems. However, even this explanation is quite nebulous and lacking in definition. Planning is a complex process that does require a lot of thinking; knowing what to think about is crucial. To facilitate this thinking, nine thinking tools and five planning templates are presented in the rest of this chapter to facilitate the planning process.

## Nested goals and planning

The macro, meso and micro terms introduced earlier indicate that short term cycles of development should be connected to medium term cycles, which are in turn connected to longer term cycles of development. In coaching terms this would mean that a single coaching session should always have a connection to the longer term objectives. This approach should prevent the irrelevant fire fighting of micro issues that can distract coaches away from the longer term goal.[2] Abraham and Collins (2011b) termed this approach as Nested Goal Setting and Planning, where short term goals should be nested within medium and then long term goals. Subsequently, planning should also follow this route. However, they expanded beyond the usual approach of performance goals setting to examine what sort of goals should be set, and how the plans would then reflect the type of decision that would then be taken. They identified that goal setting and planning decisions at the macro are typically strategic and political in nature; that is they are more likely to be about achieving long term targets. They typically involve long timeframes, often affected by internal and external key stakeholders.

Meso goal setting and planning then becomes socio-motivational and tactical in nature; that is this level focuses on creating optimal environments for the achievement of goals. As such annual planning with in-built meso cycles for participant development would be a typical meso goal setting and planning activity to engage in. However, planning for the engagement of those who will affect the motivational and learning environment, such as parents or other coaches, may also be useful.

Finally, at the micro level, goals and planning would be far more pedagogical and session (or sessions) based in nature. With greater focus on individual development or performance improvement, this level of goal setting and planning often becomes the public face of coaching.

Abraham and Collins (2011b) also make one further distinction; the type of thinking also changes with the stage of planning. They argue that the macro and meso level of goal setting should predominantly be where deliberate thinking and problem solving should occur. Completing this level of thought, they argue, should set coaches up for engaging both efficient and

| Level | Objectives | Timeline and Activity | | |
|---|---|---|---|---|
| | | Meso Year 1 Objectives | Meso Year 2 Objectives | Meso Year 3 Objectives |
| Macro, 4 year: Strategic & Political Goals | • Transition 2/3 of current players into U16s<br>• Align player capabilities and outcomes with club and NGB policy at each sub age group<br>• Work within budget constraints<br>• Benchmark player development progress against comparable clubs | • Recruit 3 players<br>• Build realistic plan and attain expected player progression across developmental targets<br>• Develop reputation of quality within benchmark clubs | | |
| | | Meso/Micro Objectives Week 1–12 | Meso/Micro Objectives Week 13–24 | Meso/Micro Objectives Week 25–36 |
| Meso Seasonal: Socio, tactical, motivational | 1. Create and deliver annual plan with team individualised targets against club defined age and stage targets<br>2. Create and administer tests of development drawing on game and training behaviour<br>3. Engage parents in establishing and understanding club philosophy to player development with associated expectations | 1. Playing when in-balance (6 weeks) and playing when out of balance (6 weeks)<br>1. & 2. Conduct needs analysis process to establish each individual player's age/stage developmental curriculum needs (p-b, p-s & p) and align with tech and tact curriculum<br>3. Parent education meeting to set expectations | | |

| Micro Sessions | Develop session and meeting plans with requisite aligned objectives and practice, behaviour and curriculum detail | 1 | 2 | 3 | 4 | 5 | 6 | 7 | 8 | 9 | 10 | 11 | 12 |
|---|---|---|---|---|---|---|---|---|---|---|---|---|---|

*Figure 2.2* An exemplar nested plan for a U12 academy football team. NB some boxes have deliberately been left empty to encourage readers to think how they might continue (or start) the process for themselves.

accurate intuitive decision making in micro situations. Furthermore, well thought through macro and meso plans also offer a template against which reflections on progress and development can be made. This should allow for meaningful, as opposed to knee jerk, adaptations to plans to be made when, inevitably, progress doesn't occur as expected. An exemplar nested diagram is shown in Figure 2.2.

## Constructive alignment

Educational psychologist John Biggs (2003) developed the concept of constructive alignment as a method to develop and achieve specific learning objectives in adult education. This process offers greater pedagogical insight (as opposed to strategic and political) to the development of learning programmes. The process of constructive alignment begins with the question 'what do coaches want their participants to be able to know and do as a result of coaching?' The intended learning objectives that arise from an analysis of participants' needs relative to the sporting context become the basis for designing long, medium and short term plans that will enable these objectives to be achieved. These objectives provide a key reference point from which coaches can monitor and adjust the effectiveness of their plans, delivery and reflections. While Biggs developed his ideas for adult learners, the concept is transferable to the development of young people.

As a planning tool, constructive alignment can be used to develop programmes from both a macro/meso level or from a sessional micro/meso level. For example, Figure 2.3 displays an approach to think through and create programme-level development outcomes and what

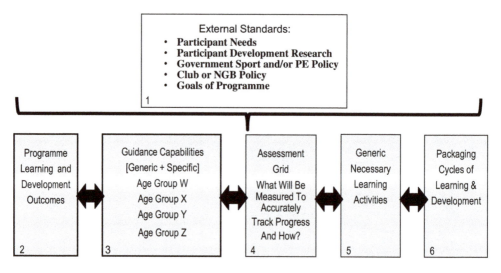

*Figure 2.3* A schematic process to develop a constructively aligned programme.

the aligned required support will be. The principle of constructive alignment in Figure 2.3 focuses first on creating development outcomes (box 2) that:

- are meaningful to participants, typically defined by their own developmental needs;
- meet important standards relative to the programme that they are in;
- meet the level of learning required to be evidenced and recognised by key stakeholders external to the immediate coaching environment (e.g. funders, managers, parents).

Second, constructive alignment relies on there being a learning environment that allows the learner to construct their learning to achieve learning outcomes. This second requirement is reflected in boxes 3–6. Finally, as displayed in box 1, coach decisions about learning outcomes and learning environments should be made against a set of external standards to assure the quality of course development process.

Whereas Figure 2.3 looks at constructive alignment from a top down macro perspective, the principle can also be used from a bottom up micro sessional perspective to inform practice. Understanding of how each coaching interaction is nested within the long, medium and short term objectives enables coaches to make more informed adjustments from predetermined plans based on observations, evaluations and reactions to 'goings on' (Abraham and Collins 2011b; Jones and Wallace 2006). At the micro level of constructive alignment (see Figure 2.4) the coach's primary task is to engage participants in practices that facilitate their progress towards the objectives of a session that align with the goals of the meso cycle. We therefore suggest that good coaches deliberately plan, manipulate and 'align':

- practice structure (such as focus on single or multiple skills; opposed or unopposed practice; blocked, variable or random practice; drill, conditioned or small sided game, and so on);

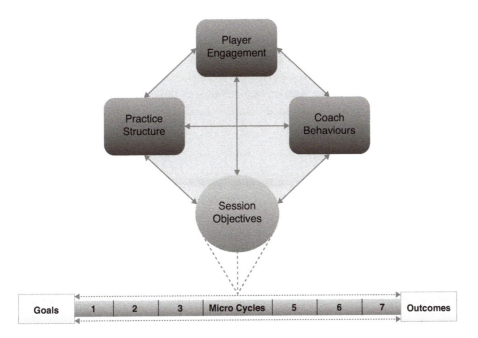

*Figure 2.4* A summary of the required alignment to consistently achieve session objectives that align with micro, meso and ultimately macro cycle objectives (Muir 2012).

■ coach behavioural strategies (that is timing and type of feedback; open or closed questioning; demonstrations; and hustles and instructional prompts, and so on).

By doing so they will maximise the opportunities for participants to engage, learn and achieve the objectives of the session and progress towards achieving the meso and ultimately macro goals of the programme (Biggs and Tang 2011; Muir, Morgan, Abraham and Morley 2011).

The concept of constructive alignment at this more micro level provides a useful framework of questions to consider when planning delivery programmes:

■ What are the long, medium and short term learning objectives and how can they be broken down into macro, meso and micro cycles?
■ What will participant engagement look like when the objectives have been achieved (for example, different components of performance relating to technical/tactical, movement, physical, psychological and social capabilities)?
■ What methods of assessment can be used to generate feedback and measure progress against the objectives?
■ How will feedback be used to make decisions regarding the focus of the programme and prioritisation of time, space and resources in relation to the different components of performance?
■ How will each micro cycle (for example, training session, competition, review session) contribute to the objectives of the meso cycle?

**23**

The overall concept of constructive alignment provides a framework to guide coaches' planning and promote connections between factors that affect the development of macro and micro goals and their achievement. Indeed, coaches who spend time considering these factors are more likely to be attentive to participants' and stakeholders' needs and more focussed with programme development, delivery and refinement through more deliberate planning and reflection leading to better informed intuitive practice.

## Who, what, how and why

While the concepts of nested planning and constructive alignment offer mechanisms to support thinking about planning, they don't necessarily help with what coaches should think about. This is filled with the concepts of who, what and how as illustrated in Figure 2.5. Focusing more explicitly on the meso and micro elements of nested planning, the who-what-how model identifies that coaches can structure their coaching decisions by considering what the requirements are of the participant (who), what the sport specific demands are for that participant (What) and what coaching behaviours, practice and task designs should be employed to facilitate the development of the participant (How).

There are too many theories and research that could be unpacked from each of these boxes for one chapter; in fact the majority of the content of this book could be tied to one or more of these concepts. Consequently, and in keeping with the longer term planning focus of this chapter so far, the focus will be on the what and who elements, and how these might be extracted to structure thinking about setting goals and planning. In so doing we draw on the major review of participant development completed by Bailey *et al.* (2010) and the subsequent

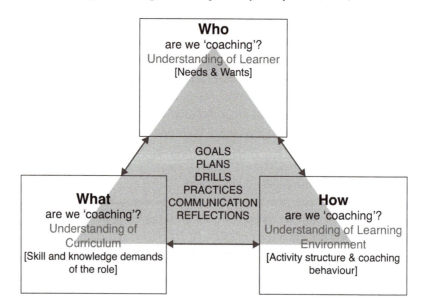

*Figure 2.5* Summary model of the interaction between who, what and how when making goal and planning decisions. Adapted from Abraham and Collins (2011a) and Muir *et al.* (2011).

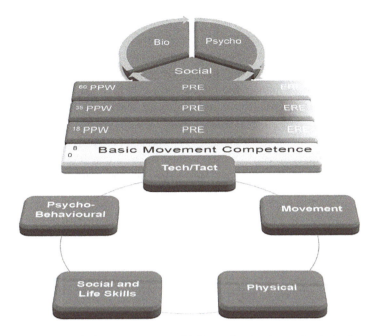

*Figure 2.6* An integrated view to support thinking about who and what when developing coaching curriculum. Adapted from Bailey *et al.* (2010) and Collins *et al.* (2012).

papers that have come from this review, that is Collins *et al.* (2012) and MacNamara *et al.* (2011). This work offers three broad conceptual views that usefully tie in with the what and who of coaching and can therefore offer structure to the planning process. These broad concepts are captured in Figure 2.6.

## The who

The first and broadest basis of this work suggests that the development of all people is a bio-psycho-social process. It further suggests that during the development of young people the influence of these three processes will vary. For example, within the bio, the neuromuscular skeletal system develops at different rates and this impinges on the child's all-round development. During adolescence there are major shifts in social influencers on children from parents to peers. During peak learning and pressure moments children's capacity to cope and even excel will draw heavily on their psycho-behavioural and psycho-social skills (Bailey *et al.* 2010; Collins *et al.* 2012; MacNamara, Button and Collins 2010a). As such this conceptual overview provides a structure that can guide thinking about, understanding of and planning for the who – especially if this thinking is guided by appropriate background reading in these areas.

The second core concept offered by Collins *et al.* (2012) offers an overview perspective about why people (the who) may choose to take part in sport. The importance of this understanding is crucial in allowing coaches to recognise motivation of their participants and match their coaching accordingly. Indeed, it allows coaches to make judgements about whether there is sufficient alignment of participant motivation to their own reasons for coaching.

**25**

Within their model they identify that initial involvement in sport is about developing a baseline of skills built around getting a sense of ownership and connection with not just one sport but a number of sports. From a motivation point of view this has been described as children engaging with a situational motivation and progressing to an ownership based on improved knowledge and understanding developed through play and/or structured play (Chen and Hancock 2006; Côté, Baker and Abernethy 2003). Progressing from this stage, Collins *et al.* (2012) argue that if participants engage in sport they do so for one of three broad reasons; Participation for Personal Wellbeing (PPW), Personal Referenced Excellence (PRE) and Elite Referenced Excellence (ERE). There is of course a fourth group – those who have no motivation to take part in sport at all. This chapter focuses only on PPW, PRE and ERE. Collins *et al.* (2012) define these different motivation states as follows:

> we suggest that excellence can be usefully considered in terms of a continuum across three different 'worlds'. The first two worlds lie mainly in competitive sport, from club competitor to world class performer. These are as follows:
>
> (1) Elite Referenced Excellence (ERE): Excellence in the form of high-level sporting performance where achievement is measured against others with the ultimate goal of winning at the highest level possible
> (2) Personal Referenced Excellence (PRE): Excellence in the form of participation and personal performance, where achievement is more personally referenced by, say, completing a marathon or improving one's personal best
> (3) Participation for Personal Well-being (PPW): Taking part in physical activity to satisfy needs other than personal progression. Typical motivations for PPW might include the improvement of one's social life (for example, making and keeping friends), the enhancement of one's social identity (by being a member of a high status group or club), personal renewal (through activity which is fulfilling) and the maintenance of aspects of self-concept (staying in good shape).
>
> (pp. 228–229)

There are two points of clarification offered within the model, however; first that motivation is context dependent; in other words, a participant could have a PPW approach to one sport, a PRE to another and an ERE to yet another. Second, motivation can change over time; that is a participant may start with a PPW motivation in a sport but find a connection with the sport and thus change his or her approach to a PRE and maybe even an ERE and eventually return to a PPW approach. In other words there is a fluidity within a participant's motivation, perhaps even within the same sport. Finally, all three broad motivations fit with Deci and Ryan's (2008) view that people have three fundamental needs – for autonomy, for relatedness and for competence – since all three can (should) be met in each world.

The third core concept refers more broadly to the what, that is the content that can actually be taught to/learned by the participant (who). Five broad areas of what could be taught to participants are suggested: Technical/Tactical Skills, Movement Skills, Physical Skills, Psycho-behavioural Skills, Lifestyle and Social Skills. In essence these five areas offer a starting point from which annual learning and performance goals can evolve and curriculum be developed.

Interestingly, despite each area having a substantial research and applied knowledge base aligned with them, developing coaching content and/or filling time are often some of the biggest problems faced by coaches, especially novice coaches. Despite often having played the sport that they coach for many years, coaches can struggle to develop a coherent curriculum for their participants. The source of this problem goes back to the preference of humans to work on intuition rather than well thought out plans. Coaches often prefer to intuitively recreate drills they have been exposed to rather than critically considering who they are coaching, what they want to coach and how to do that most effectively. As such coaches often have poorly developed performance models of what their sport requires and how that changes across years of development. Just as 10 year old children wouldn't be expected to be taught maths designed for 15 year olds and vice versa, the same is also true for sport. Consequently, for many coaches developing a greater understanding of the demands of their sport and how these relate to and change with developing participants is crucial in developing long term plans.

## Understanding the what

There isn't enough scope within this chapter to unpack the 'what' of every sport for every participant at every stage of his or her development. However, there are a number of conceptual ideas that can guide thinking and further exploration of content by coaches in each of the five areas.

### *Movement skills*

The most common terminology used with movement skills is Fundamental Movement Skills (FMS). FMS have been described as the 'building blocks' that enable young and more mature participants to successfully take part in the vast majority of sports and games (Payne and Issacs 1995). Stodden et al. (2008) argues that without this repertoire of movement competences, a child's opportunity to engage in a wide range of physical activities throughout his or her life is limited. Therefore, a young person's coach needs to ensure that children are given sufficient opportunity to acquire and develop these movement competences such that they can then be transferred and applied to a range of sporting activities and contexts.

Recognised motor development models, such as those devised by Gallahue and Ozmun (2006) and Haywood and Getchell (2005) classify FMS into Stability, Object control and Locomotor skills (SOL).

- Stability skills involve axial movements (i.e. movements around the x, y and z axis that create three-dimensional movements) where some degree of gaining and maintaining equilibrium is required in relation to the external forces such as gravity or being pushed/pulled. Typical skills would encompass twisting, turning, pivoting, stretching, bending, pulling and pushing.
- Object control skills involve fine and gross motor manipulation and include throwing, catching, bouncing, kicking, volleying and striking.
- Locomotor skills refer to a movement that transfers the body from one fixed point to another and covers walking, running, hopping, skipping and jumping.

**27**

Both models, and others like them, describe when these SOL skills should be acquired, linked and then applied to enable progression from fundamental into more specialised and sport specific functional skills. In theory a person should be able to refine and perform more complex movement skills as one progresses from early, to intermediate and then to the later stages of movement development. For example, Burton and Millar (1998) identify that basic skills such as running, throwing, twisting could be practiced in isolation for early learners, in simple combination such as a zig zag run, running and pick up a ball and so on. This could be developed into more complex specialised and functional combinations such as one player supporting another rugby player running with a ball, taking a pass and running again.

The decision coaches need to make is how does SOL relate to their sport and how can the development of fundamental movement skills fit with their sport? How can these movement skills facilitate the development of participants who have a full repertoire of skill?

## *Physical skills*

An aligned view on skill development comes from those who have an integrated view on the role of strength and fitness. The first part of this aligned view is recognising that improving the physical development of children and adolescents is an important factor in increasing sport participation and performance. However, recent research in youth strength and conditioning (Faigenbaum, Lloyd and Myer 2013; Lloyd *et al.* 2013) has highlighted the importance of not treating children like 'miniature adults' in the development of such skills.

To support coaches in making appropriate judgements about developing physical skills in a developmentally appropriate manner, a new model has recently been developed. Termed the Youth Physical Development (YPD) model (see Lloyd and Oliver 2012 for more information), it was developed to be used by strength and conditioning coaches and sports coaches to support a long term approach for improving physical development between the ages of 2 to 21 years. The YPD model focuses on the qualities of fundamental movement skills, sport-specific skills, mobility, agility, speed, power, strength, hypertrophy, endurance and metabolic conditioning with an emphasis placed on certain qualities at particular ages and stages of development. For example, between 5 and 11 years of age, it is recommended boys work on Fundamental Movement Skills, Mobility, Power, Agility, Speed and Strength; whereas between 12 and 15 years of age, Sport Specific Skills, Agility, Speed, Power, Strength and Hypertrophy are the focus for physical development. For example, simply asking children to hop on one leg will create overload and therefore some physical adaptation. Equally, the capacity of a 12 year old girl to complete a 20 metre lofted pass in football is dependent on her capacity to generate the force through the kick to complete the outcome. Engaging in relevant strength, power, and mobility development can all facilitate the successful execution of a skill that is being developed.

While there are obvious links therefore between physical development and movement and or technical skills, it remains essential to consider the individual(s) a coach is working with when planning accordingly. A number of factors, such as maturation status, gender, training age and the ability of youth participants all need to be considered in the 'who' aspect of coaching, with the ability of an individual or group ultimately determining what is planned and programmed. For example, adolescent athletes who cannot demonstrate the fundamental movement skills required to further develop physical characteristics should not proceed with this process until

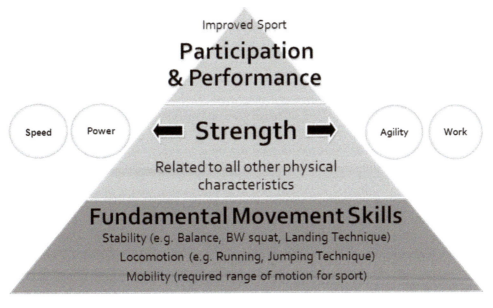

*Figure 2.7* Physical performance pyramid.

competency is demonstrated (for example, the ability to perform a body weight squat prior to weight training to develop lower body strength). This approach is illustrated in Figure 2.7, which outlines the physical performance pyramid. Athletes must be able to demonstrate prerequisites in the fundamental movement skills of stability (for example, balance, landing mechanics, stability based exercises), locomotor (for example, running and jumping technique) and mobility (where range of motion is required for sports and activities) before proceeding to more advanced physical development training. Therefore, this should be the focus for coaches working with young people, regardless of age and stage. Once these skills have been demonstrated, athletes can then concentrate on more strength based work due to its relationship with all other physical variables such as speed, power, agility and work capacity. For example, if an adolescent athlete has missed the FMS development stage (in which the body weight squat should form part of this phase as a lower body stability exercise), or has failed to continue to undertake FMS activities into adolescence (and has decreased mobility and stability due to growth and maturational processes), then this athlete should focus on mastering technical competency and mobility in the body weight squat prior to loading the movement for strength development. This is therefore where coaches must plan and focus the attentions according to the individual(s) they are working with to optimise long term physical development.

### Technical/tactical skills

There is some irony that for most coaches this is the most important knowledge base required for creating ideas that can be used to create goals and curriculum, yet is often the knowledge base that coaches lack the most (Abraham *et al.* 2006; Schempp *et al.* 2006). It is equally ironic therefore that this is the section that this chapter can least deal with, simply because there are just too many sports to examine. There are, however, some generic ideas that can be used to help coaches think about the problem.

Drawing on the work presented related to FMS, coaches can examine the demands of their sport by considering what the requisite Stability, Object control and Locomotor skills actually are, and how these change over time as young people get better. The SOL concept with the associated change from basic, to linked, to complex and specialised skills can either be used to critique ideas offered in sport specific text books or even in creating a checklist against which young participants can be observed. Beyond this there is a growing range of sport specific research, typically within the biomechanics and motor control domain, which can offer more in-depth views on technical requirements.

In a similar fashion, the tactical elements of sport are also difficult to unpack simply because they are so diverse in nature. But again there are some generic concepts that can be used to encourage critical thinking. The first step is to consider what tactics are (see Chapter 8 for further information on tactics). Typically, many will see this as simple ideas such as formations or strategies; however, there is a more fundamental point to tactics if they are viewed through a decision-making lens. In short they are the structures that guide decisions taken to achieve the goal of the sport. Consequently, a key question that all coaches need to ask themselves is what is the goal of my sport? The next questions would be what are the things that will help participants achieve that goal and what are the things that will hinder the participants achieving that goal? Finally, all of these questions should be put into the context of the age and stage of the participants being coached.

In keeping with this approach, research has consistently shown that sport intelligence is one of the defining differences between expert, sub expert and competent and novice performers (MacMahon and McPherson 2009). Returning to the earlier comment regarding not teaching maths for 15 year olds to 10 year olds, the same is also true in sport. Too often young participants are treated like young adults when tactics are taught. Sports can be incredibly complex and dynamic environments. Coping with this level of complexity is, unsurprisingly, difficult for young participants unless the problems that they are trying to solve become easier and are adhered to (that is, coaches don't try to fire fight every small problem that comes along). There is a trend in team sports to move to smaller sided games, since this not only reduces the number of problems that have to be solved, but also increases the opportunity to solve them. Therefore, progressing from the 'what is the goal of my sport' question, coaches need to decide what the problems are that the young participants need to overcome, in what order to present them to their young participants and the knowledge that they will require to solve the problems. Furthermore, they need to question whether all of their participants share the same ideas about how to solve the problems and have the same capacity to answer them (that is, consider the who). In other words, do they have a shared mental model of what they are trying to achieve and how they are trying to achieve it (Richards, Collins and Mascarenhas 2012)?

Finally, the intrinsically linked skill of accurate perception should be considered. While tactics offer guidance to the way sport based problems can be addressed, participant capacity to use tactics is fundamentally tied to their ability to perceive the correct information. Perceptual skills are the essential first stage of decision making, so while teaching participants to see, hear and feel the correct information is unusual, having clear ideas about what should be perceived is important and should be planned for.

## Psycho-behavioural skills

Psycho-behavioural development can be taken to reflect the operationalisation of psychological skills (such as goal setting, focus and distraction control and so on) to self-regulate observable learning and performance behaviours. As such, it relates to people exhibiting psychological skills through behavioural outcomes. The importance of psycho-behavioural development can probably be traced back to the work of Orlick (1988), with Collins and colleagues (Abbott and Collins 2004; Martindale, Collins and Abraham 2007; MacNamara, Button and Collins 2010a, b) amongst those who have subsequently identified the essential role that psycho-behavioural skills play in participant learning and performance in sport, music and education settings.

Typically, 'psychology'-based work has been seen as something that should be done within a classroom environment, away from the practice context, but this does little to facilitate the improvement of psychological skills in practice. While coaches are often quick to command their players to 'relax!', 'focus!', and 'talk!' during practice and competitive situations, the 'teaching' of such skills is rarely conducted within realistic contexts (if done at all). Indeed many coaches simply hope that their participants are made of tougher stuff while bemoaning them as being 'weak' or lacking focus when they don't handle challenging moments well. This situation is perhaps best summarised by Pain and Harwood (2004), who found that coaches did not want time spent on developing participants' psychological attributes to impinge upon 'coaching time' (perceiving them to be separate areas).

In contrast, we contest that psycho-behavioural content must be embedded into a coaching programme/curriculum. The fulfilment of a participant's potential is so dependent on the acquisition and implementation of a broad set of psychological skills, anything less than embedding puts that fulfilment at risk. The deliberate integration of psycho-behavioural skills into and across a core coaching programme provides a basis for the development of these skills throughout the year, therefore increasing the likelihood of them being practiced. For example, introducing and consistently promoting the requirement for participants to 'think through and mentally practice' how a drill will work and to ask questions on anything that needs clarity could usefully promote imagery, focus, goal setting – quality practice skills. Furthermore, it also gives greater meaning to the skills when they are practiced, thereby enhancing transfer of these skills across sessions and into competitive settings (Holliday et al. 2008; Weinberg and Williams 2006). The alternative, doing this work in isolation, only promotes the suggestion that it is surplus to the sport itself.

The actual psycho-behavioural skills that we suggest here are drawn from the work of Mac-Namara, Button and Collins (2010a). Reflecting their work with a range of elite performers who described their talent journey and the role of psycho-behavioural skills in their journey, ten core skills, with aligned subskills, were identified. Table 2.2 offers real world application of these skills within a professional club academy setting. Broadly, the bold skills are introduced at U9s, the underlined skills are introduced at U12s and the italic skills are introduced at U14s level. Once introduced, however, they should continue to be developed even once age transitions have been made.

**31**

*Table 2.2* Psycho-behavioural skills and sub skills. Bold skills introduced and developed 9–12 years. Underlined skills introduced and developed 12–14 years. Italic skills introduced and developed 14 onwards. Adapted from MacNamara *et al.* (2010a, pp. 82–85)

| Core psycho-behavioural skill | Aligned attributes and skills | Operationalised skill |
| --- | --- | --- |
| Commitment to the performance domain | Motivation to succeed | **Motivated to gain recognition and praise from others**<br>Continually striving to improve<br>*Desire to fulfil potential as a driving force* |
| | Determination | Willing to work outside of comfort zone to achieve excellence<br>*Not willing to accept second best*<br>*Not willing to accept failure*<br>*100% committed to the pursuit of excellence* |
| | Perseverance | **Persevered in the face of obstacles**<br>Showed a robustness during difficult times<br>*Takes responsibility for own development* |
| | Pursuit of excellence as a priority | **Decisions made taking the pursuit of excellence into account**<br>Willing to give up other activities to achieve in chosen domain<br>*Works independently without the supervision of others*<br>*Willing to make sacrifices to achieve goals* |
| | Self-determination | **Ability to adhere to performance plans**<br>Self-disciplined |
| Vision of what it takes to develop | Willing to push oneself | **Understood the importance of working hard in the activity**<br>Steps out of comfort zone |
| | Recognised the importance of looking beyond physical components of talent | **Understands that bigger does not mean better** |
| Goal setting | Goal setting for training/practice and competition | **Realistic goals set for competition**<br>Process and outcome goals set for competition<br>Engages in goal setting process with coach<br>*Ability to independently set goals for training/practice*<br>*Ability to modify goals when needed* |
| Focus and distraction control | Focus on task relevant cues | **Ability to focus on task relevant cues** |
| | Distraction control | Ability to block out distracters in the environment<br>*Ability to organise appropriate training environments* |
| Belief can excel | Confidence | **Confident in ability to succeed**<br>Confident to seek out performance and development opportunities |
| | Self-belief | Maintains self-belief even during difficult periods |

*(Continued)*

Table 2.2 (Continued)

| Core psycho-behavioural skill | Aligned attributes and skills | Operationalised skill |
| --- | --- | --- |
| Quality practice | Quality practice | **Engaged in requisite amounts of quality practice**<br>Understands the importance of quality practice<br>Understands the importance of rest and recuperation<br>*Ability to organise practice/training appropriately* |
| Coping with pressure | Ability to prioritize | Ability to recognize what has to be accomplished within certain timeframes<br>*Ability to balance competing commitments* |
| | Ability to regulate arousal | **Ability to cope with frustration**<br>Ability to stay confident in pressure situations<br>Ability to regulate arousal in pressure situations<br>Ability to cope with the expectations of others |
| | Planning skills | Organisational skills<br>*Plans in advance* |
| | Adaptability | Able to adapt to the demands of the situation<br>*Willing to change plans if necessary* |
| Realistic performance evaluations | Realistic performance evaluations | Ability to accurately recognize weaknesses and work on them<br>Understanding of the underlying factors affecting good and bad performances<br>Is self-critical regardless of performance outcomes<br>Ability to maintain realistic expectations |
| Social and communication skills | Social skills | **Ability to interact with fellow performers and support staff**<br>Ability to fit into new environments |
| Imagery | Imagery for skill development | **Imagery used for skill development** |
| | Imagery for performance preparation | Imagery used to prepare for performances<br>Imagery used as a source of confidence during performance preparation |
| | Imagery to review performance | **Imagery used to review practice**<br>Imagery used to correct errors |

## Selecting psycho-behavioural attributes

The selection of relevant psychological attributes to focus upon should consider two things:

1   the psychological demands of various aspects of the sport being played;
2   the players' age and stage of development.

As with all of the five broad *what* skills, to identify the psychological demands, coaches must first of all establish the philosophy of their sport that best suits their beliefs and clarify their understanding of their club/NGB/school's views on this. Doing so facilitates the completion of a

**33**

comprehensive review of the psychological skills required to optimally develop in and through the sport. Such knowledge is crucial so as to establish the psycho-behavioural skill work to be done is work that is:

1   introducing psycho-behavioural skill development to the learner for the first time;
2   developing and building upon some initial foundations;
3   refining some psycho-behavioural skill work that has been relatively well developed beforehand.

For example, if seeking to do some goal setting with a group of individuals who have never been exposed to goal setting before, it will be necessary to educate the participants on the benefits of setting targets, and perhaps initiating the setting of a small number of targets, before proceeding onto more sophisticated levels of goal setting. Progressing this further towards the 'refinement' stage, it might be more appropriate for coaches to create mechanisms that simply support the participants' autonomous selection, monitoring and evaluation of their own goals, relative to their short, medium and long term objectives.

## Social and life skills

Improved social skills are often a goal for coaches, but equally often improved social skills lack any distinct definition and their development is left to chance. At their best, social skills are those that allow us to engage with and flourish in everyday society. They are the attitudes and beliefs that either prevent us from or cause us to engage in anti-social behaviour. There are some coaches who are employed to use sport for broader social good, such as working with children who are at risk of offending or working with children who have suffered emotional trauma. However, going to this level of depth regarding social skills is beyond the scope of this chapter. Still, there are good reasons for coaches to develop the social skills of their participants. From a purely selfish point of view, young participants who 'behave' during coaching sessions allow sessions to retain focus on learning objectives rather than behaviour management. Indeed effective teachers will often spend the first few weeks working with a new class setting the expectations of good classroom behaviour (Fink and Siedentop 1989). Beyond this initial need for compliance, however, there are many tangible and positive reasons for working on social skills. The main one is that young participants are more able to engage in everyday life and are therefore more likely to be happy. As such, within coaching environments young participants are more likely to engage well together, support each other and solve their own problems and cooperate.

Although there is no obvious, agreed set of social skills within the research literature, there are a number of views from various authors that allow for an overview. For example, within the UK national curriculum the department of education identifies Personal identities, Healthy lifestyles, Risk, Relationships and Diversity as being key social domains for learning and development (Education 2014). Further definition can be garnered from both research and applied articles (Jones and Harcourt 2013; Jurevičienė, Kaffemanienė and Ruškus 2012; Shapiro 2004; Weinberg and Gould 2003). This definition has been captured in Table 2.3. In contrast

*Table 2.3* A tabulated summary of the work concerning social skills and their development by Jones and Harcourt (2013), Jurevičienė *et al.* (2012), Shapiro (2004) and Weinberg and Gould (2003)

| Main social skill themes | Core skills | Operationalised skill |
|---|---|---|
| Ability to adapt to contextual situations | Skills of social cognition Moral reasoning | Independence<br>Social problem solving<br>Managing conflict<br>Compromising<br>Being able to function in non-familial social contexts<br>Thinking beyond selfish needs - what is best for all involved? |
| Ability to regulate emotions | Emotional skills | Social sensitivity<br>Emotional literacy<br>Empathy perspective taking<br>Being able to persist with challenging tasks<br>Self-control<br>Recognising own strengths and weaknesses |
| Effective language skills | Participation skills Being part of group | Friendship building<br>Successful play entry behaviours<br>Engagement in complex play<br>Being able to develop positive relationships with peers and adults<br>Developing trust<br>Awareness of differences<br>Cooperation |
| | Interaction skills | Verbal assertiveness<br>Being able to listen and be attentive to learning experiences<br>Making eye contact<br>Tone of voice |
| | Communication skills | Apologising<br>Common courtesy<br>Giving and accepting compliments<br>Offering constructive opinion |
| Understanding social values | Moral behaviour Sportspersonship | Recognising difference between aggression and assertiveness<br>Developing respect<br>Fair play<br>Compassion<br>Playing to the rules<br>Responsibility |

to the work of MacNamara *et al.* referred to earlier, the information included in Table 2.3 is a summary of the work of others. There is no obvious indication as to what should be done and when. Some guidance is offered in the national curriculum work from the UK department of education (Education 2014), but even here there is no direct evidence referred to. Consequently, when it comes to planning for the social development of participants, coaches will need to decide how much emphasis they place on explicit planning of social skills (given that there is some crossover between social skills and psycho-behavioural skills) and which skills are chosen to focus on.

### Spiral curriculum – learning takes time, there is no rush

Rome wasn't built in a day and neither was a great or even an average athlete. Anderson (1982) estimates that it takes 100 hours of learning activity to create a significant shift in cognitive knowledge and understanding. Ericsson *et al.* (1993) originally estimated that about a decade of deliberate practice and learning was required to achieve expert performing status. In short, learning and development takes a long time. Unfortunately, a combination of treating young participants like mini adults and pressuring coaches to show quick results means this issue gets lost. The point of unpacking the five broad areas of Movement, Physical, Technical/Tactical, Psycho-behavioural and Social skills is to show just how much content there is that could be delivered and taught to young participants.

As was stated in both the ideas about nested planning and constructive alignment, creating a clear understanding of what the goals of coaching programmes are is crucial to developing a curriculum and assessments for that curriculum. Further to these ideas, therefore, is understanding that achieving these goals will require the participants to go through an extended period of learning, and it is understanding how learning works that can support the development of curriculum. Constructivist researchers such as Biggs and Tang (2011) talk about how learning is cumulative, that learning is best when it builds on what is already known. Similarly, cognitive researchers such as Hambrick (2003) would suggest that one of the best predictors of what makes someone more knowledgeable than someone else is prior knowledge. In other words, both theorists suggest that knowledge and understanding begets knowledge and understanding. Two further learning ideas fall out of this theoretical insight: first, learners are unlikely to exhaust all the learning opportunities from a coaching session or series of sessions at the first attempt. Second, if learning ideas are revisited, then the participant may well be in a better position to take more from the learning opportunity the second or even third time around simply because they know more.

The core conclusion from this work is that coaching curriculum should be revisited on an on-going and planned-for basis, but with additional expectations being placed on the learner when the revisiting occurs. This approach has been termed spiral curriculum by Bruner (1963), who stated that:

> The way you get ahead with learning is to translate an idea into those non-rigorous forms that can be understood. Then one can, with their (participants) aid, become more precise and powerful . . . This is most of what is meant when we speak of "spiral curriculum".
>
> (p. 530)

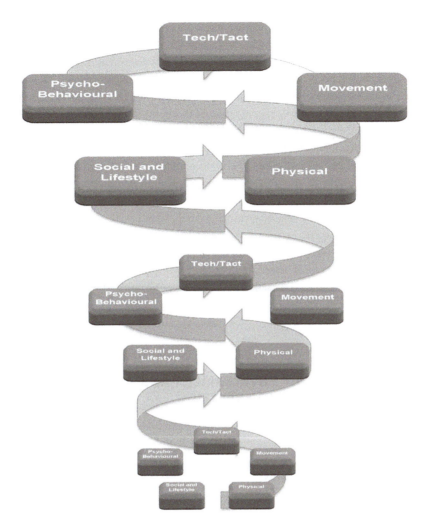

*Figure 2.8* Schematic view of spiral curriculum.

Against this definition, Figure 2.8, indeed all of the figures and the sections of this chapter, are designed in the spirit of spiral curriculum. Figure 2.8 is a concept designed to offer a way in to thinking about planning. There are even probably enough ideas included in this chapter to have a decent stab at planning a long term programme or a number of linked coaching sessions. However, they will work far better if coaches become more precise and powerful with their understanding through further reading, critical conversations with other coaches, observations of other practice and so on.

## The who revisited

As described earlier, a participant's development will be fundamentally underpinned by bio-psycho-social developments. While each of the five areas described within the 'what' offer useful insight and structure for thinking about the goals and curriculum for any plan, coaches must avoid the mistake of treating all of their participants as being the same with curriculum being equally relevant to each participant. Our experience is that most coaches will immediately agree with this challenge, since it is 'obvious' and 'common sense'. However, as stated earlier, intuition generally takes people down the road of treating participants as being the same until participants stop being the same. At this point blame is often attached to those who veer away from engaging in or developing through the curriculum being delivered. Obviously, it is not possible to totally individualise curriculum with bigger groups, nor is it actually useful to try and do so since it would take too much time and result in lost focus. However, some attempt should be made to match the curriculum designed to individual bio-psycho-social needs of the participant. Monitoring growth, maturation (psychological and biological), motivation, achievement, curiosity, prior learning, what creates meaning for the participant, responses to training and competition, social happenings, exams, point in school calendar, relationships and so on, should allow all coaches to adapt plans to meet the needs of individual participants. Furthermore, where there are more extreme changes for some individuals, the bio-psycho-social view can be used as a starting point for understanding what is going on. The constant challenge for the practicing coach therefore, is how to plan for a mixed ability group where participants can be of roughly the same age but are significantly different in their stage of development.

## CREATING THE RIGHT ENVIRONMENT AND MAKING BEST USE OF COMPETITION

So far this chapter has focused on aligning goals and planning around the who and the what. However, as emphasised in discussing Figures 2.4 and 2.5, coaches should also consider and plan for how they are choosing to engage their participants from a behaviour and task/practice design point of view. This is crucial, for the development of:

- relationships with their participants (see Chapter 7);
- the expectations/perceptions that those participants bring to the coaching environment (see Chapter 6);
- an effective skill acquisition environment (see Chapter 5).

Clearly no coach can be in total control of these issues (it takes two to tango and often there are more than two dancers), but some thoughtful consideration and planning can help. Given the scope of this chapter none of these issues can be explored in detail; furthermore, these topics are considered in more depth in other chapters of this book. In keeping with this chapter, however, there are some useful concepts that can guide thinking.

For example, in planning for meaningful relationships, coaches can consider how they are letting their participants (or parents, other coaches) know that they care for, respect and trust them (Abraham, Manley and Morgan 2012; Sagar and Jowett 2012). People's willingness to respect another person is based on their perception of the personal attributes of that person, specifically how trustworthy, hard working and knowledgeable they are.

Consequently coaches who display these attributes as well as those who are caring, display equality in their behaviour (Langdon 2007) and have shared goals[3] are more likely to form quality relationships.

In more depth, being trustworthy is dependent on being predictable; as stated by Dirks (2000), trust is 'an expectation or belief that one can rely on another person's actions or words' (p. 1004). As long as participants can trust something, then they will form expectations that will influence their behaviour. If coaches want their programmes to reflect the needs of participants who have a PPW approach, then the programmes and coach behaviour need to reflect this. Similarly if coaches want to have a programme based around a growth and excellence (that is PRE and ERE) mind-set (Collins *et al.* 2012; Olson and Dweck 2008), then that is the preach that needs to be practiced and therefore planned for.

One area where a coach's capacity to be predictable is reflected is in competition, since this is where a coach's capability is most on public show (Leary and Kowalski 1990). It is therefore worth considering the options that competition offers so that a clear view can be taken and focused on by the coach. Competition plays some role in most young participant's lives and has been identified as being crucial in the development of sport expertise (Baker *et al.* 2003). Recently, through improvements of our understanding of learning and development, the role of competition in development has become more obvious – from understanding how competition provides a template for understanding the requirements of training, that is requisite mental skills (Birrer and Morgan 2010; MacNamara *et al.* 2010a), to recognising how the naturalistic setting of competition should influence pedagogical approaches in practice (Passos, Araújo, Davids and Shuttleworth 2008; Richards, Collins and Mascarenhas 2012). As such, understanding the role of competition in a young participant's development becomes crucial, not least since today, children as young as 5 or 6 years old can find themselves engaged in competition. Furthermore, at 17 (or even younger for 'early specialisation' sports), a player may already be engaged in international competition.

Rather than assuming that competition is simply about winning, the critically aware coaches recognize that competition offers up numerous opportunities (Abraham, Collins and Martindale 2006; Grecic and Collins 2013). Competition may be an ideal time to assess: check ranking, the development of an athlete, the effectiveness of a particular part of your coaching and training through evidence of retention and transfer (see Chapter 4 for further information about the coaching context). It can be used as a motivational tool: the prize for the participant who is training and developing well, the time for the participant to demonstrate competence and ownership of his or her development, the opportunity for the participant to evaluate his or her own progress against other competitors. It can be used as a focusing tool: children will often focus more when there is greater meaning to what they are doing (Moylett and Stewart 2012). Competition can often offer this meaning, as defined through self-determination and situational motivation theory (Chen and Hancock 2006), for numerous reasons such as:

- there is less intervention from a coach (greater ownership);
- it is more game-like (opportunity to test competence);

- participants actually feel part of a team (relatedness);
- it presents a more interesting/different challenge simply because there are different players (situational motivation).

Finally, and encompassing all of the previous ideas, competition may simply be seen as a learning and development tool; it is a task or practice to be undertaken by the participant just like any other task or practice used in a training session. Indeed, in examining the development of expert performance, Baker, Côté and Abernethy (2003) demonstrated that in addition to deliberate practice, the best athletes accumulated more hours of competition.

In short, competition offers numerous opportunities to coaches to enhance the development of their athletes. However, the skill is capturing this opportunity within a coherent programme of development, and this requires planning. Too often this big picture is missed, and competition becomes the focus for setting week to week or session to session goals – otherwise known as fire fighting. Typically this simply results in an unfocused programme where quick changes in performance are taken as evidence for learning and little true development actually occurs (Abraham and Collins 2011a; Schmidt and Bjork 1992).

While it is important to think philosophically about what role competition will play within a coaching plan, it is also important to think operationally and logistically. When are the competitions, how many of them are there, can they be ranked in terms of importance or amount of challenge that they pose? The key point here is coaches should carefully consider how they can make most effective use of competition time as part of the planning process.

## SUMMARISING KEY POINTS SO FAR

Up to this point we have talked largely about the importance of planning and offered some tools to guide thinking about goal setting and planning:

- Considered, thoughtful planning can overcome and then guide intuitive practice in the moment of coaching responses.
- There is a lot of specific terminology used within the field of planning, some of which is useful to coaches of young participants, some of which isn't. However, an awareness of all specialist terms will probably be useful to aid communication.
- Planning requires thinking, but thinking is difficult in complex environments such as coaching. Consequently a range of thinking tools has been offered.
- Nested planning identifies the need for coaches to be aware of macro long term strategic and political goals within their setting. They should try to contribute to these goals. They should use these goals to then map out how a meso timeframe (a year, for example) of this long term plan which in turn can be used to map out how a micro set of sessions would be developed.
- Constructive alignment identifies that well defined goals/learning outcomes should be developed for both long term macro/meso programmes, with aligned ideas for measuring progress and methods of delivery. This alignment should then be carried through into more meso/micro programmes of session delivery.

- The bio-psycho-social model offers a way of thinking about and understanding the behaviour and development of participants (the who).
- Three worlds offers a view on why participants may be engaging in a given sport at a given moment. These reasons are PPW, PRE or ERE. Participants' reasons for engaging are fluid, meaning that reasons for engagement can change over time, within a sport and from sport to sport.
- Five skill domains offers a view that skill development demands, goals and curriculum (the what) can be drawn from any Movement, Physical, Technical/Tactical, Psychobehavioural, Social and Life skills. The precise nature of the goals and curriculum should be based on the goals identified in nested and constructively aligned planning and be relevant to the needs of the participant.
- Spiral curriculum recognises that learning is not linear but, rather, is cumulative, interconnected and evolving. Simply because a topic has been taught does not mean that it has been learned. Indeed even if there is a comprehension and effective performance of a skill or idea, it does not mean that this skill has been integrated within a participant's other skills. As such, planning for skill development should revisit and build from previous ideas.
- Careful thought is required about creating the best coaching environment, from the development of strong and respectful relationships to the optimal use of competition. Typically for young participants, competition will not necessarily be about winning but about what can be learned, even if that means learning how to win or learning from defeat.

## THE MECHANICS OF PLANNING

Contrary to some perceptions, there is no such thing as the perfect planning template. In our time working with coaches and being coaches we have seen plans that range from extremely detailed multipage booklets to a piece of A4 paper with a table drawn in pen. The reason why there isn't a perfect template is in keeping with the rest of this chapter – a plan committed to paper or computer programme is an output; it is the planning process of thinking and decision making that defines the quality of goals and plans. Indeed from this point of view the paper copy or computer file is little more than an aide memoire to help coaches remember what they were thinking when they engaged in a planning process. However, there can be more to a template than acting simply as an aide memoire. As identified in the previous summary section, there are a number of key concepts that can drive thinking about goal setting and planning, and a strong template can act as much as a aide memoire for what coaches should think about as much as what they were thinking about. As such the remainder of this chapter will focus on offering some templates and supporting ideas to help coaches plan, drawing on the major concepts presented in this chapter.

Just to be clear though, these are templates developed for a largely unspecified context, and coaching is fundamentally driven by the context that it is situated in (Jones and Wallace 2006). As such our preference would be that coaches use the templates presented as a starting point to develop their own templates to match the demands of their own context.

**41**

*Template 2.1* Nested goal setting and constructively aligned programme outcomes for a 4-year programme

| Strategic/political and theoretical expectations and benchmarks | | | | | |
|---|---|---|---|---|---|
| Programme outcomes (suggest no more than 6) | 1.<br>2.<br>3.<br>4.<br>5.<br>6. | | | | |
| Year: | 1 | 2 | 3 | 4 | |
| Expected key performance indicators (KPI) to feedback to stakeholders (e.g. programme funders, managers, parents) | | | | | |
| Major bio-psycho-social maturational considerations | | | | | |
| Expected athlete and/or team capabilities to be shared with participants (language subject to change) | Tech/tact | | | | |
| | Movement | | | | |
| | Physical | | | | |
| | Psycho-behavioural | | | | |
| | Social/lifestyle | | | | |

This template is designed to encourage coaches to think about the broad picture of what they are trying to achieve in the long term using the terminology of programme outcomes. The first box recognises that there will be strategic and political imperatives that have to be worked to. However, coaches should also have a strong view on this and this should be informed through theoretical and and good practice principles. Such views would be informed by the likely motivations and capabilities of the participants in the programme, drawing on bio-psycho-social evidence and/or the three world's theoretical ideas.

The suggested aligned six programme outcomes category is rather arbitrary and there is relatively little evidence to support this suggestion. However, the best assumption is twofold. First, it encourages people to formulate a coherent view on what a coaching programme is trying to do, thus allowing for structured and coherent thinking about how to best achieve these outcomes. The second reason is probably more strategic – fewer programme outcomes allows for an easier and concise 'sell' when presenting them to key stakeholders such as parents, participants and/or managers. The creation of well-defined programme outcomes sets platform from which aligned expected KPIs and developments in participant skills can be mapped. This table strongly aligns with the need for nested thinking and constructive alignment presented in Figures 2.2 and 2.3.

*Template 2.2* Assessing status and measuring progress

|  | Assessment method(s) | Data collected, collection method, environment and time of collection | Output and link to programme outcomes |
|---|---|---|---|
| KPIs |  |  |  |
| Bio-psycho-social maturational status |  |  |  |
| Tech/tact |  |  |  |
| Movement |  |  |  |
| Physical |  |  |  |
| Psycho-behavioural |  |  |  |
| Social/lifestyle |  |  |  |

Following the constructive alignment concept, coaches will need to monitor progress through the use of some form of assessment. This provides both information about progress and, if the systems have meaning for the participants, crucial motivation to the participants about where to direct their efforts and how well they are developing. As such this will not be a quick process; planning to develop valid and meaningful assessments will require critical and innovative thought, template 2.2 is designed to structure this critical thought.

Continuing with the flow of constructive alignment presented in Figure 2.3, template 2.3's meso cycles of goals considers the need to plan required learning activities and allocate effort. The allocation of effort is designed to encourage coaches to think about where the emphasis of development (and probably competition) for that meso cycle lies. It may be evenly spread across the five areas or more focused in just one or two – the answer to this will come from considerations about how the coaching curriculum and participant development interact in order to achieve the programme outcomes. As such the 'Goal' box (shown in template 2.3) is designed to encourage coaches to accurately define the goals that are being worked towards while also considering how these will link to past and future goals in a spiral curriculum. Finally, the required learning activities box encourages coaches to think about what type task or practice and coach behaviour is going to be required to facilitate the required participant engagement in keeping with Figure 2.4. Clearly only a limited amount of detail can be added here, but this can encourage coaches to consider that learning activities do not just have to be used once and

Template 2.3 Annual goal setting for team and/or individual

| | Meso cycle 1 | | | Meso cycle 2 | | | Meso cycle 3 | | | Meso cycle 4 | | |
|---|---|---|---|---|---|---|---|---|---|---|---|---|
| | % Allocation of effort | Goal (spiral connection) | Required learning activities and assessment points | % Allocation of effort | Goal (spiral connection) | Required learning activities and assessment points | % Allocation of effort | Goal (spiral connection) | Required learning activities and assessment points | % Allocation of effort | Goal (spiral connection) | Required learning activities and assessment points |
| Tech/tact | | | | | | | | | | | | |
| Movement | | | | | | | | | | | | |
| Physical | | | | | | | | | | | | |
| Psycho-behavioural | | | | | | | | | | | | |
| Social/lifestyle | | | | | | | | | | | | |

that there should be some level of continuation in practice design. This consideration should also account for when any of the previously considered assessment/analysis methods will be used to monitor progress.

*Template 2.4* Meso–micro planning template

| Meso cycle 1 | | Week 1 | Week 2 | Week 3 | Week 4 | Week 5 | Week 6 | Week 7 | Week 8 |
|---|---|---|---|---|---|---|---|---|---|
| Objectives (integrative statement(s) from 5 goals) | | | | | | | | | |
| Resources | Training time available | | | | | | | | |
| | Facilities available | | | | | | | | |
| | Competition focus | | | | | | | | |
| | Suggested homework | | | | | | | | |
| | Support available/ required | | | | | | | | |

Planning template 2.4 provides a further level of detail at a meso–micro level. We suggest here that the explicit goals of the meso plan may be better served as being recorded as weekly objectives. There would be no reason why the same objective couldn't cross more than one week, especially in recognition of our earlier comment about learning taking a long time. This is the first time that resources have been explicitly added. Consideration of resource can be a reality check on the level of development expected against the resources available to support that development.[4] Note that 'homework' is an explicit resource available to all coaches but, in our experience, infrequently used by coaches. Competition focus is included in keeping with the idea that coaches should actively consider how they can make best use of upcoming competitions in meeting short term objectives and longer term goals. Finally, there is a reminder that coaches may want to consider how they can make use of any support available, for example asking a parent to film a competition for use at a later debrief.

The last planning template 2.5 is an individual session planner. This represents the final template in a constructively aligned, nested planning approach. Here team and individual objectives are aligned with meso goals. These goals should then lead to the formulation of practice and task designs, alongside suggested coaching approaches and even the vocabulary that may be chosen.

*Template 2.5* Session planner

| Coach | | | Date | | Meso block | | Week | |
|---|---|---|---|---|---|---|---|---|
| **Meso block goals** | Tech/tact | Psycho-behavioural | | Physical | | Movement | | Social/lifestyle |
| | | | | | | | | |

| TEAM session objectives | | |
|---|---|---|
| Technical/tactical | Physical | Psychological/social |
| | | |

| INDIVIDUAL PARTICIPANT session objectives | | |
|---|---|---|
| Player name | Learning objective | Progress review and action plan |
| | | |

| Session structure and organisation |
|---|
| |

| Key coaching methods and vocab |
|---|
| Coaching methods:<br><br><br>Vocab: |

## HEALTH WARNING AND CONCLUSIONS

Planning is not an exact science, nor is this chapter anywhere near a complete resource of planning ideas. In fact many of the ideas offer only a conceptual level of insight to the how, what and why of planning; the rest of this book offers ideas that could be considered within any planning activity. When thinking about the use of planning to enable and inform participant and performer development and coaching, it is important for coaches to be aware of a range of participant and performer possibilities that affect its coverage and efficacy. For example, it is useful to draw on two typical yet contrasting images of talent development. One is of a naturally gifted athlete who would succeed in a chosen sport regardless of the effort put in and resources made available. For example, pundits often make comments such as 'Messi's a natural talent', implying that with these natural gifts Lionel Messi's performance success was inevitable. The other is of the master coach working miracles with individuals and teams whom no one else gave a chance, or who have been deprived of success for many years. In the first image, the coach has a limited role, accompanying the athlete on his/her path to glory. Success is inevitable, so why bother too much with planning? In the second image, the coach's knowledge and expertise reigns supreme. Planning is used as a means of structuring and implementing this knowledge, providing a kind of formalised guarantor of long term performer success.

The problem with these perceptions is that they have very little basis in reality, or research for that matter. Instead, the research suggests that talent development is a more complex set of interactions between genetics, time devoted to training and practice, psychological enablers and access to social resources such as coaching and support from the family. Many ingredients come together to produce the high performing athlete or indeed the poorly performing participant. These ingredients may be different for different participants, and come together in different times and places. In this complex interaction there are influences, not determinates; there are possibilities, not guarantees (North 2013).

There are no easy answers, but the following seems important. By simply having knowledge of the complex and multidimensional qualities of participant development and coaching, coaches can recognise that their role is important whilst repositioning themselves from 'controllers' to 'guiders/influencers' working with the resources available to them and doing the best they can. Planning should be seen as one means of assimilating information, guiding action, and minimising risk in these complex coaching environments. It should also be seen as a means of focusing self-reflection. Why didn't the planning work? What could be done better next time? There are no guarantees in participant development and coaching, but effective planning could be seen as one tool to structure coaching, minimise risks, and encourage reflection on what worked and what did not.

### Some comments from coaches

In the process of putting this chapter together we sent it to a number of experienced coaches and coach educators to get their feedback. Where possible we used their feedback in editing this chapter. However, many of their comments merit inclusion here as they may help other coaches engage in some critical thinking about the contents of this chapter:

**47**

Motivation can change over time, we've had some success with allowing kids to temporarily drop out of ERE/PRE groups into PPW group at times when 'life has got tough', for example at exam time. So instead of having to 'perform' they can just enjoy sport for a period of time and then switch back into Performance when other commitments subside. Coaches should consider how their planning and competition impacts on parents' capacity to support their kids through the sport. I don't see many, if any, kids in Triathlon whose parents aren't professional services or 'middle class', can coaches plan for those kind of barriers? Coaches should draw on the contents of this book to consider why and how they plan for talent selection, hopefully coaches would see that this doc helps propose there is a much wider issue than current Personal Best. Also coaches should consider how to plan for talent selection issues when they don't have control over the selection process/criteria.

*Tony Jolly, Head Coach Manchester Triathlon, Coach Educator for British Triathlon*

One observation I have made of many coaches and especially coaches of 12 to 18 year olds is they often don't take the big picture into account. Considering the physical and mental stress loads in general life, from something as simple as walking to school, engaging in other sports and staying up late to understanding academic and social stressors, these are all crucial in monitoring and adapting coaching plans.

Coaches should be wary of planning for and introducing mental skills, wherever possible recognize the skills that children already possess and develop in other areas of life. Children and teenagers often struggle to put things into perspective. If a coach suddenly starts to focus on mental skills in a way that the child doesn't recognize then the consequence could be that the child internalizes this to be a bigger problem than it actually is.

I would emphasise that in general most teenagers that are not in academies are still choosing what they are good at in sport and therefore planning for flexibility is key for this type of teenager. Their long term goal is more likely to be what sport or sports could I do.

*Sue Jolly (No relation to Tony Jolly). Sport Learning Consultant, Mountain Bike Coach*

I really enjoyed reading this chapter as unlike most books I have read it is clearly understandable and written in common sense plain English. The issue of experience and expertise is an interesting issue, people with expertise are those who are deliberate planners but coaches' expertise also depends on the quality and versatility of their experiences. I think you need both assets to be able to plan training/development programmes/career paths successfully – you need the experience of going a down a variety of roads in your own career with an athlete and then you need expertise to make sense of what you have experienced. Therefore experience and expertise must work together as Ericsson *et al.* (1993) said it take many hours of learning and deliberate practice (experience) to achieve expert status.

*Sue Ringrose, Head Coach, New Farm Equestrian;*
*Coach Educator British Eventing*

I think the chapter highlights key considerations and brings to life the requirement for alignment between planning processes in order to influence real-world coaching practice. From experience this is especially important within Talent Development Environments, but equally with younger groups of children in multi-skill activities where 'ages and stages' of participants are wide-ranging.

Also, youth participant development, across any 'performance level' and regardless of the intended outcomes of a coaching programme (participation/talent development), at some stage the focus turns to the needs of individuals within a group. This requires in-depth planning i.e. not only broad consideration of the way general-outcomes can be supported but also how associated learning opportunities can be afforded to individuals in the group. This individualisation may either differentiate complexity of intended-outcomes and/or address different aspects of participant development across bio-psycho-social domains for participants. Planning can accelerate participant development, as well as preparing coaches for what may come within coaching practice so that they are equipped to deal with emerging needs of the performer.

*Andy Rock, AASE Scheme Manager and Academy Coach, Leeds Rugby and Otley Grammar School*

Some ideas I would offer in addition to those included in the chapter are:

- Booking facilities and building resources require planning since both play a large part while working with young people.
- Don't assume that movement skills are completed when participants get beyond the FMS stage. Working on advanced SOL skills is important for participants to facilitate the development of sport specific techniques.
- There are major benefits in planning for subtle challenges (even losing) to create speed-bumps that are specific to a mental strength area for the athletes developing within a sport. However, developing a meaningful speed bump for an athlete requires a lot of preparation and cooperation.
- Offering formative feedback on current coaching topics within a meso cycle help you identify with current learning outcomes as opposed to what you want it to look like at the end of the plan.
- Identify what athletes arrive at your programme knowing and looking like while considering what they need to know about in the next environment on their journey.

*Stewart Wilkinson, England Rugby League Performance Coach,*
*Lecturer in Sport Coaching and Performance, University of Central Lancashire*

I enjoyed reading the chapter; you have incorporated certain areas into the planning process that often get overlooked. Of course, mainly that 'the participant comes first' or decides what happens next. It is delivered in a nice 'humanistic' and honest manner which coaches will find engaging too. LTAD is analysed in a balanced manner which takes into account early, mid and late specialisation and the main issue of competition structure. I would also encourage coaches to consider the issues of windows of bio-psycho-social issues of trainability when planning for individuals as they mature (Balyi, Way and Higgs

2013), and shift from sampling a number of sports to specializing in a few to investing in one or two (Côté *et al.* 2003).

*Ian Freeman, High Performing Coach Research and*
*Long Term Athlete Development Specialist, British Swimming*

## NOTES

1 This is not to say that winning is a 'bad thing'. Learning how to win may well be a valid goal to work on. It is when winning is at the expense of development that problems will occur.
2 This does not mean that plans should be cast in stone and be inflexible – this is addressed later in the chapter.
3 Taking on board the ideas in the three world's continuum that if coaches don't share the same goals they may want to consider if they are in the right coaching environment.
4 There would be nothing to stop coaches considering how resources could be planned for earlier in the cycle if this was thought useful.

## REFERENCES

Abbott, A. & Collins, D. (2004). Eliminating the dichotomy between theory and practice in talent identification and development: Considering the role of psychology. *Journal of Sport Sciences*, 22, 395–408.

Abraham, A. and Collins, D. (2011a). Effective skill development: How should athletes' skills be developed? In *Performance Psychology: A Guide for the Practitioner*. D. Collins, H. Richards and A. Button (Eds.) (London: Churchill Livingstone): pp. 207–230.

Abraham, A. and Collins, D. (2011b). Taking the next step: Ways forward for coaching science. *Quest* 63(4): pp. 366–384.

Abraham, A., Collins, D. and Martindale, R. (2006). The coaching schematic: Validation through expert coach consensus. *Journal of Sport Sciences* 24(6): pp. 549–564.

Abraham, A., Manley, A.J. and Morgan, G. (2012). *Aura, presence and impression management*: pp. 1–22. (London: Leeds Metropolitan University The FA).

Anderson, J.R. (1982). Acquisition of a cognitive skill. *Psychological Review* 89(4): pp. 369–406.

Bailey, R., Collins, D., Ford, P., McNamara, A., Toms, M. and Pearce, G. (2010). *Participant development in sport: An academic review*: p. 141. (Leeds: Sports Coach UK).

Baker, J., Côté, J. and Abernethy, B. (2003). Sport specific training, deliberate practice and the development of expertise in team ball sports. *Journal of Applied Sport Psychology* 15: pp. 12–25.

Balyi, I., Way, R. and Higgs, C. (2013). *Long term athlete development*. (Champaign IL: Human Kinetics).

Biggs, J. B. (2003). *Teaching for quality learning at university* (2nd edn). (Buckingham: Open University Press/Society for Research into Higher Education).

Biggs, J. and Tang, C. (2011). *Teaching for quality learning at university* (4th ed.). (Maidenhead: Open University Press).

Birrer, D. and Morgan, G. (2010). Psychological skills training as a way to enhance an athlete's performance in high-intensity sports. *Scandinavian Journal of Medicine & Science in Sports* 20: pp. 78–87.

Bompa, T.O. and Haff, G.G. (2009). *Periodization: Theory and methodology of training* (5th ed.: p. 424). (Champaign, IL: Human Kinetics).

Bruner, J. (1963). Needed: A theory of instruction. *Educational Leadership* 20(8): pp. 523–532.

Burton, A. W. and Miller, D. E. (1998) *Movement Skill Assessment*. (Champaign, IL: Human Kinetics).

Chen, A. and Hancock, G.R. (2006). Conceptualizing a theoretical model for school-centered adolescent physical activity intervention research. *Quest* 58: pp. 355–376.

Collins, D., Bailey, R., Ford, P. A., MacNamara, Á., Toms, M. and Pearce, G. (2012). Three worlds: new directions in participant development in sport and physical activity. *Sport, Education and Society* 17(2): pp. 225–243.

Côté, J., Baker, J. and Abernethy, B. (2003). From play to practice: A developmental framework for the acquisition of expertise in team sports. In *Expert Performance in Sports*. J.L. Starkes and K.A. Ericsson (Eds.) (Champaign, IL: Human Kinetics): pp. 89–135.

Deci, E.L. and Ryan, R.M. (2008). Self-determination theory: A macrotheory of human motivation, development, and health. *Canadian Psychology/Psychologie Canadienne* 49(3): pp. 182–185.

Dirks, K.T. (2000). Trust in leadership and team performance: Evidence from NCAA basketball. *Journal of Applied Psychology* 85(6): pp. 1004–1012.

Education, Department of. (2014). *Secondary national curriculum until 2014: Personal, social, health and economic education (PSHEE)*. Retrieved: 14 January 2014. www.education.gov.uk/schools/teachingandlearning/curriculum/secondary/b00198880/pshee/ks4/personal/statements

Ericsson, K.A., Krampe, R.T., Tesch-Romer, C., Ashworth, C., Carey, G., Grassia, J. and Schneider, V. (1993). The role of deliberate practice in the acquisition of expert performance. *Psychology Review* 100(3): pp. 363–406.

Faigenbaum, A. D., Lloyd, R.S. and Myer, G.D. (2013). Youth resistance training: Past practices, new perspectives, and future directions. *Pediatric Exercise Science* 25(4): pp. 591–604.

Fink, J. and Siedentop, D. (1989). The development of routines, rules, and expectations at the start of the school year. *Journal of Teaching in Physical Education* 8(3): pp. 198–212.

Gallahue, D. L. and Ozmun, J. C. (2006) *Understanding motor development* (6th edn). (New York: McGraw-Hill).

Grecic, D. and Collins, D. (2013). The epistemological chain: Practical applications in sports. *QUEST* 65(2): pp. 151–168.

Halpern, D.F. (2014). *Thought and knowledge* (5th ed.). (New York: Psychology Press).

Hambrick, D.Z. (2003). Why are some people more knowledgeable than others? A longitudinal study of knowledge acquisition. *Memory and Cognition* 31(6): pp. 902–917.

Haywood, K. & Getchell, N. (2005) *Life Span Motor Development*. (Champaign, IL: Human Kinetics).

Holliday, B., Burton, D., Sun, G., Hammermeister, J., Naylor, S., & Freigang, D. (2008). Building the better mental training mousetrap: Is periodization a more systematic approach to promoting performance excellence? *Journal of Applied Sport Psychology*, 20, 199–219.

Jones, D.F., Housner, L.D. and Kornspan, A.S. (1995). A comparative analysis of expert and novice basketball coaches' practice planning. *Applied Research in Coaching and Athletics Annual*: pp. 201–227.

Jones, L. and Harcourt, D. (2013). Social competencies and the 'Early Years Learning Framework': Understanding critical influences on educator capacity. *Australasian Journal of Early Childhood* 38(1): pp. 4–10.

**51**

Jones, R. and Wallace, M. (2006). The coach as 'orchestrator': More realistically managing the complex coaching context. In *The Sports Coach as Educator: Reconceptualising Sports Coaching*. R. Jones (Ed.) (Abingdon: Routledge): pp. 51–64.

Jurevičienė, M., Kaffemanienė, I. and Ruškus, J. (2012). Concept and structural components of social skills. *Education. Physical Training. Sport* 86(3): pp. 42–52.

Kahneman, D. and Klein, G.A. (2009). Conditions for intuitive expertise: A failure to disagree. *American Psychologist* 64(6): pp. 515–526.

Langdon, S.W. (2007). Conceptualizations of respect: Qualitative and quantitative evidence of four (five) themes. *Journal of Psychology* 141(5): pp. 469–484.

Leary, M.R. and Kowalski, R.M. (1990). Impression management: A literature review and two-component model. *Psychological Bulletin* 107(1): pp. 34–47.

Lloyd, R. S. and Oliver, J. L. (2012) The Youth Physical Development Model: A new approach to long-term athlete development. *Strength and Conditioning Journal*. 34(3), 61–72.

Lloyd, R.S., Faigenbaum, A. D., Stone, M.H., Oliver, J.L., Jeffreys, I., Moody, J.A. and Myer, G.D. (2013). Position statement on youth resistance training: The 2014 international consensus. *British Journal of Sports Medicine* 48(7): pp. 498–505.

Lyle, J. (2010). Planning for team sports. In *Sport Coaching: Professionalisation and Practice*. J. Lyle and C. Cushion (eds.) (London: Churchill Livingstone).

MacMahon, C. and McPherson, S.L. (2009). Knowledge base as a mechanism for perceptual-cognitive tasks: Skill is in the details! *International Journal of Sport Psychology* 40(4): pp. 565–579.

MacNamara, Á., Button, A. and Collins, D. (2010a). The role of psychological characteristics in facilitating the pathway to elite performance: Part 1, Identifying mental skills and behaviors. *The Sport Psychologist* 24(1): pp. 52–73.

MacNamara, Á., Button, A. and Collins, D. (2010b). The role of psychological characteristics in facilitating the pathway to elite performance: Part 2, Examining environmental and stage-related differences in skills and behaviors. *Sport Psychologist* 24(1): pp. 74–96.

MacNamara, Á., Collins, D., Bailey, R., Toms, M., Ford, P. and Pearce, G. (2011). Promoting lifelong physical activity and high level performance: Realising an achievable aim for physical education. *Physical Education & Sport Pedagogy* 16(3): pp. 265–278.

Martindale, A. and Collins, D. (2005). Professional judgement and decision making in applied sport psychology: The role of intention for impact. *The Sport Psychologist* 19(3): pp. 303–317.

Martindale, R., Collins, D. & Abraham, A. (2007). Effective talent development: The elite coach perspective in UK sport. *Journal of Applied Sport Psychology*, 19, 187–206.

Moylett, H. and Stewart, N. (2012). *Development matters in the early years foundation stage (EYFS)*. London: Early Education. Retrieved: 30 September 2014. www.foundationyears.org.uk/files/2012/03/Development-Matters-FINAL-PRINT-AMENDED.pdf

Muir, B. (2012). Using video and the coaching practice planning and reflective framework to facilitate high performance coaches development. In UK Sport World Class Performance Conference. Conference Presentation, Leeds, 26–28 November.

Muir, B., Morgan, G., Abraham, A. and Morley, D. (2011). Developmentally appropriate approaches to coaching children. In *Coaching Children in Sport*. I. Stafford (ed.) (London and New York: Routledge).

Myers, D.G. (2010). Intuition's powers and perils. *Psychological Inquiry* 21(4): pp. 371–377.

Nash, C., Martindale, R., Collins, D. and Martindale, A. (2012). Parameterising expertise in coaching: Past, present and future. *Journal of Sports Sciences* 30(10): pp. 985–94.

North, J. (2013). A critical realist approach to theorising coaching practice. In *The Routledge Handbook of Sports Coaching*. P. Potrac, W.D. Gilbert and J. Dennison (eds.) (London: Routledge): pp. 133–144.

Olson, K.R. and Dweck, C.S. (2008). A blueprint for social cognitive development. *Perspectives of Psychological Science* 3(3): pp. 193–202.

Orlick, T. D., & Partington, J. (1988). Mental links to excellence. *The Sport Psychologist*, 2, 105–130.

Pain, M. A. & Harwood, C. G. (2004). Knowledge and perceptions of sport psychology within English soccer. *Journal of Sports Sciences*, 22, 813–826.

Passos, P., Araújo, D., Davids, K. and Shuttleworth, R. (2008). Manipulating constraints to train decision making in rugby union. *International Journal of Sports Science and Coaching* 3(1): pp. 125–140.

Payne, V. G. and Issacs, L. D. (1995) *Human Motor Development: A lifespan Approach* (3rd edn). (Mountain View, CA: Mayfield).

Richards, P., Collins, D. and Mascarenhas, D.R.D. (2012). Developing rapid high-pressure team decision-making skills. The integration of slow deliberate reflective learning within the competitive performance environment: A case study of elite netball. *Reflective Practice* 13(3): pp. 407–424.

Sagar, S.S. and Jowett, S. (2012). Communicative acts in coach–athlete interactions: When losing competitions and when making mistakes in training. *Western Journal of Communication* 76(2): pp. 148–174.

Schempp, P.G., McCullick, B.A. and Sannen Mason, I. (2006). The development of expert coaching. In *The Sports Coach as Educator*. R. Jones (Ed.) (Abingdon: Routledge): pp. 145–161.

Schmidt, R.A. and Bjork, R.A. (1992). New conceptualizations of practice: Common principles in three paradigms suggest new concepts for training. *Psychological Science* 3(4): pp. 207–217.

Shapiro, L.E. (2004). *101 ways to teach children social skills*. The Bureau For At-Risk Youth. Retrieved: 9 April 2014. www.socialskillscentral.com/free/101_Ways_Teach_Children_Social_Skills.pdf

Stodden, D. F. et al. (2008) A Developmental Perspective on the Role of Motor Skill Competence in Physical Activity: An Emergent Relationship. *Quest*, 60: pp. 290–306.

Weinberg, R.S. and Gould, D. (2003). *Foundations of sport and exercise psychology* (3rd ed.: p. 585). (Champaign, IL: Human Kinetics).

Weinberg, R. S., & Williams, J. M. (2006). Integrating and implementing a psychological skills training program. In J. M. Williams (Ed.), *Applied sport psychology: Personal growth to peak performance* (5th edn). (Mountain View, CA: Mayfield: pp. 425–457).

## Chapter 3

# The importance of
# a coaching philosophy

*John Sproule*

This chapter outlines why a coaching philosophy should be couched in terms of values and principles, and the need for a sports coach to be a principled leader. The perspective that philosophy should be a pursuit of everyone, with coaching philosophy as a means of monitoring professional practice, is presented. Some critique of the UK coach education system is aligned to some suggestion for self-determination and self-regulation conceptual frameworks. Discussion of cheating, Olympism and humanism includes biological manipulation and the spirit of sport. The parameters of the humanistic approach to coaching, storytelling and the reflective process build to a recent case study of a national rugby team coach who was found to evidence a coaching philosophy communicated through value statements, ideological objectives and pragmatic intentions. The chapter concludes by highlighting the need for a strong philosophical underpinning with moral purpose to guide coaching behaviour.

### Ceteris paribus

In 1999 Lyle stated:

> When invited to, coaches are able to express their thoughts about coaching practice in a set of inter-related statements. The drawing together of these value statements about how they practice coaching is what we term 'coaching philosophies'. These value frameworks indicate to the reader what the coach believes is important in coaching.
>
> (Cross and Lyle 1999, p. 26)

Rokeach (1973) suggested a three component framework for all beliefs: a cognitive component (for example, a coach's knowledge about what is true or false); an affective component (for example, a coach taking a positive or negative position in an argument); a behavioural component (for example, the coach's action based on his or her belief[s]). Rokeach's framework of beliefs could be interpreted as including the following perspectives: a sports coach is completely responsible for his or her own actions (in other words, an existential belief); a sports coach's belief(s) could be evaluated as 'good' or 'bad'; the outcome of a sports coach's actions could be desirable or undesirable.

The values of a coach, whether they be instrumental (for example, the athlete can with certainty depend on the coach to be ready and prepared for the training session) or terminal (for example, the coach respects the opinion of the athlete), are the determinants of a coach's attitudes. If we agree that a coaching philosophy should be couched in terms of values and principles, then this requires an understanding that principles are the implementation of values, guidelines for putting values into practice, which is a guide to the coach's behaviour. For example, communication styles, decision making, feedback, goal setting, counselling, disciplinary behaviour and management will all individually and collectively reflect the coach's belief system (Cross and Lyle 1999). The values reflected by an ethical coaching culture are those of attaching importance to athletes as individuals. For example, a coach needs to be an effective leader in order to guide the individual performer/group/team towards their ultimate goal. As Albion (2006) states:

> Values-based leadership is about how you choose to express your humanity through your business. Every decision you make . . . is an opportunity to express your values.
>
> (p. 97)

The improvement in performance and the improvement in competition performance are at the heart of coaching and performance coaching respectively, and an acceptable societal ideology for personal coaching practice is surely values-laden. It is the coach's responsibility to abide by a code of conduct and behave in an ethical manner. For example, it is unacceptable to over-pressurize and abuse young people. Robinson (2010) has stated that a coaching style is the manner in which the coach delivers his or her coaching session and is partially dependent on a philosophy of coaching. However, as knowing about philosophy does not guarantee being able to practice coaching philosophy, a degree of caution is advisable.

Philosophy belongs to everyone and should, to a greater or lesser degree, be a pursuit of everyone – that is why it matters. Martin Cohen describes philosophy as a kind of manure. Pile it high, in a few places, and it simply rots and stinks. But spread it around and it becomes surprisingly useful (Cohen 2013). Thus philosophy can be a guide to action – helping to answer the perennial question 'what should I do?' John Hospers suggests that philosophy is the study of the reasons people have for thinking as they do think. Your beliefs and desires determine the reasons for your actions, and an understanding of philosophy helps you decide the 'right' thing to do (Hospers 1997). In a sense philosophy can be thinking about thinking, or *metacognition*. Metacognition involves cognitions about cognitions and is a fundamental characteristic of being human. In other words, it involves an individual thinking about their thoughts and thought processes (Hacker 1998). Most cognitive processes are accompanied by metacognitive activities that control and monitor the cognitive activities of individuals (Koriat 1998; Yzerbyt *et al.* 1998). Flavell (1979) adopts a view that metacognition involves knowledge of one's cognitive processes and products, and involves regulation, self-monitoring and evaluation of cognitive activity. The majority of writing on metacognition approaches the topic from a cognitive information processing perspective without appreciating the connection to socio-cultural influences on an individual's use of metacognitive strategies. However, as much of the coaching process involves social interactions among coaches and athletes, it is essential that coaches also understand the social dimensions of this construct and any impact on the coaching experience of athletes this may have; the philosophy of coaching is, in one sense, grounded in social-cognitive theory. Indeed, Einstein has stated that the only way to approach the core truths of reality is through philosophy. The world of coaching sport is perhaps more complex than sports coaches think it is. This could be one good reason for those involved in sports coaching to find out more about philosophy, because, as Socrates said: 'knowledge is the food of the soul'.

One of the central assumptions of many sports coaches, partly because sports SCIENCE rules, is that of cause and effect, and sometimes this lures sports coaches into believing that identical conditions will produce identical outcomes. For example, it enables them to make accurate predictions about athlete training or competitive performance. However, the coaching role goes beyond that of technical expert, and philosophy isn't just about physical theories such as Darwin's biological Theory of Natural Selection, where the fastest and strongest survive and the rest must perish. From a philosophical perspective it is reasonable to ask *Ceteris paribus,* that is other things being equal Darwin's theory is supposed to be true, unless you live in some parts of North America, where natural selection is a philosophical idea that has been rejected! Perhaps coaching and philosophy are intricately bound and as such should be considered together.

## WHAT IS A COACHING PHILOSOPHY?

In the study of coaching, where there is much emphasis on the performer, there is a tendency to privilege the technological, biophysical and scientific aspects, because they are perceived to be easier to control (Williams and Hodges 2005). Some researchers in this area have concluded that there is a clear differentiation between participation and performance coaching, but others have argued that coaching must be viewed from a more holistic perspective rather than a somewhat simplistic standpoint (Cushion 2007). Jowett (2008) emphasised that more attention has to be focused on the work of coaches and the initial introduction and basic skills of the particular sports to highlight the importance of fundamentals and to encourage the later development of higher-order skills, such as decision making and problem solving. Professional values and personal commitment should be at the core of coach education if novice coaches are to benefit from mentorship with the most 'experienced' coaches. For this to be successful the coach education process should contribute to developing appropriate knowledge, skills, attitudes, values and practices compatible with Cohen's (1995) description of philosophy for a just and equitable world ('spread it around and it becomes useful'). However, this will not happen unless the more experienced coaches are capable of providing mentor leadership aligned to a value-laden vision for improvement in outcomes for less experienced coaches, based on shared values as well as the ethical and robust evaluation of evidence based coach behaviour.

A coaching process that offers a supportive learning environment, appropriate levels of challenge for both the coach and the participants and that engenders a passion for the sport can produce positive and productive sporting outcomes. Research on the professional development of physical education teachers shows that the philosophies and beliefs of teachers are linked to their actual practice (Tsangaridou *et al.* 2003). Similarly with coaches, their coaching philosophy as determined by factors such as their values, should be reflected in their coaching style and should include socially and culturally acceptable transparent coach behaviours (Jones *et al.* 2003; Potrac *et al.* 2000). According to Weiss (2008) the development of a coaching philosophy should be grounded in developmental psychology, particularly for coaches involved in youth sport. According to O'Sullivan *et al.* (2005) a philosophy is based upon beliefs, those formed through sport as a participant and coach, and based upon educational background and life experiences. I agree with Reynolds (2005) who stated that a personal coaching philosophy can be viewed as a tool to enable coaches to question their practice and develop their own (and their performers') understanding and knowledge. This is important because coaches could simply be viewed as 'merely technicians engaged in the transfer of knowledge', or alternatively be encouraged to consider the holistic role of the coach aligned to a perceived relevance of a coaching philosophy to their own role and coaching practice (Fraser-Thomas and Côté 2009; Malloy and Rossow-Kimball 2007). Experts within coaching, teaching and instruction regularly reflect upon their beliefs and coaching philosophy as a means of monitoring their professional practice (Schempp *et al.* 2006). Coaching effectiveness is determined by use of a humanistic philosophy, focusing upon individual aptitudes and aims, whereas experienced coaches are more likely to re-examine their practice and have the previously established knowledge base to make informed change when necessary (Butler 2005). Novice coaches, on the other hand, tend to concentrate on organisational aspects as well as session content rather than question their own belief system (Cothran *et al.* 2005). Nash *et al.* (2008) examined the importance of a coaching philosophy in coaching practice. The participants (male and female) for this study were all practicing coaches from Level 1 to Level 5, with a wide range of years coaching ($\leq$ 1 year to 37 years). They found that coaches at Levels 1 and 2 generally did not exhibit an obvious awareness of their core values and coaching methods. They suggested that the acquisition of a coherent coaching philosophy would enable Level 1 and 2 coaches to approach their coaching practice with consistency and clarity. In their study the coaches at Levels 3, 4 and 5 showed evidence of a more profound consideration of their coaching philosophy and of the recognition the direct impact a coaching philosophy has on their coaching processes and strategies. Additionally, the Level 4 and 5 coaches demonstrated a conceptual awareness of key ideas related both to sport and coaching, as well as an appreciation of the social, cultural and political values associated with the practice of coaching.

## DEVELOPMENT OF A COACHING PHILOSOPHY

Since the 1950s there has been a movement away from authoritarian and paternalistic attitudes to human relations in the workplace in the UK. We have progressed to more egalitarian and respectful approaches that reflect a more holistic view of the individual, whilst still being mindful of the spirit of individualism and even hedonism that this can engender. With mentoring the unit is not the individual but the individuals, the mentor coach and the mentee coach, learning collaboratively (see Chapter 11). Such an approach will focus more on the individual need than on technical coach intervention, on long-term performer talent development than on short-term talent identification, and on a continuing coach-athlete relationship rather than on quick fix but unsustainable outcomes. Indeed, it would be naïve, in a world of multiple and relatively easy access to instant communication, not to engage in the potential of mentoring for the sharing of knowledge, information, ideas and concepts for the development and enhancement of coaching. A mentor can be someone who:

> . . . can care and who know(s) how to integrate the desire for learning that will help one to be powerful in a difficult world.
>
> (Herman and Mandell 2004, p. 10)

The emergence of mentoring as a process of human learning and discovery is significant in various coaching situations, opening up the possibility of new answers to old questions; for example, how can performance be improved in an ethical and sustainable way to escape from 'stuckness' and move forward? If coaching is considered to be a profession, then as professionals, coaches should have the authority as a profession to take responsibility for their own development in the journey towards coaching expertise. It can be argued that such a process would be enhanced with a philosophical self-(re)discovery of our core values and beliefs.

Nash and Sproule (2009) examined the transition of expert coaches through various stages in their careers. The main aim of this study was to ascertain if expert coaches could explain the process of their development to perceived expert status. The beliefs of coaches were found to play a part in their long-term development, but the coaches in their study found them difficult to articulate. Nash and Sproule reported that although the coaches had well developed beliefs regarding their coaching practice, they did not consider them to be an important aspect in framing both their role and their practice. These expert coaches did not connect their beliefs with their tangible coaching approach. Interestingly, according to the expert coaches in the study, coach education courses in their current form do not enable coaches to meet the needs of high-level performers. The key themes identified by these experienced coaches of knowledge, experience, personal qualities, networking and *philosophy* are not currently integrated into formal coach education courses in the UK. Indeed, Nash and Sproule (2012) investigated the impact of coach education qualifications on coaching practice across a range of coaching levels, sports and experiences ($n = 621$ sports coaches). Their results suggested that coaches viewed coach education courses as key providers of sport specific content. However, coach perceptions of their coach education experiences were that they were not very effective with other aspects of coaching, for example, decision making, pedagogy and sports science. The findings of Nash and Sproule (2009, 2012) suggest that if the aim of the formal coach education system is the development of expert coaches, it should be re-examined.

## COACHING PRACTICE AND COACHING PHILOSOPHY

There is an assumption that a coaching style, which has the potential to shape athletes' sport experiences, reflects the coach's philosophy or values. In simple terms a coaching style is the way in which the coach delivers his or her coaching session, and this will vary depending on the situational context, the needs of the performers, the emotional intelligence of the coach and so forth. Traditionally, coaching styles have been placed on a continuum, from the command (autocratic) style, where the coach makes all the decisions, to the democratic (interactive) style, where the athlete(s) discuss and negotiate issues/challenges, through to the laissez-faire (hands-off) style, where all authority is given to the athletes who determine goals, make decisions, and resolve issues on their own. Confounding variables with coaching styles include the necessity to distinguish between different levels of coaching, such as participation to performance coaching, or factoring in age and a developmentally appropriate approach when coaching children. However, it is entirely feasible that a coach could be authoritarian in decision making whilst at the same time be more democratic in communication style, reflecting a pluralistic coaching style that adapts to context (for example, last five minutes of a cup final compared to strategy development in a pre-season practice session). Thus, there are many factors that can influence the adopted coaching style including, for example, the emotional intelligence (EI) of the sport coach (see Chapter 10). EI is believed to be a necessary skill in today's coaching environment. Mayer *et al.* (2008, p. 511) defined EI as 'the ability to carry out accurate reasoning about emotions and the ability to use emotions and emotional knowledge to enhance thought'. Others have found positive correlations between EI and interpersonal, leadership and teamwork success (Boyatzis and Saatcioglu 2008) – essential skills for those coaching sport. It is also important for coaches to have a personal philosophy that will help relate to the world around them. Reflection and analysis lead to confrontation with one's belief systems to support and justify coaching behaviour.

It is obvious from the above that the coach's value orientations are only one influence on coaching behaviour. Interestingly, some recent studies (Bartholomew *et al.* 2011; Hodge and Lonsdale 2011; Stebings *et al.* 2011) on the operationalisation of interpersonal styles employed by coaches have drawn from self-determination theory to examine coach behaviours and the subsequent effects on athletes' sport experiences. For example, Stebbings *et al.* (2011) tested a model of perceived coach autonomy supporting and controlling behaviours on athlete outcomes such as motivation and performance. Their findings support that when coaches have high perceived autonomy supportive behaviours, they experience heightened psychological well-being in their coaching role. In turn such coaches are more likely to provide athletes with choice and responsibility and engage in open discussions with athletes regarding their feelings, ideas and opinions about training sessions and competition (that is, a democratic style). Hodge and Lonsdale (2011) reinforce the importance to the proper functioning of society that individuals act in accordance with moral values that reflect 'good deeds'. They go on to state that individuals have the ability to independently regulate their thoughts, emotions and behaviour in line with those values. This could be volitionally engaging in pro-social behaviour such as verbally encouraging an athlete, rather than resorting to antisocial behaviours such as the public humiliation of an athlete after a poor performance. Their findings highlighted the links between an autonomy-supportive coaching style, athlete motivation and pro-social behaviour of competitive sport young adult athletes. In particular they noted:

> Although controlling interactions with athletes may lead to immediate compliance, this way of relating with athletes may hinder the processes by which they accept and internalize moral values and are autonomously guided by them in their lives. Coaches should be educated about ways to improve the quality of autonomy support for their athletes and to provide a coaching style conducive to developing the athlete's sense of autonomy and self-regulation.
>
> (Hodge and Lonsdale 2011, p. 544)

**59**

If personal coaching philosophy is a statement of beliefs and attitudes relative to the purpose of coaching and the role of the coach, some would argue that coaching is primarily about the process. Why? It seems reasonable that what a coach believes about coaching can have a major impact on the performance environment; coaches tend to implement coaching practices that reflect their philosophical beliefs, and a well-reasoned personal coaching philosophy can provide a basis for appropriate action. For example, I think this must include facilitating/developing the skill of self-regulation within an athlete-centred coaching process, partly because it is now generally agreed that improving performance is more than acquiring knowledge and developing skills. According to social-cognitive researchers, self-regulation involves three or four interdependent phases (Wolters 2010). One phase is commonly referred to as the *forethought* phase, which involves planning, setting goals and selecting strategies for performance improvement. During the *monitoring* phase a coach would continually track the athletes' progress and be aware of their current performance in relation to their goals. The activities involved in the *control* phase refer to implementing and adapting strategies to complete the task. Finally, reviewing and responding to the experience makes up the *reflection* phase.

Coaching pedagogy has moved towards an understanding of athlete learning judged less as a performance outcome and more as an active process involving self-regulation – a constructive process in which athletes play an active role in their own performance improvement. Self-regulation has roots in Bandura's social-cognitive theory, which suggests that learning occurs as an interaction of three factors: personal, environmental and behavioural (Bandura 1991). Self-regulation focuses on the result of behaviour, which can be seen as the product of the athlete-coaching environment interaction. Self-regulation allows individuals to adapt to their social and physical environments; contemporary psychologists view this as a defining feature of being human (Martin and McLellan 2008). Researchers have supported the idea that the development of self-regulation should be the focus of social interaction situations (Baumeister and Vohs 2007). Additionally, researchers have highlighted that self-regulation also involves motivational and affective elements in addition to cognitive and social influences (Beishuizen and Steffens 2011; Whitebread *et al.* 2009). In trying to ensure that athletes benefit from this aspect of coaching pedagogy, it is important to understand that a progressivist coaching philosophy that includes an emphasis on self-regulation is not a unitary construct. There is no single set of strategies that should be used, but rather distinct motivational, behavioural and cognitive strategies that are appropriate for an athlete-centred coaching domain. Of course, this all assumes that coaches are free to allow their value framework to influence their coaching behaviour. However, consider the 2012–16 UK Olympic funding for performance strategy. How much does this dictate/influence the coaching style of say athletics, cycling and volleyball coaches in the UK? The influence of the 'organisation' may dictate coaching behaviour; in other words the coach may need to accede to or adopt the values of the organisation if they are to 'survive' within – a process of occupational socialisation. We assume that the statements of values indicating an acceptance of organisational values are translated into implications for coaching practice. However, contrary to ethical standards, rhetoric does not always match the reality of values and beliefs that underpin the coaching philosophy that drives sport coaching behaviours in the complexity of a social context! This view recognizes the issue of a potential conflict between a coach's beliefs and values (aspiration), accountability and the actual practice behaviours (for example, results justify the process!). The philosophy should reflect the practice, evidenced in the interpersonal behaviour (for example, degree of autonomy afforded to the athlete), direct intervention (e.g. TID selection process), the social context (for example, the highly competitive Hong Kong rugby 7s or touch rugby after work to reduce stress) and the purpose of the coaching role (for example, participation legacy from London 2012 versus winning gold at Rio 2016).

## PRIMA FACIE COACHING PHILOSOPHY, CHEATING, OLYMPISM AND HUMANISM

A coach's previous experience, knowledge, values, opinions and beliefs will influence the way he or she coaches, and all these factors that dictate the way he or she coaches can be the basis of a philosophy of coaching. In an ideal world this should lead to consistent and positive coach-athlete interactions that enhance performance and satisfy all participants during and with the outcomes of the process – that is know yourself, understand your athletes, be certain of your coaching context. Lyle (Cross and Lyle 1999) provided his own personal coaching philosophy, as a performance coach operating in a team sport, and with national and international level players. One of the beliefs he clearly expressed was 'All possible legal advantage will be sought to win important matches. Players will rarely, if ever, be expected to cheat'. Green (2004, p. 85) described cheating as 'the intentional violation of a rule, in order to gain an unfair advantage over others'. From my own perspective, the *prima facie* moral wrongness of cheating, this is disappointing because I think **ALL** who are involved in coaching sport should do so from a basis of integrity, honesty and justice. For example, players should **never** be expected to cheat by their coach, as Schermer (2008) states that cheating is primarily a matter of fairness. It is accepted that performance enhancement is a main goal of sports. Rose (2005) questioned whether is it acceptable to use cognition enhancement drugs (for example, smart drugs that can enhance memory and concentration), and whether this is a form of cheating by bypassing hard work and study. Is the use of hypoxic air machines performance enhancement through effective training or cheating (Spriggs 2005)? Or should the essence of sport be that the person with the best genetics (natural abilities, the winner of the genetic lottery) should win the competition? Perhaps we should be guided not just by the notion of fairness or justice, but by the view that:

> Keeping scores is meant to honour and promote a given type of human excellence, whose meaning is in the doing, not simply in the scored results.
>
> (President's Council on Bioethics, 2003)

Such a view is more intimately connected with virtues such as honesty and justice, with athletes having the courage not to corrupt themselves, and coaches having the courage not to violate both safety and health-related concerns and the constitutive rules (and ethos) of the sport in question. Coaching sport is also associated with developing moral values such as loyalty, fairness and cooperation. A recent study (d'Arripe-Longueville *et al.* 2010) examined self-regulatory mechanisms (for example, self-judgement of behaviour in relation to personal standards) and the likelihood of sport cheating in French adolescents. Their findings emphasised the role of affective and resistive self-regulatory efficacy (for example, to resist temptation to cheating) to improve moral functioning in sport. This highlights the important role that a sport coach has in helping youth acquire effective skills to manage the stressors related to moral dilemmas in sport – it is not just about enhancing performance. Another study (Corrion *et al.* 2010) examined cheating acceptability in physical education in French youth aged 11 to 16 years. They observed that the more participants focused on mastery goals, the less they considered cheating as acceptable. Saulsbury *et al.* (2011) investigated pharmacy students' attitude towards cheating in a university setting. Specifically, they examined whether the absence or presence of certain traits affects student propensity to cheat, including idealism (for example, the absolute adherence to ethical or honourable principles as the standard regardless of circumstances). Idealism was found to be inversely related to the likelihood of a student engaging in cheating (or tolerating peer cheating). More than 14,000 athletes have competed at the 2012 London Olympic Games. Some estimates suggest that approximately 1,000 of these Olympians will have cheated by taking banned drugs (Cooper 2012, the Lancet). They cheat, for example, to increase their explosive power and aerobic endurance, often encouraged by unscrupulous coaches – against the spirit of sport (vaguely defined as the celebration of the human spirit, body and mind). In recent years some philosophers have argued that whenever a line is set, athletes (and coaches) will push against it. Savulescu *et al.* (2004) have argued that biological manipulation is not against the spirit of sport – it is the spirit of sport! Perhaps John Lyle was not so controversial after all.

## WHY DO PEOPLE COACH SPORT AND WHAT SHOULD THOSE COACHING SPORT ASPIRE TO?

Most coaches are likely to have clear aims towards improving athlete performance, where the athlete can be a clumsy child or the elite Olympian. Appropriate principles, such as respect and equity expectation, should govern the coach-athlete relationship, and this should operate within an ethos of integrity, fairness and justice (for example, not cheating, encouraging self-regulating behaviour with a sense of right and wrong and so on). Importantly, this will be a person-centred partnership, a developmental process because, for example, coaches who understand different learning styles and preferences tend to be more effective (Cassidy, Jones and Potrac 2008). It is hoped that the majority of sport coaches are diligent, well organised, emotionally intelligent and caring individuals with a balanced, value-laden perspective to achievement and winning. For example, you can enjoy eating meat without agreeing or going along with factory farming! As Aldo Leopold stated: 'A thing is right when it tends to preserve the integrity, stability, and beauty of the biotic community. It is wrong otherwise' (Leopold 1949). Therefore, paramount values for sport coaches should reflect the rights of the individual, athlete self-regulation, athlete self-determination and athlete enjoyment. This should emerge from participation in a supportive and accountable environment that is situated in a context of the coaches' declared philosophy. Key to this is an active engagement in positive coaching experiences by the athlete, leading to increased self-esteem, that is underpinned and guided by principled coach behaviours. These benefits for the athlete will come to fruition more readily if coaches focus more on the process of coaching rather than an end justifies the means (that is, product) approach. In the current climate of (multi-) sport festivals such as the Olympic

Games where success is dependent upon position within a medal table – and to win a medal is to ensure future funding for your sport – am I adopting ideals that are too Utopian? Teetzel (2012, p. 32) highlights the fundamental principles of Olympism, such as:

> Overlapping ideas . . . , which compromise: 1) fairness, including fair play, justice, and respect for the rules, traditions, opponents, and one's self; 2) equality, including non-discrimination and respect for human rights, athletes' rights, and autonomy; and, 3) ethical behaviour, including the embodiment of virtues such as honesty, courage, excellence, and honour.

Such ideals are surely worth promoting and pursuing in sports coaching practice, but it would be oversimplifying matters to propose that process-focused sports coaching will ensure a coaching environment that facilitates an equal, fair and ethical athlete experience. Sports coaches could usefully consider the potential of Olympism as an underpinning framework for their coaching philosophy. A relevant question here might be whether such humanistic principles create difficulties for the coach involved in talent identification and development. Is it ever acceptable to lose a sense of fairness and respect within the coaching process as one progresses the coach-athlete relationship from controlling behaviour (for example, talent identification) to shared responsibility and then on to self-regulation and self-determination (for example, talent development)? The transfer of priorities from performance outcome to the person implies a leadership style of coaching firmly based on co-operation and athlete autonomy, one that goes beyond the superficial rhetoric of humanism.

However, are the parameters of the humanistic approach to coaching practically viable for performance coaching within professional and elite sport? As Côté and Gilbert (2009) have stated, the main task of a coach in such environments is to manage the talent necessary to win. There is some recent evidence that having a clear coaching philosophy based on truths, principles, attitudes and values, and guided by consistency, trust, cooperation, understanding and expectation, is a key ingredient to coaching success in the professional arena. Bennie and O'Connor (2010) investigated the coaching philosophies of six professional cricket, rugby league and rugby union coaches in Australia. They found that the development of the total person was a high priority for each coach, in the belief that if you develop the player and the person, this will likely result in on- and off-the-field success. This finding reflects a shift away from merely developing the players' competitive skills to the total development of the whole person, supporting humanistic aims. They concluded that the humanistic ideals of developing the player and the person, considered incompatible by Lyle (2002), are compatible with principles of performance sport.

## STORIES AS PERSONAL COACHING PHILOSOPHY

Carless and Douglas highlight two related justifications for the importance of a coaching philosophy:

> First, what coaches actually do in their coaching practice is understood as being unavoidably shaped by their personal values and views . . . subconscious or unconscious. . . . In

contrast . . . clearly articulating one's philosophy is a prerequisite to good practice, as it provides direction and focus in relation to how one goes about doing the job of coaching.

(2011, p. 2)

One problematic and limited view of a coaching philosophy is that it can be seen as a general set of statements that have the potential to apply to the wide range of contexts and scenarios in which a coach might work. However, it is not uncommon for there to be a lack of alignment between coaching philosophy and coach behaviour, as noted by Jenkins (2010). Cassidy *et al.* (2008) suggest that as a result, some coaches find the philosophies they have developed to be of little use in their day-to-day practice.

Jenkins (2010) suggested that reflective *storytelling* may help align and link coach actions with the values of the coach. Carless and Douglas (2011) offered three reasons in an attempt to explain why this might work for some coaches. First, they outline how stories can reflect personal embodied experience, developing an authentic philosophy grounded in real and personal coaching experiences. Second, they describe stories as socio-cultural constructions; a coach's work is shaped by social, cultural and political factors. This could be the actions of other coaches, the athletes s/he works with, the media and/or political forces. For example, consider the potentially devastating impact on a the personal aspirations of a basketball or volleyball coach following the recent announcement of Olympic and Paralympic sports funding in the run-up to the 2016 Rio de Janeiro Games, as part of the legacy of 2012 London. Basketball failed to secure any financial investment and volleyball funding was reduced from £3,536,077 to £400,000. Third, Carless and Douglas (2011) suggested storytelling as an integral strategy for self-reflection – a 'freeze-frame' through which past events may be reconsidered. One goal of this type of a coach-learning pedagogical approach would be to provide social and intellectual context to probe the coaches' knowledge and understanding of their own (and others) coaching practice. This reflective orientation has a focus on coach-learning processes concerning explanations of thoughts as well as actions. For example, this may help a coach explain why certain coach behaviours and processes are related to the successful/ unsuccessful performance outcome of one of the players. This approach has the potential to constructively inform as evidenced in emergent coaching practice (what) based on a personal value-laden coaching philosophy (why). This perspective is supported by Cushion *et al.* (2012) in their review of behaviours and practice structures for talent development coaches in youth soccer, when they concluded that:

Values are always represented in, and through, coach behavior and practice. . . . Coaches will have developed a personal set of views on coaching and 'best' ways to structure practice and behavior. . . . Without a form of reflective process, coaches simply accrue these experiences without any meaningful impact on their practice. Experiential learning is more than just doing . . . with direct and indirect guidance provided from observing and listening to others, and the context . . . to reflect critically on why they structure practice and behave as they do, and be able to make judgements that are meaningful within their particular situation and challenge.

(Cushion *et al.* 2012, p. 1638)

## ESPOUSED THEORY AND THEORY-IN-USE

Hall (unpublished doctoral dissertation, University of Edinburgh) has used post-practice video-stimulated recall and reflective interviews to examine the way in which a National rugby team's female head coach (Kate, a pseudonym) develops, understands and utilizes her philosophy in the production of her coaching practice across a whole rugby season (covering reflection-in-action; reflection-on-action; retrospective reflection-on-action). He found that Kate's philosophy existed as a triumvirate framework, communicated through descriptions of value statements, ideological objectives and pragmatic intentions. The different factors incorporated into Kate's philosophy reflected her perceptions of coaching as a 'balancing act' in which she attempted to resolve expectations about the head coach's role (being overall in charge and providing clear direction) with the uncertain, complex and contingent nature of her coaching context. Kate's value statements reflected her core values, such as respect. Her ideological objectives represented aspirational mental models of how she wanted to achieve her values, for example, by using predominantly game-realistic activities. By adopting a more pragmatic approach and being aware of the inherent variables in her particular coaching context, Kate was able to integrate her value statements and ideological objectives with her coaching practice. At the same time, she acknowledged that various factors, such as time pressures, players' skill levels, available facilities and coach-to-player ratios would support or constrain their realisation.

For example, conflict occurred in the actualisation of Kate's values and aspirations represented by judgement calls within a decision-making process (for example, creating an enjoyable and fun environment whilst also providing honest feedback to a dropped player). Additionally, Kate often incorporated experience and knowledge, developed from previous practice sessions and matches, into her planning for the next session (described as pre-flection). Hall reported that Kate's espoused theory (her coaching philosophy) and her actual coaching practice (theory-in-use) were usually shaped by greater or lesser uncertainty. For example, during normal practice sessions, Kate usually responded to players' mistakes – player performance being an uncertain variable in the coaching process – by asking questions, drawing out the improvements required from the player or his or her peers. However, during warm ups before matches, Kate's proportionate use of questioning was much less, accounting for around 1% of her total behaviours, whilst her proportionate use of concurrent correction was much larger (about 10% of total behaviours). Here, the imminence of the match and the perceived 'lack of time' for players to solve the problem themselves, led Kate to experiment with 'strategies' (coach behaviours) that diverged from her espoused theory. Interestingly, on reflection, Kate did not view this divergence as negative. In fact, she justified her actions through another ideological objective: for players to feel confident and prepared for match performance (Hall, unpublished doctoral dissertation, University of Edinburgh, 2013).

In conclusion, it is widely accepted that a coaching philosophy is grounded in the beliefs, values and principles of the sports coach, and it appears to evolve over time (Nash et al. 2008). It is a reflective means to understand, develop, guide and characterise behaviour during coaching practice whilst trying to remain true to your values (Burton and Raedeke 2008). One way to improve coaching practice is to respect and improve the coaching profession. However, transforming coaches with strategies to improve and develop their coaching is a challenge. There is an observation that luck favours the prepared mind. This requires a strong philosophical underpinning with moral purpose to guide coaching behaviour, such as the right of athletes to be treated with dignity by their coach. Therefore, development of an individual coaching philosophy could perform a gate-keeping function for entry into coaching, a kind of baseline professional competence standard grounded in values and a beliefs system. This could also be useful for the self-evaluation and reflection process of coach development towards expertise. Central to this are the notions of an empowering athlete-centred pedagogical approach, which includes planned outcomes associated with athlete self-regulation and self-determination. However, reading about the philosophy of coaching does not guarantee being able to do it.

## REFERENCES

Albion, M. (2006). *True to yourself: Leading a values-based business.* (San Francisco: Berrett-Koehler Publishers).

Bandura, A. (1991). Human agency: The rhetoric and the reality. *American Psychologist* 46(2): pp. 157–162.

Bartholomew, K., Ntoumanis, N. and Thogersen-Ntoumani, C. (2011). Self-determination theory and the darker side of athletic experience: The role of interpersonal control and need thwarting. *Sport and Exercise Psychology Review* 7(2): pp. 23–27.

Baumeister, R. and Vohs, K. D. (2007). Self-regulation, ego depletion, and motivation. *Social and Personality Psychology Compass* 1(1): pp. 115–128.

Beishuizen, J. and Steffens, K. (2011). A conceptual framework for research on self-regulated learning. In *Self-regulated learning in technology enhanced learning environments: A European perspective.* R. Carneiro, P. Lefrere, K. Steffens and J. Underwood (Eds.) (Rotterdam, The Netherlands: Sense): pp. 3–19.

Bennie, A. and O'Connor, D. (2010). Coaching philosophies: Perceptions from professional cricket, rugby league and rugby union players and coaches in Australia. *International Journal of Sports Science and Coaching* 5(2): pp. 309–320.

Boyatzis, R. and Saatcioglu, A. (2008). A 20-year view of trying to develop emotional, social and cognitive intelligence competencies in graduate management education. *Journal of Management Development* 27(1): pp. 92–108.

Burton, D. and Raedeke, T. (2008). Sport psychology for coaches. *International Journal of Sports Science and Coaching* 3(2): pp. 291–292.

Butler, J. (2005). TGfU pet-agogy: Old dogs, new tricks and puppy school. *Physical Education & Sport Pedagogy* 10(3): pp. 225–240.

Carless, D. and Douglas, K. (2011). Stories as personal coaching philosophy. *International Journal of Sports Science and Coaching* 6(1): pp. 1–12.

Cassidy, T., Jones, R. and Potrac, P. (2008). *Understanding sports coaching: The social, cultural and pedagogical foundations of sports practice.* (London: Routledge).

Cohen, G. A. (1995). *Self-ownership, freedom and equality.* (Cambridge University Press).

Cohen, M. (2013). *101 philosophy problems.* (New York: Routledge).

Cooper, C. (2012) Drug cheating at the Olympics: who, what, and why? *The Lancet,* Vol 380, Issue 9836: 21–22.

Corrion, K., D'Arripe-Longueville, F., Chalabaev, A., Schiano-Lomoriello, S., Roussel, P. and Cury, F. (2010). Effect of implicit theories on judgement of cheating acceptability in physical education: The mediating role of achievement goals. *Journal of Sports Sciences* 28(8): pp. 909–919.

Côté, J. and Gilbert, W. (2009). An integrative definition of coaching effectiveness and expertise. *International Journal of Sports Science and Coaching* 4(3): pp. 307–323.

Cothran, D.J., Kulinna, P.H., Banville, D., Choi, E., Amade-Escot, C., MacPhail, A., Macdonald, D., Richard, J.F., Sarmento, P. and Kirk, D. (2005). A cross-cultural investigation of the use of teaching styles. *Research Quarterly for Exercise and Sport* 76: pp. 193–201.

Cross, N. and Lyle, J. (1999). *The coaching process: Principles and practice for sport.* (Oxford; Boston: Butterworth-Heinemann).

Cushion, C. (2007). Modelling the complexity of the coaching process. *International Journal of Sports Science and Coaching* 2(4): p. 395.

Cushion, C., Ford, P. and Williams, A. (2012). Coach behaviours and practice structures in youth soccer: Implications for talent development. *Journal of Sports Sciences* 30(15): pp. 1631–1641.

d'Arripe-Longueville, F., Corrion, K., Scoffier, S., Roussel, P. and Chalabaev, A. (2010). Sociocognitive self-regulatory mechanisms governing judgments of the acceptability and likelihood of sport cheating. *Journal of Sport and Exercise Psychology* 32(5): pp. 595–618.

Flavell, J. H. (1979) Metacognition and cognitive monitoring a new area of cognitive-developmental inquiry. *American Psychologist,* Vol 34, No.10: 906–911.

Fraser-Thomas, J. and Côté, J. (2009). Understanding adolescents' positive and negative developmental experiences in sport. *Sport Psychologist* 23(1): pp. 3–23.

Green, S. P. (2004). Cheating. *Law Philosophy,* 23: 137–185.

Hacker, P. M. S. (1998) *Current Issues in Philosophy of Mind,* Royal Institute of Philosophy 43: p. 233.

Hall, E. *The coaching process: Ethnography of apex women's rugby union.* (Unpublished doctoral dissertation). University of Edinburgh.

Herman, L. & Mandell, A. (2004) *From Teaching to Mentoring.* (London: Routledge Falmer): p. 10.

Hodge, K. and Lonsdale, C. (2011). Prosocial and antisocial behavior in sport: The role of coaching style, autonomous vs. controlled motivation, and moral disengagement. *Journal of Sport and Exercise Psychology* 33(4): pp. 527–547.

Hospers, J. (1997). *An introduction to philosophical analysis.* (New York: Routledge).

Jenkins, S. (2010). Coaching philosophy. In *Sports coaching: Professionalisation and practice.* J. Lyle and C. Cushion (Eds.) (Edinburgh: Churchill Livingston).

Jones, R. L., Armour, K. M. and Potrac, P. (2003). Constructing expert knowledge: A case study of a top-level professional soccer coach. *Sport, Education and Society* 8(2): pp. 213–229.

Jowett, S. (2008). Moderators and mediators of the association between the coach-athlete relationship and physical self-concept. *International Journal of Coaching Science* 2: pp. 43–62.

Koriat, A., Ma'ayan, H. & Nussinson, R. (2006) The Intricate Relationships Between Monitoring and Control in Metacognition: Lessons for the Cause-and-Effect Relation Between Subjective Experience and Behavior. *Journal of Experimental Psychology,* Vol. 135, No. 1: 36–69.

Lyle, J. (2002) *Sports Coaching Concepts: A framework for coaches' behaviour.* (London: Routledge)

Leopold, A. (1949). *A sand county almanac.* (New York: Oxford University Press).

Malloy, D. and Rossow-Kimball, B. (2007). The philosopher-as-therapist: The noble coach and self-awareness. *Quest* 59(3): pp. 311–322.

Martin, J. and McLellan, A. (2008). The educational psychology of self-regulation: A conceptual and critical analysis. *The Study of the Philosophy of Education* 27: pp. 433–448.

Mayer, J., Roberts, R. and Barsade, S. (2008). Human abilities: Emotional intelligence. *Annual Review of Psychology* 59: pp. 507–536.

Nash, C. and Sproule, J. (2009). Career development of expert coaches. *International Journal of Sports Science & Coaching* 4(1): pp. 121–138.

**67**

Nash, C. and Sproule, J. (2012). Coaches perceptions of coach education experiences. *International Journal of Sport Psychology* 43: pp. 33–52.

Nash, C., Sproule, J. and Horton, P. (2008). Sport coaches' perceived role frames and philosophies. *International Journal of Sports Science & Coaching* 3(4): pp. 539–554.

President's Council on Bioethics. (Oct, 2003) *Beyond Therapy: Biotechnology and the Pursuit of Happiness.*

O'Sullivan, M. (2005). Beliefs of teachers and teacher candidates: Implications for teacher education. In *The art and science of teaching in physical education and sport.* F. Carreiro da Costa, M. Cloes and M. Gonzalez (Eds.) (Universidade De Tecnica, Lisbon).

Potrac, P., Brewer, C., Jones, R., Armour, K. and Hoff, J. (2000). Toward a holistic understanding of the coaching process. *Quest* 52(2): pp. 186–199.

Reynolds, F. (2005). Developing a formal coaching philosophy. *Brian Mackenzie's Successful Coaching.* (ISSN 1745–7513/ 25/September): pp. 1–3.

Robinson, P. (2010). *Foundations of sports coaching.* (London; New York: Routledge).

Rokeach, M. (1973). *The nature of human values.* (New York: Free Press).

Rose, S. (2005). *The future of the brain.* (Oxford University Press).

Saulsbury, M., Brown III, U., Heyliger, S. and Beale, R. (2011). Effect of dispositional traits on pharmacy students' attitude toward cheating. *American Journal of Pharmaceutical Education* 75(4): pp. 1–8.

Savulesco, J., Foddy, B. and Clayton, M. (2004). Why we should allow performance enhancing drugs in sport. *British Journal of Sports Medicine* 38: pp. 666–670.

Schempp, P., McCullick, B., Busch, C., Webster, C. and Mason, I. (2006). The self-monitoring of expert sport instructors. *International Journal of Sports Science and Coaching* 1(1): p. 25.

Schermer, M. (2008). On the argument that enhancement is 'cheating'. *Journal of Medical Ethics* 34(2): pp. 85–88.

Spriggs, M. (2005). Hypoxic air machines: Performance enhancement through effective training – or cheating? *Journal of Medical Ethics* 31(2): pp. 112–113.

Stebbings, J., Taylor, I. and Spray, C. (2011). Antecedents of perceived coach autonomy supportive and controlling behaviors: Coach psychological need satisfaction and well-being. *Journal of Sport and Exercise Psychology* 33(2): pp. 255–272.

Teetzel, S. J. (2012) Optimizing Olympic education: a comprehensive approach to understanding and teaching the philosophy of Olympism. *Educational Review*, Vol 64, Issue 3: 317–332.

Tsangaridou, N. and O'Sullivan, M. (2003). Physical education teachers' theories of action and theories-in-use. *Journal of Teaching in Physical Education* 22: pp. 132–152.

Weiss, M. R. (2008). 2007 C.H. McCloy Lecture – 'Field of dreams': Sport as a context for youth development. *Research Quarterly for Exercise and Sport* 79(4): pp. 434–449.

Whitebread, D., Coltman, P., Pasternak, D., Sangster, C., Grau, V., Bingham, S., Almeqdad, Q. and Demetriou, D. (2009). The development of two observational tools for assessing metacognition and self-regulated learning in young children. *Metacognition and Learning* 1: p. 63.

Williams, A. and Hodges, N. (2005). Practice, instruction and skill acquisition in soccer: Challenging tradition. *Journal of Sports Sciences* 23(6): pp. 637–650.

Wolters, C.A. (2010). *Self-regulated learning and the 21st century competencies.* Retrieved: 11 April 2014. www.hewlett.org/uploads/Self_Regulated_Learning__21st_Century_Competencies.pdf

Yzerbyt, V., Lories, G. & Dardenne, B. (1998) *Metacognition: cognitive and social dimensions.* (Sage: London): pp. 1–15.

# Section 2

Section 2 assesses the many coaching environments that a sport coach can encounter, in both practice and competition. Organisations such as sportscoachUK (2009) and Coaching Association of Canada, have developed a generic participant development model that is evidence-based, related to participants' needs, goals, motives and age/stage of development. These chapters make reference to the many coaching domains encountered by sport coaches in their practice.

- Chapter 4 examines the build up to competition and all the factors that the coach and coaching team must consider to optimise performance. Today's athletes, whether recreational or elite, run and swim faster, throw farther and jump higher than their competitors from the past. The coach must create a healthy competitive environment that allows the athletes to succeed, instilling confidence and further success. But how does the coach manage all the factors that contribute to successful competitive performance?

- Chapter 5 discusses the learning environment created by the coach in practice, in other words how a coach maximizes skill acquisition. Training sessions are the embodiment of the coach's art and a product of his or her holistic skills-set. They are the mechanisms through which coaches bring all the elements of effective practice together and are the points at which they impart their craft to the subject, be it a squad, a team, a team-unit or an individual athlete.

- Chapter 6 considers the motivational climate the coach creates during practice. Coaches design practice sessions, group athletes, give recognition, evaluate performance, share their authority and shape the sport setting. In doing so, they create a motivational climate that can have an important impact on an athlete's motivation. The motivation for participating in sport and striving for improvement is likely to vary considerably from person to person. Indeed, most people have multiple motives rather than single reasons. In sport, the motivational climate created by a coach in practice can influence satisfaction in team sport, achievement strategies, perceived purposes of sport and conceptions of ability.

- Chapter 7 studies the concepts of talent development within sport and the coach's role within the process. Most coaches are aware of talent identification, and with the world of elite sport becoming increasingly more competitive, many coaches are still hoping to spot that unique talent. However many coaches do not understand how to nurture and develop the talent that already exists within their participants. Talent development is a long term process and depends upon many coaches providing the age and stage appropriate contribution during the practice session as well as understanding their particular place within this process.

■ Chapter 8 analyses tactics and tactical awareness within sport coaching. Tactical knowledge is both difficult to teach and difficult for coaches to learn but an important component of the individual and team coaching toolbox. Tactical awareness is closely related to many of the aspects of expertise – decision making, problem solving, pattern recognition and speed of response.

## REFERENCE

sportscoachUK. (2009). *The Coach Development Model User Guide*. Leeds: Coachwise Business Solutions/The National Coaching Foundation.

# Chapter 4

# The competition environment

*Dave Collins and John Kiely*

## THE COMPETITION CONTEXT – FOCUS, TIME SPAN AND NESTED THINKING

No coaching book can be complete without an explicit consideration of competition. Competition is why all those involved put in so much effort to prepare and train for the best performance on a particular day. Unfortunately, however, some coaches and many athletes often get so caught up in the day to day detail that they lose sight of the 'big picture' focus on the event itself. Accordingly, as we go through the build-up to the event, and consider coaching behaviours at the event itself, we will highlight some of the difficult areas that should be avoided.

Another important factor to consider is the time span over which the event-specific preparation will take place. There is a world of difference between the planning and execution of a football coach, playing at least weekly, and an Olympic sport where planning may well take place over two quadrennials. Through a discussion of event preparation in this chapter, we will try to offer some guidelines for both, although perhaps inevitably the discussion will focus on the single big event approach rather than the almost daily grind that typifies practice in major team sports, certainly in the UK.

There is, or at least should be, one common strand across all these sport environments. Any good coach will have a number of 'agendas' running simultaneously – working for good performances in the upcoming event (however minor compared to the annual or quadrennial target) whilst also catering for the longer-term developmental needs of the athlete, squad or team. These complementary agendas will be nested within each other, as illustrated in Figure 4.1.

This example is for an Olympic sport, with the aims of the week's training, nested within a series of six weekly blocks which are, in turn, nested within the annual and quadrennial plans. In practice, at least to the casual observer, the coach will be focused mostly on the 'here and now', working with the performers on the objectives of that session. The better coaches will always have the longer term agendas at the back of their minds however, making decisions and taking actions with all these aims as a blended approach (Abraham and Collins 2011). This is always the case, often due to the externally generated expectation or coach-generated internal pressure to perform *now!* The longer term agenda is always an important factor, though, and particularly so in talent development environments (see Chapter 7). Of course, in the hectic and pressured world of professional team sports, the longer term agenda may sometimes be forgotten, especially as instant success is expected and the threat of unemployment always seems just around the corner. Even in these situations, however, the top level coach will be

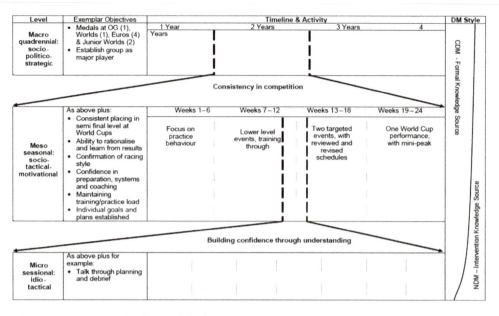

| Level | Exemplar Objectives | Timeline & Activity | | | | DM Style |
|---|---|---|---|---|---|---|
| **Macro** quadrennial: socio-politico-strategic | • Medals at OG (1), Worlds (1), Euros (4) & Junior Worlds (2) • Establish group as major player | 1 Year / Years | 2 Years | 3 Years | 4 | CDM - Formal Knowledge Source |
| | | *Consistency in competition* | | | | |
| **Meso** seasonal: socio-tactical-motivational | As above plus: • Consistent placing in semi final level at World Cups • Ability to rationalise and learn from results • Confirmation of racing style • Confidence in preparation, systems and coaching • Maintaining training/practice load • Individual goals and plans established | Weeks 1–6 Focus on practice behaviour | Weeks 7–12 Lower level events, training through | Weeks 13–18 Two targeted events, with reviewed and revised schedules | Weeks 19–24 One World Cup performance, with mini-peak | NDM – Intervention Knowledge Source |
| | | *Building confidence through understanding* | | | | |
| **Micro** sessional: idio-tactical | As above plus for example: • Talk through planning and debrief | | | | | |

*Figure 4.1* An example of nested thinking – multiple agendas in an Olympic sport (based on Abraham and Collins 2011).

planning and preparing for changes to be made in forthcoming seasons, although those plans will probably remain a closely guarded secret.

So, keeping these ideas in mind, what are the principles behind preparation for, and performance at, competition that the coach should consider and apply? The following sections will work through these chronologically, starting with the pre-event period through to 'on the day' considerations.

## BEFORE THE EVENT – PREPARING FOR COMPETITION

All of the chapters in this book address this topic in one way or another. So for the purposes of this chapter, the discussion will be limited to those factors which relate most specifically to preparation for the event; these are generally referred to by the blanket term periodisation (see Chapter 2 for further details). An awful lot has been written about periodisation, mostly focused on the physical side, by a predominantly east European set of authors who have proposed complex and involved systems. From a personal perspective, it seems that much of this work has only provided a confused picture, with too much assumption and 'sciencey' argument (Collins and Bailey 2012) overlooking some rather basic flaws. For example, we now know enough about the complexity of human systems to question the idea that reaching a peak can be reliably and consistently achieved by manipulations based on an *a priori* plan of activity. In short, people are so different and change so much from year to year that following one set of rules on the design of training, however complex, is unlikely to generate consistent and predictable results (Kiely 2012).

## Periodisation below the neck – physical aspects

Of course, there are some principles that apply to the mysterious but important concept of peaking. In general, most specialists would agree that:

- Athletes undertake smaller quantities of work at higher quality as the event approaches (less volume, higher intensity).
- Variation is important, both to avoid monotony (which just adds to the stress of the training process) and to maintain the stimulus to make the body systems adapt (which is a major aim of training).
- Recovery is as important to generating the adaptation effect as is the training itself. Accordingly, attention to recuperation and regeneration is as crucially important as working hard.

This is not a simple matter of just following a recipe, either across individuals or even following what worked for a particular person last year. The main point about the complexity described earlier is that the skilled coach will base decisions on workload almost entirely on how the individual is coping with, and adapting to, the training. Reflecting this idea, many coaches now rely on measures of 'training readiness'; literally, measures which show how well (or badly) the athlete is handling the workload. These measures may be physical (for example, standing jump), neural (for example, reaction time), psychological (for example, mood state) or biochemical (for example, salivary measures of immune function). In many professional setups, a combination of several such measures are used, with longer term data profiles indicating which particular combination is most indicative for each individual competitor. As such, the once dominant study of periodisation and tapering has been more empirically grounded in an individualised process of regular profiling, with consequent adjustments to the training load.

## Periodisation below the neck – mental aspects

In contrast, from a psychological point of view the concept of periodisation seems to offer some important implications. Four examples are presented to demonstrate this utility, starting with the systematic development of the athlete's confidence level. Following a clear and (perhaps apparently) well developed plan, the athlete comes to 'expect' that a positive performance will result. Expectancy has been shown to be a very powerful tool in sport; for example, the expectancy that drugs or legal ergogenic aids will generate an effect (Maganaris, Collins and Sharp 2000; McClung and Collins 2007) leads to enhanced performance, even when the substance is, in fact, absent. Thus, setting out the programme in advance generates positive expectations and confidence in the outcome. Figure 4.2 presents one such example.

The second psychological application of periodisation relates to the timing of the essential switch from general improvement to event-specific preparation. This is clearly illustrated in Figure 4.3, which presents one interpretation of the circumstances surrounding the shock defeat of world champion boxer Lennox Lewis by the comparative unknown Hasim Rahman.

**73**

## Fred Bloggs' Olympic Preparation

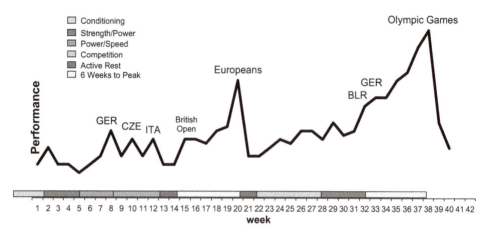

Figure 4.2 An exemplar peaking chart for a judo athlete in Olympic year (name changed).

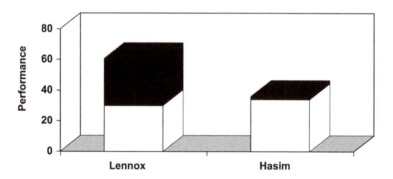

Figure 4.3 Performance potential (whole column – both black and white) minus product losses (black part) equals actual performance (in white).

As world champion, Lennox was a formidably talented boxer; Figure 4.3 highlights his very high 'performance potential', literally what he was capable of. Clearly, improving this performance potential is the main aim of coaches for most of the time: training, developing new skills and, in the case of team sports, recruiting new players to strengthen the squad. By contrast, Hasim was less talented with a much lower performance potential. On paper, and based on this big difference in potential, the contest should have been an easy victory for Lennox. Unfortunately however, at least based on media reports at the time, Lennox's preparation was less than perfect. A combination of media distractions, illness, delayed arrival at the venue and poor preparation meant that, on the night, Lennox lost a lot of his potential and his performance was under par. By contrast, Hasim's preparation was carefully designed, resulting in a performance close to, or even at, his potential. As a result, he won the contest.

Of course, the natural order was restored in the rematch, with Lennox winning in the fourth round after a much more thorough preparation minimised the 'product losses'. This resulted in a performance much closer to his potential and reflected the differences in potential between the two boxers. The message for coaches and athletes is clear. In the run-up to most events, and particularly key ones, general development (raising the performance potential) must be halted whilst the emphasis swings to specific event preparation designed to minimise product losses and ensure that the athlete performs near to, or even slightly above, his or her potential. Only when a performer decides to 'train through' and/or use the event for developmental purposes (identified up front), would skill evolution continue in the pre-event phase.

The third example is related to the previous idea but looks specifically at the improvement of skill – a clear and obvious feature of coaching in sport *but only at certain times*. The point here is that a new skill must be given time to 'establish itself', so that the athlete becomes comfortable and confident with the skill and for sufficient practice to be accrued to ensure the skill doesn't break down or regress to an earlier version under the pressure of competition. It is, therefore, particularly important to allow a sufficient period for skill change, ensuring that the new skill is automated and confidence is re-established (see Carson and

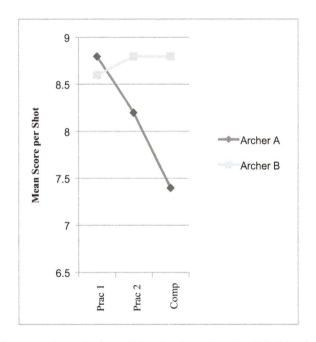

*Figure 4.4* Performance impact of practicing too long. Practice 1 in March – Both athletes practicing technically; Practice 2 in April – Athlete A still working on technical issues, whilst B has changed focus to consolidation; first competition in May.

Collins 2011 for a more detailed discussion of this idea) before it is required in the 'heat' of the event. Figure 4.4 illustrates the challenge of tinkering, experimenting or even overly zealous fine-tuning too long into the competitive season. Perhaps as a result of over-thinking (Beilock and Carr 2001), the skill doesn't work as well as it should: more thinking and more angst result, leading to a downward spiral which is both hard to break out of and ruinous to the season's performance.

There is one other motoric aspect of pre-event preparation, our fourth and final exemplar, which applies particularly to self-paced skills. The idea is based on the control differences between the state which can be achieved in training and the event itself. As a result of the adrenalin, which unsurprisingly flows in the event itself, the whole body is more 'revved up' with higher levels of muscular power available for both neurological and mycological reasons. In consequence, there is a subtle but genuine difference in the pattern of coordination between performances of a skill in training and in the event itself (MacPherson, Collins and Morriss 2008). So when developing a skill, especially a closed skill, coaches need to cater for this, accepting a slightly 'rough' version with the training body as an almost essential precursor to developing the optimum technique for the competition body. The timing of such practice, as well as the technical emphasis at different phases, represents another important feature of 'psychological periodisation'.

So, for all these and other reasons, developing a periodised plan seems to be a good idea, with significant psychological benefits for the athlete, *especially* when he or she is totally involved in the planning process (see Chapter 2). Indeed, so important are these effects that there may well be an indirect physiological benefit to the training process, due to the athlete's buy-in and confidence that the programme is going to achieve its aims. Once again, expectancy effects are immensely powerful, so it is always worth ensuring the athlete's commitment and understanding for the programme.

## THE RUN IN – USING THE LAST FEW WEEKS BEFORE COMPETITION

Clearly, by a few weeks before a competition most of the substantive work must have been completed. After all, significant fitness gains take a bit longer than three weeks. Unfortunately, however, some athletes and even a few coaches sometimes forget this and try to pack in extra training for extra gains at a time when recuperation and sharpening are much more important. This principle also applies to mental preparation. Athletes are much more likely to lose rather than gain in this period, so an emphasis on minimising product losses (see Figure 4.3) and consolidating strengths should be the focus for this potentially 'dangerous' period.

### Creating an impression

It is worth considering why this drive to work hard rather than smart might take place, especially because the answer also applies elsewhere in the performance preparation cycle. Of course, it may just be ignorance; after all, the urge to be as prepared as possible is both face-valid and very strong. In the vast majority of cases, however, the key theoretical perspective for this phase is related to self-presentation. Built on the work of Baumeister, Leary and colleagues

**76**

(for example, Baumeister and Hutton 1987; Leary and Kowalski 1990), self-presentational bias suggests that we are often most worried about what we think other people think of us than we are by our own thoughts (James and Collins 1997). As a result, we try to 'impression manage' so that we create the impression in significant others that we *think* they want. Arguably the major source of worry for most sub-elite performers, and very apparent in adolescents, there are two problems with this process. First, we get worried when we don't know what we have to show, often falling into the 'assume' trap by trying to do what we *think* is expected of us. Only slightly less potentially harmful, the second issue is even though we are now confident that we know what we should be showing, we doubt that we can.

Many of the implications deriving from this theory are well beyond the scope of this section; however, the following discussion will focus on three. First of all, consider how the athlete behaves in the crucial, pre-event phase. Rather than doing what they need to do, many will swagger about acting macho, aim for monk-like social isolation or spend so much time thinking through and rehearsing their performance that their brains almost fry; all because they *think* that's what is expected of them. Of course, one of these variations *may* be perfect for certain individuals, but they should know that and have confidence from past experimentation and experience not to conform to the expected behaviour. To avoid this common problem, coaches and athletes should work through plans well in advance of the event, discussing and considering others' views and experiences whilst also actively trying things out to arrive at their own personalised structure.

The second implication applies to coaches and support staff who, in their natural desire to be seen as fully supportive and contributing to performance, increase their efforts (and consequent demands on the athlete's time) to ever higher levels. This is an increasing problem for major professional sports, especially when teams have appointed coaching and support specialists for almost every discipline available. In attempting to make themselves 'indispensable', each specialist takes up time with the players when, in fact, the 'less is more' adage should apply. To avoid this problem, everyone has to be both clear and open as to what is and isn't required or useful. As workers at major competitions, we have both been on the receiving end of 'keep him/her away from me' requests, even though the individual concerned may be making valuable contributions at other times. So, knowing what is needed and when will be an essential feature of pre-event planning (more of this later). Recognising that the best contribution from a specialist may be made through someone else, or much earlier, is another insight which may be gained with experience, maturation, greater self-confidence or just better management (see Chapter 16, Putting it all together).

Third, and finally, consider steps that may be taken to reassure the athletes that they can actually do what is needed: as a consequence, many athletes and coaches develop 'benchmark' sessions – performances that they can use to 'prove' their readiness. For example, one javelin thrower used to throw a 'final trial', with a 700g implement, a few days before the event. Experience and preparation had shown him that he would achieve around the same distance with the full weight 800g javelin in the event as he managed with the lighter 700g in his final session. Runners can use a specific interval session or timed run, curlers a particular set of throws, lifters a run through at opening weights; the permutations are endless but the impact on the athlete's confidence (and the coach's peace of mind) can be very powerful.

**77**

## Optimising the final preparation

The main message here is that both performers and coaches should know, and be confident that they know, how they individually reach their own performance peak. As an untypical example, yet a consistent feature of elites, consider the need to be 'in character' for the optimum performance. Achieving this mental state, assuming that the athlete has taken the trouble to learn exactly what his or her own variation is, takes time and space. Well informed coaches and team managers allow for this, doing what is needed, but no more, to help their experienced and self-aware performers do what they need to do. Controlling the various distractions that occur at this time, such as media 'requests' for interviews, visiting dignitaries, opening ceremonies, who rooms with whom, athlete/family communication issues and so on, is a large part of promoting effective preparation and avoiding product losses. From a coaching perspective, and reflecting the self-presentational issues discussed earlier, sessions at this crucial stage are almost entirely and unremittingly positive; the aim being to constantly remind the athlete what is needed *and* that he or she can achieve it. Only under very particular circumstances is it worth continuing to work on weaknesses so close to the event, and in this case it is even more important for the athlete to be involved in the decision-making process: more on this later.

The coach also needs to strike a careful balancing act between conserving/hoarding energy and staying sharp. As a result, activity at this stage should be high in intensity but the volume should reflect the challenges of the forthcoming event. Thus, distance runners will still run distance, judo players will do practice bouts at high intensity but neither will be to the levels of the upcoming competition. Matching the timing and rhythm of these practices to the timing of the event itself is also sensible. So, if the athlete is required to run heats early in the morning (or at least early for the normal wake up), then do practices at the same time. Many coaches forget about the need to fit the athlete's daily (circadian) and other rhythms to the event template; after all, that can't be done the other way around. In certain circumstances, this can mean that the athlete 'time slips' whilst remaining in his or her home training environment, thus doing the time adjustment whilst also maintaining the advantages of the familiar home training environment. For example, a boxer training in Scotland for a fight in New York gradually adjusts his daily pattern to New York time (five hours behind the UK) whilst putting his heaviest sparring sessions on at 3 a.m. UK time to match his bout.

Finally, and while enabling the optimum blend of space and focus to enable effective self-preparation, coaches need to achieve another balancing act between distraction and loss of focus. Even highly committed athletes need to switch off sometimes. Resting is strangely tiring, however, especially when you are used to a daily dose or two of hard training. Once again, the perceptive coach will be very aware of the need for balance.

All these processes and considerations also apply to the much shorter time scales associated with professional sport. For example, many premiership clubs will require their players to stay in a team hotel the night before a game, even when it is a home fixture. Of course, taking all this trouble then insisting on filling the time available with team meetings and other potentially 'impression managing' interventions ('look I am doing EVERYTHING possible for our performance') is just one situation where theory and practice don't quite marry up.

The extra challenges of catering for all the factors described above in each individual, whilst also enabling the optimum team preparation, is another balancing act. Each individual has to have his or her own needs met, while also perceiving that everyone else's preparation has also been perfect. This is yet another feature of the Shared Mental Models (SMMs) (Richards, Collins and Mascarenhas 2012; Richards, Mascarenhas and Collins 2009) which characterise effective performance in team sports.

## AT THE EVENT

As with the run up to the competition, the event itself is another balancing act for the coach. In this case, the best option is to offer just enough communication. Less is almost always more and silence is often golden, due to the insecurities which the athlete may feel at this crucial stage. In an almost reverse impression management process, the athlete becomes hyper-aware of the coach's behaviour, often misinterpreting the signals he or she receives. This is an interesting manifestation of free-floating anxiety: 'I feel worried – WHY do I feel worried – AHHH! because the coach thinks . . . so I'm no good' (see Srivatava 2013 for a discussion on how pervasive and powerful this can be, albeit in a non-sports setting). Once again, clear and open communication between coach, athlete and other members of the team is crucial to avoid the negative spiral which can result from misinterpretation of observed behaviour: for example, 'why are you eating? – well, why are you watching?'

As another consequence of this misinterpretation, many coaches find themselves in a conflict of interest when they are asked to coach rival athletes in the same event. Major events are increasingly limited on accreditations, the essential pass which offers coaches the necessary access to their athletes in warm up and in the stadium. As a result, unless the athlete is a genuine medal hope, he or she may have to accept coaching support from a sport-employed coach who may also be responsible for rivals or several others in the same event. Once again, early and open communication is essential if athlete and coach are to achieve an effective working relationship.

As mentioned earlier, coaches must plan and accommodate the media circus, countering the almost inevitable product losses that can accrue. An overlooked issue here is the negative effects this can have on those who are *and* those who are not the focus of the media attention. Those who are want to avoid the limelight; those who are not feel inadequate or 'put down' by the lack of attention they perceive and often misinterpret.

## Prior planning to avoid product losses

As mentioned earlier, there are physical issues as well as these 'perception' mental challenges. In multi-event days for example (heats in morning and semis in the afternoon or multiple bouts/repechage and so on), athletes need to carefully plan for refuelling and rest during the day. This might mean carrying fluids and snacks into the 'closed' areas of the event (where access is limited to competitors and officials) so that refuelling can start immediately after the end of the heat. Similar procedures are required in weight control sports, where athletes must put as much extra weight on as practical once they have 'made weight'.

Also within this plan, the coach must allow for the effective build up to the next round, ideally working on the basis of well documented experience as to whether the athlete will have time for a cool down, refuel and warm up. Abbreviated versions of each must be developed and deployed if time is short. Good distraction and relaxation strategies should be practiced and employed if time is available. In the latter case, previous experience will suggest how long a block of time each individual requires to facilitate a 'genuine break'. If the sport is even remotely tactical, the warm up must allow for some preparation time to develop an event or fight plan. Laptop computers/tablets, in conjunction with databases and handheld cameras, have revolutionised this preparation period, enabling athletes to watch upcoming opponents, then evolve from template plans in discussion with a prede-termined panel of support staff. Why this isn't a consistent part of footballers' preparation for penalty shoot outs remains a mystery; there are still players who seem to do little but lie on their backs whilst the ill-prepared coach asks for volunteers to take penalties. The comparative frequency of this sort of behaviour is an excellent example of how much fur-ther some coaches have to go.

The bottom line is that all these processes need evolution and practice. Athlete and coach confidence in their efficacy is almost as important as their actual impact. Accordingly, coaches must anticipate the types of systems which will be required at the top level, plus associated skills and resources, then start to evolve them as a systematic feature of the athlete's develop-ment. Earlier comments about support suffocation also apply here. Support staff must know when they aren't needed and be prepared to take a back seat, equipping and empowering others to provide that aspect of support. Of course, these same considerations also apply to the coach. For example, half-time briefings on effective tactics, both offensive and defensive, may best be communicated by performance analysts rather than coaches. Physiotherapists or soft tissue therapists might play an important part; strength and conditioning specialists could usefully manage aspects of the warm up. The main point is that, whatever is decided upon, the procedure and the provider are matters of well established and thought through individual preference, not just tradition ('We've always done it this way') or ego salving.

## After the ball is over

After the event is finished, it also helps to have well developed and established recovery and cool down strategies. Physically, these enable the athletes to get the after-effects out of their bodies, enabling the earliest possible return to training or commencement of preparation for the next event. Psychologically, such systems ensure that the event is 'put to bed' quickly and effectively. Win or lose, the event is reviewed, necessary lessons are learnt and the athlete can focus completely on the next challenge.

The tight schedules and short lifespan of competition mean that any athlete must be able to 'get back on the job', even after a major win such as an Olympic Games, Wimbledon or a Champions/Heineken League victory. Time for celebration is short and consistency is all. The coach must play a central part in this, helping the athlete to celebrate (once again, even elite athletes are human), then recover and refocus. Indeed, recuperation and regeneration has almost established itself as a spate discipline in sport science; albeit that this is predominantly physiological and training recovery focused.

## COACHING CONSIDERATIONS ACROSS THE PROCESS

The preceding sections should have highlighted the levels of challenge that the coach faces in achieving optimum performances in competition. Accordingly, this final section will highlight the skills and techniques that are needed to facilitate the delicate balancing act that has been exemplified. This will be covered in four interlinked sections, starting with practical considerations and techniques for debriefing and developing competitive skills in training, then turning to the higher order considerations of decision making and planning.

### Debriefing and revisions

As Aldous Huxley somewhat misogynisticly observed 'experience is not what happens to a man; it is what he does with what happens to him'. The point is that just being there doesn't automatically confer development; rather, this depends on how carefully and thoroughly the occurrences are reviewed and analysed to generate changes for future trials. It is so with coaches and competition – a recognition that seems to have been covered by the current fascination with critical reflection in coaching and other support professions.

Carefully considered debriefing is an essential component for securing lessons for the future. At the time of writing, the England cricket team are completing a disastrous tour of Australia in early 2014. Clearly, debriefing is essential; some would even say overdue. Notably, however, this debrief, as with all others, must avoid three traps if accurate and effective information is to accrue. First, the debrief must be honest and open, contextualised against the circumstances surrounding the event but still completed without vested or other political interests 'polluting' the interpretations. The second issue is a particular problem for high profile sports. Before a single line has been written or individual consulted, the media will have completed their own 'thorough and authoritative' review. Unfortunately, this is often riddled with self-interest, but the power of such statements can have an overwhelming impact. For this reason, many professional sport coaches place high importance on media management as a means of promoting job survival or even as a coaching tool (Cruickshank, Collins and Minten 2014). The final consideration is the one which can often negate, or at least severely limit, the impact of critical reflection; namely, the criteria against which to judge the object of reflection (Martindale and Collins 2013). So in the cricketing example, extensive comparative data about diverse aspects such as tour preparation, coping with pressure, team culture and leadership must all be used as the ruler against which the circumstances of the case are measured. This idea is important across the coaching spectrum, and underpins the application of professional judgement and decision-making principles (Abraham and Collins 2011; Martindale and Collins 2013) that can be applied to all aspects of the process.

If these three principles are catered for, genuine and meaningful data should result. It is then a case of making the necessary changes, but in a way that preserves the good features of the situation. After all, change is a delicate process and needs careful handling (Cruickshank and Collins 2012). Given the essential need to maintain a cutting edge, however, coaches at the top level must constantly explore change to keep ahead of their rivals. Accordingly, the skills of careful review and change management become particularly important for staying at the top.

## Competition in practice

Seeing that every other aspect of a sport is rehearsed, it seems logical that competition is no different. Competition simulations can be used to develop and practice routines, systems and tactics. They can also help to 'problem solve', offering the chance to collect data to address issues which could not be measured in actual events (Collins, Doherty and Talbot 1993). The main concern in such simulations is ensuring sufficient arousal and challenge to make things realistic. There are some 'cunning plans' to do this, however. For a start, aspects can be changed, such as the previously cited example of using a lighter javelin. Conditioned games, carefully briefed opposition and competitive tasks interspersed with hard physical training can all be used to good effect. In fact, this last element is part of a common mental training approach called 'combination training' (Collins and Collins 2011), which combines practice of difficult technical challenges with physical challenge – another form of competitive simulation.

## Developing decision making

Much has been made of the coach's decision making in this chapter; indeed, we would suggest that the way in which the coach makes decisions, and how he or she ensures that this process is continuous, is the major characteristic of coaching expertise (Quick, Kiely and Collins, in review). The other crucial decision makers in the picture are, of course, the athletes. In some sports, communication and simplicity make active decision making by the athlete a small concern. In track and field, for example, coach and athlete can communicate easily on technical matters ('make that run-up slightly longer') or not at all on tactics ('make your break now') once the event has started.

In other sports, however, developing and empowering athlete decision making is essential to performance. Unless competitive execution is to be only a pre-choreographed sequence (and for some coaches it is), the athlete's decision making must be a major thrust of training; this aspect is particularly important for team sports. This crucial topic is covered in detail elsewhere (Richards *et al.* 2009, 2012, in press). For the present purpose, however, consider the core principles of developing decision making in athletes; in its simplest form, this process leads to the development of a Shared Mental Model or SMM, whether between coach and athlete or, more commonly, between coach and the different members of a team. The essentials are as follows:

- All must have the ability to pick up and similarly interpret cues in the situation. This will involve the capacity to scan the environment in different ways and at different times (Mortimer 2002).
- A similar 'cross team weighting scale' must be applied in the decision-making process itself. All involved must have a similar idea of the relative importance of factors and desirability of outcomes.
- This enables each member to anticipate the actions of others and to take actions which proactively support the team tactic (Kleinman, Pattipati, Luh and Serfaty 1992).
- Ideally, the SMM will have been developed almost totally through collaboration, ensuring both buy-in to, and confidence in, the resulting plan.

Application of these principles generates a SMM between team members; not necessarily the ultimately optimum plan but certainly one which, when executed consistently and with full focus, will be highly effective. It is also important to note that any SMM developed is team specific; change members of the team and the SMM must be redeveloped.

Of course, all these ideas depend on having a coach who is sufficiently open minded and empowering to hand power to his or her athletes. Perhaps surprisingly, this is not necessarily a ubiquitous characteristic, even at the top level. Coaches can be very arrogant and controlling (Collins, Abraham and Collins 2012), although the power of expectancy means that this autocratic style can often be effective as athletes are 'convinced' that their coach's word is *the* way forwards. All other things being equal, however, developing the athlete to go further than you can take them would seem to be both a logical and an ethical way to proceed.

## Putting it all together

We will not anticipate the final chapter of this book, in which some thoughts are offered on how the whole process can be optimally integrated. For the moment, however, readers should recognise the need for careful and critical planning and review if the complex system of myriad factors is to be exploited. Good luck with your competition preparation.

## REFERENCES

Abraham, A. and Collins, D. (2011). Taking the next step: Ways forward for coaching science. *Quest* 63: pp. 366–384.

Baumeister, R. F. and Hutton, D. G. (1987). Self-presentation theory: Self-construction and audience pleasing. In *Theories of Group Behavior.* Mullen, B. and G. R. Goethals (Eds.) (New York: Springer): pp. 71–87.

Beilock, S. L. and Carr, T. H. (2001). On the fragility of skilled performance: What governs choking under pressure? *Journal of Experimental Psychology: General* 130: pp. 701–725.

Carson, H. J. and Collins, D. (2011). Refining and regaining skills in fixation/diversification stage performers: The Five-A Model. *International Review of Sport and Exercise Psychology* 4(2): pp. 46–167.

Collins, D., Abraham, A., and Collins, R. (2012). On vampires and wolves: Exploring and countering reasons for the differential impact of coach education. *International Journal of Sport Psychology* 43: pp. 255–271.

Collins, D. and Bailey, R. (2012). 'Scienciness' and the allure of second-hand strategy in talent development. *International Journal of Sport Policy and Politics.* DOI:10.1080/19406940.2012.656682.

Collins, D. and Collins, J. (2011). Putting them together: Skill packages to optimize team/group performance. In *Performance Psychology: A Practitioner's Guide.* Collins, D., A. Button and H. Richards (Eds.) (Oxford: Elsevier): pp. 363–401.

Collins, D. J., Doherty, M. D. and Talbot, S. (1993). Performance enhancement in moto cross: A case study of the sport science team in action. *The Sport Psychologist* 7: pp. 290–297.

Cruickshank, A. and Collins, D. (2012). Culture change in elite sport performance teams: Examining and advancing effectiveness in the new era. *Journal of Applied Sport Psychology* 24: pp. 338–355.

Cruickshank, A., Collins, D. and Minten, S. (2014). Driving and sustaining culture change in Olympic sport performance teams: A first exploration and grounded theory. *Journal of Sport and Exercise Psychology* 36(1): pp. 107–120.

James, B. and Collins, D. (1997). Self-presentational sources of competitive stress during performance. *Journal of Sport and Exercise Psychology* 19(1): pp. 17–35.

Kiely, J. (2012). Periodization paradigms in the 21st century: Evidence-led or tradition-driven? *International Journal of Sports Physiology and Performance* 7(3): pp. 242–50.

Kleinman, D., Pattipati, K., Luh, P. and Serfaty, D. (1992). Mathematical models of team performance: A distributed decision-making approach. In *Teams: Their Training and Performance.* Swezey, R. and E. Salas (Eds.) (Norwood, NJ: Ablex Publishing Corporation): pp. 177–218.

Leary, M. R. and Kowalski, R. M. (1990). Impression management: A literature review and two-component model. *Psychological Bulletin* 107: pp. 34–47.

MacPherson, A. C., Collins, D. and Morriss, C. (2008). Is what you think what you get: Optimizing mental focus for technical performance. *The Sport Psychologist* 22: pp. 304–315.

Maganaris, C. N., Collins, D. and Sharp, M. A. (2000). Expectancy effects and strength training: Do steroids make a difference? *The Sport Psychologist* 14: pp. 272–278.

Martindale, A. and Collins, D. (2013). The development of professional judgment and decision making expertise in applied sport psychology. *The Sport Psychologist* 27: pp. 390–398.

McClung, M. and Collins, D. (2007). Evaluating the contribution of expectancy to improved performance with ergogenic aids. *Journal of Sport and Exercise Psychology* 29(3): pp. 382–394.

Mortimer, P. (2002). Developing decision making. In *Rugby Tough.* Hale, B. D. and D. Collins (Eds.) (Champaign, IL: Human Kinetics).

Quick, S., Kiely, J. and Collins, D. (in review). Telling the pros from the joes: Characteristics of coaching expertise. *Journal of Applied Sport Psychology.*

Richards, P., Collins, D. and Mascarenhas, D. (2012). Developing rapid high pressure team decision making skills. The integration of slow deliberate reflective learning within the competitive performance environment: A case study of elite netball. *Journal of Reflective Practice* 13(3): pp. 455–469.

Richards, P., Collins, D. and Mascarenhas, D. (in press). A framework for developing team decision making: Integrating knowing what to do and when to do it. *Journal of Applied Sport Psychology.*

Richards, P., Mascarenhas, D.R.D. and Collins, D. (2009) Implementing reflective practice approaches with elite team athletes: Parameters of success. *Reflective Practice* 10(3): pp. 353–363.

Srivatava, R. (2013). Free-floating anxiety. *The Lancet* 381(9880): pp. 1808–1809.

## FURTHER READING

Collins, D., Button, A. and Richards, H. (2011). *Performance psychology: A practitioner's guide.* (Oxford: Elsevier.)

Hale, B. D. and Collins, D. (2002). *Rugby tough.* (Champaign, IL: Human Kinetics).

# Chapter 5

# The practice session
## Creating a learning environment

*Terry McMorris*

This chapter will examine how the coach can create an environment that facilitates athlete learning and will begin by looking at what is actually meant by learning or acquiring sports skills. This is followed by a discussion on how the coach can create a climate of learning and an examination of ways in which the quality of learning and coaching are ensured. Finally, a look at coach and athlete commitment will lead into a discussion on how the coach creates a motivational climate during practice in Chapter 6.

## ATHLETE LEARNING

Learning has been defined as 'a relatively permanent change in performance resulting from practice or past experience' (Kerr 1982). Kerr's interpretation explains a great deal about learning and that performance is not truly indicative of learning. Most people have heard about beginner's luck. The novice golfer who hits the ball straight down the middle of the fairway is likely to put the next shot out of bounds. Performance is 'a temporary occurrence fluctuating from time to time: something which is transitory' (Kerr 1982, p. 5), whereas athletes perform a learned skill 'relatively permanently' or consistently. When considering learning academic skills rather than sports skills, once a person has learned something they would not expect to occasionally get it wrong; yet when it comes to sports skills that is not the case. Maria Sharapova isn't expected to get every first serve in the service court and it is generally accepted that Lionel Messi will not always hit the target. This is not because there are different standards for athletes compared to scholars; it is because of the difference between the nature of a sports, or psychomotor, skill compared to an academic skill. Academic skills are purely cognitive and rely on brain activation, but psychomotor skills require both activation of the brain and the body. As a result, there are thousands of interconnections between neurons, and connections between neurons and muscles and joints, when performing a psychomotor skill. Just think of how many joints, muscles and nerves are involved in a fairly simple task like throwing a ball. Getting just one small part wrong will affect the outcome. These nerves, muscles and joints are known as *degrees of freedom* – the more that are involved, the more likely the skill will go wrong. This issue will be discussed later in the chapter.

Another interesting phrase used by Kerr (1982) are the words 'resulting from practice or past experience' (p. 5). By learning from practice, Kerr was probably meaning what is called 'explicit learning'. This refers to what might be considered the 'normal' way of learning;

students are given overt, or explicit, instructions and told to concentrate on the task at hand. By learning from past experience, Kerr was stating that it is also possible to learn from analysing past performances. As with learning by practice, Kerr inferred that learning occurs by making explicit rules about a skill and using these rules to guide learning and performance. More recent research, however, has shown that it is also possible to learn at a subconscious level, with what is now referred to as 'implicit learning'. A great deal of learning from past experience is implicit. Little thought is given to what has been done or seen, but repeated exposure to a skill can lead to the acquisition of that skill. Cognitive neuroscientists have even shown that explicitly and implicitly learned skills are recalled in different ways to one another and probably stored differently in the brain. As illustrated in the next section, it is possible to organise practices in such a way that skills will be implicitly learned, so learning implicitly can be through both practice and past experience.

The reason for including references to explicit and implicit learning is not purely academic, nor is it intended to confuse. A large amount of research has examined the effects of explicit compared to implicit learning of skills. Both ways work, but there is evidence to show that implicitly learned skills are less susceptible to breakdown under stress.

---

**Key points box 5.1**

- Learning is 'a relatively permanent change in performance resulting from practice or past experience' (Kerr 1982)
- Performance is 'a temporary occurrence fluctuating from time to time: something which is transitory' (Kerr 1982)
- Explicit learning is conscious and depends on forming rules
- Implicit learning is subconscious and based on repeated exposure to a skill

---

## MAJOR THEORIES OF LEARNING

This section will examine some of the major theories of learning. The first set of theories examined, Fitts and Posner's (1967) Three Stage Theory, Schmidt's (1975) Schema Theory and Anderson's (1982) Adaptive Control of Thought (ACT*) Theory have many similarities and can be described as cognitive theories. The final theory, Dynamical Systems Theory, is very different in origin and underlying philosophy but, like all of the theories, it places a strong emphasis on the need to practice.

### Fitts and Posner's three stage theory

Fitts and Posner (1967) claimed that learning takes place in three stages – cognitive, associative and autonomous. In the cognitive stage the person tries to make sense of instructions. They make a great deal of use of verbal labels. This does not mean that instruction needs to be verbal, but simply that the individual uses verbalisation to aid memory. For those skills requiring perception and decision making, there are often mistakes made and the person attends to irrelevant as well as relevant stimuli. The motor component is characterised by crude and uncoordinated movement.

Practice leads to the development of explicitly learned rules or knowledge of what to do. When someone is at this stage they are said to be in the associative stage, sometimes referred to as the intermediate stage. Further practice is required to perfect the skill and develop the consistent coordinated movement that demonstrates learning. When the person can perform consistently, and with little overt cognitive activity, they are said to have reached the autonomous stage.

## Key points box 5.2

- Cognitive stage
  - Use of verbal labels
  - Thinks about the skill
- Associative or intermediate stage
  - Physical practice very important
- Autonomous stage
  - Consistency
  - Limited cognitive input

## Schmidt's schema theory

According to Information Processing theorists, learning is achieved through the acquisition of a whole range of what Keele (1968) called 'motor programs' (the American 'programs' is normally used rather than the British 'programmes'). Keele defined motor programs as being 'a set of muscle commands that allow movements to be performed without any peripheral feedback' (Keele 1968, p. 367). While Keele believed that motor programs were specific to each skill, in other words a motor program would be required for kicking a static ball, another for kicking a ball moving towards a player, another for kicking a ball going away from a player and so on, Schmidt (1975) believed that motor programs were general rather than specific. This claim is widely accepted today. Schmidt saw a generalised motor program as being a schema, which he described as 'a set of generalised rules or rules that are generic to a group of movements' (Schmidt 1975, p. 232). Consequently, it is not necessary to store millions of motor programs but rather store fewer, generalised programs. A program for kicking would be all that is required, and it does not even have to be kicking a ball specifically. The same program or schema can be adapted to kicking in taekwondo or karate.

Schmidt claimed that two kinds of schema are developed; these he called the recall and recognition schemas (or schemata). The recall schema is responsible for the choice and initiation of action, while the recognition schema evaluates the ongoing movement and makes appropriate changes in the action. Schmidt stated that the learning of the recall and recognition schemas are brought about by the development of the general rules that evolve during practice. In developing the recall schema, athletes and players remember the desired outcome, the initial conditions, the response parameters and the sensory consequences. An example of initial conditions would be the position of the individual's body parts when preparing to make a catch in the outfield during a game of cricket. The speed, line and length of ball flight would also be initial conditions. Response parameters, sometimes called response specifications, are changes in the specifics of the action that are necessary if the outcome is to be successful. These parameters will depend on the contextual situation. The parameters will be different if the initial conditions change. For example, to kick a static football, say while taking a corner kick, the response parameters will be different to those required when running towards an approaching ball. Importantly, it is not necessary to have previously experienced the exact initial conditions or response parameters. If a recall schema has been developed, the brain can automatically adjust to the new situation. This explains how it is possible to perform novel skills or improvise in novel situations, something that the original motor program theory could not.

Similarly, with the recognition schema, the desired outcome, initial conditions and the sensory consequences are remembered. It is the latter that are the most important for the recognition schema. The sensory consequences are what the movement feels like. As with the recall schema, it is not necessary to have experienced the exact same sensory consequences to know if the movement is performed as desired. The development of the schema determines if the actions performed are within the correct boundaries. Anyone who plays striking games, such as tennis, cricket, golf or baseball, will know when a strike is good, without having to see where the ball goes, just from the feel of the movement. They will also know when they have under hit or over hit a shot.

The development of the schemas is controlled by error labelling. For fast movements, sensory information is fed back to the brain and spinal cord, known as the Central Nervous System (CNS), after the completion of the action. Any mismatches between the desired and actual outcomes are labelled as being errors and are used to alter the schemas, ready for the next time the individual needs to achieve the desired goal. This also occurs for slow movements until the recognition schema has been developed, then the sensory information is fed back to the CNS and the movement is continually altered during performance to achieve the desired outcome.

## Key points box 5.3

- A schema as a set of generalised rules or rules that are generic to a group of movements
- Recall schema
- Choice and initiation of action
- We remember:
  - desired outcomes
  - initial conditions
  - response parameters or specifications

- changes to specifics necessary for success
- sensory consequences
- feel of the movement
■ Recognition schema
■ Evaluates ongoing movement
■ Makes changes to action if necessary
■ We remember:
  - desire outcomes
  - initial conditions
  - sensory consequences
■ Error labelling
  - we learn from mistakes by changing the schema

## Adaptive control of thought (ACT*) theory

Anderson's (1982) Adaptive Control of Thought (ACT*) theory probably provides a better explanation than the other theories of how decision-making skills are acquired. Care should be taken with ACT* because it was developed to explain how children acquire language skills. According to Anderson, first stage of learning involves the acquisition of declarative knowledge or knowledge of what to do. He believed that declarative knowledge is acquired prior to what he termed procedural knowledge. Procedural knowledge is not merely making the correct decision but knowing how to ensure that the outcome of the action is met. Research into implicit learning has shown that often sports performers can have procedural knowledge without declarative knowledge.

Although ACT* theory has been largely discredited with regard to learning motor skills, many coaches and psychologists believe that it provides a good explanation of how people learn decision-making skills. Anderson believed that when learning to make decisions, people predetermine what they will do in any given situation. He claimed that problems are solved by saying, 'if A happens then I will do B'. This is declarative knowledge; as people practice more and more, they need to do this less and less until they respond automatically when they perceive the situation. This is procedural knowledge.

### Key points box 5.4

■ Declarative knowledge
  - knowing what to do
■ Procedural knowledge
  - being able to perform the skill
■ Declarative knowledge leads to procedural knowledge
■ Declarative rules:
  - 'if A happens then I will do B'

## Dynamical systems theory

Dynamical Systems theory is very different to the cognitive theories outlined above. To the cognitivists, learning is about developing memory and is primarily a function of the brain. To the Dynamical Systems theorists, memory is of little use in the learning of motor skills, as people have no recourse to memory while performing skills. All that is required from the brain is to know what goal is to be achieved. With this information, individuals will search the environment for the optimal conditions that allow them to achieve their goal. These are called affordances, and they do not require a motor program or any other central representation to perform the necessary movement. This is taken care of by the interaction between the affordance and the individual. The nature of this interaction is determined by what the Dynamical Systems theorists call constraints.

Constraints have been divided into task, environmental and organismic constraints. Task constraints are basically the rules of the activity. For example, the bowler in cricket is prohibited from using a throwing action; this affects how he or she interacts with the environment. Environmental constraints in sport are factors such as the weather or size of the playing area, while organismic constraints are the physiological and psychological attributes of the performer. According to the Dynamical Systems theorists, once an affordance has been recognised, the individual will naturally self-organise to meet his or her goal or, in their words, realise the affordance. Self-organisation refers to the coordination of the nerves, muscles and joints that is the degrees of freedom.

---

### Key points box 5.5

- Memory plays little or no part in learning
- We learn by interacting with the environment
- We search the environment for affordances
- Affordances
  - opportunities to achieve our goals
- Constraints determine what we can do
  - task constraints
  - for example, rules of the sport
  - environmental constraints
  - for example, space available
  - organismic constraints
  - for example, height, weight and so on
- Movement depends on self-organisation
  - co-ordination of nerves, muscles, joints and so on
- These make up our degrees of freedom

## A LEARNING CLIMATE

This section will examine how the coach provides a learning climate for the athlete. Of course, the motivational aspects covered in the next chapter are also key with regard to the learning climate, but for now the focus is on motor behaviour issues. Good coaches begin creating the climate by ensuring that their instruction is of the highest quality. This is covered in the first subsection. The second subsection will look at the types of practice that can be used, and how the learner's attributes and the nature of the task combine to determine the coach's choice of practice environment.

## Instruction and demonstration

Most coaches tend to begin coaching sessions with some form of instruction. It is common to hear the coach say, 'Today we are going to learn to . . .'. The coach then gives some form, or forms, of instruction, which are aimed at facilitating the athlete's learning. There are basically three types of instruction – verbal, visual and verbal plus visual. Another word for visual instruction is, of course, demonstration. A great deal of research has been carried out on the efficacy of these different instructional methods. First, they all tend to work but not necessarily for all skills. For example, some skills are very difficult to articulate and are far more easily taught using demonstration. When coaches use verbal instruction they must be sure that the learners understand the words used. With beginners one cannot use jargon; they simply will not understand what is meant. With more experienced athletes using jargon is fine, but jargon is not the only problem. Children often have limited vocabularies, so the coaches must choose their words very carefully. It is not easy to articulate how many sports skills are performed. Try it for yourself. Choose a couple of skills from your own sport and try to write down a list of instructions for a beginner.

Due to the problems of articulating sports skills, most coaches prefer to use demonstrations. However, even demonstrations will not solve all problems. It is not possible to be certain that the learners are focusing on the key factors as to how the skill is performed. Moreover, it cannot be assumed that their perceptual skills are such that they accurately perceive what they have seen. Perception and seeing are not the same. All of the learners will receive the same visual information, but they will not all perceive it accurately. It is not uncommon to be in situations where several people witness an event but their accounts of what happened vary greatly. This has led coaches to advocate the verbal plus visual method of instruction. The verbal part consists of the coach drawing the learner's attention to the key points. This aids the athlete's perception of how the skill is performed.

One of the areas concerning demonstration that has been of interest to coaches and psychologists is just how good the demonstration has to be. This will obviously be a major issue when coaching advanced skills, which may be beyond the coach's own ability level. The use of demonstrations by other athletes has been shown to be beneficial, but is not always possible. The use of videos of expert performers has also been shown to be successful. Surprisingly perhaps, it does not appear that demonstrations need to be perfect, but they do need to have some quality. Some coaches overcome limitations by demonstrating in slow motion. If, however, speed is an essential factor in the skills, for example, change of pace when dribbling in football, basketball or hockey, there may be problems. If learners have only seen a slow motion demonstration, this important point may be missed. In some cases, however, it may be necessary to slow performances down or the action will be too fast for the athlete to perceive it accurately. In such cases a full-speed action should also be demonstrated.

---

### Key points box 5.6

- Instruction
- Verbal
  - not all skills can be verbalised
- Visual (demonstration)
  - quality of demonstration is a factor
- Visual plus verbal
  - verbal should draw the learner's attention to the key points in the demonstration

---

## Dynamical systems theory and instruction

The use of instruction outlined above is geared to explicit learning and is favoured by cognitivists. It is about the learner developing rules for performing the action. To Fitts and Posner (1967) this is in the cognitive stage of learning, while Schmidt sees this as the early stages of developing recall and recognition schemas. The Dynamical Systems theorists advocate that the coach simply sets the learner a task. The coach then manipulates the constraints to guide the athletes towards organising their own limbs to perform the skill in their own way.

A variation of this type of approach is the use of an external focus of attention. For example, a coach might ask a javelin thrower to focus on the finishing position of his or her hand. According to Dynamical Systems theory, self-organisation of joints, muscles and nerves will automatically take care of how the hand gets to its final destination. This is the opposite of what most coaches do when using explicit instruction, where they ask the learner to focus internally on the feel of the movement or the nature of how he or she performs the task. This is known as an internal focus. Research comparing external and internal foci has tended to show that the former is more advantageous, however caution is advised as much of the research has been undertaken with skills that arguably lend themselves to this approach.

---

### Key points box 5.7

- Practice is organised in order to allow learners to become attuned to the affordances to be able to achieve their goals
- External focus of attention:
  - focus on outcome or an end point rather than mechanics of movement

---

## Practice

Once the coach has provided the athlete with instruction, it is essential that the learner then practices the skill. In fact, one cannot really separate practice from learning. To the cognitivists, it is during practice that schemas are formed, while, to the Dynamical Systems theorists, it is during practice that a search of the environment is performed for the opportunities to carry out a skill. They call this process 'becoming attuned to the affordances'. Although the cognitivists and the Dynamical Systems theorists are coming from different starting points, they have some similar beliefs about practice. Most importantly, both groups believe that learning is not possible without practice – a lot of practice. How the coach organises this practice will play a major role in setting a learning climate.

## Types of practice

One of the first issues to be researched with regard to practice was the use of massed versus spaced practice. The research was undertaken in laboratories, using tasks that have little in common with sports skills. Massed practice refers to situations where the athlete practices a skill over and over again with little or no gap between trials. Spaced practice is, in its literal sense, where the interval between the trials is greater than the time it takes for one trial to be completed. In reality, it is when practice is interspersed with rest periods or breaks. This can help guard against boredom and fatigue, but research has generally shown that there is no difference in learning resulting from the two types of practice.

A far more important factor than whether massed or spaced practice is used is when to use whole, part or part-progressive practice. Whole practice refers to practicing a task in its entirety, for example, throwing the javelin or taking a penalty flick in hockey. This is fairly straightforward, but whether practice is whole or part becomes confusing when using small-sided games, such as 6-a-side hockey. Is this whole or part practice? The best explanation of whether it is whole or part practice is probably how it relates to the learner. For an adult, playing 6-a-side hockey is not whole practice. For an 11-year-old, however, it can be classed as whole practice because the level of development of the 11-year-old means that playing 11-a-side is not an appropriate task.

Using whole practice means that everything happens in the environment in which it will be performed. The learner not only gets to practice the technique but also learns how and when to use that particular technique. To the cognitivists, whole practice is also good in helping the learner to develop schemas. Learners cannot simply repeat a specific motor program but must constantly recall and re-assess the desired outcome, the initial conditions, the response parameters and the sensory consequences. There are drawbacks, however, particularly when learning team games. The amount of information that the learner must deal with when playing a full version of a game can be overwhelming for the beginner. This is particularly important if the learner is a child, with limited selective attention and past experience. In these cases it is better to use part practice.

Part practice refers to breaking down a skill into its parts and practicing each part in isolation. So a triple jumper might practice the hop or the step or the jump separately. A common example is the swimmer who works on legs only or arms only. While this allows them to concentrate on specifics, problems can occur when they have to put the parts together. Sometimes it can be very de-motivating. A tennis coach was recently observed having young players practice throwing the ball up for a serve. However, the coach did not let them hit it. They just threw it up, let it bounce, picked it up and threw it up again. To say that the youngsters were bored would be an understatement. Advanced performers, however, will practice part of a skill if they know that getting that part correct will allow them to perform the whole skill better. Hence many coaches use whole-part-whole practice. With whole-part-whole practice, the performers make an initial attempt to perform the whole skill. The coach then highlights the area or areas that are causing concern and has the athlete practice those parts of the skill in isolation. Once the performer reaches a good enough level on the weaker parts, they return to practicing the whole skill.

Rather than use purely part practice, many coaches use part-progressive practice. This refers to breaking down a skill into its component parts, beginning by practicing a specific part, adding another part to it, then another and so on until they reach the whole. This type of practice may be familiar to many. To develop passing and support play in hockey, the coach might start by having beginners practice passing to one another in a static situation. They then have to pass and move, which forces their partner to look to see where they have gone before making a return pass. These changes in initial conditions necessitate changes in response parameters and sensory consequences – this fits in with developing a schema for passing.

As they become more proficient, performers can move onto a 4 v 1 keep-ball game. This is quite easy even for beginners, but when they progress to 3 v 1 it is more difficult and forces them to take up better support positions, again building up the schema. They can progress to 3 v 2 keep-ball and then a 3 v 3 small-sided game. Each step increases the difficulty and allows the further development of the schema.

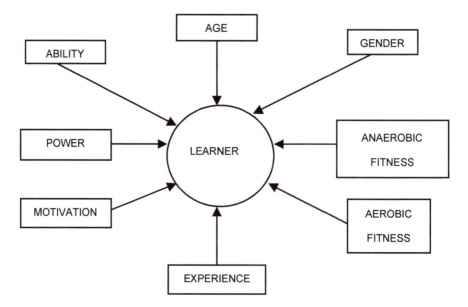

*Figure 5.1* Key factors which the coach must take into consideration concerning the learner when deciding which type of practice to use.

*Table 5.1* Factors affecting choice of practice type

| Learner | Task | Type of practice |
| --- | --- | --- |
| Beginner | Simple | Whole |
| Beginner | Large perceptual and/or decision-making demand | Part-progressive |
| Beginner | Complex movement demand | Part-progressive |
| Experienced | Simple | Whole |
| Experienced | Large perceptual and/or decision-making demand | Whole-part-progressive-whole or Whole-part-whole |
| Experienced | Complex movement demand | Whole-part-whole |

The great advantage of part-progressive practice is that coaches can make sure that they are not asking too much of the learners, that they are not overloading them intellectually or physically. As the learners develop one part of the skill, the next can be added until they are able to practice the whole skill. This type of practice is particularly useful in team games. If a child learning to play hockey is having difficulty controlling the ball with the stick, it is pointless to ask them to make decisions about when and where to pass the ball, at the same time as controlling it. However, as they learn to control it, decision-making elements can be slowly introduced.

The problem facing the coach is to decide which type of practice is best suited to any given situation. Figure 5.1 illustrates the key factors the coach must take into consideration with regard to the learner. Table 5.1 provides a general guideline for such a decision with regard to the learner and task.

## Key points box 5.8

- Massed practice
  - practice with little or no gap between trials
- Spaced practice
  - practice is interspersed with rest periods or breaks
- Whole practice
- practicing the skill as a whole
- Part practice
  - breaking the skill down into parts
- Part-progressive practice
  - gradually putting the parts together to reach the whole
- Whole-part-whole practice
  - begin with the whole
  - break down into parts
  - slowly add parts together
  - return to whole

## QUALITY OF LEARNING AND COACHING

In the previous section, the types of practice available to the coach were examined. However, even choosing the correct type for any given athlete-task interaction does not, in itself, ensure quality of experience. This section will look into the number of factors that must be taken into account regardless of the type of practice chosen. These factors are not only linked to the previous section but are also very much related to the first section on athlete learning.

### Variability of practice

Variability of practice means practicing the skill using a variety of task and environmental demands. If a coach is introducing the basketball chest pass to beginners, the coach will have them pass to each other from 5, 10, and 15 m rather than just one distance. The table tennis player, learning the topspin drive, will be asked to hit shots across the table and down the line, while the novice badminton player may be asked to serve short or long.

There is a strong theoretical underpinning for the use of variability of practice. According to Schema Theory, when variable practice is used, the initial conditions, response parameters and the sensory consequences are altered. Football players practicing free-kicks do not constantly use the same distance or angle from the goal. By starting at different angles and distances from the goal, they build up a store of differing initial conditions – to score, they must alter the response parameters. A long kick requires the application of more power and a longer leg movement. Similarly, the sensory feel of the movement will differ, albeit subtly. It is the ability to recognise these subtle differences that have ensured the success of the likes of David Beckham and Cristiano Ronaldo.

Research has generally supported the use of variability of practice, but for children only. It would appear that while children are in the developmental process of building up schemas, adults have probably gone through these processes during their childhood. Therefore, varying practice has less of an effect. Nevertheless, most coaches advocate variability of practice even for experienced athletes. One would find it strange to see a basketball team practicing the jump-shot from the same spot throughout a session.

---

### Key points box 5.9

■ Variability of practice
  • practicing the skill using a variety of task and environmental demands
■ Induces errors, therefore:
  • allows error labelling to take place
■ Change schemas by:
  • altering initial conditions
  • response parameters
  • sensory consequences
■ Research only supports this for children

## Practice scheduling

Practice scheduling refers to whether practice is blocked, random or serial. Blocked practice is when the learner practices one skill continually with no interference from the performance of other skills; for example, the basketball player may repeatedly practice the set-shot. When undertaking random practice, the athlete will perform two or more skills having random trials on each skill; for example the footballer may practice shooting and heading at goal. Serial practice is a version of random practice. The learner practices more than one skill and practice is interspersed between the skills but in a serial order; for example, the rugby player might practice tackling for a set number of trials, followed by passing, followed by kicking and then back to tackling. The cycle is then repeated.

Research has repeatedly shown that scheduling can have an effect on learning quality. In a typical experiment comparing learning using blocked, random and serial practice, the experimenter will examine how the use of scheduling affects the learning of a chosen skill immediately post-practice (a measure of performance) and following a retention test taken after a period of no practice (a measure of learning). Figure 5.2 shows the effect of blocked, random and serial practice on performance and learning of a passing skill in football – blocked practice

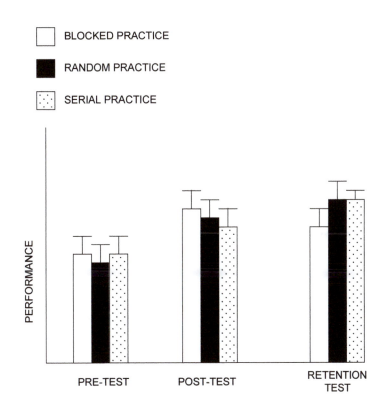

Figure 5.2  The effect of blocked, random and serial practice on the performance and learning of a sports skill.

improved immediate post-practice performance. However, random and serial practice were better for learning. Battig (1979) claimed that with random and serial practice, practicing the other skills has a negative effect on performance but a positive one on learning, something he referred to as the contextual interference effect.

Although it is fairly self-evident how practicing skills other than passing would have a negative effect on immediate performance, it is not evident how it would have a positive effect on learning. Shea and Morgan (1979) claimed that, when practicing in the blocked situation, learners work out a strategy for performing the skill (Fitts and Posner's cognitive stage) and repeatedly use that strategy. However, when practicing randomly and serially, learners use more strategies to carry out the skill rather than sticking to one plan as in the blocked situation. In fact, what is learnt while performing the other skills might even be used to develop strategies for the skill being measured. This is known as elaboration theory. Lee and Magill (1983) put forward the theory of action plan reconstruction, which has its base in Schema theory. They claimed that the learner experiences partial or total forgetting of a skill during the periods when they are working on the other skills. As a result, they have to re-plan the way in which they will perform the skill when they return to it, that is re-draw their action plan. This aids the development of schemas. There is no research evidence to support one theory more than the other.

Research into contextual interference has shown an interaction between the contextual interference effect and the types of task used. If two or more tasks that are very different to one another (that is not using the same schema) are practiced, then the contextual interference effect has generally been demonstrated. If tasks require variations of the same schema, the contextual interference effect is not shown. So in the example given in Figure 5.2, the learners were being tested on passing but were also practicing dribbling and tackling, which are very different skills. Had they been practicing passing, shooting and taking corners, the contextual interference effect would not be observed. This is probably because using the same schema, as passing, shooting and corner taking do, would not result in elaboration or action plan reconstruction.

## Key points box 5.10

- Blocked practice
  - practices one skill with no interference from the performance of other skills
- Random practice
  - practice on two or more skills having random trials on each skill
- Serial practice
  - practice on two or more skills in serial order
- Research shows that:
  - performance immediately after practice is best enhanced by blocked practice
  - learning as measured by a retention test shows random and serial practice to be better than blocked

- Contextual interference effect
  - practicing more than one skill has a negative effect on performance but a positive one on learning
- Theories of the contextual interference effect:
  - elaboration theory
  - what is learned from performing each skill can be used to develop strategies for performance of all of the skills
  - action plan reconstruction
  - partial or total forgetting of a skill occurs when learner is working on the other skills

## Conditioned games

A method of practice that naturally incorporates variability and contextual interference is the use of conditioned games. At their simplest level these can be small-sided games, for example, 8-a-side rugby, or smaller versions of the real game, such as mini-tennis. Top football and rugby players often play conditioned games as part of practice, in the form of one- and two-touch football or touch rugby. Conditioned games are also popular with Dynamical Systems theorists. By definition, conditioned games use task, environmental and organismic constraints, which will develop the learner's ability to recognise affordances and develop his or her own self-organised movement skills. Examples of the use of task constraints are not running with the ball in basketball, to develop passing skills, or having the rule that goals can only be scored with headers in football, to develop heading ability. Stopping players from calling for a pass in football or hockey is an example of an organismic constraint used to develop the players' ability to look up and perceive the situation for themselves. A good example of an environmental constraint in football, hockey and basketball would be to play on a narrow field or court in order to develop the players' ability to use the full playing surface. Can you think of others that you have seen? Can you make some up yourself?

### Key points box 5.11

- Constraints can be manipulated during conditioned games
- Task constraints
  - one-touch football
  - touch rugby
- Environmental constraints
  - narrow playing area in team games
  - smaller net in tennis
- Organismic constraints
  - no one allowed to speak while playing
  - walking rugby

## Feedback

While the subsection on instruction refers to the initial direct input from the coach, this section deals with coach input both during and following practice. However, feedback is more than just coach input. Feedback is all information resulting from an action or response. It can be visual, proprioceptive, vestibular or auditory. In other words, it is what we see, feel and/or hear. Feedback can be from within the performers themselves, what we call intrinsic or inherent feedback. It can also be extrinsic or augmented feedback. This kind of feedback is normally verbal or visual but can be in other forms such as biofeedback. Moreover, although it normally comes from the coach, feedback can come from any external source.

Feedback has been divided into Knowledge of Results (KR) and Knowledge of Performance (KP). KR is post-response information concerning the outcome of the action, knowing whether a goal is scored or not, or the time it took to run the 100m. KP consists of post-response information concerning the nature of the movement. The most obvious type of KP is the 'feel' of the movement or, in line with Schema theory, knowledge of the sensory consequences. KP can, and does, come in many forms, such as videos of a performance. Bio-mechanical methods of providing KP can also be used, for example, measuring force using specially designed platforms (called force platforms).

Later in this section there will be a discussion of some of the research findings concerning the timing and precision of feedback. However, before that, it would be useful to comment on one of the major skills of the coach, namely observation. If the coach fails to observe correctly, the feedback will be inaccurate and useless. In fact, it could be detrimental to the performer.

### Key points box 5.12

- Feedback is all information resulting from an action or response. It can be visual, proprioceptive, vestibular or auditory
- Intrinsic feedback
  - from within the learner
- Extrinsic or augmented feedback
  - from outside of the learner
- Knowledge of Results (KR)
  - post-response information concerning the outcome
- Knowledge of Performance (KP)
  - post-response information concerning the nature of the movement

## Observation

Observation is a perceptual skill that is dependent on information held in short-term memory and a comparison of that information with information held in long-term memory concerning similar previous experiences. From this it should be obvious that observational skills can be

Table 5.2 Checklist used when observing performance of a soccer player kicking a ball along the ground (from McMorris, T. and Hale, T. 2006. *Coaching science: Theory into practice.* Chichester: Wiley. Printed with permission)

| Check | Correct action | Common faults |
| --- | --- | --- |
| 1 Is the point of football contact correct? | Instep of foot contacts ball in its mid-point | Kick with toe<br>Kick with inside of foot<br>Contact beneath mid-point<br>Kick with outside of foot<br>Contact to side of mid-point<br>Contact above mid-point |
| 2 Is angle of approach correct? | Approach at a slight angle (about 10 degrees from an imaginary line drawn vertically backwards from ball) | Straight approach |
| 3 Is the follow through correct? | Follow through should point to where the player wants the ball to go | Follow through to left or right of target<br>No follow through |
| 4 Is the body position correct? | Shoulder on same side as non-kicking leg should be at angle of about 45 degrees to the ball | Square on position (shoulder 90 degrees to the ball) |
| 5 Is the head still? | Head should be down and over the ball and remain in that position | Head jerked back on contact<br>Head facing upwards before and on contact |

learned just the same as physical skills. Coaches should constantly practice their observational skills, but how many really do? Learning observational skills follows a similar process to developing a recall schema. The novice coach may well rely heavily on checklists – lists of the key points to look for when observing a skill being performed. They need to follow a systematic approach (Table 5.2 provides a checklist for a coach observing shooting in football). As the coach becomes more experienced, sometimes the error is obvious and is perceived immediately. This, however, is not always the case and it may become necessary to use the checklist approach, although the list will by now be held in long-term memory. In other words, there will be no need for a paper list.

Observation in real time is often very difficult, so coaches may use video as an aid. This can also be used to provide feedback to the athlete (see Chapter 13). More sophisticated biomechanical analyses can also be used to provide the coach with the information necessary to provide insightful feedback. Information concerning speed, velocity, acceleration, deceleration and force are all available to the coach via biomechanical analyses. Of course, these are not available to all coaches, but at the top level they are essential in many sports.

---

## Key points box 5.13

- Observation is a perceptual skill and depends on:
  - information held in short-term memory
  - information about past experiences held in long-term memory
  - a comparison of the two sets of information
- Observation can be improved with practice
- Aids to observation
  - checklists
  - video
  - biomechanical analysis

## Timing of feedback

The time lapse between an athlete performing a skill and the athlete receiving feedback from the coach is called the feedback delay. The actual length of the time is surprisingly of little or no importance, but any activity taking place during this delay, what is referred to as interpolated activity, can have a negative effect. Interpolated activity can interfere with the athlete's recall of what he or she did. Unfortunately it is unavoidable in many situations. Interpolated activity will also affect learning if it takes place between the athlete being given feedback and repeating the skill. This is known as the post-feedback delay. Unlike with the feedback delay, the length of the post-feedback delay is important. If the time period is too short, the learner does not have time to consolidate the information in memory and create a new response.

Another aspect of the timing of the presentation of feedback is that of frequency. In other words, is feedback supplied following every practice trial or after 50% or 25%? Recent research on this topic has been somewhat contradictory. One of the problems with research in this area is that much of it refers to laboratory skills and may not apply to sports activities. I strongly suspect, however, that frequency depends on the nature of the skill and the performers' own characteristics, particularly their level of competence. Research has generally advocated what is known as the *fading technique,* i.e. beginners receive a lot of feedback, probably after each trial, but feedback is given less and less often as the athlete improves. Ideally there will come a time when extrinsic feedback is no longer required.

## Key points box 5.14

- Feedback delay is the time lapse between an athlete performing a skill and receiving feedback.
- It is of little importance unless:
  - any activity is undertaken during the delay
  - this is called interpolated activity

- The post-feedback delay is the time between the athlete being given feedback and repeating the skill
- It is affected by:
  - interpolated activity
  - length if time
  - if it is short, the learner does not have time to create a new response
- The fading technique refers to the amount of feedback following each trial of the skill:
  - beginners need frequent feedback
  - experts need little
  - as learners improve, frequency should be gradually faded

## Precision of feedback

First and most importantly, the feedback needs to be intelligible to the athlete. In the previous section, the use of biomechanical information for the coach and athlete is advocated, but it is of little use is if it is so precise that a PhD in physics is required to understand it (unless, of course, the coach and/or the athlete have a PhD in physics). In providing feedback, the coach must take into account the athlete's attributes and the skill being learned.

A way of dealing with the problem of providing redundant feedback is to use what has been termed bandwidth feedback. As previously noted in the first section of this chapter, it is not possible to repeat motor skills precisely every time. The use of bandwidth feedback takes this into account. The coach sets parameters for performance. If performance falls outside of the parameter, feedback is given. If the performer is within the parameter or bandwidth, nothing is said. As the performer becomes more and more proficient, the bandwidth is reduced in size. This kind of feedback has generally, although not unequivocally, been seen to be the most beneficial. It should be remembered that, by using bandwidths, the coach is in fact giving feedback after every trial. If the coach says nothing, the learner knows that he or she was within the bandwidth, which is a form of KR.

## Key points box 5.15

- Precision of feedback
- Can be too much detail:
  - needs to be intelligible to the learner
  - bandwidth feedback is when the learner only receives feedback
  - when performance falls outside of a chosen bandwidth
  - the bandwidth can be shortened as the learner improves

## Prescriptive versus descriptive feedback

Prescriptive feedback refers to feedback that informs the learner as to what they must do to improve performance. Descriptive feedback is merely a commentary on what happened. A learner might see a video of themselves performing a skill, for example. Beginners need prescriptive feedback. They do not have sufficient knowledge to know how to correct a fault. Experienced performers can, and will, tell you what needs to be done to correct an error. They may still require help to determine what exactly did happen, hence the need for descriptive feedback. Sometimes they do not even need descriptive feedback.

---

### Key points box 5.16

- Prescriptive feedback refers to feedback which informs the learner what to do in order to improve performance
- Learners require prescriptive feedback
- Descriptive feedback refers to when the athlete is simply given information concerning outcome
- Descriptive feedback is all that is necessary with elite performers as they are capable of developing their own action plan

---

## COMMITMENT

The idea that athletes must be committed to practice and must work hard over a period of time was known to the ancient Greeks and the Romans. Even St. Paul refers to it in one of his letters. In more recent times, claims concerning the amount and nature of practice needed before an individual becomes expert has been promulgated (for example, Ericsson, Krampe and Tesch-Römer 1993). Working in the performing arts, particularly music, Ericsson and colleagues found that elite performers had undertaken practice over a period of 10 years and/or spent about 10,000 hours practicing. Moreover, they claimed that the practice:

- required time and energy from the learner and also access to coaches and training facilities;
- was not inherently motivating in itself;
- required effort.

Ericsson called this type of practice deliberate practice. Examining deliberate practice in sports settings, Janet Starkes and colleagues (for example, Helsen, Starkes and Hodges 1998) found a similar situation, except that in sports situations deliberate practice can be enjoyable and possibly inherently motivating. They also subdivided effort into physical and mental. Although the theory of deliberate practice has been accepted by motor behaviourists to a large extent, there has been some criticism. Most of the research requires athletes to fill in questionnaires concerning their habits over their career. This method is very subjective and open to some creative remembering, especially if the athlete knows about the theory of deliberate practice. Probably the most serious criticism is that almost all of the research has been undertaken with successful athletes, ignoring those who have practiced hard without achieving success. However, recent research (for example, Ford and Williams 2012) has shown differences in level of expertise reached due to different amounts of deliberate practice carried out by performers, but again this was derived from information provided by the retroactive completion of questionnaires. There can, however, be little doubt that practice, and a lot of it, is necessary for success.

**Key points box 5.17**

- Deliberate practice requires:
  - time and energy from the learner
  - access to coaches and training facilities
  - effort
- Deliberate practice may not be inherently motivating

## Performance profiling

One way of creating a committed learning environment is the use of performance profiling (see Butler and Hardy 1992), a process originally developed by Richard Butler, who was at the time sports psychologist to the British boxing team. This profiling was used successfully by Butler and coach Ian Irvine. First, the coach and athlete(s) determine what factors are advantageous to be a good performer in their sport. Second, the athlete rates him/herself on each of the factors and draws a profile similar to that in Figure 5.3. Third, the coach also evaluates the athlete on each factor. The coach and player then discuss what factors need to be improved upon and the extent to which they must be improved. They will not expect to reach a perfect 10 in all areas. Butler suggested dividing areas into physical, technical, psychological, coordination, strategy and character. Figure 5.3 shows a performance profile for technical factors for a professional footballer. Each factor has an optimal score for that particular athlete and a score for where he or she is now. The aim is to reach the optimal. Note that the optimal for each athlete will differ, depending on the athlete's innate abilities. A small footballer like Jermaine Defoe would not expect to reach 10 for heading, whereas someone like the much taller Andy Carroll would. Butler particularly stressed the use of this visual profile as he believed that this helped the athletes to picture where they are and how well they are progressing.

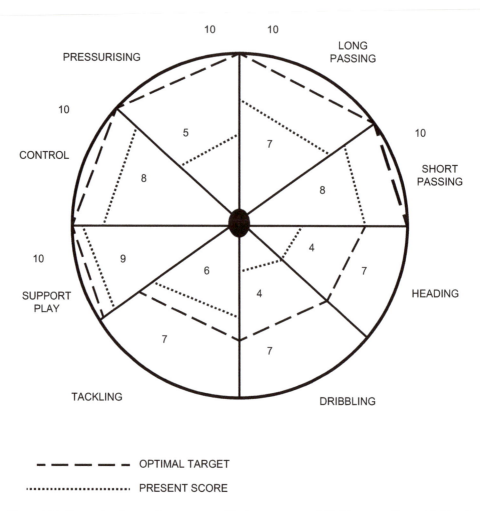

Figure 5.3 Example of a performance profile for a soccer midfield player (from McMorris, T. and Hale, T. 2006. *Coaching science: Theory into practice.* Chichester: Wiley. Printed with permission).

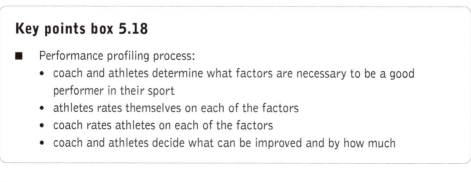

**Key points box 5.18**

■ Performance profiling process:
   • coach and athletes determine what factors are necessary to be a good performer in their sport
   • athletes rates themselves on each of the factors
   • coach rates athletes on each of the factors
   • coach and athletes decide what can be improved and by how much

## Measuring learning

If athletes are going to be committed they need to know how well they are progressing. Indeed the coaches also need to know this or else they too might lose commitment. This means that learning must be measured in some way. Unfortunately measuring learning is notoriously difficult. The extent of learning can only be measured by performance, which is transient and not a true measure of learning. In fact, learning can only be inferred based on performance. First, a measure of performance *before* the athlete begins practice is required. However, just how performance is measured can be problematic. There are some skills that easily lend themselves to measuring. To measure how good an athlete is at running 100 m, simply time them, but over several runs not just one. One performance may well give a false impression. While track and field athletics may be easy to measure, how can team games players' performance be measured? There are some skills tests used by coaches that have been examined for validity and reliability, but, in reality, not that many. Valid and reliable tests for skills like decision making are even more difficult to find. It is necessary sometimes to simply use coach assessment, that is, give a subjective mark out of 10 or use a performance profiling chart.

Once a test or assessment has been chosen, the athlete is given a pre-training mark. Then the practice sessions begin. At pre-chosen times, further assessment is made, but again the problem of performance versus learning occurs. Figure 5.2 illustrates the difference between immediate post-training performance and performance on the retention test, which indicates learning. To show improvement over a series of tests, plot performance curves.

Figure 5.4b shows a positively accelerated curve. There is an overall general improvement, but that improvement is slow at first and then accelerates. Figure 5.4a demonstrates

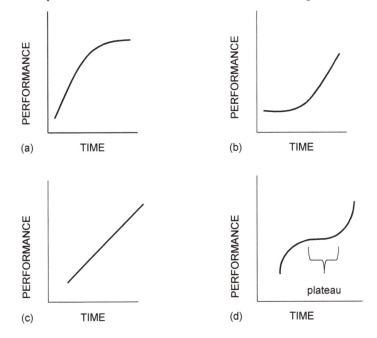

Figure 5.4 Examples of learning curves: (a) a negatively accelerated curve, (b) a positively accelerated curve, (c) a linear 'curve' and (d) an example of a plateau in learning.

a negatively accelerated curve. There is an early improvement, but then performance tapers off somewhat. Figure 5.4c shows a linear improvement with practice, a rare occurrence except with simple skills. Figure 5.4d depicts the effect of what is referred to as a plateau in learning. This is quite a common occurrence in learning and is probably something many have experienced. There comes a point when practicing does not appear to be having any effect – this is the plateau. With further practicing, there is a breakthrough and more learning is demonstrated.

**Key points box 5.19**

- We can only infer learning based on performance
- Measurement should take place several times as performance is transient
- Performance profiles can be used as a means of measuring learning
- We can plot performance curves

## CONCLUSION

If we are to achieve a relatively permanent change in the performance of our athletes, we need to ensure that instruction, verbal or visual or both, is clear and unambiguous. Plenty of opportunity for practice must be provided. Coaching is about the athlete learning, not the 'wise' words of the coach. Practices should be enjoyable but challenging and as realistic as possible. Feedback should be such that gradually the performers require less and less from the coach and can perceive errors themselves. Making errors is part of developing a schema. Coaches should practice their own observational skills to aid their athletes. Finally, learning needs to be measurable in some form.

## REFERENCES

Anderson, J. R. (1982). Acquisition of cognitive skill. *Psychological Review* 89: pp. 369–406.

Battig, J. W. (1979). The flexibility of human memory. In *Levels of processing in human memory*. Cermak, L. S. and Craik, F.L.M. (eds.). (Hillsdale, NJ: Erlbaum): pp. 23–44.

Butler, R. J. and Hardy, L. (1992). The performance profile: Theory and application. *The Sport Psychologist* 6: pp. 253–64.

Ericsson, K. A., Krampe, R. T. and Tesch-Römer, C. (1993). The role of deliberate practice in the acquisition of expert performance. *Psychological Review* 100: pp. 363–406.

Fitts, P. M. and Posner, M. I. (1967). *Human performance.* (Belmont, CA: Brooks/Cole).

Ford, P. R. and Williams, A. M. (2012). The developmental activities engaged in by youth elite soccer players who progressed to professional status compared to those who did not. *Psychology of Sport and Exercise* 13: pp. 349–52.

Helsen, W. F., Starkes, J. L. and Hodges, N. J. (1998). Team sports and the theory of deliberate practice. *Journal of Sports and Exercise Psychology* 20: pp. 12–34.

Keele, S. W. (1968). Movement control in skilled motor performance. *Psychological Bulletin* 70: pp. 387–403.

Kerr, R. (1982). *Psychomotor learning.* (Philadelphia: Saunders).

Lee, T. D. and Magill, R. A. (1983). The locus of contextual interference in motor skill acquisition. *Journal of Experimental Psychology: Learning, Memory and Cognition* 9: pp. 730–46.

McMorris, T. and Hale, T. (2006). *Coaching science: Theory into practice.* (Chichester: Wiley).

Schmidt, R. A. (1975). A schema theory of discrete motor skill learning. *Psychological Review* 82: pp. 225–60.

Shea, J. B. and Morgan, R. L. (1979). Contextual interference effects on the acquisition, retention and transfer of a motor skill. *Journal of Experimental Psychology: Human Learning and Memory* 5: pp. 179–87.

## Further reading

McMorris, T. (2004). *Acquisition and performance of sports skills.* (Chichester: Wiley).

Schmidt, R. A. and Wrisberg, C. A. (2008). *Motor learning and performance.* (Champaign, IL: Human Kinetics).

# Chapter 6

# The practice session
## Creating a motivational climate

*Kevin Morgan and Mohamad Faithal Haji Hassan*

The motivational climate created by coaches has a significant influence on participants' motivation, the quality of their involvement, their emotional responses and the likelihood of their continued participation or 'drop out' from sport (Duda and Balaguer 2007). In short, coaches really matter in the world of sport and they can make all the difference to the enjoyment, motivation and long term investment of athletes. The aim of this chapter is to provide guidance for coaches on how to foster a positive motivational climate in their practice sessions to maximise the effort, persistence and learning of their athletes.

Motivational climate is a term that originated from achievement goal theory (AGT) (Nicholls 1989). As an introduction, a brief explanation of AGT theory is provided and how it links to individual differences in athletes' perceptions of the motivational climate. Different types of motivational climate will then be considered, along with the coaching behaviours that foster these climates and the associated motivational responses of the athletes. Finally, the role of significant others, such as parents and peers, and how they and other factors might influence perceptions of the motivational climate will be covered. Throughout the chapter, theory and research evidence will be presented to justify and explain the practical implications for coaches in designing their coaching sessions.

## TYPES OF MOTIVATIONAL CLIMATE

Before identifying and explaining the different types of motivational climate in sport, it is important to understand the theoretical background of AGT (Nicholls 1989). According to Nicholls, in achievement situations such as sport, where the aim is to demonstrate ability, two different concepts of ability prevail – a 'task involved' concept where the aim is to achieve mastery, improve against previous performances or perfect a skill; or an 'ego involved' concept, where the individual judges his/her ability relative to others. If an athlete is ego involved then the primary goal in that situation is to outperform others and to be the best. For example, a field hockey player who is ego involved in a team training session would be aiming to demonstrate superior ability to other teammates by exerting the minimum effort required. On the other hand, a task involved athlete is focused on self-referenced goals and the aim is to learn and improve on previous best performances. In this instance, the same hockey player would be primarily focused on improving his or her own level of performance, regardless of the performance of other teammates. According to Nicholls (1989), these two states of goal involvement are transitory, and an individual's goal involvement in a particular situation is held to be the function of the individual's disposition towards particular achievement goals (goal orientations) and the situational factors (motivational climate). Furthermore, Nicholls (1989) contends that an important relationship exists between goal involvement and perceptions of ability, which has a mediating effect on an individual's motivational responses.

According to Nicholls (1989), if a person is highly task involved, then perceived ability is not relevant since the criteria for success is self-referenced rather than normative. Achievement behaviours will, therefore, be positive in that the person is more likely to persist in the face of difficulty, exert effort, choose challenging tasks and be interested in the activity (Roberts 2001). On the other hand, when an individual is highly ego involved, perceived ability is of greater importance because the demonstration of normative ability is now salient. If perceived ability is high, then adaptive (positive) motivational behaviours are predicted because it is more likely that high comparative ability will be demonstrated. On the other hand, if perceived ability is low, and the person is ego involved (focused on comparisons with others), then more negative behaviours such as challenge avoidance, lack of effort, reduced persistence and the devaluing of tasks are predicted (Roberts 2001).

Individual differences in their proneness to be task or ego involved are termed achievement goal orientations and result from childhood socialisation at home, or in learning situations such as school and sport (Nicholls 1989). Nicholls contends that task and ego goal orientations are independent constructs so that individuals can be high or low in both, or high in one and low in the other. Research has shown that a high ego orientation is associated with an emphasis on social comparison and the desire to demonstrate high ability (or avoid demonstrating low ability) relative to others (Duda and Nicholls 1992). A high task orientation, on the other hand, is associated with an emphasis on gaining skills or knowledge and with improving on previous best performances. Roberts (2001) suggests that goal orientations are not 'traits'; rather they are considered to be cognitive schema subject to change over time. They do, however, have some stability over time and are difficult to change in the short term (Duda and Whitehead 1998).

More recently, Elliott and colleagues (Elliott 1999; Elliott and Church 1997; Elliott and MacGregor 2001) have focused on 'approach' and 'avoidance' behaviours associated with achievement goals and developed the 'trichotomous' and 'two-by-two' models of goal orientations. The trichotomous model identifies three types of goals – task-approach goals, in which the focus is to demonstrate self-referenced competence; ego-approach goals, which focus on demonstrating normative referenced competence; and ego-avoidance goals, where the concern is to avoid demonstrating normative incompetence. The two-by-two model also divides the task goal into approach and avoidance behaviours. To illustrate these four goals, a track athlete may enter a competition with the goal of not performing poorly in relation to others (ego-avoidance goal), or poorly in relation to his or her own personal best time (task-avoidance goal). Alternatively, the athlete may be concerned with wanting to win every race (ego-approach goal), or simply wanting to improve on his or her personal best time (task-approach goal).

In addition to an individual's goal orientations, Ames (1992) argued that parents, teachers and coaches create motivational climates that affect a participant's goal involvement in achievement settings. Ames (1992) talks about 'choice points' sport coaches have that are crucial in determining the motivational climate. By setting certain explicit expectations and giving instructions, cues and rewards, the coach structures the motivational climate to be task or ego involving. Participants recognize that ability is assessed in an ego or task involving way and, consequently, they are more likely to develop achievement goals consistent with the prevailing conception of ability (Ames 1992). In this way, sporting participants become socialised into either task/mastery or ego/performance goals of action (Ames 1992). For example, a coach who is constantly talking about winning and losing is more likely to foster an ego involving climate, whereas a coach who focuses more on improvement and progress is more likely to facilitate a mastery climate.

Individual differences in susceptibility to task or ego involvement (goal orientations) are not to be denied, but research in physical education and sport (for example, Dorubantu and Biddle 1997) has shown that the motivational climate created by significant others can be more influential in determining motivation. Motivational climate, therefore, is defined as a situationally induced psychological environment directing goals of action (Ames 1992). When an emphasis is placed on effort, improvement, cooperation and self-referenced goals, then a task-involving (mastery) climate develops (Ames 1992). In such a climate, individuals typically adopt adaptive achievement strategies such as working hard, selecting challenging tasks and demonstrating persistence (Ames 1992). In contrast, when the emphasis is placed on social comparison and winning competitions, an ego involving (performance) climate develops. In this case, individuals often adopt maladaptive (negative) achievement strategies such as lack of effort and resilience, particularly when perceptions of their own competence are low, in an attempt to protect themselves from demonstrating low ability (Ames 1992).

The majority of research focusing on motivational climate in sport settings has captured perceptions of the climate via one of two versions of the Perceived Motivational Climate in Sport Questionnaire (PMCSQ 1 and 2) (Walling, Duda and Chi 1993; Newton, Duda and Yin 2000). Such measures provide an effective means for coaches to assess their athletes' perceptions of the motivational climate they are creating in their practice sessions. Using these measures, along with other questionnaire-based measures of goal orientations and cognitive and affective motivational responses, correlational research in sport and PE (for example, Carpenter and Morgan 1999) has revealed that perceptions of a mastery (task) climate relate to a higher task orientation, greater feelings of satisfaction and less boredom, higher perceived ability and intrinsic motivation. It is also believed that effort and ability are causes of success and a more positive attitude toward the activity. In contrast, a perceived performance (ego) climate has been related to higher levels of ego orientation, less enjoyment, greater boredom, the belief that ability leads to success and is negatively related to attitude and the belief that success is due to effort. For sport coaches, understanding and creating a mastery motivational climate is, therefore, central to athlete learning and motivation.

## CREATING A MASTERY MOTIVATIONAL CLIMATE

Coaches design practice sessions, group athletes, give recognition, evaluate performance, share their authority and shape the sport setting. In doing so, they create a motivational climate that can have an important impact on an athlete's motivation and learning. Ames and Archer (1988) were the first to identify the theoretical dimensions of a mastery involving climate and

*Table 6.1* Dimensions of a mastery goal (Ames and Archer 1988)

| Theoretical dimensions | Mastery goal |
| --- | --- |
| How is success defined? | Individual improvement |
| What is valued? | Effort, self-referenced progress |
| How is the learner evaluated? | Progress, effort |
| How are mistakes viewed? | Part of learning |
| Why engage in the activity? | Develop new skills |
| Why does the learner feel satisfied? | Personal best, challenge |
| What are learners focused on? | Learning of skills |
| What is the teacher focused on? | Development, learning |

*Table 6.2* TARGET structures

| TARGET description | Coaching strategies |
| --- | --- |
| Task | • Design tasks for variety, differentiation and inclusion<br>• Shared goals between coach and athletes<br>• Encourage athletes to set their own self- or group-referenced goals for improvement |
| Authority | • Athletes involved in decision making and task design |
| Recognition | • Private individual recognition and feedback on improvement and effort |
| Grouping | • Mixed ability, co-operative groups |
| Evaluation | • Self-referenced based on performance, improvement and effort scores<br>• Athletes keep personal diaries to record performances |
| Timing | • Flexible time to complete tasks<br>• Promotion of maximum participation within lessons |

to translate these into teaching parameters (see Table 6.1). These parameters are also relevant to a wide range of achievement situations including sport, and are an effective way of evaluating motivation in sport coaching contexts (Ames 1992).

Extrapolating from Ames and Archers's (1988) work in the classroom to the sport setting, the environment in which the participants learn and practice is vitally important. For example, in the context of swimming, the coach can emphasise a mastery climate focused on individual improvement, personal best times and technique development. This type of motivational climate fosters personal challenge in small achievable steps, stresses learning and fosters enjoyment of personal achievement for all levels of ability (Ames 1992).

Ames (1992) identified six areas of the teaching and learning environment that can influence achievement goals and used the acronym TARGET, first identified by Epstein (1989) in the context of developing effective schools and students, to represent the task, authority, recognition, grouping, evaluation and time structures of the learning environment (see Table 6.2). Each of these structures will now be considered in relation to fostering a mastery motivational climate in the sports practice sessions.

## Task

The design of activities in coaching sessions is a crucial aspect in engaging the participants, maintaining their concentration and interest, and maximising their effort and improvement. According to Ames (1992), the design of tasks can influence levels of interest and perceptions of ability. Consequently, practices should be designed for variety, interest and personal challenge. The use of a variety of activities within a coaching session would provide the opportunity to improve on multiple skills and potentially increase participants' interest. This would also decrease the possibility of social comparison between athletes, as there would be less opportunity to compare performances with those of others. A multiple 'stations' format to practice sessions is an example of this.

Introducing innovative or more novel tasks into practice sessions would potentially increase enjoyment and interest and broaden the learning experiences of the athletes. For example, playing 'ultimate frisbee' as a warm up activity in a soccer training session would provide a 'fun' element whilst still focusing on invasion games principles such as possession, creating and denying space, support and pressure. The activities should be also designed to maximise intrinsic appeal and to help athletes appreciate the value of what they are learning in order to enhance intrinsic motivation and interest in the long term (Ryan and Deci 2000).

Additionally, the task goals should be clearly identified at the start of the sessions and shared between coach and athletes to help foster a mastery climate that focuses on self-evaluation and personal challenge. This will ensure that the athletes have ownership of their own goals and fully understand what is expected of them. Individual differentiation and personal challenge is difficult to achieve in coaching sessions where differences in individual ability, playing experience, knowledge and understanding exist. To ensure that tasks are individually challenging for all, athletes should, therefore, be coached to set their own self-referenced goals and to monitor the progress towards achieving these goals within practice sessions. For example, tennis players can be encouraged to self-evaluate the success rate of their volleys in a training session and to set themselves targets to improve this level of performance.

## Authority

The authority structure relates to the balance of decision making between coach and athlete during the practice sessions. To emphasise a mastery climate coaches should give athletes the opportunity to take on leadership roles, make real choices and encourage them to participate in decision making. The degree to which a coach involves athletes in decision making is directly related to positive motivational responses such as feelings of self-competence, responsibility and independence and greater levels of determination and engagement in learning (Ames 1992). Providing athletes with an element of choice within coaching sessions, therefore, is one way to achieve a mastery authority structure. Such choices could include the level of difficulty, for example, giving the players the authority to decide on the number of defenders or the size of the working space in a practice designed to improve possession in an invasion game, such as basketball.

Several teaching styles from Mosston and Ashworth's (2002) Spectrum allow for shared decision making in physical education and sport coaching settings. The Spectrum is a

*Table 6.3* Mosston's teaching styles. Adapted from Mosston and Ashworth (2002)

| Style A | Command | Coach makes all the decisions |
|---|---|---|
| Style B | Practice | Learners practice coach prescribed tasks |
| Style C | Reciprocal | Learners work in pairs, one as the coach and one as the learner |
| Style D | Self-check | Learners evaluate their own performance against criteria |
| Style E | Inclusion | Coach provides alternative levels of difficulty for the learners |
| Style F | Guided discovery | Coach plans a target and leads the learners to discover it |
| Style G | Problem solving | Coach presents a problem and learners find their own solutions |
| Style H | Individual | Coach proposes subject matter, learners plan and design the programme |
| Style I | Learner initiated | Learners decide content and plan and design the programme |
| Style J | Self-teaching | Learners take full responsibility for the learning process |

continuum of teaching styles categorised according to the decisions made by the teacher and learner before, during and after the activity. At one end of the Spectrum is the command style in which the teacher/coach makes all the decisions across all three phases. At the other end of the Spectrum is the learner initiated style in which the learner makes almost all the decisions and the teacher/coach acts as a consultant. Between these two styles, Mosston and Ashworth (2002) have systematically identified a series of other styles, each with its own decision-making anatomy (see Table 6.3). Styles such as reciprocal, inclusion, guided discovery and problem solving are particularly focused on learner authority within sessions. For example, in a reciprocal or peer teaching situation, athletes can be set the task of coaching another member of the group with the aim of increasing the amount of individual feedback provided and also improving their own level of knowledge and understanding of the techniques and skills. Clear criteria and coaching points need to be made available by the coach, so that the feedback given by the peers is technically accurate. Athletes also need to be taught how to provide effective and constructive feedback to make this a positive mastery climate. Furthermore, in such a scenario, coaches should provide feedback to the athlete acting as the 'coach' and not directly to the peer being coached, otherwise the authority of the athletes is undermined (Mosston and Ashworth 2002). Previous research (Morgan, Kingston and Sproule 2005) has demonstrated that reciprocal and guided discovery teaching styles foster a more mastery involving motivational climate than the more traditional command/practice style.

**115**

## Recognition

The type of rewards, reasons for rewards and the distribution of rewards have important consequences for athlete's interest, satisfaction and feelings of self-worth (Ames 1992). To foster a mastery motivational climate, recognition and rewards from the coach should be focused on individual effort and improvement, rather than comparisons to the performance of other athletes. This provides equal opportunity for all athletes to be recognised for their accomplishments, not just the high achievers, because everyone can try hard and there's always room for improvement.

Although often given with good intention, extrinsic rewards can undermine the intrinsic interest in the task (Ryan and Deci 2000), so the focus should be on intrinsic rewards, such as satisfaction and enjoyment of the tasks, and of personal progress. Further, when rewards are given publicly and on a differential basis they invite social comparison and emphasise an ego involving climate. To foster a mastery climate, rewards should be private between coach and athlete, whenever possible, so that feelings of satisfaction derive from improving personal standards rather than doing better than others (Ames 1992).

In sport coaching settings with large group numbers, providing individual feedback privately and distributing this equally amongst the participants is a difficult challenge, but coaches should aim to achieve this as much as possible. Feedback can then be tailored to the individual athlete and address his or her performance specifically, rather than the performance of others, which happens when general group feedback is provided. By providing one-to-one feedback the coach recognises every athlete's individual role and personal accomplishments, and the focus should be on effort and improvement in the subsequent attempts. In practical terms, with young athletes, simple strategies such as 'two stars and a wish' can be employed in giving feedback, where the coach identifies two aspects of good practice and then gives the athlete one aspect to improve upon. Such feedback is specific and positive and provides key points for improvement as well as recognising the athlete's strengths, which can enhance confidence and perceived ability.

## Grouping

The basis by which athletes are grouped is particularly salient in determining the motivational climate in practice sessions (Ames 1992). When athletes work as a whole group, or in groups based on ability, it is easier to make comparisons with others. On the other hand, when coaches promote mixed ability and varied grouping arrangements it is more difficult for athletes to interpret performance comparatively and, consequently, this is more likely to evoke a mastery involving climate. However, there are circumstances in sport where ability groups may be preferable due to the nature of the activity. For example, in a middle or long distance running session focused on pace judgement, athletes of lower aerobic capacity than others in the group would probably be unable to maintain the same pace as the more able runners and would, therefore, be likely to perceive this as an ego involving situation. Varied grouping arrangements are, therefore, encouraged with groups formed on the basis of a variety of criteria such as friendship, common interest, positional or technical requirements of the sport and when appropriate, achievement level.

The key emphasis within groups should be on cooperation rather than competition, thus allowing the coach to create a learning environment that promotes the social construction of knowledge. For example, in certain circumstances, athletes can learn from each other within practice sessions just as effectively as they can from the coach, particularly when there are experienced performers in the group. This type of learning environment, however, should be carefully constructed and facilitated by the coach rather than just assuming it will happen by chance. Developing athlete leaders within groups will assist this process, as will grouping athletes into units that work well together and complement each other's strengths and limitations. Grouping arrangements should also be varied within and between sessions to promote social interaction and cohesion.

## Evaluation

Evaluation is one of the most salient features of achievement situations such as sport; consequently, athletes' motivation to learn can be easily undermined by how evaluation occurs. Evaluation that emphasises normative comparisons evokes a state of ego involvement that can impair participants' self-worth, intrinsic interest and perceived ability (Nicholls 1989). The mere availability of social comparison information, however, is not the main concern; rather, it is when this normative information is emphasised that motivation can be undermined (Treasure 2001). When evaluation is based on improvement, progress towards individual goals, participation and effort, individuals are more likely to be mastery involved (Ames 1992).

In a mastery climate, evaluation should be formative (ongoing) and self-referenced with a focus on individual progress and effort. Consistent with the recognition structure, evaluation should be communicated privately, without comparison to others, to emphasise a mastery climate. Furthermore, effort should be recognised and rewarded and mistakes regarded as part of the learning process, rather than an indication of failure (Ames 1992). Effective evaluation strategies for the promotion of a mastery involving climate include informing athletes of the criteria against which they are being evaluated and including them in self- and peer evaluation. By becoming more aware of their own and others' strengths and weaknesses, athletes are more likely to understand their performance and be able to set themselves targets for improvement. A personal diary approach is one way of emphasising self-evaluation, for example, in strength and conditioning training or running activities.

## Time

The pace of instruction and the time allotted for completing practices significantly influences motivation (Ames 1992). Strategies for promoting a mastery climate involve adjusting time for participants who have difficulty completing the practices and allowing athletes flexible time to complete their own schedules. This approach allows athletes to progress at an optimal rate for their own learning. This flexibility also increases opportunities for athletes to engage in meaningful learning activities and gives them autonomy in making decisions that can enhance their motivation. However, depending on the maturity and experience of the athletes, this flexibility also has the potential to allow athletes to lose focus and for the pace of the sessions to drop to unsatisfactory levels. Coaches should, therefore, closely monitor practices that allow athletes flexible time to ensure that they remain on task and are progressing at a rate that is optimum for their learning.

**117**

As a general principle then, the pace of the sessions should be flexible and based on individual learning needs. Coaches should avoid practices where the athletes have to wait in lines and should try to maximise activity time in their sessions, thus encouraging active learning. The use of extension tasks for those who finish the task early, and additional time for those who require it, are important strategies in implementing this structure. Coaches can also allow athletes to decide on how long to spend on the various tasks within sessions, provided that they have enough flexibility themselves in the length of the sessions. This would be similar to a practice style in Mosston and Ashworth's (2002) Spectrum (see Table 6.3).

## The interrelationship of the TARGET structures

Treasure (2001) has identified the interrelationship between the TARGET structures as an important issue for future research into the effectiveness of intervention programmes in sport. According to Ames (1992), the TARGET structures should not be viewed as independent contributors to motivation, but rather they should work in concert in a coordinated fashion towards the same mastery goal. If these requirements are not met, then the mastery focus of one structure may be undermined by the ego strategies in another. Ames, therefore, argued that the TARGET structures are interdependent, but posed the more specific question of whether the TARGET structures operate in an additive or multiplicative fashion. If they are additive then they become complementary and inadequacy in one structure can be compensated for by strengths in another. If, on the other hand, the structures are multiplicative, they cannot compensate for each other. As a result, when a multiplicative relationship exists, for example, if the coach sets differentiated mastery based tasks, but emphasises normative, ego involving standards for evaluation, the athlete will not be able to foster perceptions of a mastery climate. In contrast, if an additive relationship exists between these two structures, the mastery involving tasks could compensate for the ego involving feedback and allow a mastery climate to prevail. Previous research (Morgan, Sproule, Weigand and Carpenter 2005) has suggested an additive relationship between the TARGET structures in a physical education context, with the recognition and evaluation structures having the greatest impact on perceptions of the motivational climate. However, further research is required to investigate this interrelationship in sport coaching situations.

## TARGET intervention studies

To date, only a limited number of studies have attempted to manipulate the motivational climate in the field, and these have been primarily limited to the physical education context. In the first of these studies, Treasure (1993) adapted the TARGET structures to develop an intervention programme which promoted mastery and performance climates in school soccer lessons. The results revealed that those subjects who participated (ego) in the mastery condition perceived the climate to be more mastery involved and reported more adaptive cognitive and affective responses than those in the performance condition. Specifically, pupils in the mastery condition perceived the climate to be focused on skill improvement and effort, preferred more challenging tasks, attributed success more to effort and were more satisfied and interested in the activities in comparison to pupils in the performance condition. Further, participants in the performance condition reported that deception was a key to success, thus accepting that 'cheating' to win was an acceptable part of competing.

A study by Solmon (1996), where pupils participated in juggling classes in either mastery or performance conditions, provided further support for the TARGET structures in creating a mastery climate in PE. Teachers in the mastery condition stressed individual challenge, improvement and self-referenced criteria for success. In contrast, the emphasis in the performance condition was on normative (comparisons with others) criteria for success. The results showed that pupils in the mastery condition showed higher persistence at difficult tasks than those in the performance condition. Further, participants in the performance condition were more likely to attribute success to normative ability than were participants in the mastery condition. Further, Morgan and Carpenter (2002) investigated the effects of manipulating the motivational climate in PE lessons to be mastery oriented on students' perceptions of the motivational climate, achievement goal orientations and cognitive and affective responses. Secondary school pupils (aged 12–14) were involved in a mastery intervention programme that implemented the TARGET teaching structures in track and field athletics. Results revealed students' perceptions of the existence of a mastery climate and significant increases in their task orientation, preference for challenging tasks, satisfaction and positive attitude, as a result of experiencing the mastery programme.

To date, little is known about the impact of coach created motivational climate in organised sport coaching settings (Duda and Balaguer 2007). According to Ntoumanis and Biddle (1999), sport and PE represent different physical activity contexts, and they are most likely to differ in reasons for participation, meaning attached to involvement, variability in physical competence and how they are socially influenced by the teacher or coach. Indeed, given that a major focus of sport coaches is to prepare their athletes for competition with the aim of outperforming the opposition, it would seem particularly salient to investigate the TARGET structures in sport coaching. Currently, however, there is a dearth of research into coaches' implementation of the TARGET structures in competitive sport settings and their perceptions of how these behaviours may impact on athletes' learning and performance.

In a first attempt to address this gap in the research, Hassan (2011) conducted an in depth qualitative investigation of coaches' TARGET behaviours in the performance environment. The purpose of the study was to examine sport coaches' perceptions, understanding and application of the TARGET structures in the sport coaching context and to explore their relevance and implementation. The coaches were involved in coaching a variety of performance sports including: athletics, cricket, football, netball, rugby, strength and conditioning and trampolining. The following section identifies the findings of Hassan's study in relation to the individual TARGET structures and the real life issues coaches face in implementing these structures into their coaching sessions.

## The application of TARGET to sport coaching (Hassan 2011)

In relation to the task structure, consistent with Ames's (1992), all the coaches agreed and understood the importance of athletes being fully aware of their team and individual goals. The coaches recognised that by involving the athletes in the goal setting process, they were able to establish more realistic goals, make learning more interesting, increase variety and personal challenge, and develop effective task strategies. Furthermore, they felt that this involvement and shared 'goal setting' gave the athletes greater self-confidence and allowed them more opportunities to have control over their own development.

Consistent with the differentiation of tasks to challenge various levels of ability, and a multi-dimensional task structure (Ames 1992), the coaches endeavoured to present a variety of tasks in their practice sessions based on individual goals, the specific needs of team units, or positional requirements within the team. They also unanimously agreed that athletes should be given a variety of activities during training sessions to enhance and maintain their interest and learning. These findings are consistent with the research of Keegan, Harwood, Spray and Lavallee (2009), who found that variety, fun and an optimum level of challenge were important factors in motivating early career sports participants.

Contrary to the total focus on mastery goals, however, the majority of the coaches also believed that competitive goals were important in the sporting environment. This is consistent with Hardy *et al.* (1996), who suggested that ego goals are essential for the long term achievement of elite athletes, and Keegan *et al.* (2009), who found that ego involved competitive tasks can enhance athletes' motivations in training and are good practice for competition. However, Boardley and Kavussanu (2010) warn that such ego involvement can affect the athletes' moral behaviour, potentially developing anti-social behaviours such as cheating that may negatively influence their motivation and learning in the practice environment.

The giving of authority to athletes resulted in a mixed response from the coaches. All agreed that athletes should be allowed to be actively involved in the learning process through discussion and decision making, and that by giving authority to athletes they would develop a sense of ownership for their learning and become more independent (which was considered particularly essential in sports where athletes must perform their activity unaided by the coach). According to Kidman (2001), athletes will be more motivated regarding their learning, have greater understanding of skills and tactics, and develop greater decision-making ability if they are given involvement in their own development. Indeed, shared leadership and empowerment can enhance athletes' self-awareness, self-sufficiency, teamwork and subsequent on-field success (Kidman 2001). In this respect, the coach becomes more of an orchestrator, as opposed to being controlling and autocratic (Jones and Wallace 2006). However, consistent with Jones and Standage (2006), the concept of empowerment and athletes' autonomy within the coaching process was not unproblematic amongst the coaches in Hassan's (2011) sample. Some argued that authority needs to be given with great care to avoid any unnecessary complications, such as a shift in power from the coach to the athletes and the attendant perception of the coach losing control. The coaches also suggested that the transfer of autonomy should be done in stages, and according to the athletes' level of performance. For example, experienced athletes can be given more autonomy compared to less experienced, or much younger, athletes who require more guidance. Additionally, in sports that involve high risk activities (for example, trampolining and rugby), health and safety were major concerns for the coaches and consequently the athletes' age and experience were important factors for them to consider before the delegation of authority could be permitted.

In relation to the recognition structure, all of the coaches agreed on the main principle that athletes should receive equal recognition for their individual effort, skill development and accomplishments (Ames 1992). This is consistent with the research of Keegan *et al.* (2009), which highlighted equal treatment and perceived fairness as key factors in motivating athletes. There was some disagreement with the private versus public nature of the recognition, with time constraints being identified as a major factor in inhibiting private feedback. The coaches generally concurred that positive feedback could be given publicly, provided that there was equal opportunity to receive this and that it was evenly distributed amongst the group. This is consistent with Covington and Beery (1976), who established that when there is equal opportunity for all to receive rewards (that is when they are based on effort and improvement), the potentially negative effects on individuals' perception of self-competence are avoided. However, the coaches in Hassan's (2011) study felt strongly that negative and more corrective feedback should be given privately to avoid feelings of embarrassment and shame by the athletes, something that could potentially reduce their confidence and motivation. The theme of 'positivity' has been highlighted by Keegan, Harwood, Spray and Lavallee (2010) as a key element in enhancing athletes' motivation.

The grouping structure focuses on athletes' ability to work cooperatively in small mixed ability groups and to vary the grouping arrangements within and between sessions (Ames 1992). Keegan *et al.* (2009) identify emotional and moral support from peers as having a positive influence on athletes' motivation and suggest that collaboration, where peers work together to help each other, can increase the chances of performing well or improving. When asked about this structure, the coaches in Hassan's (2011) study felt that it was helpful to have more experienced and able athletes helping out the less experienced, especially when the numbers in the group were high. They also felt that it was beneficial to change groups frequently for the players to have different experiences within practice sessions to enhance their learning.

Contrary to a mastery grouping structure, the coaches suggested that, in certain situations, the confidence of the less able athletes can be undermined if they are grouped with more able performers. Furthermore, the more able performers can sometimes become frustrated in this situation, as they are not being challenged at their optimum level. Some of the coaches, therefore, felt that their athletes benefitted from participation with and against similar ability athletes to increase their level of challenge. This is identified as 'positive rivalry' by Keegan *et al.* (2009). The coaches in Hassan's (2011) study also believed that when some lower ability athletes participate in a group of more able performers, it can potentially undermine their confidence and perceived competence. Finally, the team sport coaches reported that for certain practice situations, their groups were best formed based on playing positions, or units, as opposed to ability, in particular when it involved more technical and tactical sessions.

Evaluation that is based on improvement, individual goals, participation and effort is more likely to develop an athlete's motivation (Ames 1992). In accordance with Ames, the coaches agreed that it is important to create a climate where the athletes feel that mistakes are part of learning and recognise that they are being evaluated on personal effort and improvement. The coaches also agreed that their athletes should learn to self-evaluate and reflect on their own performances, rather than relying totally on coach feedback. However, they also felt that less experienced athletes needed significantly more support and guidance in this process than more experienced performers.

All the coaches unanimously agreed that they aimed to allow flexible time for athletes to learn at different rates in training. Despite this, however, they all recognised the restrictions on the time and the venues that they had to work within, and they agreed that they needed to consider the age and ability of the athlete and the situational constraints before deciding on the flexibility of this structure. They agreed that it depended on the situation and how many athletes they had in the group as well as their age, experience, personality and ability level. Furthermore, with younger players they needed to be stricter with the time structure, whereas, with the older and more able players, they could allow greater flexibility due to their higher levels of maturity and responsibility.

The findings of Hassan (2011) identify some important differences between a performance sport coaching environment and the educational domain from which TARGET emerged. Future research should consider these differences in more depth by critically investigating each of the TARGET structures individually in the sport coaching setting, as well as other pedagogical skills that impact on athlete motivation. Practitioner based, action research studies, involving both coaches and athletes, in collaboration with researchers, would provide much needed insight into coaching pedagogy and the TARGET structures.

## Objective coach created climate

Research into motivational climate in sport and PE settings has focused predominantly on the social-psychological environment, that is the perceived motivational climate. More recently, drawing on the TARGET structures (Ames 1992), research has attempted to measure the 'objective' climate created by PE teachers (Morgan and Kingston 2008; Morgan, Sproule, Weigand and Carpenter 2005) and sport coaches (Hassan 2011), using the Behavioural Evaluation Strategies and Taxonomies (BEST) software (Sharpe and Koperwas 1999). This research involved the use of a computer-based observational measure of the teaching/coaching behaviours that influence perceptions of the motivational climate – a measure first developed by Morgan, Sproule, Weigand and Carpenter (2005). This measure allows researchers to film PE lessons and sport coaching sessions and to code the teaching/coaching behaviours as 'mastery' involving, 'performance' involving or 'neither'. Furthermore, the computer software allows practitioners to view their own teaching behaviours from video footage and to evaluate themselves against Ames's (1992) guidelines for fostering a mastery climate, thus encouraging reflective practice and assisting coaches to become more aware of and to self-regulate their own coaching behaviours.

Recently, Hassan (in press) used this behavioural measure of motivational climate to develop a collaborative action research based intervention programme with sport coaches. As part of the intervention, the researcher conducted a series of video recordings of practice sessions led by three different coaches over a period of five months. Hassan then worked closely with the coaches during the intervention, through discussions and reflective sessions, to change their behaviours to be more mastery focused. The findings revealed a significant increase in coaches' application and athletes' perceptions of mastery TARGET behaviours. Additionally, athletes significantly increased their task (mastery) goal orientations. Furthermore, there were significant decreases in athletes' perceptions of performance (ego) focused TARGET behaviours and ego goal orientations. Given that previous research (for example, Morgan and Carpenter 2002; Morgan, Kingston and Sproule 2005) has identified the positive influences of a mastery climate on participants' motivational responses, this study suggests that an intervention programme of this nature can positively influence participants' motivation levels and enhance their learning experience in sport coaching situations.

## Motivational climate created by parents and peers

In addition to the coach, there are significant others such as parents and peers who can influence the social-psychological environment in sport coaching contexts. In athletes' formative
years, their parents play a huge role in influencing their perceptions of success and failure and
in forming their view of themselves as competent and socially acceptable (White 2007). As
White (1998) contends, parents who promote sporting competence and normatively based
ability will see one set of responses from their children, whereas those who promote personal
mastery and effort will see another. Parent created motivational climate, therefore, has huge
implications for the socialisation of children into sport. Research (for example, White 1998)
investigating the relationship between athletes' perceptions of the motivational climate created by their parents and their own achievement goal orientations, has found that individuals
high in task (mastery) orientation perceived that their parents valued a climate that focused
on learning, enjoyment and high effort (mastery involving). In contrast, athletes high in ego
orientation perceived their parents to emphasise a climate where success was related to exerting low effort and worrying about mistakes (ego involving).

The practical implications for coaches of the parental influences on athletes' perceptions
of the motivational climate are based around educating parents on how to communicate with
their children during and after competitions and practice sessions. Discussions with parents
about the TARGET structures will help to foster a more mastery involving climate not only
in a sporting context but also in other achievement domains such as education. Indeed, the
TARGET structures were also identified by Epstein (1989) as structures to assist learning and
motivation in the family domain and can have a very positive effect on people's lives and family relationships in general. Suggesting that parents ask about improvement and effort when
their children arrive home after practice sessions and competitions, rather than whether they
simply won or lost, is one example of how parents can promote a more mastery focused
motivational climate. Both are natural questions to ask, but in the first instance the athlete's
perception is that improvement (mastery) is the most important aspect, whereas in the second, the message is that winning (ego) is the most important thing.

Peer influence is also a significant factor in how individuals perceive the motivational climate
in individual and team sports. Ntoumanis and Vazou (2005) identified eleven dimensions that
influence peer climate: improvement, equal treatment, relatedness support, autonomy support,
cooperation, effort, intra-team competition, intra-team conflict, normative ability, mistakes
and evaluation of competence. The improvement dimension is the extent to which peers provide feedback to improve fellow athletes' skills and performance. Equal treatment is related to
athletes' perceptions of equal importance and non-preferential treatment amongst their peers.
Relatedness support is about making peers feel part of the group and creating a friendly atmosphere. Autonomy support refers to athletes feeling that their peers allow them to have input
into decision making. Cooperation is the extent to which athletes help each other to improve
and learn. The effort dimension refers to whether athletes emphasise to their peers the importance of trying their best. Intra-team competition is the promotion of competition by peers, and
intra-team conflict refers to negative and conflicting behaviours, such as blaming teammates or
emphasising their weaknesses. Normative ability refers to perceived peer influence on comparative ability and a preference to work with the more able athletes. The mistakes dimension relates

to positive and negative peer reactions to making mistakes, and evaluation of competence refers to whether peers use self-referenced or normative criteria to evaluate their teammates.

In practical terms, the coach can influence the peer created motivational climate by emphasising the TARGET structures and encouraging a mastery focused climate in peer interactions. For example, in group work, or peer evaluations, the coach can ask peers to focus on self-referenced improvement in their feedback and to encourage and praise each other. Further, cooperative group learning (in the grouping structure) can be used to emphasise relatedness support between peers, making them more likely to feel accepted and related to their peers (Ntoumanis and Vazou 2005). The climate that peers create among themselves is, therefore, influenced by coaches and the climate that they foster.

## Other considerations in creating a positive motivational climate

It is acknowledged that TARGET may not cover all of the aspects that coaches need to consider in creating an effective motivational climate. Indeed recent research (Keegan *et al.* 2009, 2010) has suggested that other factors such as social goals, in addition to achievement goals, play an important part in athletes' motivation. In addition, this same research found that single coach behaviours were rarely associated with consistent motivational effects, suggesting that the relationship between coach behaviours and athletes' motivation is moderated by a number of interpersonal and contextual factors such as the relationship between the coach and athlete, consistency in coach behaviours and the training versus the competition environment. The one exception to this in the research of Keegan *et al.* (2009, 2010) was the theme of 'positivity', which was consistently identified with a positive effect on athletes' motivation.

Athletes' perceptions of coaches' supportive and caring behaviours towards them have also been shown to have a positive impact on their motivation, whereas controlling behaviours and exerting pressure have been associated with negative motivational responses (Garcia, Bengoechea and Strean 2007). Additionally, coaches' belief in athletes' capabilities and connection with them were identified as positive aspects of adolescents' developmental experiences in sport (Fraser-Thomas and Côté 2009). Therefore, in addition to implementing the TARGET structures, the social side of coaching should be recognised as crucial in fostering a positive motivational climate for athletes. Future research should, therefore, consider how TARGET combines with social factors and other pedagogical skills in coaching situations to influence athletes' motivation.

## REFERENCES

Ames, C. (1992). Achievement goals, motivational climate and motivational processes. In *Motivation in sport and exercise*. Roberts, G. C. (ed.) (Champaign, IL: Human Kinetics): pp. 161–176.

Ames, C. and Archer, J. (1988). Achievement goals in the classroom: Students' learning strategies and motivational processes. *Journal of Educational Psychology* 80: pp. 260–267.

Boardley, I. D. and Kavusannu, M. (2010). Effects of goal orientation and perceived value of toughness on antisocial behavior in soccer: The mediating role of moral disengagement. *Journal of Sport & Exercise Psychology* 31(2): pp. 176–192.

Carpenter, P. J. and Morgan, K. (1999). Motivational climate, personal goal perspectives, and cognitive and affective responses in physical education classes. *European Journal of Physical Education* 4: pp. 31–41.

Covington, M.V. and Beery, J. (1976). *Self worth and school learning.* (New York: Holt, Rinehart and Winston).

Dorobantu, M. and Biddle, S. (1997). The influence of situational and individual goals on intrinsic motivation of Romanian adolescents towards physical education. *European Yearbook of Sport Psychology* 1: pp. 148–165.

Duda, J. L. and Balaguer, I. (2007). Coach created motivational climate. In *Social psychology in sport.* Jowett, S. and Lavallee, D. (eds.) (Champaign, IL: Human Kinetics): pp. 117–130.

Duda, J.L. and Nicholls, J.G. (1992). Dimensions of achievement motivation in schoolwork and sport. *Journal of Educational Psychology* 84: pp. 290–299.

Duda, J.L. and Whitehead, J. (1998). Measurement of goal perspectives in the physical domain. In *Advances in sport and exercise psychology measurement.* Duda, J.L. (ed.) (Morgantown, WV: Fitness Information Technology): pp. 21–48.

Elliott, A. J. (1999). Approach and avoidance motivation and achievement goals. *Educational Psychologist* 34: pp. 169–189.

Elliott, A. J. and Church, M. A. (1997). A hierarchical model of approach and avoidance achievement motivation. *Journal of Personality and Social Psychology* 72: pp. 218–232.

Elliott, A. J. and McGregor, H. A. (2001). A 2 x 2 achievement goal framework. *Journal of Personality and Social Psychology* 80: pp. 501–519.

Epstein, J. (1989). Family structures and student motivation: A developmental perspective. In *Research on motivation in education.* Ames, C. and Ames, R. (eds.) (New York: Academic Press) 3: pp. 259–295.

Fraser-Thomas, J. and Côté, J. (2009). Understanding adolescents' positive and negative developmental experiences in sport. *The Sport Psychologist* 23: pp. 3–23.

Garcia Bengoechea, E. and Strean, W.B. (2007). On the interpersonal context of adolescents' sport motivation. *Psychology of Sport and Exercise* 8: pp. 195–217.

Hardy, L., Gould, G. and Gould, D. (1996). *Understanding psychological preparation for sport: Theory and practice for elite performers.* (Chichester, UK: Wiley).

Hassan, M. F. (2011). Developing a mastery motivational climate in sports coaching. Unpublished doctoral dissertation, University of Wales Institute, Cardiff.

Hassan, M. F. and Morgan, K. (In press). Effects of a mastery intervention programme on the motivational climate in sport coaching. *International Journal of Sport Science and Coaching*, 10(2).

Jones, R. L. and Standage, M. (2006). First among equals: Shared leadership in the coaching context. In *The sports coach as educator: Re-conceptualising sports coaching.* Jones, R. L. (ed.) (London: Routledge): pp. 65–76.

Jones, R.L. and Wallace, M. (2006). The coach as 'orchestrator'. In *The sports coach as educator: Re-conceptualising sports coaching.* Jones, R. L. (ed.) (London: Routledge).

Keegan, R. J., Harwood, C. G., Spray, C. M. and Lavallee, D. E. (2009). A qualitative investigation exploring the motivational climate in early-career sports participants: Coach, parent and peer influences on sport motivation. *Psychology of Sport and Exercise* 10: pp. 361–372.

Keegan, R. J., Spray, C. M., Harwood, C. G. and Lavallee, D. E. (2010). The motivational atmosphere in youth sport: Coach, parent, and peer influences on motivation in specializing sport participants. *Journal of Applied Sport Psychology* 22: pp. 87–105.

**125**

Kidman, L. (2001). *Developing decision makers: An empowerment approach to coaching.* (Christchurch, NZ: Innovative Print Communications).

Morgan, K. and Carpenter, P.J. (2002). Effects of manipulating the motivational climate in physical education lessons. *European Journal of Physical Education* 8: pp. 209–232.

Morgan, K. and Kingston, K. (2008). Development of a self-observation mastery intervention programme for teacher education. *Physical Education and Sport Pedagogy* 13: pp. 109–129.

Morgan, K., Kingston, K. and Sproule, J. (2005). Effects of different teaching styles on the teacher behaviours that influence motivational climate in physical education. *European Physical Education Review* 11: pp. 257–286.

Morgan, K., Sproule, J., Weigand, D. and Carpenter, P. J. (2005). A computer-based observational assessment of the teaching behaviours that influence motivational climate in physical education. *Physical Education and Sport Pedagogy* 10: pp. 83–105.

Mosston, M. and Ashworth, S. (2002). *Teaching physical education* (5th Ed.). (San Francisco: Benjamin Cummins).

Newton, M. L., Duda, J. L. and Yin, Z. (2000). Examination of the psychometric properties of the perceived motivational climate in sport questionnaire-2 in a sample of female athletes. *Journal of Sport Sciences* 18: pp. 275–290.

Nicholls, J. G. (1989). *The competitive ethos and democratic education.* (Cambridge, MA: Harvard University Press).

Ntoumanis, N. and Biddle, S.J.H. (1999). Affect and achievement goals in physical activity: A meta-analysis. *Scandinavian Journal of Medicine & Science in Sports* 9: pp. 315–332.

Ntoumanis, N. and Vazou, S. (2005). Peer motivational climate in youth sport: Measurement development. *Journal of Sport & Exercise Psychology* 27: pp. 432–455.

Roberts, G. C. (2001). *Advances in motivation in sport and exercise: Conceptual constraints and convergence.* (Champaign, IL: Human Kinetics).

Ryan, R. N. and Deci, E. L. (2000). Self determination and the facilitation of intrinsic motivation, social development and well being. *American Psychologist* 55: pp. 68–78.

Sharpe, T. and Koperwas, L. (1999). *BEST: Behavioral evaluation strategy and taxonomy software.* (New York: Sage Publications, Inc).

Solmon, M.A. (1996). Impact of motivational climate on students' behaviors and perceptions in a physical education setting. *Journal of Educational Psychology* 88: pp. 731–738.

Treasure, D. (1993). A social-cognitive approach to understanding children's achievement behavior, cognitions, and affect in competitive sport. *Unpublished doctoral dissertation.* University of Illinois, Urbana-Champaign.

Treasure, D. (2001). Enhancing young people's motivation in youth sport: An achievement goal approach. In *Advances in motivation in sport and exercise.* Roberts, G. C. (ed.) (Champaign, IL: Human Kinetics): pp. 79–100.

Walling, M.D., Duda, J.L. and Chi, L. (1993). The perceived motivational climate in sport questionnaire: Construct and predictive validity. *Journal of Sport and Exercise Psychology* 15: pp. 172–183.

White, S. A. (1998). Contextual influences and goal perspectives among female youth sport participants. *Research Quarterly for Exercise and Sport* 69: pp. 47–57.

White, S. A. (2007). Parent created motivational climate. In *Social psychology in sport.* Jowett, S. and Lavallee, D. (eds.) (Champaign, IL: Human Kinetics): pp. 131–143.

# Chapter 7

# The practice session
## Talent development

*Russell Martindale*

One important role for any sports coach is to nurture the potential of young people and help maximise the natural talents they were given. Part of this role includes the identification and development of that talent, which could be interpreted as helping to find and guide those who have the aptitude and desire to reach an elite level within performance sport.

Performance sport and the search for excellence forms only a part of the coaching fabric, as it is inextricably linked to sport participation and related recreational activities. This becomes apparent when reviewing the lives and experiences of those who have made it to the very top in sport. At one stage even they were only involved in sport for fun. Due to the experiences, opportunities and support they were given, in combination with their aptitude and desire, over time they developed into, and succeeded as, elite sportsmen and women. This means that every coach, whether it be a volunteer coach with an under 8's cricket team or a national head coach, has some role to play in the development of talent and, perhaps more importantly, young people in general.

In fact, the course of a young person's sporting life can be shaped significantly as much (and perhaps more) at an early age, as it can be at a later stage in development. The influence of PE teachers or 'early' coaches as the inspiration for many budding youngsters, before aspiring for excellence within sport, is reported on many occasions.

Conversely, there are also reports of young people being demotivated, burning out or dropping out due to excessive pressure and lack of appropriate support. As such, it is important to understand how talent develops across the lifespan, including the characteristics of those that 'make it', to gain insight and ideas from the experiences and support processes that appear to facilitate development. This will help clarify the role of the coach at various stages of development and enable coaches to work with more confidence, backed by evidence to support their practice.

This chapter will start with an overview of talent development. Specifically, this will outline the various phases and transitions involved in the progression of talent and the associated qualities, support and experiences that appear to facilitate development. Second, the chapter will examine common pitfalls in talent identification and development, such as early selection and specialisation, reliance on performance and anthropometrics as indicators of 'talent', short termism and outcome focus. Third, the chapter will provide implications for the philosophy and role of the coach, including the relative emphasis on talent identification and/or talent development, and the holistic role of the coach within the 'talent development environment'. Some practical examples will be discussed in relation to the promotion of important psychological characteristics within the coaching process, against a backdrop of effective goal setting, review and athlete support, and the use of challenge to facilitate psychological growth, transfer of skills and self-regulation.

## THE NATURE OF DEVELOPMENT

### It's a long-term process

One thing that those involved in talent development research have agreed upon is that it takes time to become world class at anything, including sport. For example, Ericsson and colleagues (1993), developed a rule of thumb called the '10,000 hour rule'. This highlighted the evidence that suggested at least 10,000 hours of deliberate practice were required to become an expert in any domain. An important feature of this practice is that it involved specific criteria (see below) to be considered deliberate practice:

- Deliberate practice is designed specifically to improve performance – specific goals, feedback and opportunity for repetition.
- Deliberate practice is not inherently enjoyable (although sometimes it can be in sport) but effortful.
- Deliberate practice is motivated by wanting to achieve excellence.

Indeed, stagnation and limitation in performance and developments were seen as a lack of motivation to engage in further deliberate practice, as highlighted in the following quote:

> The development of typical novice performance is prematurely arrested in an effortless automated form, experts however, engage in an extended, continued refinement of mechanisms that mediate improvements in their performance. Most amateurs do not improve their performance only because they have reached (in their minds) an acceptable level!
>
> (Ericsson et al. 1993, p. 363)

The implications for this theory are that the earlier an individual is engaged in deliberate practice, the better they will become, because they have the opportunity to spend more time engaging deliberately. Of course, this has further implications for the identification and selection of talent and also has been used as evidence for the need for early specialisation and high work ethic from the outset.

### Specialisation versus diversification

It is important to bear in mind that much of the subsequent talent development research puts this theory into its appropriate context. The research highlights that a significant proportion of elite athletes, especially those that have longevity within the sport, were late specialists in the activity that they eventually excelled in, and had a history of widespread participation at early ages in a variety of sports and activities. Many of those who specialised and engaged in serious, deliberate training at early stages dropped out in the development phase through demotivation or burnout.

Furthermore, the 10,000 hour rule has been shown to not always be necessary, and that experience and skills developed through hours performing and practicing in different domains can transfer across to allow 'fast tracking' of performance development within a new sport. Research in the UK has shown that approximately half of all successful elite athletes started life as pre-elites in a different sport before transferring across at a relatively late age (approximately 14 years old). This highlights the need for a more complex and holistic consideration of the journey to elite status rather than assuming a need for specialising early and engaging in deliberate practice.

## The need for staged progression

Work led by Bloom (1985) and Côté (1999) provided a more holistic picture of the nature of talent development by providing an understanding of the nature of progression as a staged process. In other words, it had started to emerge that for successful progression through the whole process, suitable foundations had to be laid effectively in a step by step manner. This foundation would facilitate progression through each subsequent stage. For example, without developing the necessary intrinsic motivation and love for the sport at early stages, it would not be possible to engage in the required amounts of deliberate practice over a long period of time, which would be necessary to be successful later on. Bloom noted:

> There are many years of increasingly difficult stages of talent development before mature and complex talent will be fully attained . . . without the purposeful step by step talent development process, it is unlikely that even the individuals we studied (top world 25) would have reached the high levels of talent development reported.
>
> (1985, p. 14)

More specifically, Bloom's (1985) model of talent development identified three stages to progression – an Initiation Stage, a Development Stage and a Mastery Stage. Importantly, the transition between each of these stages was not triggered by chronological age or some pre-determined cut off point, but was initiated by certain tasks being complete, relationships formed and attitudes developed or learning achieved. The stages were characterised at three levels:

- athlete qualities
- coach qualities
- parent qualities.

An athlete in the Initiation Stage could be described as playful, joyful and excited by participation in the activity, with very little emphasis placed on competition. This general atmosphere was reinforced by the coach who tended to adopt a kind, cheerful and caring approach, with a very process oriented philosophy to coaching. This helped the children build and develop crucial motivation as well as fundamental skills and attributes.

> These are crucial years, even more crucial than those that follow, because it is during this period that our subjects became interested and caught up in the sport of swimming. In time that interest became self motivating. Had there been no excitement during the early years, and no sense that the young swimmer was very successful, there would have been no middle or later years.
>
> (Bloom 1985, p. 141)

Parents were strongly involved in the socialisation of their children into the activity at this stage. They shared the excitement of participation, maintained a very supportive and positive role and proactively sought out an appropriate mentor/coach. Peers also play a crucial role in sport socialisation as well. The progression from Stage 1 (Initiation) to Stage 2 (Development) was, in part, characterised by the development of an athletic identity: children realising that they were no longer children who swim, they were swimmers. However, there was often a combination of features that triggered this change, including information related to the competence of the child. For example, a period of accelerated development often occurred and/or the child was labelled as having 'potential' or 'talent'. Attitudes could also spontaneously change, such as an increase in commitment or task/achievement orientation. Sometimes a new, more technical coach was introduced, triggering the move from Initiation to Development.

The Development Stage was characterised by more serious achievement orientation, the athlete being more engaged and committed to pursuing excellence and his or her talent identified in some capacity. The coach tended to be more knowledgeable and demanding and developed a strong personal interest in the athlete as well as the capacity to command respect. The parents started to make more sacrifices and take more of an organisationally supportive role in the sense of helping to restrict unnecessary activities and helping with transport and time management. The transition into the Mastery Stage was often triggered by an unexpected success or turning point. This was often in combination with sport becoming *the* priority in life and as a result of a strong independence emerging. Competition became a yardstick for success and often a master coach was introduced to facilitate this transition to expert status. In the Mastery Stage itself, fine tuning performance is a huge driver for hard work, and the strengthened obsession with the sport fuels this commitment. The coach is increasingly demanding and often has a strong love/hate relationship with the athlete, while parents take on a lesser role, providing financial or emotional supportive where necessary.

However, it is important to note that this work is specific to a North American population, and as such, it is important to recognise cultural differences. For example, in the UK, over half of all elite athletes under 25 years of age are still financially dependent on their parents, with limited access to facilities and 'master' coaches, and a very different University sporting infrastructure and support process. Indeed, the emphasis on 'transitions' and occurrence of more varied pathways is also important to note. Having said this, the detailed and holistic description of the three stages and associated transitions includes behavioural (for example, increasing commitment, becoming more obsessed), cognitive (for example, increasing task orientation, developing an athletic identity) and social factors (such as more technical coaching, less parental involvement, being identified as talented), that all provide useful insight into *possible* requirements and potential pitfalls to successful development.

## The role of deliberate play and deliberate practice

Building on this more generic work by Bloom, Côté and colleagues investigated a more sport-specific model of talent development, with retrospective interviews with elite junior rowers and tennis players. In a similar vein, three stages of development emerged: the sampling years (aged 6–12), the specialising years (aged 13–15) and the investment years (aged 16+). There are many similar concepts to Bloom's model, such as the nature of the atmosphere at different levels and triggers to stage movement. However, Côté's model is sport-specific in nature and explicitly rooted in the theoretical concepts of deliberate play, deliberate practice and 'number of other sporting activities'. Deliberate play contrasts with deliberate practice in that it is defined as activities that maximise inherent enjoyment, are focussed on process and experimentation and are loosely monitored with no immediate focus on correction. As the names of the stages suggest, at the earliest phase of development a wide range of activities were sampled, leading to the development of a range of fundamental movement skills and informal, perhaps unconscious, searching for what sport is most enjoyable and/or suitable. Critical incidents that triggered change and moved a child into the specialisation stage included positive coach experiences, encouragement from siblings, enjoyment and/or success. Furthermore, it emerged that the 'split' between deliberate play and deliberate practice changed through the stages. In the sampling stage there was a high frequency of deliberate play and low deliberate practice, through the specialising years there was a similar amount of each, and through the investment years deliberate practice dominated. Latterly, maintenance and career discontinuation stages have also been added to the stage model of athletic development.

## Varied pathways: the need to consider individual differences

These stage models provide a useful breadth of information about what experiences, support processes and training may help to facilitate development in an effective manner. However, more recent research has highlighted a more idiosyncratic and individualised nature of many development pathways and the crucial nature of transitions and challenges (Collins and MacNamara 2011). Essentially, developing athletes must successfully negotiate and adjust effectively to these challenges to be successful. As such, these challenge points are perhaps worthy of greater emphasis rather than the stages per se. For example, results from some UK based research suggest many athletes do not consider themselves to have passed through the stages outlined above in a linear or straightforward manner, while many more transition and challenge points were highlighted. Given the apparent complexity of the route to elite status, aspiring athletes must be able to make the most of developmental opportunities when they arise (such as the first time appearance at new level of competition), adapt quickly to difficult circumstances and setbacks (training/work balance, injury) and negotiate transitions (for example from junior to senior) if they are to maximise their potential and progression.

**131**

Generally, there are considered to be a significant number of 'normative' transitions, those that can be considered to be standard for most, if not all, developing athletes. These can be predicted and therefore planned and prepared for. For example, the transition from junior to senior sports is considered to be one of the most difficult 'normative transition' to deal with successfully, and is clearly crucial for the progression to elite sport performance. However, Wylleman and Lavallee (2004) established the 'developmental model of athlete transitions', and showed that athletes face a range of challenge points when their lives are considered as a whole. As well as Bloom's talent development stages, there are stages and transitions in athletes' psychological, psychosocial and academic-vocational development. So for example, the transition from junior to senior sports may coincide with transitions in other spheres of life (for example, from school to college or university), adding life stress and making it even more challenging to cope successfully. Furthermore, there are also other much more individualised and unpredictable transitions called 'non-normative' transitions. These could be related to any life sphere – for example, injury, de-selection, relationship or family stresses, financial or academic pressure – and are often more difficult to cope with due to their unexpected initiation and consequences. As such, it is clear that the developmental pathway is complex, individualised and filled with multiple challenges and opportunities that developing athletes must overcome and make the most of. This puts emphasis on the need for preparation for and support prior to, during and post transitions to ensure that progression is not stalled or halted due to inadequate coping skills or support. This means that part of the role of the coach is to be aware of current and potential transitions and challenges for their athletes and be able to prepare them physically and mentally to be ready for what comes next. As such, individualised athlete attention and psychological skills development is one of the many crucial skill sets that coaches need to maximise their effectiveness.

## COMMON PITFALLS IN TALENT IDENTIFICATION AND DEVELOPMENT

### Over emphasis on talent identification and early outcome success

Identifying talent within sport is considered to be one of the Holy Grails of coaching. Indeed, often much more emphasis is put on trying to identify talent than trying to develop it. Within many sports there are both formal and informal methods for attempting to identify talent. This ranges from the subjective opinion of a coach or selection panel, an organised system of scouts, through to more 'scientific' testing procedures. Most sports tend to adhere to a system of selecting young players in different age groups into a tiered system of 'elite performers/teams' (for example, club, regional and national level representation). These opportunities often involve additional training, coaching and competition above and beyond the normal opportunities afforded to 'less talented' peers. The selection processes are often subjective and based on physical attributes and one off measures of proficiency or performance opportunities. Furthermore, the rationale for selection is often not clear but tends to revolve around selecting the most 'talented' performers at a given time, where kudos is given to the team or performers and associated coaches who win the tournament or competition that year.

## Future potential versus current performance capability

The definition of talent is often closely linked to performance capability but, importantly, less related to future potential. However, many perceive these two concepts to be the same. While of course there is no reason why someone couldn't have performance capability and future potential at any one time, it is important to recognise they are not necessarily synonymous concepts. This is particularly so at early ages where performance characteristics still have much development opportunity.

This focus on performance as a key selection criterion has resulted in some interesting and worrying consequences. For example, a phenomenon 'relative age effect' is common in many sports. This evidence shows that a larger proportion of children selected into more 'elite' teams/opportunities at age group level are born early in the selection year for strength sports. A larger proportion of those born late in the selection year are selected for gymnastic type sports. In other words, age differences (that is up to a year apart in any given age band) and maturational differences (potentially much more than one year apart) play a large role in performance capability and therefore the likelihood of selection through childhood and adolescence. Taking this further, many young people have been shown to rely on the physical advantages that made them 'good performers' at young ages (for example, relative physical prowess) and fail to learn the skills required at a later phase (such as tactical awareness, technique, performing under pressure), particularly where strong, knowledgeable guidance is not available. Ironically, a reverse relative age effect has been shown to exist in some sports, resulting in those younger peers who did make it into the system early being more likely to make it to an adult elite level. This initial 'disadvantage' may force the athletes to adapt and develop in the face of additional challenges and work hard to cope with training and performing against older and physically more developed peers from a young age. This highlights a very salient point in that many features of performance are trainable from early ages, and as such, a motivation and capacity to develop is far more important than having an ability to outperform peers at development stages if long term success is the goal.

## The role of the self-fulfilling prophecy

Furthermore, talent or performance can be misleading when you take into consideration the past experiences of the players. In fact, one piece of research by Ward and Williams (2003) concluded that the higher skill levels of 'elite' soccer players as young as eight are likely to be as a result of the 200 hours of expert coaching they have received as opposed to any genetic superiority. As such, it is important to understand and take into account the nature of development, the goal and need for selection and subsequent development opportunities.

The theory of 'self-fulfilling prophecy' provides a good rationale and important considerations for coaches when assessing and working with young developing performers. It builds on the idea that perceptions of competence and 'potential' are important from both the athlete's perspective ('I could be quite good at this' or 'I am good at this') as well as a coach's perspective ('that athlete has potential or talent'). Indeed, Bloom highlights the fact that

**133**

while being good in early phases of development is not well correlated with ability or success in any other later stage, perceptions of competence or being identified as someone with potential can be important, if not crucial precursors to commitment to later stages and the pursuit of excellence.

> Being good in one phase of the learning may not have a high relation to being good at a later phase, even though both phases are in the same talent field. . . . Precociousness in a talent field is not to be dismissed, it can only be realistically viewed as an early stage in talent development.
>
> (Bloom 1985, p. 538)

The self-fulfilling prophecy outlines how a coach's perception of a young person can have significant bearing on both the perceptions of competence and subsequent behaviour of an athlete and his or her eventual success. As such, it is important from a coach's perspective to have an open mind to athlete potential and provide equal opportunities where possible. For example, evidence has shown that athletes and young people in different contexts (such as school) who are perceived to have greater potential receive more instruction and feedback (of a more individualised and higher quality style), warmer interaction and acceptance, higher expectations and more opportunities to practice and learn. This differential interaction leads to changes in the athlete's own perceptions of competence and commitment, in addition to more tangible reduction in practice opportunities and feedback information. Research has outlined that those who are perceived to have greater potential make better gains in ability over a period of time, even if 'high potential athletes' are categorised randomly by researchers. So it is clearly important to provide equal opportunities to athletes within the context of the nature of talent development and what constitutes having 'potential'. Otherwise, significant others (for example, coaches, parents, teachers) may have a negative influence on an athlete's development, albeit inadvertently, without providing a realistic opportunity for the development of ability and self-motivation.

## Recognising and managing unhelpful pressures

Given the complexity and context of how young people's talent develops, for example, the disparity between performance and potential, the non-linear nature of development (such as early developers, late developers, sport transfers, changeable performance capability) and the importance of 'setting up' and supporting the process effectively, it is important to consider other external influences on coaches practice.

In many situations, coaches working across a range of different age groups feel pressure for their children to 'win'. However, from the literature previously outlined, winning at early ages or selecting those children who are more likely to win at age group level is not the same thing as planning and preparing youngsters for long term development and success, and in many cases, it is often an unhelpful pressure. As such, the more influences that support a long term successful outcome the better. However, invariably this isn't the case. For example, there may be explicit pressure from a governing body to produce certain results; to get funding or support, there is a goal of four medals at the U16 European championships, or for youngsters to be selected for a regional age group squad, they must gain a certain performance time at a national competition. It could even be an implicit pressure, for example, perceptions of a coach's ability are often linked to 'the outcomes' that the coach's teams or athletes achieve at competitions. So for coaches to achieve recognition and be perceived as a 'top coach', they may need to select and train youngsters to win as opposed to having a more long term plan to help youngsters grow, develop and move successfully on to the next phase. For coaches with ambitions to coach at a more senior level, this is often a way (or sometimes the only way) to enhance their credentials as far as potential employees are concerned.

Another concern relates to the pressure that sports have to recruit young people. Quite often someone who is an outstanding performer in one sport is also an outstanding, or certainly very good, performer in other sports. Such performers will be highly sought after by many different sports. This, in combination with a general culture of outcome/win focus at every age group, game and competition that is available, puts a lot of pressure on young people to be available for selection but also increases the risk of burnout and injury. Of course, it is not only the multi-sport context of this participation; it is also the multi-level nature of sport participation. For example, a young person may play for a school, club, region and country all within the same season. Without sports and organisations working together with the best interests of the young person at heart, it can lead to too much too soon, resulting in enhanced risks of over playing, de-motivation, injury and burnout.

## PROMOTING THE CHARACTERISTICS OF EFFECTIVE DEVELOPERS

### Holistic fundamental skills base

While it can be useful to focus on what is wrong or challenging with the system, it is perhaps more valuable at an individual coach level to try to understand some of the more 'controllable' factors regarding enhancing athletes' potential to succeed. To help with this, it is important to understand the typical characteristics of those who have potential to improve and progress effectively and then consider the extent to which these factors can be developed.

A key feature of people who are able to show potential is the capacity to learn and develop. There are a number of factors related to this within a sport context, including physical and psychological attributes, appropriate support and opportunities. Physically, it has been shown that fundamental movement skills and coordination form a crucial platform from which more sport specific skills can be developed robustly. As such, it is clearly worth spending time putting these in place before putting too much focus on sport specific skills. Although it also makes sense for this to happen at early stages – even at later stages, particularly where shortfalls exist – it is worth promoting and reinforcing fundamental movement skills. Therefore, this area of development affords an opportunity for all sports to work together, even if benefits are not immediate for the specific sport. In other words, everyone is developing the platform for potential, and when children choose certain sports to participate in, they will be more successful if they begin with good fundamentals regardless of where or who they learnt them from.

**135**

## Building for the long term

Of course this philosophy of putting the foundations in place applies right through the system, including the development of performance capability over the long term. For example, increasing training load can easily enhance fitness. However, if appropriate techniques or strengthening does not happen first, then potential is limited (even if a faster short term performance increase is likely). Increasing training load in this case will only take a person so far and will also increase the chances of injury occurring. Leading on from this, performance at later stages is also a consequence of acquiring a package of holistic skills. As such, ensuring that a range of sport specific skills is put into place, such as technical, tactical, physical and psychological skills, is crucial. This is an important point because many coaching sessions and programmes are often reported as being somewhat uni-dimensional, dominated by technical development in team sports, for example, or physical fitness in endurance sports.

Furthermore, it has been shown that different performance factors are more important at different ages, adding more complexity to the picture. For example, hard physical running may be more likely to lead to victory at younger ages, and decision making and good technique, post-adolescence. As such, if a coach has a strong win focus, then selection and training may be dominated by different factors year on year. However, if the coach has a long term development vision, they are likely to present a more coherent development programme throughout the system aimed at developing well prepared adult, elite performers in the long run, albeit at the risk of slower or lesser age group performances per se.

## The role of psychological characteristics

In relation to psychology, the capacity to learn and develop is crucial. For example, on a basic level, someone who is not committed or motivated will not make as many steps towards maximising his or her potential to the extent that someone who is committed and motivated will. As such, these factors would usually be facilitated by the coach. Indeed, research has already shown the importance of intrinsic motivation development, which is crucial at early stages. This can be facilitated through the age groups into elite sport, even when there are huge extrinsic pressures and rewards available, which can often reduce intrinsic motivation. Theory suggests that promotion of perceived competence, autonomy and relatedness facilitates the development and maintenance of intrinsic motivation.

In addition to this, learning ability has been shown to be underpinned by the ability to self-regulate thinking and emotions. For example, skills such as planning, monitoring, realistic self-evaluation, curiosity and confidence are all associated with effective learning outcomes. Indeed, part of the process to transitioning to the Mastery Stage in Bloom's model involved a move towards becoming a self-regulatory, independent athlete learner. However, it is important to note that other research suggests this process usually starts much earlier in the Development phase. Importantly, many of these skills and attributes can be taught, learnt and reinforced in practical ways. Finally, the journey to reaching elite status is never smooth. The psychological skills required to succeed relate not only to learning capacity but also to the ability to handle pressure, allowing someone to make the most of opportunities when they arise, adapt quickly to challenging circumstances and negotiate change as it occurs.

## How psychological characteristics develop

Interestingly, recent research has highlighted that psychological skills develop over time and through a variety of means. For example, Gould *et al.* (2002) highlighted a number of sources of psychological development, including the community, individual personal reflection, non-sport and sport personnel and the sport process itself. However, the biggest influences seemed to be family and coaches. These sources facilitated development both directly, through teaching or facilitating 'lessons learnt', and indirectly, through modelling or unintentionally creating 'psychological' environments. Furthermore, Bull *et al.* (2005) highlighted influences on the development of mental toughness in cricket to include family background, (for example, parental influence and childhood circumstances), opportunities to survive early setbacks, exposure to foreign cricket and being in an environment where success had to be earned.

Taking this further, Collins and MacNamara (2011) highlight the necessity for coaches to challenge people to develop and use psychological skills and self-regulation at an appropriate level. This requires using both natural life challenges (for example, exams, transitions between schools) and intentionally created challenges (such as training with a mixed age range, playing out of position, challenging physical or psychological drills or experiences). They recommend a more systematic and intentional approach to psychological skills development including:

- teaching relevant skills;
- facilitating the application of the skills through challenging situations;
- modelling the skills;
- reflection and refining of skills as part of an ongoing process of development;
- encouraging transfer of skills across contexts.

Indeed, this process can be well facilitated by coaches. The nature of the most pertinent psychological skills and ideas for development will be covered later.

## ROLE OF THE COACH IN TALENT DEVELOPMENT: PHILOSOPHY AND GOALS

In summary, it seems that the literature provides a good understanding of many of the requirements of athlete development, from novice level through developmental into elite and beyond. Furthermore, the literature also highlights some of the potential pitfalls, including:

- lack of understanding/emphasis between 'potential' and 'performance outcome', particularly at young ages;
- overlooking the importance of individualising practice and allowing for variability in development and performance;
- uni-dimensional training programmes, with a lack of structured emphasis on holistic development, in particular a psychological input;
- overtraining and playing;
- a culture where 'winning' at every level seems to be prioritised and reinforced at a number of levels.

**137**

**KEY FEATURES**

**KEY METHODS**

| KEY FEATURES | KEY METHODS |
|---|---|
| **Long Term Aims & Methods** | • Develop a Long Term Vision, Purpose & Identity |
| **Wide Ranging Coherent Messages & Support** | • Provide Coherent Philosophies, Aims & Methods at a Variety of Levels (e.g. Parents, Coach Content, Practice & Reward Systems, Selection, Funding, Competition Structure, NGBs)<br>• Educate Parents, Schools, Peers, Coaches & Important Others (and encourage positive contributions!)<br>• Utilise Role Models at a Variety of Levels<br>• Set Up a Variety of Support Networks Over the Long Term (e.g. Peer, Coach, Sport Staff, Family)<br>• Provide Forums for Open & Honest Communication Patterns, Formal & Informal Coach/Athlete Interactions at a Variety of Levels |
| **Emphasise Appropriate Development NOT Early Success** | • Re-Conceptualise 'Winning' as Success at Developmental Stages<br>• Provide Clear Expectations, Roles, & Meaning Within the 'Big Picture' at Every Level<br>• Provide 'Stage Specific' Integrated Experiences & Teaching With Explicit Links to Performance<br>   ○ Fundamental Physical & Sport Specific Skills (Technical, Tactical, Mental, Physical, Perceptual)<br>   ○ Fundamental Mental Skills (Learning & Development, Life, Performance Related)<br>   ○ Balance<br>• Encourage Increasing Responsibility & Autonomy in Learning/Development<br>• Develop Intrinsic Motivation & Personal Commitment to Process<br>• Promote Personal Relevance, Athlete Understanding & Knowledge |
| **Individualised & Ongoing Development** | • Provide Accessible Opportunities & Fundamentals to as Many Youngsters as Possible<br>• Provide Flexible Systems to Allow for Performance & Physical Development Variation<br>• Identify, Prepare for, and Support Individuals Through Key Transitions<br>• Provide Individualised Programmes & Regular Individual Goal Setting & Review Processes |

*Integrated, Holistic & Systematic*

*Figure 7.1* A summary of the key features of effective TDEs.

As such, it is important that this knowledge informs a coach's philosophy, driving coaching practice and decision making. Ultimately, it seems that it is worth considering the acronym TID (talent identification and development) as TiD (TALENT identification and DEVELOPMENT), where identification is an important but smaller part of the process, managed in an on-going and open way, and where effective development is emphasised. In a well-run development environment, talent will emerge and be identified over time. To help summarise, on the basis of the key issues emerging from the talent identification and development literature, Martindale and colleagues (2005) developed guidelines to highlight key considerations when setting up talent development environments (TDEs). These are outlined in Figure 7.1. They have also developed and validated the Talent Development Environment Questionnaire (TDEQ), which can be used by coaches or those in charge of organising and running TDEs to gain feedback from their athletes on the key features of practice that have been identified as useful facilitators of talent development (Martindale *et al.* 2010). This holistic structure can be used to guide practice and decisions, but it would be implemented most effectively with special consideration of the systematic development of key psychological attributes. This aspect of development is considered next.

## IDENTIFYING AND PROMOTING THE PSYCHOLOGICAL CHARACTERISTICS OF DEVELOPING EXCELLENCE (PCDEs)

### What are the PCDEs?

There have been a number of psychological skills and attributes identified in the literature that have been shown to be associated with effective progression and performance. While it is difficult to prioritise certain skills and strategies over others, a relatively consistent set of skills termed the psychological characteristics of developing excellence have emerged from focussed research in this field (Abbott, Collins, Martindale and Sowerby 2002; MacNamara *et al.* 2010). These include:

- self-motivation;
- commitment and role clarity;
- goal setting and self-reinforcement;
- quality practice;
- effective and controllable imagery;
- realistic performance evaluation and attribution;
- coping under pressure;
- social skills.

Committing time to understanding, identifying and promoting these characteristics within individuals will enable developing athletes to make the most of their development, coaching and performance opportunities whilst coping more successfully with the inevitable ups and downs of sport and life. In other words, by doing this, coaches will be investing effort into developing the attributes that facilitate self-regulation, learning, development, progression and performance. Ultimately, this will maximise the chances of effective talent development and long term success.

### Context specific nature of PCDEs

It is important to outline that the way in which these characteristics are embodied is often highly context specific. For example, commitment in a 14-year-old regional rugby player will be very different to the required commitment in an 18-year-old professional. Perhaps training five hours a week would be appropriate at 14, including appropriate rest, cross train-ing and balanced competition schedule, but this would clearly not be sufficient for a young professional player. Indeed, the nature of the application of some of these characteristics also changes. For example, self-regulation and independence will become more pertinent as an athlete matures and develops, a feature that would need to be incorporated, encouraged, and facilitated through the operationalisation and development of the PCDEs. As such, this con-text needs to be recognised appropriately and in keeping with the context and long term goals of the player. Furthermore, commitment may well 'look' different in different sports. For example, in judo, a 'committed' player may be one who is able to keep going hard in practice, address identified weaknesses and show progress and maintain a healthy diet; while in curl-ing a 'committed' player may train independently of organised squad sessions, demonstrate consistent effort by consistent preparation and support the efforts of others. Along with sport specific aspects of these psychological characteristics, as with any development process there are likely to be individual specific contexts as well, although clearly, many will cross over as generally relevant between sports. This encourages the development of a general awareness of expectations for athletes at their current levels and as they develop further. This is useful not only to provide clarity for the athletes and to help identify appropriate role models, but also to develop coherent understanding between coaches, parents and significant others.

## Profiling

One way of starting the process of incorporating PCDEs into practice is to profile these characteristics for individuals on a more generic level – the sport-stage context. This starts by using the eight PCDEs identified above as a framework for identifying relevant behaviours that could be considered to embody each characteristic.

It would be useful to do this in conjunction with other coaches to help brainstorm the most relevant and pertinent aspects. This template can then either be adapted over time or to suit individuals more specifically. Below are some examples of each of the characteristics and behaviours that may represent them appropriately within a practical setting.

*Self-motivation:*

- practices away from team training;
- enjoys practicing and competing.

*Commitment and role clarity:*

- listens, takes advice, asks for advice;
- consistently and appropriately warms up and cools down.

*Goal setting and self-reinforcement:*

- sets process, performance and outcome goals with coach;
- independently and realistically self-reinforces achievements.

*Quality practice:*

- maximizes understanding about why things are done as they are in training;
- independently evaluates training and competition performance.

*Effective and controllable imagery:*

- takes time in training to use imagery to prime new movements or techniques;
- uses imagery to learn to deal with difficult situations.

*Realistic performance evaluation and attribution:*

- realistically evaluates performance regardless of win or loss;
- evaluates why he or she does well or not.

*Coping under pressure:*

■ shows confident behaviour under pressure;
■ maintains a consistent pre-event routine regardless of importance of event.

*Social skills:*

■ can ask the coach questions which help to get useful feedback about how to do better;
■ can interact effectively with teammates in order to help the learning process.

Although all of these characteristics are important for development, and as such need to be facilitated and reinforced through practice, it is worth periodically identifying the priority for individuals and/or the development environment more generally. So once these characteristics have been identified and operationalised appropriately, performance profile techniques can help pinpoint the main focus for development, the process for which is outlined next.

1    Brainstorm the key behaviours associated with each PCDE.

This is often more challenging than it initially seems; brainstorming in groups helps to develop clarity by bouncing ideas off like-minded people. Get the athletes involved, use their attributes to put together ideas and use role models as templates to work from. Think about someone who has become successful in the sport and consider what he or she was like as a developing performer. Be as specific and 'observable' as possible. Record these ideas in a format similar to that in Figure 7.2.

2    Rate how important each of the behaviours is to developing full potential in the long term (0–10) and record it under Importance.
3    Rate the ideal score required on each behaviour to develop full potential in the long term (0–10) and record this under Ideal Performer.
4    Rate where the athlete is currently between 1 and 10, and record that under Current Score. NOTE: This could be done by the athletes themselves and/or the coach(es), and/or the parent(s) and so on. It is interesting to find out how different people define the priorities and rate what level they think has been achieved to date. Often, people do not independently come up with the same results, at least initially.
5    Identify the most important factors to work on by performing a simple calculation:

*(Ideal Score − Current Score) × Importance Score = Profile Score*

The most important factors to work on will have the highest Profile Scores.

## Promoting and reinforcing PCDEs

An advantage of clearly identifying the behaviours associated with effective talent development, and the reasons behind why they are required, is that people are more likely to understand what is expected and will be more likely to 'buy in' to their importance.

| Self-Motivation | Importance (0-10) | Ideal Performer (0-10) | Current Score (0-10) | Profile Score |
|---|---|---|---|---|
| Practices away from team training | 10 | 10 | 7 | 30 |
| | | | | |
| | | | | |
| **Commitment and Role Clarity** | Importance (0-10) | Ideal Performer (0-10) | Current Score (0-10) | Profile Score |
| maintain a healthy diet | 9 | 10 | 6 | 36 |
| | | | | |
| | | | | |
| **Goal setting and Self-Reinforcement** | Importance (0-10) | Ideal Performer (0-10) | Current Score (0-10) | Profile Score |
| address identified weaknesses and show progress | 10 | 10 | 7 | 30 |
| | | | | |
| | | | | |
| **Quality practice** | Importance (0-10) | Ideal Performer (0-10) | Current Score (0-10) | Profile Score |
| keep going hard in practice | 10 | 10 | 3 | 70 |
| | | | | |
| | | | | |
| **Effective and Controllable Imagery** | Importance (0-10) | Ideal Performer (0-10) | Current Score (0-10) | Profile Score |
| Takes time in training to use imagery to prime new movements or techniques | 10 | 10 | 7 | 30 |
| | | | | |
| | | | | |
| **Realistic performance evaluation and attribution** | Importance (0-10) | Ideal Performer (0-10) | Current Score (0-10) | Profile Score |
| Realistically evaluate performance regardless of win or loss | 9 | 10 | 3 | 63 |
| | | | | |
| | | | | |
| **Coping under pressure** | Importance (0-10) | Ideal Performer (0-10) | Current Score (0-10) | Profile Score |
| Show confident behavior under pressure | 10 | 9 | 5 | 40 |
| | | | | |
| | | | | |
| **Social skills** | Importance (0-10) | Ideal Performer (0-10) | Current Score (0-10) | Profile Score |
| Can interact effectively with team-mates in order to help the learning process | 10 | 9 | 6 | 30 |
| | | | | |
| | | | | |

*Figure 7.2* Profile of psychological characteristics of developing excellence.

This helps reduce second-guessing by athletes, coaches or parents and provides clarity on what to look for, who might make a good role model and what to encourage and reinforce.

While there are many ways to facilitate the *development* of PCDEs, it seems that a practical approach is likely to lead to the greatest effect. This would involve coaches and significant others using a combination of teaching skills and strategies, designing challenges and/or using natural life and sport challenges to test, develop and refine the application of mental skills in a transferable, self-regulating way across different life domains of the athlete. Using role models is crucial to highlight, reinforce and motivate developing performers to commit to mental development, as is a consistent goal setting and review process. Indeed, understanding the principles of effective goal setting will help structure a positive development process of these characteristics. For example, research highlights a number of important considerations such as:

- setting specific goals;
- setting moderately difficult but realistic goals;
- setting long and short term goals – stepping stones to success;
- setting a combination of process, performance and outcome goals;
- always setting both training and competition goals;
- recording goals and seeking feedback on progress;
- identifying strategies to help achieve success;
- fostering individual commitment to goals and ensuring adequate support is available.

## Two-factor process: coach behaviours and coach systems

One way to think about this systematically is to consider a two-part process of development: first, the manner in which the coach interacts with the athlete, and second, the structures/systems within the talent development environment itself. To simplify, these two features can be termed coach behaviours and coach systems. For example, if a key behaviour has been identified as 'work hard at their own level', it may be agreed that for athletes to show this they need to set self-referenced goals, train, review and reward themselves based on a realistic perspective of their current stage of development.

One example of coach behaviours and coach systems that could encourage this is as follows: coach behaviour – provide individualised, goal related feedback; in other words provide feedback that is related to the quality of training, effort and progression in relation to the personal goals that have been set. This would need to be in combination with coach systems – monthly review meetings where the coach and the athlete sit down together to discuss goals, progress and evaluate feedback specifically in relation to what was set previously. This combination approach is illustrated in Figure 7.3.

Of course, these two elements do need to work coherently together. For example, a monthly meeting in which feedback is given unrelated to goals set or not referenced to processes within the athletes control would not facilitate the desired behaviour. As such, it is very important to see these processes as a working partnership. In fact, the more avenues in which this behaviour is reinforced (for example, role models, during training

**143**

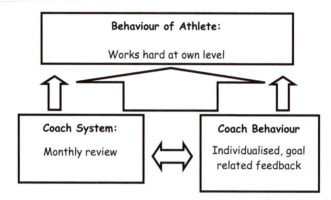

*Figure 7.3* An example of a coach system and coach behaviour that promote the required
behaviour (see Collins *et al.* 2010).

introduction talks, meetings, post-match conversations, parents and so on), the more
likely consistent results will emerge.

## Integration of concepts and keeping it simple

Finally, there is rarely only one answer, and as the coach will know their athletes better than
others they may have important insight into what is appropriate and required for progress. Of
course, there will also be sport specific and other context specific factors to be considered,
including individual coaching style preferences. Some of the behaviours that are identified
may well be relevant for more than one PCDE. For example, 'turning up on time to training' may relate to commitment, motivation and quality practice. In other words, promoting
certain behaviours may have multiple positive side effects and encourage integration with
one another, something that is helpful and the coach should be aware of. The more simple,
straightforward and integrated the behaviours, coach behaviours and coach systems are, the
more likely they will be successful and consistently used over time. The following examples
(Examples 7.1–7.4) and a blank template (Template 7.1) from Collins *et al.* (2010) illustrate
this potential similarity.

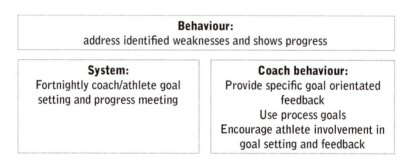

*Example 7.1*

| Behaviour: |
| :---: |
| Practice away from team |

| System: | Coach behaviour: |
| :---: | :---: |
| End of session debrief – including probable content for next session and therefore relevant tasks to practice | Ask individual athletes about extra practice<br>Praise fast learning due to extra practice<br>Provide role model examples of importance of extra work |

*Example 7.2*

| Behaviour: |
| :---: |
| Turn up to training sessions on time |

| System: | Coach behaviour: |
| :---: | :---: |
| Pre-published session start and finish times<br>Organised pre-session activity for early arrivals | Adhere strictly to start and finish times |

*Example 7.3*

| Behaviour: |
| :---: |
| Coherent understanding of athlete role (coach/athlete) |

| System: | Coach behaviour: |
| :---: | :---: |
| Team meet – clarify training and competition expectations and roles<br>Monthly individual review meeting | Clearly define roles and expectations<br>Be consistent |

*Example 7.4*

*Template 7.1* Blank template example

COMMITMENT BEHAVIOUR:

| Coach systems | Coach behaviours |
| :--- | :--- |
|  |  |

## CONCLUSION

Talent identification and development is an important part of youth sports coaching. Coaches and significant others at early stages play as important a role as those coaching or supporting at an elite level. Understanding the way in which young people develop to an elite level is central to designing effective training, competition and support programmes. Crucially, there appear to be many common pitfalls and misconceptions about the necessary requirements and characteristics of talented youngsters (such as early selection and specialisation, win focus). In short, it is important to take a long term perspective and recognise the necessity to build foundations for future development in a step by step manner. However, this is not to say that everyone develops in the same manner. Research suggests that development is often idiosyncratic and transitions between the various stages in development are likely to be the key challenge points and drivers to successful development.

Within this structure, providing coherent and consistent messages to young people throughout development is important, as is consideration of a holistic package of skills. Of course, performance, and the manner in which athletes apply themselves, is crucial at every stage. However, many people become too focussed on the outcomes of competition and training (for example, who won). Outcome focus has been shown to be negative and not particularly relevant for developing athletes. In fact, many successful elite athletes attribute their success to being able to stay self-focussed even under immense pressure to win. Building on this psychological perspective, the psychological characteristics of developing excellence have been shown to be key in the facilitation of self-regulating individuals capable of effective learning, performing consistently under pressure and ultimately developing successfully through to the elite level. As such, it is recommended that coaches consider systematically incorporating such psychological skills development and the necessary challenge to athletes into training. Some of the practical ideas presented in this chapter will help start this process.

## REFERENCES

Abbott, A., Collins, D., Martindale, R. and Sowerby, K. (2002). *Talent identification and development: An academic review.* (Edinburgh: sportScotland).

Bloom, B. S. (1985). *Developing talent in young people.* (Ballantine: New York).

Bull, S., Shambrook, C., James, W. and Brooks, J. (2005). Towards an understanding of mental toughness in elite English cricketers. *Journal of Applied Sport Psychology* 17: pp. 209–227.

Collins, D. and MacNamara, A. (2011). The rocky road to the top: Why talent needs trauma. *Sports Medicine* 42(11): pp. 907–914.

Collins, D., Martindale, R.J.J., Button, A. and Sowerby, K. (2010). Building a physically active and talent rich culture: An educationally sound approach. *European Physical Education Review* 16(1): pp. 7–28.

Côté, J. (1999). The influence of the family in the development of talent in sport. *The Sport Psychologist* 13: pp. 395–417.

Ericsson, K. A., Krampe, R. T. and Tesch-Romer, C. (1993). The role of deliberate practice in the acquisition of expert performance. *Psychological Review* 100: pp. 363–406.

Gould, D., Dieffenbach, K. and Moffett, A. (2002). Psychological characteristics and their development in Olympic champions. *Journal of Applied Sport Psychology* 14: pp. 172–204.

MacNamara, Á. and Collins, D. (2010). The role of psychological characteristics in managing the transition to university. *Psychology of Sport and Exercise* 11: pp. 353–362.

Martindale, R., Collins, D. and Daubney, J. (2005). Talent development: A guide for practice and research within sport. *Quest* 57: pp. 353–375.

Martindale, R.J.J., Collins, D., Wang, J., McNeill, M., Sonk Lee, K., Sproule, J. and Westbury T. (2010). Development of the talent development environment questionnaire (TDEQ) for sports. *Journal of Sports Sciences* 28(11): pp. 1209–1221.

Ward, P. and Williams, A. M. (2003). Perceptual and cognitive skill development in soccer: The multidimensional nature of expert performance. *Journal of Sport and Exercise Psychology* 25: pp. 93–111.

Wylleman, P. and Lavallee, D. (2004). A developmental perspective on transitions faced by athletes. In *Developmental sport and exercise psychology: A lifespan perspective*. M. Weiss (Ed.) (Morgantown, WV: Fitness Information Technology): pp. 507–527.

## FURTHER READING

Baker, J., Cobley, S. and Schorer, J. (2012). *Talent identification and development in sport: International perspectives*. (London: Routledge).

Collins, D., Richards, H. and Button, A. (2012). *Psychology for physical performance*. (Kidlington: Elsevier).

## WEB LINKS

www.sportni.net/NR/rdonlyres/991FF96E-C6DB-4700-A900-F4DF2732E81A/0/Participant DevelopmentinSport.pdf. Retrieved: 13 April 1014.

This link provides access to SportsCoachUK's 2010 report: 'Participant Development in Sport: An Academic Review'. It outlines the main research findings and provides clear implications for participant development in sport and/or physical activity involvement.

www.sportscotland.org.uk/sportscotland/Documents/Resources/DevelopingthePotentialof YoungPeopleinSport.pdf. Retrieved: 13 April 1014.

This link provides access to a sportScotland report outlining a pilot project with young people aiming to provide them with the skills to fulfil their potential through a sport context. Implications for all those involved with youth sport at any level.

Chapter 8

# Coaching tactics

*Shirley Gray and Edward Hall*

This chapter will focus on coaching tactics for games and highlight the importance of developing coach knowledge, particularly tactical knowledge, if coaches aim to improve their players' tactical and decision-making abilities. Details of game tactics, with reference to how tactics can be modified according to the developmental needs of the player, will also be provided. This chapter will also describe some of the approaches for developing player tactical performance that are available to coaches and the theories that explain how their players learn tactical skills. Finally, some practical examples are provided to demonstrate how coaching practices might be organised.

## COACH KNOWLEDGE AND COACH KNOWLEDGE DEVELOPMENT

What does it take to become an expert coach? In defining the characteristics of an expert coach, many researchers have attempted to distinguish between the skills, knowledge and experiences of experienced coaches compared to beginner, or novice, coaches. An interesting finding from this research is that expert coaches have spent many years as players, not just in one sport but, on average, in at least three sports accumulating more than 13 years playing experience (Gilbert, Côté and Mallet 2006). Perhaps less surprisingly, research has also uncovered that expert coaches have had more experience coaching and more time developing their coaching through reflective practices within authentic learning environments (Nash and Sproule 2009). Additionally, they have attended more coach education courses, spent more time learning from others, encountered and solved more problems and, as a result, have had many opportunities to enhance and deepen what they know about coaching, including the tactical components of coaching.

Emphasising the importance of the coach's tactical knowledge, Horton and Deakin (2008) reported that a highly regarded collegiate basketball coach spent approximately double the amount of time working with players to develop the tactical components of the game compared to providing instruction on technique. They also described their own investigation where they observed and interviewed five national coaches in the sports of basketball, soccer and wheelchair basketball. They found that tactical instruction constituted almost half of the time that the coaches spoke to athletes, supporting the notion that tactical instruction, and therefore tactical knowledge, plays a key role in coaching at an elite level.

It appears, therefore, that expert coaches have more coaching knowledge than novice coaches and that, as coaches become more expert, the role of tactical knowledge plays a greater role in their coaching practice. This knowledge enables the coach to make sense of the chaotic ebb and flow of tactical action information and make decisions, even during fast-paced competitive games involving numerous players. In describing coaches' decision-making skills from the bench during game play, Piltz (2004) explains how a more sophisticated level of game knowledge enables them to:

- observe the players of both teams;
- understand the patterns of play;
- evaluate the effectiveness of the game plan;
- decide on possible changes;
- predict the opposition's strategy and plan ahead;
- communicate information/plans effectively.

Expert coaches thus have more knowledge (particularly tactical knowledge), more connections between bodies of knowledge and a greater depth of knowledge representation used for problem solving compared to novice coaches. They use this knowledge to develop cognitive rules, or schemata, to make sense of the game or practice situations and inform their decision making. By contrast, novice coaches tend to make decisions based on specific, superficial and often isolated incidents during the game, without reference to such schemata. Take for example the game of field hockey. The novice coach notices the team cannot get the ball outside of their defensive circle and so spends the next training session going through tackling and/or clearing drills that develop and improve these basic skills. However, the more experienced coach may use his or her understanding of the game and previous knowledge to conclude that tackling and clearing skills are not the problem; the failure to clear is a result of the midfield players off the ball not moving to provide a target for the defending players. Consequently, this coach may work on movements and positioning off the ball, counter attacking and/or speed of transition when turning defence into attack. This is because experts are more proficient at recognising larger patterns of play within the game, patterns that are often linked to the team system, strategy or tactics (these terms will be clarified later on in this chapter). It is important to understand the significance of coach knowledge, not only because it is related to the degree of success experienced by the coach, but also because it helps to understand the process of coaching and how coaches learn; consequently, it can be used to develop future expert coaches.

## Knowledge development

One of the most important sources of learning for the coach is the workplace itself. Within the coaching environment, coaches have opportunities to reflect on their own practice, discuss issues with their athletes, observe other coaches and draw upon their previous coaching (and playing) experiences. These actions enable coaches to develop and even transform what they know about coaching practice, their athletes' learning and the activity itself.

Cassidy and Rossi (2006) expand on the notion of learning in the workplace by discussing the concepts of apprenticeship, mentoring and communities of practice as important sources of coaching knowledge and competencies. When coaches work with other coaches, they share and construct knowledge together, deepening their expertise and shaping their future actions. Additionally, many coaches are influenced as players by early role models and mentors who provide them with an initial framework for coaching. Bloom *et al.* (1998) state that previous coaches not only taught 'them the technical, tactical and physical skills but also shared philosophies, beliefs and values about coaching and dealing with people' (p. 273).

In attempting to explain how coaches use these experiences to develop their coaching knowledge, Nash and Sproule (2009) refer to situated learning theory. Situated learning theory advocates that connecting learning to coaches' interests and experiences increases the contextual relevance of knowledge. It is closely associated with the notion of constructivism in which 'learning is conceived as an active, constructive, collaborative and context-bound activity' (Kwakman 2003, p. 153). From this theoretical perspective, the coaching context is critical to the development of the coach's knowledge because of the key role that social interactions play in learning. Consequently, learning takes place in authentic settings and requires cognitive processes that promote the construction of new knowledge based upon the foundation of existing knowledge. Through social interaction, authentic activity and participation within communities of practice, coaches construct meaning in practical ways (Nash and Sproule 2009).

## Coach knowledge: declarative and procedural knowledge

To explain how coach knowledge develops and is structured, Abrahams and Collins (1998) refer to Anderson's Theory of Knowledge Acquisition (1982). This theory attempts to explain the content, structure and the development of knowledge and describes two forms of knowledge: declarative and procedural.

Declarative knowledge is an accumulation of a propositional network of facts (Anderson 1982), sometimes known as factual knowledge or conceptual knowledge. Due to the conceptual nature of this knowledge, it is usually evidenced by what coaches say about coaching or what they write about coaching (also known as 'why knowledge'). Although it is possible to produce action using declarative knowledge, because of the amount of interconnected pieces of information it is represented by, and the amount of space this takes up in working memory, this action takes time. This is an important issue in relation to decision making in coaching, as decisions often have to be made under challenging time constraints. To overcome these problems, declarative knowledge is reduced through the process of composition and proceduralisation, thus developing procedural knowledge (also known as 'doing knowledge'). Composition refers to the capability for several productions to be collapsed into one macro production (Anderson 1982). Proceduralisation refers to the capability for declarative knowledge to be removed from the conditions of a production (Abrahams and Collins 1998, p. 61). In other words, composition occurs when declarative knowledge is reduced to specific rules, or schemata, which are applied to solve the problem more efficiently. Proceduralisation is when declarative knowledge is removed and all that is left are the conditions of the problem and the solution. Importantly, this means that procedural knowledge is developed upon a foundation of declarative knowledge that through time, experience and learning becomes reduced to a series of if-then-do productions. Procedural knowledge needs little or no declarative knowledge to be stored in the working memory, which leaves capacity for a quick decision and/or attending to more than one piece of information at the same time. However, experts use both declarative and procedural knowledge to solve problems in a breadth-first manner (Abrahams and Collins 1998). This is where the coach identifies a number of rules, or possible solutions, to a problem and reflects upon each before deciding upon the most appropriate solution for the specific situation. This is critical when coaching tactics and decision making in games where there are often a number of possible solutions to a given tactical problem.

Understanding how coach knowledge is both developed and applied is a key consideration for those responsible for developing coach education programmes. It not only highlights that coaching and sports knowledge should be central to the coach education process, it also suggests that the development of both declarative and procedural knowledge is critical in the development of expert coaches. This is especially true for coaches who have extremely fixed beliefs about what coaching is and who have well-established methods for what they believe to be effective coaching. When these beliefs are found to be weak or inaccurate, coach education programmes should focus more on exposing and challenging those beliefs. This then has the potential to provide coaches with the tools to critique their practice, create new knowledge and develop new beliefs (Abrahams and Collins 1998). Unfortunately, this approach to coach education is not the norm because it is a highly time-consuming process. Coach education programmes tend to focus on coaching theory, sports specific techniques, tactics and supervised practice. However, they are often criticised for their inability to modify coaches' behaviour or philosophies once they have returned to their real coaching situation. More cognitively challenging coach education programmes appear to carry greater potential for providing coaches with the knowledge, including tactical knowledge, and skills to transform their coaching practice.

## UNDERSTANDING TACTICS IN GAMES

This section focuses more specifically on understanding game tactics and how they relate to player decision making in games. The games referred to are games that generally fall into one of three categories – team invasion games, central net/wall games or striking and fielding games. The games within these categories are highly dependent on tactical understanding, tactical awareness and the efficient execution of tactical skills.

### Team invasion games

Team invasion games involve one team having possession of an object (usually a ball) and in some manner moving that object through the opposing team's territory towards a goal or target so that they can score a point, goal, basket, try or touchdown. Examples of invasion games include soccer, rugby, field hockey and basketball. As one team has possession of the object, the opposing team endeavours to defend their territory so that the attacking team is unable to score. Additionally, the defending team aims to dispossess the attacking team so that it can move the object into the opposing team's territory with the intention of scoring. To win the game, one team must score more points than the other within the boundaries of the rules, the playing area and the time limits of the game.

## Central net and wall games

Central net and wall games include tennis, table tennis, volleyball and squash. Players do not interact in the same way as in team invasion games as they are usually separated by a boundary and/or a net. The games within this category vary according to the size of the court, the height of the net (if a net is part of the game), the object and whether or not the object is allowed to bounce. The aim of these games is to send an object into the court of the opposition so that it cannot be returned and the point is won.

## Striking and fielding games

Striking and fielding games include cricket, rounders, baseball and softball. As with team invasion games, they involve two teams playing in opposition to one another. However, there is less direct interaction between players in striking and fielding games as the attacking and the defending teams have very different objectives. When one team is attacking, the players have to strike the object, for example batting in cricket. When the other team is defending, the players are fielding the object, for example catching the ball in cricket. Only the batting team can score by playing the ball into a space away from the fielding team to create an opportunity for completing a 'run' or as many 'runs' as possible. Meanwhile, the defending, or fielding, team has to retrieve the ball as quickly as possible and send it back to a specified area to reduce the amount of time the attacker has to score. If the ball reaches that area before the player completes a 'run', then that player is deemed to be 'out'. In most striking and fielding games, the attacking player is also 'out' if one of the fielders catches the ball before it touches the ground.

## Game tactics

In all three games categories, players have to solve problems; problems relating to interpreting tactical information, the amount of space and time available and the choice of action to apply within the given situation (Grehaigne, Richard and Griffin 2005). Importantly, the success of the final decision made on the field of play is directly related to the player's tactical understanding of the situation. Even if the player produces a technically accurate motor-skill performance, this can only be deemed to be effective if the selection of the motor-skill is appropriate for the given tactical problem. Understanding game tactics, therefore, is a critical component of effective game performance and, therefore, a critical component of coaching games.

## Game tactics

Game tactics are directly linked to the rules of the game, the game principles and the selected team strategy. Often the terms 'tactics', 'strategy', 'principles' and 'rules' are used interchangeably, referring to the way in which the player or team will organise play to outwit and outplay the opponents. However, Grehaigne *et al.* (2005) suggest that tactics differ from rules, principles and strategy in that they are represented by the player in his or her actions and, therefore, are also directly related to the competency level of the player. Although the tactic applied by the player is often directly related to the predetermined game plan, or strategy, because of the ever-changing nature of the game, the tactical decision made can also be unrelated to strategy. For example, the coach of a rugby team may decide upon a second half strategy of keeping the ball tight amongst the forwards; but at times during the game, the fly half (number 10) may decide that, because of lack of forward support (possibly due to fatigue), the best option is to kick the ball long and out to the corners to ease the pressure and gain territory. This is a game tactic, but one that deviates somewhat from the team strategy.

The terms tactics, strategy, principles and rules and the relationship between these terms will be illustrated in the context of the game of tennis.

Rules ⟶ Principles of Play ⟶ Strategies ⟶ Tactics

*Figure 8.1* Relationship between tactics, strategy, principles and rules.

## TENNIS

**Rules:** The rules of the game govern how the game can be played. Players have to manage their performance according to the size of the court, the height of the net and the scoring system. For example, in tennis the serve must land inside the service box, the ball can only bounce once on the court and if the ball is played into the net or bounces outside of the court, then the opposing player wins the point.

**Principles of play:** Although the rules of tennis give the game its basic shape, to be effective within the game there has to be even more structure to the game. This is achieved through the application of game principles. Game principles are general game playing rules (they do not directly relate to boundaries, net or scoring) that provide the game with structure, enabling the player to reach the goal of winning the point or the game. Principles are rules that, if the players abide by them, will help achieve the goals more effectively. The basic principles that apply to the game of tennis are:

■ consistently returning the ball and moving to to cover (or defend) the centre of the opponent's target;
■ placement of the ball into the opponent's area of play to make it difficult to return;
■ control the flight of the ball using force (power), spin or deception to make a ball difficult to return.

**Strategy:** The strategy selected by the player is in some way informed by the principles of play. However, strategy elaborates on the principles of play by making connections with the knowledge and ability of the player, the opposition and the playing conditions. For example, a player may know that his or her opponent has a lower level of cardiovascular fitness or speed around the court. As a result, the player may plan in advance of the game to make the opponent move as much as possible along the baseline to induce fatigue and force an error.

| Central Net/Wall: **tennis** | Team Invasion: | Striking and Fielding: |
|---|---|---|
| Rules: **court, net, scoring, etc.** | | |
| Principles: **return the ball, move opponent, etc.** | | |
| Strategy: **play to the corners, play to the opponent's weakness, etc.** | | |
| Tactics: **play to the corners, move to the net if opponent slow to reach the ball, etc.** | | |

*Figure 8.2* Template for completion.

**Tactics:** Tactics are the actions carried out on the court to implement the strategy. A number of different tactics can be applied to implement the strategy. Furthermore, the tactics can become disassociated with the strategy according to the changing conditions caused by the players, previous decisions and the match conditions (for example the weather or decisions made by the referee/umpire). If the strategy of the player is to make the opposition move around the court, then the tactic could be to play the ball to alternate sides of the baseline. The tactic could also be to play the ball deep and then to play a disguised drop shot. Importantly, the tactics used by the player are directly linked to the information available to the player at that moment in time, as well as the player's technical abilities during the game.

Can you think of examples of each from another game? Perhaps a game from one of the other games categories? (See Figure 8.2.)

## TACTICS CONTINUED

Grehaigne *et al.* (2005) refer to the concept of action rules to help to explain the situated nature of applying tactics. Action rules are rules that make connections between game conditions and possible actions. They are directly linked to game tactics and are used to solve game problems. For example, in a team invasion game such as field hockey, if the defending team has been drawn towards one side of the pitch (as a consequence of the strategy adopted by the attacking team), then the tactical decision for the ball carrier would be to work out how to move the ball to the other side of the pitch to exploit the space. The position of the defenders around the ball and the availability of their teammates to receive a pass, in other words the game condition, would dictate the action selected to switch play.

In one situation the defenders are in front of the ball and the passer has an outlet to pass deep. Therefore, in this situation, the action rule, or the tactic, would be to turn and play the ball deep for the teammate to make the switch pass.

Direction of attack

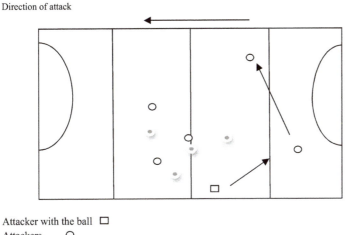

Attacker with the ball   □
Attackers        ○
Defenders

In another condition (see below), there may be space for the ball carrier to cut inside and play the switch pass themselves.

Direction of attack

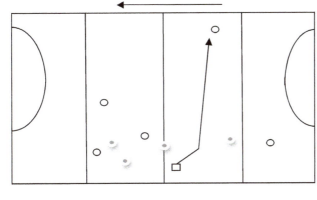

Attacker with the ball   □
Attackers       ○
Defenders

*Figure 8.3* Example of tactical play.

Both situations represent action rules, or tactical play, and both allow the player to play according to the team strategy.

## Decision making

Although action rules are useful to explain the application of tactics in games, they represent a fairly simplistic notion of tactical decision making; this is somewhat deceiving because decision making in games is a fairly complex process. To participate effectively in games, players must execute a variety of complex, goal-related motor skills within the context of a highly dynamic environment, under the combined pressures of time, space and within the boundaries set by the game rules and principles of play. Importantly, skill proficiency on its own does not equate to overall games proficiency. Critically, games proficiency involves making the appropriate decision about when and how to execute the skill to achieve the desired outcome both on- and off-the-ball in attack and defence, batting or fielding.

> Decision-making skill is the ability of a player to quickly and accurately select the correct option from a variety of alternatives that may appear before the ball is hit or kicked or an opponent moves.
>
> (Farrow and Raab 2010, p. 137)

Decision making in games begins when the performer searches for and selects relevant pieces of information about the game environment. Research has demonstrated that expert games players can not only gather more meaningful information more quickly than novice games players, but that they can use this information more effectively to make more appropriate decisions about what to do and how to do it. Experienced, or more accurately, expert players quickly recognise patterns and movements, not because they have greater memory, but because they have more detailed sport specific knowledge. Often this has been developed from a young age as they have taken part in a number of different games, usually from within the same games category. McPherson (2010) explains that this knowledge can be thought of as a 'specialised system of units of information (or concepts) that are stored in the long-term memory (LTM) and accessed when needed' (p. 157). McPherson (2010) also suggests that the decisions made on the field of play are directly linked to the player's declarative and procedural knowledge.

In the context of games play, declarative knowledge is factual information relating to the rules of the game, principles of play, strategy – and thus also includes tactical knowledge. This type of knowledge is important in decision making because it is the foundation upon which effective decision-making skills are developed. Expert performers have more sophisticated levels of declarative knowledge and are able to use this to create conceptual relationships between the tactical problems they are faced with in games and the possible ways of solving these tactical problems. For example, in soccer, if a striker is attempting to score a goal against a goalkeeper, he or she should understand at least some, or even all of the following: how the angles change when the goalkeeper moves, how the angles change when the player on the ball moves, options available when the angles are large, options available when the angles are small. Through time and exposure to the game (practice), the expert performer not only develops a deeper understanding of these principles but is also able to reduce and operationalise this knowledge to form procedural knowledge.

Procedural knowledge from a games playing perspective takes the form of a series of 'if-then-do' productions (for example, if the goalkeeper stays on the line, then shoot early). These scenarios are portions of knowledge that are directly applied to the situation, reducing demands on the performer and increasing the efficiency of performance. Novice performers, however, do not have the same depth of declarative knowledge as expert performers, nor are they able to identify the portion of their knowledge base (procedural knowledge) to carry out the task effectively. This can result in an incorrect response or a delayed and ineffective response.

In summary, developing a player's proficiency in games depends to a large extent on the parallel (and preferably linked) development of his or her knowledge about the rules, principles of play, strategy and tactics as well as the techniques required. Certainly, without the development of both declarative and procedural knowledge, the performer's ability to access the game will be seriously limited – important information for coaches to consider when planning a practice session.

## Defensive and offensive tactics in games

> Tactics are the individual and collective ways used by a team to try to best employ player skills in order to make the overall strategy work either by scoring or preventing goals.
> (Carling *et al.* 2005, p. 129)

It is important for coaches to remember that performance in games involves both decisions about what to do in attack and in defence. Such understanding of offensive and defensive tactical play is beneficial for coaches as it enables them to be more systematic in relation to their observations during training and games. It also helps coaches plan future player and team development sessions, and allows them to observe and recognise game patterns as well as game irregularities. This information can be used to provide player feedback and prepare training sessions.

In their book *Teaching Sport Concepts and Skills: A Tactical Games Approach,* Griffin, Mitchell and Oslin (1997) present a model of teaching games that focuses on the notion of solving tactical problems. In doing so, they categorise the tactical problems, both offensive and defensive, from each games category. This provides coaches with useful information about what tactics are, how they can be organised and how they can be taught. For team invasion games, the offensive tactical problems include maintaining possession, attacking the goal, creating space and using space. In defence, the tactical problems identified by Griffin *et al.* (1997) include defending space, defending the goal and winning the ball. For central net and wall games, the offensive tactical problems are setting up the attack, winning the point and attacking as a pair or team. The defensive tactical problems are defending space on own side of net, defending against an attack and defending as a pair or team. For striking and fielding games, the offensive tactical problems are getting on base, moving the runner and advancing to the next base. The defensive tactical problems are defending space by positioning, defending the bases and defending space as a team.

Grehaigne *et al.* (2005) take a slightly different and more detailed approach to the categorisation of tactical situations as they describe the concepts of action rules and principles of action (possible actions) in both attack and defence. As mentioned earlier, action rules are rules that relate to the game situation and are used to generate appropriate action.

The principal source of knowledge used to make the action decision is the player's tactical knowledge, therefore the action rules and the actions described by Grehaigne *et al.* (2005) reflect game tactics (see Table 8.4). Moreover, in adopting a games categories approach, the authors suggest that one rule, or a set of rules, can be applied to, or associated with, a class of games play problems.

| Offense action rules describe: | Defence action rules describe: |
|---|---|
| • Keeping the ball<br><br>• Playing in movement<br><br>• Exploiting and creating available space<br><br>• Creating uncertainty | • Defending the target<br><br>• Regaining possession of the ball<br><br>• Challenging the opponent's progression |

*Figure 8.4* Action rules.

For each action rule, they provide a list of possible options for action (or principles of action), which are more or less related to the three games categories (see Table 8.5). For example:

| *In offense:* | *In defence:* |
|---|---|
| • **Keeping the ball:** Keeping the ball away from one's opponents and close to oneself (team invasion games).<br>• **Playing the ball in movement:** Varying the rhythm and intensity of the moves (all three categories).<br>• **Exploiting and creating available space:** Using the depth and width of the field or court (all three categories).<br>• **Creating uncertainty:** Luring opponents into one zone to conclude in another (all three categories). | • **Defending the target:** Moving the ball away (all three categories).<br>• **Regaining possession of the ball:** Recovering the ball as close as possible to the opponents' goal (team invasion games).<br>• **Challenging the opponents' progression:** Reducing time, space and options (all three categories). |

*Figure 8.5* Options for action.

A model used in higher education to help future teachers of Physical Education (PE) understand offence and defence games and tactics to some extent brings together the two models described above. It adopts a similar structure to that proposed by Griffin *et al.* (1997), but with some of the detail provided by Grehaigne *et al.* (2005). This model emphasises three tactical components, beginning with a **game objective** (linked to the principles of play), followed by a description of **tactical situations** relating to that game objective and some of the **tactical options** available to the player within that situation. An example of the offensive and defensive tactical components for striking and fielding games can be observed below. The list of options is by no means exhaustive; they are simply presented as an introduction to understanding tactics and tactical play. PE students will soon be expected to add to and elaborate on the simple options that were initially presented to them, and this could help coaches develop tactical knowledge.

## Striking and fielding games

| Game objective | Tactical situation | Possible tactical options |
|---|---|---|
| Score runs/Win the game | Create time | Play the ball long<br>Play the ball into space<br>Vary the direction of the strike |
| | Use time efficiently | Move quickly once ball is played<br>Don't move (opt to strike again) |
| | Be ready, anticipate and react | Adopt a ready position (to strike/to run)<br>Anticipate the delivery<br>Observe the fielders (space/weakness) |

*Figure 8.6* Offensive tactics.

| Game objective | Tactical situation | Possible tactical options |
|---|---|---|
| Get the striker/ team out | Cover space | Position defenders to cover as much as the field as possible<br>Place fielders strategically according to strengths and weaknesses |
| | Reduce time | Move quickly to receive<br>Anticipate and react |
| | Send ball quickly to target | Receivers on (move to) base/targets<br>Throw direct<br>Send ball to target as a team (move and communicate) |

*Figure 8.7* Defensive tactics.

Once familiar with this model in the context of simple generic games from each category, more adult game forms are presented (as well as observation and discussion of game performance) to further develop both coaches' and players' understanding of specific game tactics. Importantly, coaches can also be encouraged to discuss the specific contexts in which each tactical option might be applied. Examples of this elaboration for offensive play in badminton and defensive play in field hockey can be seen in Tables 8.6 to 8.9.

| Tactical situation | Specific tactical options | Contexts |
|---|---|---|
| Get the shuttle over the net | Ready position<br>Base position<br>Reach and contact the shuttle<br>Play the shuttle early | Beginner player<br>Strong opponent<br>High tempo game |
| Make your opponent move | Play the shuttle into space<br>Play the shuttle to the back of the court then the front<br>Deceive your opponent by playing overhead clears and then a net shot<br>Deceive your opponent by playing high serve then a low serve<br>Deceive your opponent by adding disguise to the shot | Building to attack<br>Opponent is fatigued<br>Ineffective movement by opponent to the back of the court |
| Attack | Play a smash, drop shot or net shot into space<br>Play drop shot and net shot as close to net as possible<br>Play to opponent's backhand side | Opponent not returned to base position<br>Opponent base position deep on court<br>Opponent has demonstrated a weak backhand shot |

Figure 8.8 Offensive tactics in badminton.

| Tactical situation | Specific tactical options | Contexts |
|---|---|---|
| Close the attacker's space | Move towards the ball carrier, stick low to block the pass<br>Mark the player without the ball (front side/goal side)<br>Cover the space in behind the tackling defender<br>Defend the space in the circle as a unit, tight with no gaps | Inside defensive half<br>Attacker is a strong runner with the ball<br>Player off the ball waiting for the pass is in a goal scoring position |
| Put the attacker under pressure | Tackle early (jab/block)<br>Fake tackle then wait for error<br>Shadow<br>Stay goal side to ball carrier to anticipate cut back | Attacker makes mistakes under pressure<br>Attacker keeps head down under pressure and doesn't see the pass |
| Make the attacker move away from the target | Move towards the player from goal-side, forcing wide<br>Position stick to block the inside pass<br>Position body and stick to channel the ball carrier onto cover defender | Attacker is effective from the middle of the pitch<br>Attacker is strong and quick but runs with head down so doesn't see second defender |

Figure 8.9 Defensive tactics in field hockey.

## Tactical understanding: developmental considerations

Not only is it important that coaches have an in-depth understanding of both the offensive and defensive tactics involved in the games they coach, it is also important that they understand how tactics and decisions can vary according to the complexity of the situation that they create during practice. This knowledge is particularly important for those coaches who work with beginners and children as they attempt to develop their tactical understanding in an authentic, progressive and developmentally appropriate way.

For example, the notion of keeping possession of the ball in basketball could be presented to beginners simply by asking them to dribble away from other players during a warm-up activity. In this situation, the other players are not actually trying to steal the ball; they are simply trying to keep possession of their own ball. The reduced pressure means that each player has the physical time and space to control the ball, but importantly, they also have the mental time and space to reflect on what keeping possession means, why it is important and how they achieve it. Often this reflection is encouraged through coach questioning or by modifying the practice – pedagogical issues that will be explored in more depth later on in this chapter.

Below are some examples of how tactical knowledge can be presented in a more simple way and developed as the player and the game form progresses.

| Basketball: Keeping possession of the ball | |
| --- | --- |
| Simple tactical situation<br><br><br><br><br><br>Complex tactical situation | As an individual, keep your ball whilst moving into space away from the other players.<br>As a team (of three players), keep possession of the ball against the defensive team (of one or two players).<br>As a team (of three players), keep possession of the ball against the defensive team (of one or two players) and move towards the target as quickly as possible.<br>3v3 game. Keep possession and move towards the target to score. |
| **Tennis: Make your opponent move** | |
| Simple tactical situation<br><br><br><br><br><br>Complex tactical situation | Make your partner move away from base position during a cooperative rally.<br>Make your opponent move out to sidelines during a cooperative rally.<br>Make your opponent move out to sidelines during a cooperative rally. As soon as one player reaches the sideline, play the point out.<br>Baseline game. Make your opponent move to force an error and win the point. |
| **Softball: Send the ball quickly to the target** | |
| Simple tactical situation<br><br><br><br><br><br>Complex tactical situation | Retrieve a ball and send it to your partner as quickly as possible.<br>As a team (of three), retrieve a ball and send it to the designated area as quickly as possible.<br>As a team (of five), retrieve a ball and send it to the designated area(s) as quickly as possible.<br>Game: the objective of the game is for the fielders to retrieve the ball and send to a target(s) as quickly as possible. |

*Figure 8.10* Developing tactical knowledge.

## TASK

Take a tactical situation from the game of your choice and work out ways in which it could be presented in a simple way, within a simple context, and then progressively be made more complex.

## Approaches to coaching game tactics

This section describes the ways in which many coaches attempt to develop their players' performance abilities. Some of the approaches described will be familiar because students will either have been coached in this way, or have coached in this way. This is because, as alluded to at the start of this chapter, a great deal of coaching knowledge and coaching practice is based on personal experience. That is not to say this personal coaching style or previous experience of coaching is wrong. The intention of this section is to raise awareness of alternative coaching approaches for developing tactical play in the hope that it inspires an exploration of the possibilities and enhances coaching knowledge and practice.

### *Traditional approach*

Traditionally, games have been taught using a coach-centred, skill-focused approach with the aim of developing and refining specific game skills within the context of the game. Only once the skills have been practiced (and learned) are players provided with opportunities to apply the skills in the game. This is often the case with coaches who work with children in the early stages of learning the game, although this approach is also frequently used with coaches who work with adult players.

With this traditional approach, skills are usually practiced through repetition and progressive tasks that move from closed to open situations. As such, players can focus on key technical components of the skill and replicate a model performance provided to them by the coach or another player. Coaches facilitate this process by providing feedback to their players, feedback linked to the predetermined technical components of the skill. Coaches deliver their sessions in this way because they believe that the development of motor skill is critical to game performance and that without motor skill ability, the players will not be able to play the game.

Although many coaches appear to have experienced a great deal of success with this approach, and many players enjoy being coached in this way, there are a number of problems associated with this style of coaching, particularly in relation to developing players' tactical, or decision-making abilities. In adopting this skills-first approach, games players can find it difficult to transfer their previously 'learned' skills into the game. This is due to the fact that skills are practiced in isolation from the game context so players do not develop an understanding of the situations during the game that necessitate the application of such skills. In other words, they do not develop tactical knowledge or decision-making skills. By focusing on performing the technical aspects of the skill in a context removed from the game, players are not encouraged to consider and reflect upon the tactical context that relates to the specific skills being practiced. Moreover, they are not faced with dynamic situations that require them to reach a particular tactical, game-specific goal under the pressures of space and time. Instead, players focus solely on the correct execution of technique in a practice or drill situation that does not reflect the tactical demands of the game in any way. An example of this is when players of team invasion games, such as field hockey or soccer, are encouraged to dribble in and out of cones to refine their ball control technique. The cones do not move and, therefore, present a predictable and unrealistic environment that does not encourage the players to look up or recognise game structures or movements on which they can base their subsequent decision-making actions.

It is rare that a coach will spend an entire session working on specific skills in isolation from the game; many coaches will progress towards small-sided games and then into a game at the end of the session. At this point in the session, coaches who adopt this 'coach-centred' approach will continue to deliver technical feedback to the players, providing the main source of player knowledge. This means that they tell the players exactly what they should be doing in each situation. This usually comes in the form of procedural knowledge, or 'if-then-do' productions. In rugby for example, the coach may suggest in a two versus one situation that 'if' the defender comes to the ball carrier, 'then' the ball carrier should pass to the free player. One of the problems with developing procedural knowledge in this way is that it is not based upon a foundation of declarative knowledge. By coaching procedural knowledge in the absence of declarative knowledge, players learn what to do in a specific situation but are often unable to adapt when the situation changes (even slightly). Furthermore, when the players are reliant on the coach as their prime source of knowledge, they may become unable to perform as effectively when the coach is removed from the performance context. This can include the game context where it is almost impossible for the coach to give specific instructions to players each time they have a tactical decision to make.

One final issue with adopting a skills-first or skills-focused approach to coaching games is that the focus of learning and performance is on how the individual performs on-the-ball skills. This is problematic because the majority of a player's performance during games from all of the games categories takes place off-the-ball. It is extremely important to develop off-the-ball skills (both in offense and defence) so that players learn to prepare for their next decision and, in team games, develop their performance as a team. In all games, off-the-ball movement can have a positive effect on how a player receives the ball in terms of body position, time and space. This in turn, can influence the player's subsequent on-the-ball decisions. Additionally, when players know and carry out their role effectively off-the-ball, they are more likely to make decisions according to their team's strategy. In team games, effective off-the-ball movements also provide the ball carrier with more appropriate decision-making options.

Importantly, developing players' off-the-ball movements is as important for coaches who work with young children and beginners as it is for coaches who work with more expert players. When young children understand their role off-the-ball, they are more likely to understand the tactical components of the game and, in team games, how they contribute to the team performance. This has the potential to make them feel more satisfied with their role in the game, even though they may have not had much contact with the ball. This could have a positive impact on their intrinsic motivation and, in turn, their persistence in learning.

**163**

## *Alternative approaches to coaching games*

The alternative approaches to coaching games are generally described as player-centred and game-focused approaches. They stem from an idea that originated in the 1980s from two academics from Loughborough University, Rod Thorpe and David Bunker. They developed a games teaching approach called Teaching Games for Understanding (TGfU). The founders of this approach were concerned that pupils were leaving school with little success in playing games and knowing little about games. As a result, they aimed to challenge traditional games coaching by developing a more tactical approach where the goal of understanding the game through games play was the primary focus, rather than the acquisition of sport specific skill. Although TGfU evolved from concerns about the way games were being taught in schools, the principles that underpin TGfU in relation to learning and performance apply to the coaching context.

The model Thorpe and Bunker created consists of six stages of development (Figure 8.11). Within the first stage, players are presented with a game form that is consistent with their age and experience. For beginner players, this can involve the application of the concept of simplification. This is where the game specific movements are removed from the learning context and usually replaced by the skills of catching and throwing. This makes it easier for the players to focus their attention on aspects of the game other than the technical components. The next stage highlights the importance of understanding the rules of the game and the ways in which the rules give the game shape. This stage is known as the game appreciation stage. The third stage of the model is where players are introduced to game tactics through the development of their understanding of game principles, strategy and, of course, tactics. This tactical awareness then leads to a focus on decision making, where players are encouraged to think about what decision to make and then how to make it. It is at this point that players are directed towards the game-specific motor skills that they require to make the decisions on the field of play. Crucially, the players already understand why they are learning specific movements and the need to be able to apply those movements in a variety of dynamic, decision-making or tactical contexts. The final stage of the model is the performance stage, the point at which the coach might assess the player against relevant and appropriate criteria. That is to say, criteria that reflect the game and the learning process that the players have experienced through this TGfU approach.

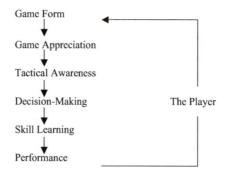

*Figure 8.11* Six stages of development.

Another similar approach to games coaching is the Tactical Approach (Griffin *et al.* 1997). The aim of the tactical approach is to combine the acquisition of motor skills and cognitive skills, both on- and off-the-ball. Unlike TGfU, the coach's primary role is to facilitate the concurrent development of game knowledge and game movements. The coach selects the tactical problem to be addressed and the player has to develop an understanding of the tactical problem by working out which appropriate game specific motor skills will be required to solve the problem. These skills are developed through question, answer and active participation in the game or game-like activity. The teacher has a less direct role in the learning process and players are given more responsibility for their own learning.

## The role of the coach

With coaching approaches such as TGfU and the Tactical Approach, the coach has a more 'hands-off' role in the coaching and learning process (see Chapter 1). Instead of providing the players with knowledge about how to perform skills in different situations, the coach has a less direct role, employing pedagogical techniques such as modified games, problem-solving tasks and questioning. The intention with these techniques is to encourage players to explore the game environment, to recognise tactical situations and work out for themselves the most appropriate tactical option and, with the Tactical Approach in particular, the most appropriate skill to execute according to their own strengths and weaknesses.

## Modified games

Modified or conditioned games are particularly useful in developing players' tactical abilities. In a modified game the rules, the court/pitch dimensions and even the equipment is adapted to suit either the developmental needs of the player, or to focus on a particular tactical aspect of the game. Simplifying the game but retaining key game-like features is important because it provides the player with time and space (both physically and mentally) to consider, execute and evaluate the tactical options available. Decision-making in games is complex and requires the player to recognise the problem, gather information about the problem, identify possible solutions, make a decision and then put the decision into action (Griffin and Sheehy 2004). Modified games offer players opportunities to carry out these tasks in meaningful learning environments that players find interesting and enjoyable and that allow them to draw upon previous game experiences to help solve tactical problems and make tactical decisions.

Games modification, for example, might be useful when coaching the game of cricket. The coach may wish to develop the batters' understanding of, and tactical abilities to, decide when to run and when not to run. In doing so, the coach modifies the game by limiting the fielding options, for example by reducing the number of fielders or restricting their movements. This should encourage the batters to recognise that their decision is based on how much time they have in relation to the line, distance and trajectory of the ball as well as the decisions and positions of the fielders. It may also encourage the batters to play certain shots (perhaps their more successful shots, high percentage shots or shots that play towards an area of weakness in the fielding team) to become more confident about running.

**165**

The tactical complexity of this game could be simplified even further for beginners, where the coach may simply wish to encourage the players to understand that particular types of shot will create more time to make the run (playing the ball into space). The game could be further modified by slowing down the delivery (perhaps by changing the type of ball), giving the batters more time to play the ball to different targets before beginning their run. This provides the batter with knowledge of the relationship between shot selection and the number of runs scored.

The two cricket scenarios described above highlight the idea discussed earlier which suggested that coaches should understand the ways in which tactics can be simplified so that they match the players' problem solving abilities. As the players' tactical understanding and ability increases, so the coach can increase the tactical complexity of the modified game. Understanding tactical complexity, therefore, allows the coach to coach at a developmentally appropriate level (Griffin and Sheehy 2004).

## Problem solving and questioning

Both of these modified games encourage the players to consider the relationship between the game context and the opportunities they have for action, as well as the impact their action has on the game. These processes can be enhanced further when the coach presents additional problem solving tasks, or poses questions to the players about the situation, their actions or both. Take the first example where the coach aims to develop the players' ability to make decisions about when to run and when not to run. The coach could set the initial task of asking the player to make a run off every contact with the ball. This experience will then provide a platform for reflection and discussion about the shots that resulted in runs and those that did not.

Take the second example, where the coach aims to encourage the players to understand that certain types of shot will create more time to make the run. The coach could ask questions at various points during the game such as, 'how many runs did you make when you hit target A?' or 'what shots did you play when you did not manage to make any runs?' Such questions help to guide the player to identifying solutions to tactical problems and are extremely beneficial when working both with beginners and more experienced players.

Higher order thinking is encouraged through effective questioning, thus promoting reflective thinking, decision making and communication (See Chapter 10). It is important, therefore, that coaches develop their ability to question players and enhance their problem solving skills, tactical knowledge and decision making. Questions should be worded in such a way that the player understands the questions, and the questions should relate to the goal of the session. If the goal of the session is to develop tactical understanding, then the questions asked by the coach should be related to the game tactics.

This section has primarily focused on introducing more player-centred, game-focused approaches to coaching tactics in an attempt to invite readers to reflect on their own experiences and practices, and perhaps begin the process of transforming the way they coach. In doing so, it highlights once again, the importance of both coach and player knowledge in the development of tactical knowledge and decision making in games. This suggests that a more hands-off, problem solving approach may be more effective in the development of tactically aware and proficient games players. McPherson (2010) provides a useful summary of the key considerations that will facilitate this process:

- Take into account what aspects of knowledge base you are focusing on when designing a practice. Keep in mind that different players in different positions will require different things.
- Reward good decision making.
- Devise practice games that simulate games situations that promote the use of tactical knowledge and skills.
- When learning a tactical skill, other skills may suffer; allow players practice time to learn how to allocate attention resources and so on.
- Allow time for players to analyse their own and other players' tactical behaviours.
- Analyse players' performance skills periodically during practices and completion. Use video to play back to the players – they may not always be aware of what they are doing. This can also be used to help them to develop profiles about their own performance.
- Embrace and use technology (see Chapters 14 and 15).

The final two points here are important in relation to developing player performance and also in relation to how the coach gathers information about player performance. Gathering information about players' tactical performance is not easy due to the complex visual nature of games play and the somewhat subjective nature of tactical decision making. Although many experienced coaches will simply observe a game and pinpoint tactical strengths and weaknesses with great precision, there are a number of resources that they can access to evaluate their team's or athlete's performance. However, many of the options available to them focus very much on the player's performance of specific motor skills during the game, rather tactical decision-making performances.

An alternative option for coaches who wish to understand and evaluate their team's tactical performance is to consider using instruments such as the Team Sport Assessment Procedure (TSAP) (Grehaigne et al. 1997) or the Games Performance Assessment Instrument (GPAI) (Griffin et al. 1997). The TSAP was designed to analyse players' offensive play by measuring player involvement and player efficacy. The data gathered using this procedure is based on two aspects of game play – how the player gains possession of the ball and how the player distributes the ball (or shoots). From these game components a set of performance indices are derived, including conquered ball, received ball, offensive ball, successful shot and lost ball. These indices are used to compute a performance score based on the player's observed behaviours. The GPAI is a similar measurement tool, designed to measure a range of game performance components, for example, decision making, skill execution support, cover and guard. One of the advantages of using this tool is that it can be adapted to measure one or more of these specific aspects of game performance, which are usually directly related to the coaches' learning objectives. A set of criteria is developed for each component and a score is calculated based on a simple tally system to record the number of observed inappropriate/unsuccessful or appropriate/successful applications of each component during games performance (both on- and off-the-ball). It is important that coaches are able to evaluate their players' tactical knowledge, or decision making, if they are to be sure that effective learning has taken place as a result of their coaching.

## PLAYER LEARNING: A THEORETICAL PERSPECTIVE

This section will briefly outline three of the key theories of learning that underpin many of the coaching styles adopted by sports coaches today and that relate well to the coaching approaches described earlier in this chapter. The intention is not to pitch one theory against the other in an attempt to compete for relevance or superiority. Indeed, they all offer a useful, and at times similar, insight into the relationship between player learning and the coaching environment. The purpose of the following section is to provide readers with different ways of viewing the coaching and learning process so that they can understand in more depth their own practice and become inspired to further their knowledge of each theory.

### Information processing theory

Farrow and Raab (2010) suggest that the ingredients for becoming an expert decision maker include perception, attention, memory and skill execution. From this perspective, learning in games is cognitive in nature and can be explained using information processing theory. Information processing looks inside the mind of the player to explain how he or she learns to execute movements and make tactical decisions. It explains how players select and organise incoming information from the game environment and relate it to their previous experiences. Consequently, memory, meaningful information and prior experiences all play a key role in learning and decision making in sports.

Information processing theory is a cognitive theory of learning that is linked to the way in which we understand how computers work. In other words, data from the game environment is input by the players through their senses and is then interpreted by the central nervous system (CNS) so that the appropriate movements can be organised. The output is the execution of the movement itself.

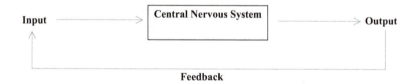

*Figure 8.12* Information processing.

Perceptual abilities differ from player to player, which means that each player will interpret game information in a different way. Perceptual skills are critical to games performance because they enable players to focus their attention on relevant pieces of information within the game environment. Research indicates that more experienced players are better than novice players at focusing their attention on relevant 'cues' because they hold more information in their long-term memory (LTM) about past game experiences and use this to compare to the incoming information stored, albeit briefly, in the short-term memory (STM) (McMorris and Hale 2006). This interaction between the LTM and the STM is known as working memory and results in both movement selection and storage of additional information in the LTM for future use. Once the movement is initiated, players begin to process feedback about the movement and the outcome of the movement. This information can also be stored in the LTM to inform future performances. Consequently, the more individuals practice, or the more experience individuals have, the more information players have to base their perception and their decision making on during future performances.

From an information processing perspective, the coaches adopt a more direct and hands-on approach to coaching. Their role is to provide sufficient practice opportunities so that relevant information can be stored in the LTM by:

- assisting the player in managing information by first breaking it down into manageable chunks (the size of the chunks will vary according to age and experience);
- drawing the player's attention towards relevant cues during performance or demonstrations;
- reinforcing positive or appropriate behaviours through the use of feedback.

## Constructivism

Constructivism is another cognitive theory that attempts to explain how players learn. From a constructivist perspective, 'learning is conceived as an active, constructive, collaborative and context-bound activity' (Kwakman 2003, p. 153). As with the development of coaching knowledge discussed previously in this chapter, player knowledge is socially constructed and developed by engaging in authentic activity. New knowledge and personal meaning are created by selecting, organising and integrating incoming knowledge and experience with prior knowledge and experience (Griffin and Sheehy 2004).

Constructivism places the learner at the centre of the learning process and encourages critical thinking, critical inquiry and problem-based learning (Macdonald 2004). The coach can support the development of these skills by making player knowledge explicit and providing opportunities for players to share their knowledge with others, thus forming a community of practice. As with the game-focused approaches described earlier in the chapter (for example TGfU), players should be placed in game situations where they are faced with tactical problems to solve and where coaches use questioning to guide the solutions to the problems. Importantly, when these learning environments are created, content is more meaningful, learned more easily and learners are therefore more motivated (Macdonald 2004).

## Dynamical systems theory

One of the problems with both information processing theory and constructivism is the emphasis that they place on the role of memory and prior knowledge in learning and decision-making. In highly dynamic and fast-moving games, the dynamical systems theorist would argue that memory and prior knowledge are of little use. Additionally, although constructivism provides a useful explanation of how game knowledge is acquired, it does not provide adequate information in terms of how functional movements emerge during performance. Instead, dynamical systems theorists suggest that decision-making movement occurs as a result of direct perception – the environment, the rules of the game, the equipment, the position and

**169**

movements of the other players directly provide the individual with opportunities for move-ment, otherwise known as affordances, without the need for cognitive processing (McMorris and Hale 2006). Moreover, games are viewed as complex dynamical systems that are highly adaptive, sensitive to change and characterised by the propensity for patterns of movement to emerge, or self-organise (see Chapter 5).

The dynamical systems theorist approach to understanding performance in games is based on the concept that behaviours and patterns emerge as a result of the interaction of a number of constraints found within the players, the game/task and the environment. The player inter-acts with the game environment to search for functional movements that meet the demands of the task at hand. Moreover, when players become attuned to key pieces of environmen-tal information, they begin to develop information-movement couplings that regulate their behaviour. Examples include the soccer player who is able to move to trap the ball as it swings through the air; or in rugby, the player with the ball who makes the off-load pass just as the defender commits to the tackle. Key to developing these couplings is exploration. Exploratory behaviour, or trial and error in learning, enables learners to identify sources of information that support their own unique possibilities for movement; with experience comes the ability to know where in an environment to search for affordances that will allow players to achieve their goal (McMorris and Hale 2006).

In terms of applying dynamical systems theory to coaching tactical decision making in games, there are a number of similarities with the constructivist approach. There is a move away from a coach-centred approach, towards an approach which encourages the player to search for the most appropriate movement solutions to a game problem. Practice, therefore, is organised in a way that allows the performer to search for all of the appropriate variations in skill to reach a specific game-related objective. The coach monitors and guides the players' search rather than giving specific information about what to do and how to do it. Additionally, the coach can guide the search for movements by manipulating the task constraints within the practice. This can be achieved by changing the size of the playing area, the number of players, the rules of the game and the equipment used; all very similar to the concept of modified games described earlier in the chapter.

## PRACTICE IDEAS FOR DEVELOPING TACTICAL SKILLS

The final section of this chapter will provide the reader with some examples of the ways in which tactical skills can be developed. The intention is not for coaches to replicate these practice ideas per se, but to think about how they relate to the coaching approaches high-lighted earlier in the chapter, how they relate to theory and how they relate to their own practice. It is hoped that coaches will then reflect on these issues to consider the ways in which they might develop their own practice to enhance their players' tactical understanding and decision making. Although only three examples are provided, the principles that underpin the practice ideas can be transferred between games within each game category, as can many of the observation and discussion tasks.

The practices below are described according to the **objective** of the task followed by the **tactical problem to be solved,** both of which should be presented and understood by the players before they begin play. The **organisation** of the practice is then described, including an explanation of the role of the attackers and the defenders. Finally, suggestions for **observation tasks** and **questions** to initiate discussion are offered in an attempt to enhance the players' tactical knowledge during the exercise. This knowledge development has the potential to have a positive impact on the players' decision-making skills during play. Importantly, coaches should consider the age and experience of the learners before presenting the observation tasks and tactical questions. Additionally, as readers reflects on each scenario, they should consider how the tactical problem could be made simpler or more complex according to the developmental stage of their athletes. Readers are also encouraged to consider the impact this would have on the way in which the game is organised (or modified).

## Example 1: developing simple tactical understanding in generic games

**Practice objective:** To develop players' understanding of keeping possession of the ball in team invasion games.

**Tactical problem:** Work out the most effective ways of keeping the ball away from the defending players.

**Practice organisation:** This practice can be carried out either in the context of a specific team invasion game, or the practice area can be split so that some of the players perform with a soccer ball and some with a field hockey stick and ball. Any two team invasion games can be selected, but coaches should consider the size of the playing area as well as the surface to take player safety into account.

**Modified game:** Five attackers and three defenders. All of the attackers have a ball.

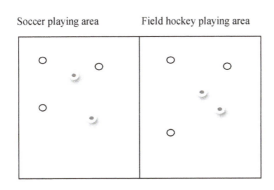

Attackers ○
Defenders ●

Defenders: try to get as close to the players with the ball as possible. Do not try to steal the ball (the defenders can be made to walk initially). Stay with them for three seconds then move to another attacker.

Attackers: move with the ball so that the defenders cannot get close to you.

*Figure 8.13* Template for task.

**Observation tasks:**

■ Observe one attacker and identify three things that the attacker does that allows him or her to stay away from the defender for more than five seconds.

**Discussion task/questions:**

■ Defenders explain to the attackers what made the task easy for them and what made it more difficult.
■ How did you know where the defender was? Why is this important?
■ How did you decide where to move?
■ What made this task easy/difficult?
■ Why is it important not to let the defender get too close to you?

## Example 2: developing tactical understanding in basketball

**Practice objective:** To understand the concept of defending the space under the basket as a team.

**Tactical problem:** What is the most effective way of organising your defensive team to force the attackers to shoot from close to, or outside, the 3-point line?

**Practice organisation:** Depending on the ability and experience of the players, this practice can start with a team of three, four or five. It can also be organised so that there are either more attackers than defenders or more defenders than attackers. The size of the playing area can also be manipulated.

Begin the practice with a rebound off the backboard to be retrieved by the new attacking team. As soon as the ball is released towards the backboard, the new defending team should move to defend their basket. The game is then played out.

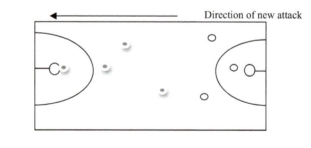

Defenders: force the attackers to shoot from close to the 3-point line.
Attackers: attack the basket and make the shot as early as possible.

*Figure 8.14* Template for task.

**172**

## Observation tasks:

- Observe the defending team and identify how they position themselves to defend the basket area.
- How many shots come from close to the basket? How many shots come from close to the 3-point line?
- What skills to the defenders exhibit when the shots are made from close to the 3-point line?

## Discussion task/questions:

- Attackers explain to the defenders what made the task easy for them and what made it more difficult.
- After three attacking plays, discuss the strengths and weaknesses of the defensive strategy you adopted. Develop the weaknesses for the next three attacking plays.
- What was the most effective defensive strategy and why?
- What are the skills you exhibited to make the defensive strategy effective?
- Why would you choose to adopt this strategy during a competitive game of basketball?

## Example 3: developing tactical understanding in badminton

**Practice objective:** To understand when to attack using the smash.
**Tactical problem:** What are the situations during your games when the smash is most successful?
**Practice organisation:** This practice can be played on either a half court or a full court depending on the ability or experience of the player. Players should alternate the serve. Play a rally of overhead clears. The player who serves can play a smash instead of a clear at any time. The player receiving the smash should attempt to return the smash and then the practice begins again. If play breaks down before the smash, begin the rally again.

## Observation tasks:

- Observe the movement of the player just before he or she plays the smash.
- Observe the flight of the shuttle just before the smash.
- How many smash shots are successfully returned? How many smashes are not effectively returned?

## Discussion task/questions:

- Can you explain why you decided to smash?
- Describe your movement pre-smash when the smash was effective.
- Describe the flight of the shuttle pre-smash when the smash was effective.
- Describe the situations when you decided not to smash.
- How will this practice influence your game performance?

# REFERENCES

Abraham, A. and Collins, D. (1998). Examining and extending research in coach development. *Quest* 50: pp. 59–79.

Anderson, J. R. (1982). Acquisition of a cognitive skill. *Psychological Review* 89: pp. 369–406.

Bloom, G. A., Durand-Bush, N., Schinke, R. J. and Salmela, J. H. (1998). The importance of mentoring in the development of coaches and athletes. *International Journal of Sport Psychology* 29: pp. 267–281.

Carling, C., Williams, M. A. and Reilly, T. (2005). *Handbook of soccer match analysis: a systematic approach to improving performance*. (Oxon: Routledge).

Cassidy, T. and Rossi, T. (2006). Situating learning: (re)examining the notion of apprenticeship in coach education. *International Journal of Sports Science and Coaching* 1(3): pp. 235–246.

Farrow, D. and Raab, M. (2010). A recipe for expert decision making. In *Developing sport expertise: researchers and coaches put theory into practice*. Farrow, D., Baker, J. and MacMahon, C. (eds.) (NY: Routledge).

Gilbert, W., Côté, J. and Mallett, C. (2006). Developmental paths and activities of successful sport coaches. *International Journal of Sports Science and Coaching* 1: pp. 69–76.

Grehaigne, J. F., Godbout, P. and Bouthier, D. (1997). Performance assessment in team sports. *Journal of Teaching in Physical Education* 16: pp. 500–516.

Grehaigne, J. F., Richard, J. F. and Griffin, L. L. (2005). *Teaching and learning team sports and games*. (NY: Routledge Falmer Taylor and Francis Group).

Griffin, L. L. and Sheehy, D. A. (2004). Using the tactical games model to develop problem solvers in physical education. In *Critical inquiry and problem solving in physical education*. Wright J., Macdonald, D. and Burrows, L. (eds.) (London: Routledge): pp. 33–48.

Griffin, L., Mitchell, S. and Oslin, J. (1997). *Teaching sport concepts and skills: a tactical games approach*. (Champaign, IL: Human Kinetics).

Horton, S. and Deakin, J. M. (2008). Expert coaches in action. In *Developing sport expertise: researchers and coaches put theory into practice*. Farrow, D., Baker, J. and MacMahon, C. (eds.) (NY: Routledge).

Kwakman, K. (2003). Factors affecting teachers' participation in professional learning activities. *Teaching and Teacher Education* 19: pp. 149–170.

Macdonald, D. (2004). Understanding learning in physical education. In *Critical inquiry and problem solving in physical education*. Wright, J., Macdonald, D. and Burrows, L. (eds.) (London: Routledge): pp. 16–29.

McMorris, T. and Hale, T. (2006). *Coaching science: theory into practice*. (London: John Wiley & Sons).

McPherson, S. L. (2010). Tactics: using knowledge to enhance sport performance. In *Developing sport expertise: researchers and coaches put theory into practice*. Farrow, D., Baker, J. and MacMahon, C. (eds.) (NY: Routledge).

Nash, C. S. and Sproule, J. (2009). Career development of expert coaches. *International Journal of Sports Science and Coaching* 4(1): pp. 121–138.

Piltz, W. (2004). *Reading the game: a key component of effective instruction in teaching and coaching*. In 2nd International Conference: Teaching Games and Sport for Understanding. Proceedings (pp. 79–89).

# Section 3

Coaches must be supported and well informed if they are going to be able to meet the needs of the population they are coaching. Understanding how coaches learn and develop can help this development process. Coaching is not an easy task, although it can be extremely rewarding, and sport coaches need to be aware, and take advantage, of many opportunities to upskill. This section uses the experiences and real life dilemmas of coaches to demonstrate the links between theory and practice and, most importantly, to show how theory informs practice.

■   Chapter 9 evaluates the ways in which coaches can learn and develop with specific emphasis on critical thinking skills and decision making. Critical thinking is the process of applying reasoned and disciplined thinking to a subject, in this case sport. These skills are essential for development and, like other skills, they improve with practice. Critical thinking includes a complex combination of skills and can be acquired through experience as well as formal education processes.

■   Chapter 10 examines the many benefits of highly developed emotional intelligence. Developing better coaches means they remain in post longer, are more effective and feel better about their jobs. It has been found that Olympic athletes, world class musicians, and chess grand masters all have one specific attribute in common: all participate in consistent and repetitive training over a prolonged period of time. This implies they have an emotional strength in the area of self-discipline. Coaches with a high level of emotional intelligence will be more effective, able to motivate and relate better to players and support staff, have improved problem solving and decision-making capabilities and be able to resolve conflicts in the workplace. An important aspect of emotional intelligence is the notion that it is trainable, and therefore, coaches could seek to enhance it.

■   Chapter 11 discusses mentoring as a coach development tool. Within the practical coaching situation, mentoring can be a valuable tool for coaches, enabling them to learn by relating theory into actual coaching environments. The mentor can be instrumental in helping to develop many skills necessary for self-development, for example, decision making, self-reflection and critical thinking. Although mentoring has recently become a buzzword in industry, education and sport coaching, as with many recent innovations the implementation and subsequent evaluation are often lacking.

■   Chapter 12 reviews reflective practice in the context of sport coaching. Reflective practice can refer to the ability to analyse one's own practice, the incorporation of problem solving into learning by doing or application of critical theory to the examination of professional practice. The importance of reflection as part of the learning process has been emphasised by many investigators. Studies have indicated that when coaches have been exposed to the principles of reflective practice, they are more likely to consider their coaching practice in a wider context use of coaching portfolios or journals.

- Chapter 13 investigates communities of practice as a coach development tool. Exponents of situated learning within coaching argue that through social interaction, authentic activity and participation within communities of practice, sport coaches are better able to construct meaning in practical ways so that knowledge can be applied outside of formal learning settings. The culture created and sustained within an organisation has a significant effect upon the engagement of individuals within the organisation and their subsequent commitment to the philosophy and goals espoused by the establishment.

The authors feel strongly that coaches need to know how to coach before gathering sport-specific information, for example, skills practices. This 'how to' approach should address fundamentals of planning, pedagogical or presentation skills, as well as aspects of participant preparation. At this early stage the basics of reflective practice should be introduced, possibly focussing on session and coach evaluation. The purpose, at this point, should be to familiarise the coach with the process and to engage with the concept as a developmental tool. Much can be learned from other professions, for example, teaching and the medical professions, about the implementation of these systems.

## Chapter 9

# How coaches learn and develop

*Christine Nash*

Think about the following example: during a field hockey game, a defence player misses a tackle that leads to the opposition scoring a goal. A novice coach may wish to solve this problem by practicing tackling in training, whereas a more expert coach may note that the problem occurred not just because of a missed tackle but also due to a lack of cover and players being out of position. During training, rather than concentrate on the surface issue of one missed tackle, the coach attempts to solve the more abstract problem of poor positional play.

To absorb, analyse and apply all their knowledge, coaches must have some understanding of how to 'sift' and 'prioritise their thinking' to develop the most appropriate coaching intervention. As described in this example the coach may be involved in a multitude of distinct activities, but the basic task is to develop and improve the performance of teams and individuals. The coach has to develop a season's plan, improve techniques, skills and tactics for participation and competition, enhance all aspects of mental and physical preparation and manage the individual or team in competitions. To do this effectively, the coach must use many different types of knowledge to solve problems and ultimately make decisions. Although this chapter will not attempt to define coach education with any precision, it will examine how coaches learn and apply these skills within the coaching environment. Coach education is operationalised by relying on how coaches go about their practice. In other words, if those involved in practice describe it as coach education, then it is coach education. The main advantage of operationalising, rather than defining, coach education is that by relying on self-identification, it is the practitioners who are describing what constitutes coach education rather than researchers. It is therefore more inclusive of those working in the field of coach education. A negative consequence of operationalising the term this way is that if those involved in practices describe it as coach development or coach*ing* education rather than coach education, then these practices may be excluded.

Operationalising coach education resulted in countless programmes being identified as coach education, including:

- coach qualification/accreditation courses;
- programmes for developing coaches;
- courses and programmes sponsored by national sporting/coaching associations in conjunction with tertiary institutions;
- undergraduate degree programmes specifically in sports coaching, or endorsed in sports coaching;

- post-graduate courses in coach education, through either specific or general post-graduate degrees in sports coaching;
- continuing or ongoing professional development courses in either sport related contexts or other areas, such as IT, as identified by coach review.

These programmes can be grouped into two main categories:

1    Formal coach education, such as programmes organised and delivered by sport or coaching organisations or educational institutions. These courses may operate at a variety of levels, both undergraduate and postgraduate. The educational qualifications may or may not directly correspond to a sporting or coaching organisation qualification. For this reason, coaches are advised to check that this formal qualification is going to both help their development and be recognised in their field.

2    CPD/professional learning that may or may not accrue coach qualification/accreditation points. Benefits of CPD programmes are said to be improved retention, enhanced learning and raised standards (Nolan 2004; Whitmore 2002), whilst more recent research has demonstrated that the introduction of compulsory CPD requirements has provided, not surprisingly, 'motivation' to participate in CPD activities (Sturrock and Lennie 2009). Effective CPD in the field of coaching should engender a sense of responsibility for both participating in and valuing CPD, where coaches control and self-regulate their CPD. The institution and implementation of a CPD framework will also meet the acknowledged coaching workforce needs in the UK, which indicate that there are clear and consistent signs of skills shortages and gaps in knowledge in the coaching profession (North 2009).

There is evidence to suggest coaches are able to bring elements from other areas of learning to benefit their coaching. Callary and colleagues (2011) highlight the example of a ski coach using knowledge gained from a mechanical engineering degree. The coach considers this degree to be more beneficial to enhancing his or her knowledge base than traditional degrees such as sports science or physical education.

As discussed earlier coaches can also learn in a more *ad hoc* manner. As more attention is paid to sports coaching and coach education, it is possible that discussions will turn to what sort of coach education is required to prepare particular coaches. Feiman-Nemser (2012) observed that when these discussions occurred within teacher education people tended to emphasise conceptual or structural issues. Contemporary developments in coach education, such as the involvement of the tertiary education sector, universities and colleges, can be viewed as structural issues. These often reflect economic and political considerations rather than 'clear thinking' about what coaches 'need to know' or how they can be assisted to acquire this knowledge. Lyle (2002) noted that coach educators will increasingly be required to clearly define and articulate the rationale for their programmes. For example, Campbell (1993) contended that coaches need to have sport specific technical and tactical knowledge as well as general performance related knowledge. Despite arguing for a common core of knowledge, in highlighting the similarities and differences between various coach education programmes across the world, Campbell exposed the limitations of assuming that there was, or ever could be, one universal subject matter in coach education.

In their analysis of published coaching education research from 1995 to 2005, McCullick, Mason, Vickers and Schempp (2006) found only nineteen articles were published during this period. They went on to say that understanding how youth sport coaches construct coaching knowledge will assist directors of youth sport and designers of coach education programmes to plan learning outcomes that will enhance the generation of coaching, and coaches', knowledge. When Cushion, Armour and Jones (2003) discussed various professional development strategies such as apprenticeship and mentoring, and the role of experience in learning to be a coach, they reflected a practical orientation to coach education, which emphasises the case for informal or experiential learning.

## HOW COACHES LEARN

Coach learning tends to be idiosyncratic – few coaches follow a systematic development route that is standardised for coaches within different sports and stages of development. Few coaches attribute their development to coach education programmes (Jones and Wallace 2005), as many have decided that formal qualifications have little value in developing their knowledge in coaching (Mallett *et al.* 2009). Currently there is no evidence base linking coach education to improved coaching, although anecdotal support exists. Coaches also develop at different rates, which may be dependent upon their own interest in learning but also the appropriateness of learning opportunities available. There does appear to be a number of individual routes to becoming an elite coach, including interaction with other coaches, reflection and mentoring (see Chapters 11, 12 and 13). Given the recent proliferation of coach education opportunities, both formal and informal, there is still little evidence that elite coaches engage with existing coaching awards as tools for their development (Irwin, Hanton and Kerwin 2004).

From previous chapters this would infer that sport coaches need to be aware of learning theory, motivational climate and knowledge construction as well as the technical detail of their sport. Understanding age-related changes as well as perceptions, physical competencies, emotions, social influences and achievement behaviours is critical for the effective coach. A coach also needs to develop communication and decision-making skills along with management and analytical proficiency. This would be very difficult to include within existing coach education programmes for a number of reasons, namely the length of the courses and the course deliverers. It is difficult, if not impossible, to teach learner autonomy through conventional didactic teaching methods, which most coach education courses are for pragmatic reasons, such as cost, organisation and delivery. It is also difficult to teach and learn the skills necessary to become a self-directed learner.

It is also useful to consider why coaches may learn and what they expect from more formal coach learning experiences. This expectation was summed up by a soccer coach with over twenty years experience of coaching who felt: 'my expectations are very low. I have attended so many of these courses over the years – some of them I know the script by heart. You have to go, you can't get out of it. They are relentless at tracking you down and for what? Just to get that all-important tick in the box to allow me to keep coaching'. However, his perception was not shared by a tennis coach with similar levels of coaching experience, who thought: 'I've been on some great courses – not all of them and some that I did not appreciate until a while afterwards. But if you attend with an open mind, looking to get something from it, you probably will, even if that is chatting to other coaches over coffee'. The views of these two experienced coaches suggest there is a wide range of expectations, experiences and value.

There appear to be an equally wide range of reasons as to why sport coaches undertake various forms of formal coach learning, from professional development opportunities to full time higher education courses. An unpublished survey (2013) of 260 experienced sport coaches from a wide variety of sports found that over 90% of these coaches undertook learning opportunities to improve coaching effectiveness and personal practice. Interestingly, the least popular response was coach certification and assessment reasons (see Figure 9.1).

Given that sport coaches want to improve coaching effectiveness and personal practice, it may be useful to examine some of the recent research in this area. Horn (2008) proposed a model of coaching effectiveness based upon three principles. First, that coach behaviour is influenced by personal characteristics, beliefs and goals, and second, that the athletes are subsequently influenced by the coaches' behaviour. Finally, the coaches' effectiveness is influenced by the individual differences of the athletes and the particular coaching situation. More recently, Côté and Gilbert defined coaching effectiveness as:

> The consistent application of integrated professional, interpersonal, and intrapersonal knowledge to improve athletes' competence, confidence, connection, and character in specific coaching contexts.

> (Côté and Gilbert 2009, p. 316)

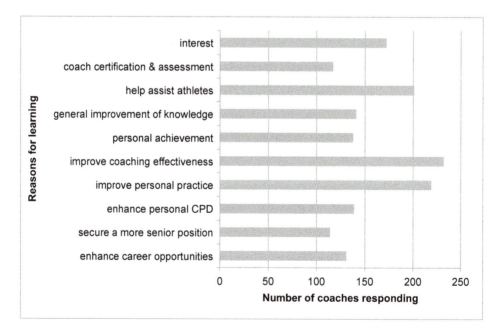

*Figure 9.1* Reasons for participating in coaching opportunities.

This definition of coaching effectiveness highlights the importance of coach knowledge, learning and the application within particular coaching environments. Werthner and Trudel (2009) also linked the concept of coaching effectiveness with coaching contexts and the need to demonstrate practical coaching competence. In their example, the Coaching Association of Canada had revisited their national coaching education programme to ensure that coaches were able to coach rather than be assessed on their knowledge of coaching.

Coach development is a long and complex process (for example, Knowles *et al.* 2005; Nash *et al.* 2009), which is pursued in individual and *ad hoc* ways (for example, Nash, Horton and Sproule 2011; Nelson and Cushion 2006). A number of critiques have demonstrated the low impact of formal provision (see Nash and Sproule 2012; Nelson *et al.* 2006). A survey was administered to 472 practicing coaches in a variety of sports. Follow-up interviews were conducted with ten coaches. Results showing these coaches were dissatisfied with aspects of coach education were compiled. Coaches were concerned with three key aspects:

1   Quality of coach educators: many of the soccer coaches felt that coach educators lacked credibility as they were not 'known' players. Other coaches cited lack of contextual or practical awareness and inability to elaborate on certain aspects or answer questions adequately.
2   Transparency of assessment: often coaches felt the assessment task was not sufficiently defined and there were no clear pass or fail criteria. There was also the suggestion that successful coaches had been identified before the assessment.
3   Course delivery: there were two main concerns expressed here that were diametrically opposite. Some coaches felt that the coach educators delivered the course 'by rote' whereas others felt that the coach educators did not stick with the task.

(Nash, Horton and Sproule 2011)

Coach educators felt that there were difficulties with the coach education process, especially with the content that they were expected to cover. Many of these difficulties reflected the technical nature of course content, especially in football and rugby, as few courses concentrated on the 'how' of coaching rather than the 'what' of coaching. Some courses brought together coaches with vastly different levels of experience and expertise, causing problems for coach educators as group work and discussions were challenging. Some coaches were required to attend coach education courses and continuing professional development events and therefore did not engage with the course content. Coach educators felt they accepted the role of assessor with little training or understanding of the criteria for success.

## THE ROLE OF THE COACH EDUCATOR

As mentioned earlier, formal coach education courses have not been linked to improvement in coaching practice, a key outcome for coaches undertaking coach education and development. Cassidy *et al.* (2008) assert that well structured and well delivered coach education programmes are necessary to coach learning and development, however much of the success, or otherwise, of said programmes can be the impact of the coach educator. One coach educator, who worked within a specific team sport in the UK, considered that his role as a coach educator was 'to pass on what I have learned during my 25 years within *"the sport"*. Things have to be done a certain way and I have followed the tutor pack to the letter. I also make sure that the trainees do things the correct way – set up the area, lay out the cones and check the equipment. It is important that we maintain standards and make sure that the coaches know how we do things'.

A more helpful approach might be to consider the coach educator as a facilitator of learning experiences and opportunities, through which skills can be developed. Skills such as analysis, decision making, critical thinking and evaluation all encapsulate the need to reflect and make sense of what has been learned. Consider the view of this experienced coach educator, who operates over a wide variety of contexts, sports and countries and had also considered all the coach learning contexts, saying 'the role and function of a coach educator is an individual actively involved in supporting the initial training and ongoing professional development of coaches from beginner coach to master coach. In the formal learning environment they can wear a variety of hats including tutor, assessor and verifier. In the informal environment, potentially a more powerful learning environment because of its context specific and applied nature, they act as mentors supporting experiential learning and encouraging critical reflection on action, challenging thinking and practice where appropriate to develop meaningful and relevant personal development plans'. These thoughts reflect the International Council for Coaching Excellence (ICCE) view around the role of the coach educator. The ICCE consider the coach educator to be an international part of the coaching process, so much so that they have designed a career pathway for coach developers to supplement the long term development of coaches (ICCE 2012).

The very nature of coaching requires the coach to make decisions about the quality of athletes' performances in relation to numerous parameters, for example, technical features, tactical considerations, psychomotor skills and psychological readiness through the unstructured and structured collection of information. Gilbert *et al.* (2012, p. 211) highlight the difficulties for coaches and coach educators, saying that 'Coach education programs seldom make explicit connections between athlete and coach development, nor do they provide much guidance on how to design authentic assessments that connect the two'. Think of the last coach education course attended; did it:

- consider coaches' knowledge and experience?
- link the coach development to actual practice?
- include contextalisation?
- offer opportunities to ask questions and discuss difficulties?
- compare and contrast the quality of interventions used in various contexts?

All learning, except for simple memorisation, requires the learner to actively construct meaning and contextualise it, not merely accumulate bits of information and isolated skills. The process of transition from a novice coach to expert seems less than clear, and in some respects under-researched. The role of the coach educator should be as co-creator of knowledge about teaching and learning, as well as sports specific knowledge. The focus of the coach education courses should be to provide opportunities for coaches to construct knowledge, not just receive it. In describing a route for developing coaching expertise, Salmela and Moraes

(2003) suggested formal coach centred training and education in a range of settings alongside interaction with peers. This seems to reinforce the experiential approach recently advocated in the literature (for example, Cushion *et al.* 2003; Gilbert and Trudel 2005) and specify a 'situated learning' approach in the coaches own workplace (Lave and Wenger 1991). By situating learning within social and cultural contexts, the individual is less involved with objective de-contextualised knowledge acquisition, but is constructing knowledge through direct experience of coaching practice (Gilbert and Trudel 2001). This can be viewed as an active process, with coaches seeking out information related to the task and the given context, and testing this within the context formed by the task and the environment. Situated cognition theory suggests knowledge is jointly constructed by interacting with the situation in which one confronts a problem. The role of coach education, and therefore coach educators, within this process is to facilitate construction of knowledge through experiential and contextual practice in coaching environments. An example of this was given by a newly qualified soccer coach, saying, 'I really thought my first coaching course was great. It covered everything I needed to know about coaching'.

Many entry-level coaches share this viewpoint; for example, consider the recently qualified basketball coach who said, 'I loved the course – everything was well organised and easy to use when I am coaching back at my club'. A recent study examining the learning processes of a novice swimming coach highlighted that often coaches accept information at face value, input into their sessions with no reflection or contextualisation and do not question the information provided (Nash and Sproule 2011). Perhaps the introduction of critical thinking skills into coach education could aid the process.

## CRITICAL THINKING SKILLS

Critical thinking is the process of applying reasoned and disciplined thinking to a subject, in this case sport coaching. These skills are essential for coaching development and, like other skills, they improve with practice. Critical thinking includes a complex combination of skills and can be acquired through experience as well as formal education processes. For example, degree study in any discipline is aimed at developing these critical thinking skills, and once developed they can be transferred between disciplines. Think about the soccer coach, working at the top level within the professional game who says, 'I've never known a coach education course to focus on critical thinking skills. It's a vital, vital area because in the modern game it's a multi-million pound industry and these decisions could make or break your club'. He added, 'I feel that I was at the top of the tree in terms of football courses and thought how am I going to develop. To attend a university course was a conscious decision to add to the knowledge that I've gained through football'.

Coaches would be expected to have declarative knowledge about the specifics of their sport, for example, skills and tactics as well as procedural knowledge regarding the pedagogical process (see Chapter 7). This information, necessary for coaches' development, should be available at appropriate stages throughout their career but should be introduced in the early stages of a coaching career (Lavallee 2006; Mallett and Côté 2006; Schinke *et al.* 1995). Coaches' knowledge would tend to guide their actions, and to be able to effectively organise, integrate and use all these knowledge sources requires the use of critical thinking skills.

Critical thinking is generally thought of as having two specific parts:

1   information generating and processing skills;
2   the habit, based on intellectual commitment, of using and acting on these skills.

So critical thinking skills are more than just the mere acquisition and retention of information alone; they involve the application of the appropriate information in a specific situation or to solve a particular problem. Think of all the uses within coaching – what drills to choose to assure the end result in practice, how to best present information to a group or individual performer and what tactics and strategies to utilise within a competitive environment. Consider the following:

■   **Critical thinking is not a matter of accumulating information.**
    Many coaches have good memories and know a lot about their sport but critical thinking is more than that.
■   **Critical thinking is not a domain-specific skill.**
    The ability to think clearly and rationally is important in many lines of work, and has been studied extensively within medicine and law (Gupta and Upshur 2012; McGee *et al.* 2013). Once coaches develop critical thinking skills, they can be applied in a variety of situations and contexts.
■   **Critical thinking is very important in the new knowledge economy.**
    There are many sources of information available, and many coaches use the Internet as a coaching tool (see Chapter 14). With the plethora of information in a variety of formats available to download and use, the evaluation of these sources is essential.

The ability to think rationally, know where to access specific information and then evaluate these sources is a valuable tool in developing coaching practice. Critical thinking also has many benefits as well as directly impacting decision making. Critical thinking can be beneficial to the decision making process because it provides background information and options available before making important choices.

## DECISION MAKING

Decision making has been identified as one of the key functions within sport coaching, and it is not simply about making decisions but making correct decisions. Coaches are asked to make decisions in a variety of situations, for example what practices to include in training sessions, how long to continue with a specific practice activity, whether to concentrate on quality or quantity of training, when to offer feedback to performers and what type of feedback. Coaches also have to make quick decisions in competition regarding tactics, substitutions and positional play, often leading to them being characterised as a 'master of the instantaneous response' (Launder 1993, p. 2).

Decision making is clearly linked to critical thinking and problem solving, as the appropriateness of the decision has to be weighed against the evaluative process that is involved.

When a problem is presented, basic elements are identified and a solution is created from knowledge stored in the memory. In studies comparing experts to novices, experts' knowledge is structured to allow easier recall from memory, experts sort problems into categories according to features of their solutions and experts develop routines to allow processing capacity to be focussed on constantly changing situations (Guest *et al.* 2001; Kreber 2002). Decision making is said to be a cognitive activity, selecting the most appropriate course of action from a repertoire of alternatives, given the specific situation. Think of the difference that a coach can make to the outcome of a game by calling a time-out or making a substitution, seemingly at random.

The questions that then have to be asked are how does a coach develop decision-making skills, and when these skills are developed does the subsequent decision making appear to be spontaneous? In less exact sciences that best describe coaching, there may not be one decisive rule to solve problems – several broad problem-solving rules may be needed to resolve the overall problem. Coaches may also use Moderately Abstract Conceptual Representations (MACRs), the abstract concepts both allowing more working memory to be utilised and contributing to the notion of automaticity (Nash and Collins 2006; Zeitz 1997). These MACRs allow coaches to have a more flexible approach and react to certain situations as they are not storing rigid schema. Developing this ability requires the integration of a number of sources of knowledge; it is not a function of increasing or decreasing certain behaviours. Rather it is the knowledge of making correct decisions within the constraints of the session, demonstrating again that coaching is not a behaviour to be copied but a cognitive skill that can be taught (Lyle 2002).

Now consider the question asked about the last coach education course attended:

- Were you encouraged to think critically
  - □ about yourself?
  - □ about your coaching practice?
  - □ about the course?
- Were you given the opportunity to review decisions you had made in your coaching?
- Were you given the opportunity to make decisions in the course?

## LINKING CRITICAL THINKING AND DECISION MAKING

Given the types of situations that coaches face on a daily basis, the need to be able to think critically, make complex decisions and then implement these decisions in a timely manner is fundamental to coaching. Critical thinking involves the use of questioning, most often self-questioning, which can take a variety of forms (see Chapter 12).

Critical thinking is often considered to be an activity that is undertaken in isolation; however, linking the two cognitive processes of critical thinking and decision making can lead to improved judgement. This relates closely to the concept of meta-cognition, which can be simply defined as thinking about thinking, but it also helps coaches develop an overall understanding by making connections and links. For example, activities such as planning how to approach a practice within coaching, then monitoring comprehension and improvement and eventually

*Table 9.1* Critical thinking skills

Think about whether you agree with these four statements:

1  I prefer being given the correct answers rather than figuring them out myself.
2  I don't like to think a lot about my decisions as I rely only on gut feelings.
3  I don't usually review the mistakes I have made.
4  I don't like to be criticised.

If you answered –yes– to all questions, then you probably need to work on your critical thinking.

evaluating progress are meta-cognitive in nature. Think about the initial example given at the start of this chapter about poor positional play – how does the coach move from recognising issues and problems at an individual level to considering the team as a whole?

Knowing the principles of critical thinking is not enough; as with many other sport skills, it requires practice. Morgan and colleagues (2013) reported the use of discussion, debate and role-play within assessed coach education. Coaching has increasingly been presented as a cognitive activity that requires critical thinking and decision making as well as the ability to view the coaching remit holistically. Problem-based learning (PBL) had been suggested as an answer to these wider issues, but the flexibility and time pressured situations experienced by many coaches renders the PBL approach insufficient to meet the meta-cognitive demands (Jones and Turner 2006). According to Morgan *et al.* (2013), ethno-drama is a form of theatre that enables the re-enactment of both emotional and contextual complexities of lived experiences, in this case within sport coaching. These ethno-dramas were based on real-life experiences and designed to challenge coaches in three key areas:

1   Coach–athlete and athlete–athlete relationships were examined with the key areas of selection of players and resulting issues.
2   Coach relationship with support staff was evaluated with divergent philosophies and methods as the primary focus.
3   Coach's interactions with others, for example, board members, with issues such as power and negotiation being important.

The participating coaches found these ethno-dramas stimulated thought and discussion that both informed and changed their perspectives on coaching issues. They also considered that this approach had enhanced their creativity, critical thinking and decision making.

Critical thinking cannot be prevalent in individuals at all times; everyone is subject to episodes of undisciplined or irrational thought. The quality of critical thinking is therefore typically a matter of degree and dependent on, among other things, the quality and depth of experience in a given domain of thinking or with respect to a particular class of questions. No one is a complete critical thinker, but only to a certain degree, with individual insights and blind spots and subject to some tendencies towards self-delusion. Within sport coaching, the inclusion of critical thinking skills – decision making, problem solving, reflection and reasoning – in coach education should enable coaches to develop the skills of independent learning.

## CREATIVITY AND INNOVATION

Some people believe that critical thinking hinders creativity because it requires following the rules of logic and rationality, and creativity might require breaking rules. This is a misconception. Critical thinking is quite compatible with thinking 'outside-the-box', challenging consensus and pursuing less popular approaches. If anything, critical thinking is an essential part of creativity because critical thinking is necessary to evaluate and improve creative ideas.

According to Mumford *et al.* (2012), creativity occurs when issues are novel and complex, often ill-defined and poorly structured, which tends to describe the context of sport coaching. Sternberg (2003) considers creativity to be a key determinant in expertise, and a fundamental characteristic of this creative process is generating novelty from within habitual forms of activity (Glăveanu 2012). In other words, if sport coaches can critically question their practice, then they may be able to challenge traditional methods and innovate. The creative achievements in the case of more 'routinized genres' such as science reside in 'small deviations from artistic ideals or paradigmatic work' (Dalton 2004, p. 609). Creativity relies on the 'spontaneous micro-adjustments of a highly prepared interpretation'; this idea could be applied to sport coaching, provided sports coaches have the necessary tools to develop this type of thinking (Chaffin, Lemieux and Chen 2006, p. 200).

## REFERENCES

Callary, B., Werthner, P. and Trudel, P. (2011). A brief online survey to help a sport organization continue to develop its coach education program. *International Journal of Coaching Science* 5(2): pp. 31–48.

Campbell, S. (1993). Coaching education around the world. *Sport Science Review* 2(2): pp. 62–74.

Cassidy, T., Jones, R. and Potrac, P. (2008). *Understanding sport coaching: The social, cultural and pedagogical foundations of coaching practice*. (London: Routledge).

Chaffin, R., Lemieux, A., and Chen, C. (2006). Spontaneity and creativity in highly practiced performance. In *Musical creativity: Multidisciplinary research in theory and practice*. I. Deliege and G. A. Wiggins (Eds.) (London: Psychology Press): pp. 200–218.

Côté, J. and Gilbert, W. (2009). An integrative definition of coaching effectiveness and expertise. *International Journal of Sports Science and Coaching* 4(3): pp. 307–323.

Cushion, C. J., Armour, K. M. and Jones, R. L. (2003). Coach education and continuing professional development: Experience and learning to coach. *Quest* 46: pp. 153–163.

Dalton, B. (2004). Creativity, habit, and the social products of creative action: Revising Joas, incorporating Bourdieu (English). *Sociological Theory* 22(4): pp. 603–622.

Feiman-Nemser, S. (2012). Beyond solo teaching. *Educational Leadership* 8, Academic OneFile.

Gilbert, W., Dubina, N. and Emmett, M. (2012). Exploring the potential of assessment efficacy in sports coaching. *International Journal of Sports Science and Coaching* 7(2): pp. 211–214.

Gilbert, W. and Trudel, P. (2001). Learning to coach through experience: Reflection in model youth sport coaches. *Journal of Teaching in Physical Education* 21: pp. 16–34.

Gilbert, W. and Trudel, P. (2005). Learning to coach through experience: Conditions that Influence reflection. *The Physical Educator* 62(1): pp. 32–43.

Glăveanu, V. (2012). Habitual creativity: Revising habit, reconceptualizing creativity. *Review of General Psychology* 16(1): pp. 78–92.

Guest, C. B., Regehr, G. and Tiberius, R. G. (2001). The life long challenge of expertise. *Medical Education* 35: pp. 78–81.

Gupta, M. and Upshur, R. (2012). Critical thinking in clinical medicine: What is it? *Journal of Evaluation in Clinical Practice* 18(5): pp. 938–944.

Horn, T.S. (2008). Coaching effectiveness in the sport domain. In *Advances in sport psychology*. T. S. Horn (Ed.) (Champaign, IL: Human Kinetics): pp. 239–267.

International Council for Coaching Excellence and the Association of Summer Olympic International Federations. (2012). *International sports coaching framework*. (Champaign, Illinois: Human Kinetics).

Irwin, G., Hanton, S. and Kerwin, D. (2004). Reflective practice and the origins of elite coaching knowledge. *Reflective Practice* 5(3): pp. 425–442.

Jones, R. and Turner, P. (2006). Teaching coaches to coach holistically: Can problem-based learning (PBL) help? *Physical Education and Sport Pedagogy,* 11, 2: pp. 181–202.

Jones, R, & Wallace, M (2005), Another bad day at the training ground: coping with ambiguity in the coaching context, *Sport Education And Society*, 10, 1: pp. 119–134.

Knowles, Z., Borrie, A. and Telfer, H. (2005). Towards the reflective sports coach: Issues of context, education and application. *Ergonomics* 48: pp. 11–14, 1711–1720.

Kreber, C. (2002). Teaching excellence, teaching expertise and the scholarship of teaching. *Innovative Higher Education* 27: pp. 5–23.

Launder, A. (1993). Coach education for the twenty first century. *Sports Coach* 16(1): p. 2.

Lavallee, D. (2006). Career awareness, career planning, and career transition needs among sports coaches. *Journal of Career Development* 33(1): pp. 66–79.

Lave, J. and Wenger, E. (1991). *Situated learning: Legitimate peripheral participation*. (Cambridge, UK: Cambridge University Press).

Lyle, J. (2002). *Sports coaching concepts: A framework for coaching behaviour*. (London: Routledge).

Mallett, C.J. and Côté , J. (2006). Beyond winning and losing: Guidelines for evaluating high performance coaches. *The Sport Psychologist* 20(2): pp. 213–221.

Mallett, C., Trudel, P. Lyle, J., & Rynne, S. (2009). Formal vs. Informal Coach Education, *International Journal Of Sports Science & Coaching*, 4, 3: pp. 325–334.

McCullick, B.A., Vickers, B., Mason, I., & Schempp, P.G. (2006, July). *An Analysis of Published Coaching Education Research 1995–2005*, AIESEP World Congress. (Jyvaskyla, Finland).

McGee, J., Guihot, M. and Connor, T. (2013). Rediscovering law students as citizens: Critical thinking and the public value of legal education. *Alternative Law Journal* 38(2): p. 77.

Morgan, K., Jones, R. L., Gilbourne, D. and Llewellyn, D. (2013). Changing the face of coach education: Using ethno-drama to depict lived realities. *Physical Education and Sport Pedagogy* 18(5): pp. 520–533.

Mumford, M., Hester, K., Robledo, I., Peterson, D., Day, E., Hougen, D. and Barrett, J. (2012). Mental models and creative problem-solving: The relationship of objective and subjective model attributes. *Creativity Research Journal* 24(4): pp. 311–330.

Nash, C. and Collins, D. (2006). Tacit knowledge in expert coaching: Science or art? *Quest* 58: pp. 464–476.

Nash, C., Horton, P. and Sproule, J. (2011). *The effectiveness of coach education interventions.* Coaching Association of Canada: 2011 Petro-Canada Sport Leadership sportif conference.

Nash, C. and Sproule, J. (2012) Coaches perceptions of coach education experiences. International Journal of Sport Psychology 43: 33–52.

Nash, C.S., Sproule, J., Callan, M., McDonald, K. and Cassidy, T. (2009). Career development of expert coaches. *International Journal of Sports Science & Coaching* 4(1): pp. 121–138.

Nash, C., Sproule, J. and Horton, P. (2011). Excellence in coaching: The art and skill of elite practitioners. *Research Quarterly for Exercise and Sport* 82(2): pp. 229–238.

Nelson, L. and Cushion, C. (2006). Reflection in coach education: The case of the national governing body coaching certificate. *Sport Psychologist* 20(2): pp. 174–183.

Nolan P. (2004). The changing world of work. *Journal of Health Services Research Policy* 9(Suppl. 1): pp. S3–S9.

North, J. (2009). The coaching workforce 2009–2016. (Leeds: Sport Coach UK).

Salmela, J. H. and Moraes, L. C. (2003). Development of expertise: The role of coaching, families, and cultural context. In *Expert performance in sports: Advances in research on sport expertise.* J. L. Starkes and K. A. Ericsson (Eds.) (Champaign, IL: Human Kinetics).

Schinke, R. J., Bloom, G. and Salmela, J. H. (1995). The career stages of elite Canadian basketball coaches. *Avante* 1(1): pp. 48–62.

Sternberg, R.J. (2003). *Wisdom, intelligence, and creativity synthesized.* (New York: Cambridge University Press).

Sturrock, J.B.E. and Lennie, S. C. (2009). Compulsory continuing professional development: A questionnaire-based survey of the UK dietetic profession. *Journal of Human Nutrition and Dietetics* 22: pp. 12–20.

Werthner, P. and Trudel, P. (2009). Investigating the idiosyncratic learning paths of elite Canadian coaches. *International Journal of Sports Science and Coaching* 4(3): pp. 433–449.

Whitmore, J. (2002). *Coaching for performance: Growing people, performance and purpose.* (London: Nicholas Brealey Publishing).

Zeitz, C. M. (1997). Some concrete advantages of abstraction: How experts' representations facilitate reasoning. In *Expertise in context: Human and machine.* P. J. Feltovich, K. M. Ford and R. R. Hoffman (Eds.) (Cambridge, MA: AAAI Press/The MIT Press): pp. 43–65.

# Chapter 10

# Emotional intelligence

*Áine MacNamara and John Stoszkowski*

Sport is undeniably an emotional experience; therefore, understanding the emotional expertise that a coach requires to optimise performance is essential. In recent years, it has been suggested that coaches with a high level of emotional intelligence (EI) will be more effective, be able to motivate and relate better to players and support staff, have improved problem solving and decision making capabilities and be able to resolve conflicts in the workplace. This chapter provides an overview of the theoretical foundation of EI and considers the importance and practical application of the 'skill' of EI in the field of sports coaching.

## INTRODUCTION

An emerging body of research suggests that emotional intelligence (EI) contributes to effective work performance (Cherniss and Adler 2001; Mayer, Salovey and Caruso 2000; Goleman 1998a). The impact of EI on performance in teams has also been investigated recently (Jordan, Ashkanasy, Härtel and Hooper 2002; Druskat and Wolff 2001). EI traditionally has been defined as 'the subset of social intelligence that involves the ability to monitor one's own and others' feelings and emotions, to discriminate among them and to use this information to guide one's thinking and actions' (Salovey and Mayer 1990, p. 189). More recently this definition has expanded to include 'motivation, non-ability dispositions and traits, and global, personal and social functioning' (Mayer *et al.* 2000, p. 268). Given the importance of emotions for sport, and the criticality of interpersonal dynamics, EI is a major consideration. Developing better coaches means they remain in post longer, are more effective and feel better about their jobs. It has been found that Olympic athletes, world class musicians and chess grandmasters all have one specific attribute in common: all participate in consistent and repetitive training over a prolonged period of time. This implies they have an emotional strength in the area of self-discipline. Coaches with a high level of emotional intelligence will be more effective, be able to motivate and relate better to players and support staff, have improved problem-solving and decision-making capabilities, and be able to resolve conflicts in the workplace. An important aspect of emotional intelligence is the notion that it is trainable, and therefore, coaches could seek to enhance it. As the ability of coaches to recognize their own or their players' emotions or moods plays an important role in leadership, including emotional intelligence, training and support develops abilities such as self-awareness, self-management, self-motivation, empathy and social skills.

Sport is undoubtedly an emotional experience and emotions play an important role for both coaches and athletes. The emotional bond, trust, empathy and interpersonal expertise that a coach possesses and demonstrates with his or her athletes is central to performance efficacy. As such, understanding the emotional expertise that a coach requires to build and maintain relationships, and to successfully assess and affect social situations, may be the differentiating factor between good and poor performances (Chan and Mallett 2011).

In fact, there is little doubt that the coach's and athlete's emotional state influence performance (Butler 1996) through both cognitive and physical functioning (Jones 2003). Therefore understanding the role of emotions in sport is central to optimising performance. Given that emotions play such an important role, the recent upsurge in interest in EI in sport is unsurprising. This chapter provides an overview of the theoretical foundation of EI and a consideration of the importance and application of EI in sport coaching.

## WHAT IS EI?

EI was established as a popular area of research during the 1990s and has since emerged as an important construct (Meyer and Zizzi 2007; Petrides, Furnham and Frederickson 2004). Emotions undoubtedly play a significant role in the development and performance of athletes, coaches and others members of the support team (Botterill and Brown 2002; Jones 2002; Meyer and Fletcher 2007; Vallerand and Blanchard 2000). Emotional intelligence has been defined as an individual's ability to perceive, utilize, understand and manage emotions (Mayer and Salovey 1997). Simply, emotional intelligence can be understood as the capacity to deal effectively with one's own and others' emotions (Palmer and Stough 2001) through the ability to recognize one's own emotional state (that is how one is feeling), sense emotions in others and build productive relationships with others. As described in the introduction to this chapter, EI should be viewed as a skill that can be developed; as such, it is not inherent in us but can be taught, learnt and developed.

Research and work in EI first appeared in the late nineteenth and early twentieth centuries when Darwin (1872) referred to it as emotional expression before Thorndike (1920) described a person's ability to engage in adaptive social interactions as social intelligence. Subsequently, Gardner (1983, p. 243) described a person's capacity to 'know oneself and to know others' as intrapersonal intelligence (understanding yourself) and interpersonal intelligence (understanding others). However, it was not until the 1990s that the construct became widely accepted as an important area, with the term 'Emotional Intelligence' first established by Salovey and Mayer (1990, p. 189), who defined it as 'the subset of social intelligence that involves the ability to monitor one's own and others' feelings and emotions, to discriminate among them and to use this information to guide one's thinking and actions'. As such, EI was said to refer to an individual's ability to perceive, monitor, employ and manage one's own and others' feelings and emotions (Mayer and Salovey 1997). Despite this background, the concept of EI was largely unexplored academically until the mid 1990s when increasing interest and popularisation of the concept exposed the subject to a wider audience. According to Goleman (1998a), EI refers to an individual's ability to recognize his or her own emotions and those of others. Subsequently, Goleman and colleagues went on to conceptualize an emotionally intelligent person as an individual who 'demonstrates the competencies that constitute self-awareness, self-management, social awareness, and social skills at appropriate times and ways in sufficient frequency to be effective in the situation'

(Boyatzis, Goleman and Rhee 2000, p. 344). These competencies will be discussed later on in the chapter.

To date, research findings have consistently associated high levels of EI with successful performance in a wide range of settings. For example, EI has been linked to better performance outcomes in academia (for example, Parker, Hogan, Eastabrook, Oke and Wood 2006; Parker, Summerfeldt, Hogan and Majeski 2004), while emotionally intelligent individuals have been shown to be better able to deal with job-related pressure, stress and conflict resolution in the business environment (for example, Zeidner, Matthews and Roberts 2004; Jordan, Ashkanasy and Charmaine 2002; Jordan and Troth 2002). Similarly, research in health settings suggests that higher levels of EI are associated with enhanced psychological well-being and frame of mind in different areas of human functioning (for example, Pau and Crocker 2003; Shutte, Malouff, Simunek, McKinley and Hollander 2002; Slaski and Cartwright 2002), while it has been suggested that high levels of EI play a key role in successful and effective leadership (Riggio and Reichard 2008; George 2000; Megerian and Sosik 1996).

Although the role of emotional intelligence has predominantly been examined outside of the sporting domain, it has been suggested that commonalities and parallels exist between the attributes required for successful performance in disciplines such as leadership, business and sport (April, Lifson and Noakes 2012; Jones 2002). Perhaps unsurprisingly, these findings have led researchers to investigate the potential application of EI in sport, where EI has been associated with optimal performance states and superior sports performance (for example, Meyer and Fletcher 2007; Meyer and Zizzi 2007; Zizzi, Deaner and Hirschhorn 2003). However, EI research that has been undertaken in the sporting domain has, at times, produced somewhat inconclusive findings (Meyer and Zizzi 2007). For example, Zizzi et al. (2003) found only moderate evidence for a link between emotional skills and athletic performance in college basketball players. However, several of the discrete components of EI (such as perceiving emotion, managing emotion) have been identified as important in maximising sport performance elsewhere (Jones 2003; Lazarus 2000; Ravizza 1998). Alongside this, the application of EI in effective sports coaching practice has come into increasing focus (for example, Afkhami, Mokhtari, Tojjari, Bashiri and Salehian 2011; Chan and Mallett 2011), although a paucity of research still exists. For instance, Thelwell, Lane, Weston and Greenlees (2008) discovered a significant relationship between EI and coaching efficacy and suggest that coaches who exhibit high levels of EI are in a better position to regulate the emotions of their participants and, as a result, support participants more effectively (Thelwell et al. 2008).

## THEORETICAL APPROACHES TO EI

Despite these positive results, and the apparent importance of EI in a variety of contexts, it must also be noted that a variety of viewpoints and theories currently exist on what exactly comprises the EI domain (Locke 2005; Matthews, Zeidner and Roberts 2004; Zeidner, Matthews and Roberts 2001). As a result, the EI field is characterised by divergence and an array of terminologies, with no mutually agreed upon theoretical model or framework of the concept (Landy 2005; Davies, Stankov and Roberts 1998). In addition, as yet, no published study has supplied an EI measure that is comprehensively accepted as valid for measuring EI in sport (April et al. 2012). Nevertheless, three main models or approaches have emerged that inform the research on the application of EI – trait based approaches, mixed model approaches and ability model approaches.

## Trait based approaches to EI

Trait based approaches conceptualise EI as an individual's ability to self-perceive emotions in direct relation to his or her experiences across different situations (Petrides and Furnham 2001). As such, those who are said to be high in trait EI believe that they are in touch with, and in control of, their emotions. This can be measured through self-report measures such as the Emotional Intelligence Scale (EIS) questionnaire (Schutte *et al.* 1998), which incorporates 33 items across six factors:

- appraisal of own emotions
- appraisal of others' emotions
- regulation of emotions
- optimism
- social skills
- utilisation of emotions.

Using a 5-point Likert scale for each item (1 = strongly agree to 5 = strongly disagree), the EIS assesses how able an individual is in identifying, understanding, utilising and regulating emotions (Meyer and Fletcher 2007). Recently, the EIS has been used in EI research in sport (for example, Lane, Thelwall, Lowther and Davenport 2009; Thelwell *et al.* 2008), and peer-reviewed literature has shown it to possess adequate-to-moderate internal consistency reliability and test-retest reliability (Tett, Fox and Wang 2005; Schutte *et al.* 1998).

## Mixed model approaches to EI

Mixed model approaches (for example, Goleman 1998b; Bar-On 1997) view EI as competency based and suggest that EI encompasses a multi-factorial combination of both trait mental abilities and self-reported state personality characteristics (Sternberg *et al.* 2000). For example, Bar-On (1997) identified five areas of functioning related to an individual's ability to succeed:

- intrapersonal skills (emotional self-awareness)
- interpersonal skills (interpersonal relationships)
- adaptability scales (problem solving)
- stress-management scales (impulse control)
- general mood (optimism).

These functional areas can be measured using the Emotional Quotient Inventory (EQ-I) (Bar-On 1997), a 133-item self-report measure (Mayer, Caruso and Salovey 1999). Similarly, Goleman (1998b) proposed a model of EI comprising of 20 behavioural competencies across four separate domains:

- self-awareness – for example, knowing one's emotions;
- self-management – for example, regulating one's emotions;
- social awareness – for example, recognising emotions in others;
- relationship management – for example, handling relationships with others.

Goleman (1998b) measured EI using the Emotional Competence Inventory-2 (ECI-2), a self-report measure of 110 items within the four domains. However, although widely accepted in mainstream literature, researchers have questioned the reliability and validity of mixed model approaches as definitions are often inconsistent, measures overlap and conclusions lack scientific rigor (Meyer and Zizzi 2007; Conte 2005; Matthews *et al.* 2004). In this regard, Matthews *et al.* describe Goleman's (1998b) model as 'too open-ended and loosely specified to constitute a good scientific theory' (Matthews *et al.* 2004, p. 15). It must also be noted that although Goleman (1995) suggests that EI can be learned and developed, perhaps contradic- torily, the mixed model promotes EI as a trait-like construct (Meyer and Fletcher 2007).

## Ability model of EI

Finally, the ability model approach (for example, Mayer and Salovey 1997) has received scholarly recommendation (Daus and Ashkanasy 2005) and conceptualizes EI as a dynamic set of mental abilities or skills (or states), distinct from personality, that an individual needs to encode the information in emotion to direct subsequent cognition and motivate behaviour (Mayer 2001). As such, EI is said to be an individual's ability to successfully manage the inter- action between emotion and cognition (Chan and Mallett 2011). Mayer and Salovey (1997) put forward an ability model of EI consisting of four integrated branches:

- perceiving emotions – for example, the ability to identify and label emotions in oneself and others;
- use of emotions – for example, the ability to utilize emotions to direct attention and influence thinking;
- emotional understanding – for example, the ability to interpret emotions and their fluctuations;
- managing emotions – for example, the ability to regulate emotions in oneself and others.

A key caveat of the ability approach, and one that has direct relevance for the development of sports coaches, is that EI is viewed as a dynamic and malleable skill that can be learned, developed and improved over time (Meyer and Fletcher 2007; Mayer 2001). A popular assess- ment inventory of the ability model of emotional intelligence is the Mayer-Salovey-Caruso Emotional Intelligence Test (MSCEIT: Mayer, Salovey and Caruso 2002), which contains 141 items divided into the four proposed branches of EI and can be administered online (Mayer *et al.* 2002). However, the objectivity of the MSCEIT has been called into question due to the rigid nature of content measures and disagreement over their associated definitions (Petrides, Pita and Kokkinaki 2007). In addition, it is not readily available and requires training before it can be administered.

## EI COMPETENCIES

Reflecting the arguments made in the previous section, EI can be understood as composing several competencies that are related to performance (Goleman, Boyatzis, and McKee 2002). The competencies of perception, understanding, utilising and managing emotions effectively, both in the self and others, are the core competencies of EI. These basic competencies can be understood as follows. Competency in the perception of emotion can be understood as the ability to recognize emotion related cues, both visual and audio, of others and awareness of one's own body states relating to emotions. Competence in understanding one's own and other's emotions can be demonstrated by knowing the causes and consequences of different emotions and the ability to differentiate between various emotions. The ability to harness the effects of emotions by using emotions is an EI competence. Finally, managing emotions in the self and others requires the ability to regulate emotions so that they are compatible with the performance environment, requirements of the situation and the particular goals of the individual.

Building on these basic competencies, Goleman's (Goleman *et al.* 2002; Goleman 2001) competency theory of EI includes 20 competencies that are grouped into four categories. Central to this categorisation is that EI competencies are not innate talents but learned abilities. These four domains are further categorised into Personal Competence and Social Competence (Goleman *et al.* 2002). The theory postulates that the more competencies one has, the more emotionally intelligent the individual is. In the following sections these competencies will be discussed with specific relevance to their role within sport coaching.

Personal Competence capabilities determine how we manage ourselves and are categorised by two domains and their associated competencies:

- self-awareness – emotional self-awareness, accurate self-assessment, self-confidence;
- self-management – emotional self-control, transparency, honesty/integrity/trustworthiness, adaptability/flexibility, achievement/drive for performance, initiative, optimism.

(Goleman *et al.* 2002)

Self-awareness is a key component of an emotionally intelligent coach and is central to effective leadership (Chan and Mallett 2011). Self-awareness is the ability to understand your own moods and emotions, both in terms of their effect on you, and their effect on your athletes. Highly self-aware coaches are confident, have a realistic view of their abilities, and aren't afraid to admit their mistakes. Chan and Mallett further suggest that self-awareness plays a critical role in sport coaching and argue that being self-aware about competence is critical 'for producing high performance in a competitive and scrutinising environment' (Chan and Mallett 2011, p. 353).

Once coaches have the ability to understand their own moods and emotions, that is self-awareness, they must learn to regulate their emotions if they are to become an emotionally intelligent coach. Self-regulation refers to one's ability to control or redirect disruptive impulses and moods. In a coaching setting, this can be operationalised as a coach who leads with integrity, is open to change and promotes a trustworthy environment. Given the importance of the coach as a role model for athletes, the ability of the coach to model appropriate

**195**

behaviour, such as calmness and rational thinking in the face of adversity, sets an example for athletes to do the same.

Social Competence capabilities determine how relationships are managed and are contained within two domains:

- social awareness – empathy towards others, awareness of organizational-level currents, decision networks and politics, service to others;
- relationship management – inspirational leadership, influence tactics, developing others, change catalyst, conflict management, building bonds, teamwork and collaboration/cooperation.

(Goleman *et al.* 2002)

Empathy can be understood as an interpersonal component of EI and goes beyond sympathy, which refers to a general feeling of concern for others, to literally sharing the feelings of others. This has important implications in a coaching setting given the crucial role that interpersonal dynamics play. Coaches who have the ability to empathize are able to build strong relationships with their athletes, and have athletes who are more satisfied with their sport experience. Coaches have been shown to be effective when they establish emotional connections and strive to understand others; empathy is a key antecedent of this behaviour. Coaches who are able to show their athletes that their feelings matter, and that they can relate to their concerns, will be able to influence them to perform to their optimal and cope with performance stressors.

The culmination of the previously discussed components of EI (that is, self-awareness, self-regulation and empathy) is social skill. Although the focus of much coach education and training is on the technical, tactical and physical components of performance, the importance of social skills in managing relationships should not be overlooked. Coaches who are socially skilled are proficient in managing and maximising relationships. The socially skilled coach is able to build strong relationships with athletes that contribute to their ability to perform. Competencies will be discussed further in the context of coaching later in the chapter. However, it is important to point out that at this stage the evidence basis for EI, in sport and other domains, is in its infancy and further empirical evidence is needed to ground this work.

## MEASURING EMOTIONAL INTELLIGENCE

Emotional intelligence, as described elsewhere in this chapter, has been conceptualised using different theoretical frameworks. As such, the development of a variety of different instruments to measure EI, both self-report and performance-based measures, is a significant limitation in this field as it makes comparisons between studies difficult. Some of the criticisms of measurement issues are highlighted next.

### Ability model measures conformity, not ability

One criticism of the works of Mayer and Salovey comes from a study by Roberts *et al.* (2001), which suggests that the EI, as measured by the MSCEIT, may only be measuring conformity.

The MSCEIT employs a consensus-based assessment and, as such, since the scores are negatively distributed scores, differentiates between people with low EI better than people with high EI.

## Ability model measures knowledge but not actual ability

A further criticism of the measures associated with the ability model of EI is levered by Brody who claims that, unlike tests of cognitive ability, the MSCEIT 'tests knowledge of emotions but not necessarily the ability to perform tasks that are related to the knowledge that is assessed' (Brody 2004, p. 234) . Following this, an individual may know how he or she should behave in a certain situation, but the extent to which the individual carries out the reported behaviour is not tested. As such, the MSCEIT is actually testing knowledge rather than actual ability.

## Issues with self-report measures

As with all self-report measures, there are issues with socially desirable responding where test-takers respond in ways that represent themselves with an excessive positive bias (Paulhus 2002). There is considerable evidence to support these limitations with self-report measures such as those used to measure EI (for example, McFarland and Ryan 2000; Zerbe and Paulhus 1987). Further, given the highly evaluative contexts in which EI is assessed (for example, employment settings, high-performance settings and competitive sport), the problems of socially desirable responding are obvious (Paulhus and Reid 1991).

## The predictive power of tests is questionable

Although EI appears to be a useful construct there seems to be a tension between 'the commercial wing' and 'the academic wing' of the EI movement. Landy (2005) suggests that the former makes expansive claims on the applied value of EI, while the latter is trying to warn users against these claims. Reflecting the former, Goleman asserts that 'the most effective leaders are alike in one crucial way: they all have a high degree of what has come to be known as emotional intelligence. . . . emotional intelligence is the sine qua non of leadership' (Goleman 1998b, p. 94). Coming from an academic perspective, Mayer cautions 'the popular literature's implication – that highly emotionally intelligent people possess an unqualified advantage in life – appears overly enthusiastic at present and unsubstantiated by reasonable scientific standards' (Mayer 1999, p. 50). This presents an interesting problem; there appear to be significant questions about the robustness and rigour of EI studies (Mills 2009; Barbuto and Burbach 2006; Schulte 2002) and, as such, much of the evidence is currently, at best, questionable and should therefore be interpreted with caution.

## IMPORTANCE OF EI FOR COACHING

Coaching is a primarily social occupation and the coach must form many relationships to ensure the production of high-level performance, for example coach–athlete, coach–management, coach–parent, coach–team. Central to the formation of these productive relationships are feelings and emotions and, as such, the focus for coach education needs to move beyond sport-specific knowledge and pedagogy skills to include a consideration of the 'softer skills' that contribute to optimal coaching performance. As such, EI may be useful for facilitating improved interpersonal relationships that lead to improved performance. It is worth considering how the various EI abilities that have been proposed could translate into appropriate behaviours, informed by the individual's ability to perceive, use, understand and manage emotions. Due to the relative lack of research in sport, EI literature in business, leadership and other domains is referred to when presenting a case for the importance of EI for sport coaching. To understand why coaches need emotional intelligence, begin by asking why coaches need to be able to identify, use, understand and manage emotions. Exemplars from coaching practice are used throughout this section to illustrate the role of EI in this context.

A leader's ability to identify his or her own emotions and feelings has been shown to allow the leader to accurately identify the emotions of peers and groups, to express emotions accurately and to differentiate between emotional expressions (Caruso, Mayer and Salovey 2002). Empathy, the ability to understand and experience another person's feelings or emotions, is an important component of EI and facilitates a leader's social support and positive interpersonal relationships (George 2000). In fact, empathy has been shown to have the strongest correlation with perceived effective leadership (Kellet, Humphrey and Sleeth 2006). This suggests that a coach's ability to perceive others' feelings and empathize with them may establish an affective bond that is beneficial for leadership. Given the leadership role that a coach fulfils, this should have important implications for the coach's ability to interact with a group.

The ability to accurately perceive emotions is critical for enabling the positive management of interpersonal relationships (Chan and Mallett 2011) and is clearly important for the relationship between the coach, athletes and other key stakeholders. Take, for example, the coach who has identified a limitation in her athlete's tactical approach to performance when facing a particular opponent in tennis. Believing that the issue stems from a technical weakness, she decides to implement a series of challenging drills during the next training session. The athlete, who is normally an optimistic, bubbly and outgoing person, is unusually quiet and trudges onto the court with slumped shoulders and a distinct lack of enthusiasm. In this scenario, if the coach is not adept at 'reading' nonverbal channels of emotional expression (for example, tone of voice, body language, gestures and facial expressions), she may not recognize that the athlete is nervous or lacking in self-confidence about performing such challenging skills or drills. Similarly, an athlete may display subtle indications of engagement in, or enjoyment of, a particular activity through emotional expression such as levels of eye contact or changes in posture for example. As such, the ability to recognize these moods and emotions would allow coaches to respond in an appropriate manner by adapting their leadership style, planning for a session or addressing the emotional climate in response to the needs of their athletes (Chan and Mallett 2011).

The use of emotions to enhance cognitive processes and decision making is also an important consideration for coaching (George 2000). This ability would allow coaches to understand and motivate others by making emotions available, engaging in multiple perspectives that facilitate more flexible planning as well as more creative, open-minded, and broader thinking and perspectives (Caruso et al. 2002; George 2000). Understanding EI provides functional insights into human behaviour and perceptions. This understanding includes the ability to recognize relationships between emotions, determine emotions' underlying meaning, comprehend complex feelings and recognise and accept emotional fluctuation (Caruso *et al.* 2002). Therefore, if a coach is able to identify, use and understand emotions, he or she will be better able to facilitate the effective management of emotions. For example, a golfer has identified several tournaments within the competitive schedule as the prime focus for performance during the upcoming season. Although the golfer performs well in the early part of the season, in the two tournaments prior to the first identified 'major' the player performs poorly and is eliminated early. During this time, the player experiences a subtle shift in emotion from optimism, to fear, to eventual frustration and anger. In this scenario, a coach who is adept at managing emotions would be able to help dissipate and alleviate the effects of these negative events, and provide redirection and focus towards more positive events and moods such as the self-belief and confidence that was generated in the early part of the season (Caruso *et al.* 2002; George 2000). Mayer and Salovey (1997) term this as meta-regulation of mood. Indeed, EI leadership prescribes not just the ability to manage self-feelings and moods, but the ability to manage the moods and emotions of others (George 2000).

The empirical evidence has also demonstrated the strong relationships between emotional intelligence and performance, the existence of a relationship between emotional intelligence and leadership style and the need to combine emotional intelligence abilities and competencies with leadership skill. Goleman *et al.* (2002) provide this linkage with the EI based model of leadership described in a previous section. Similarly, in a field study on the emotional dynamics of self-managed groups, Pescosolido (2002) reports that emergent leaders within groups adopt the role of managing the group's emotional state. As such, the emergent leader may not be the designate 'head coach' but perhaps another member of the support team, an athlete, or mentor. The leader uses his or her emotionally intelligent behaviour (for example, empathy, emotional perception of self and others, emotional management of self and others, emotional expression, emotional communication, inspirational leadership, role modelling) to communicate messages to group members regarding group performance and contextual events. For example, a football team has a crucial match that they must win to avoid relegation to a lower division. Five minutes into the game, the team loses possession cheaply in their opponents' half of the pitch and several players are caught out of position. The opposition breaks quickly and, after several missed tackles and a defensive mix up, score a controversial goal that appeared to be offside. The reaction of the head coach or 'leader', who is watching from the dugout on the touchline, is crucial in this situation and one of two possible scenarios will ensue. In the first scenario, the coach suddenly runs toward the pitch to berate the striker who initially gave the ball away. His arms flail and his face is contorted with anger and frustration as he stomps down the touchline gesticulating furiously and pointing at the players he feels were to blame. For the remainder of the first half, he marches nervously up and down the touchline barking seemingly random instructions at the top of his voice. This coach's behaviour, which plays an important role in setting the behaviour and tone of the group, does not bode well for the team's chances of victory due to what Goleman *et al.* describe as 'emotional contagion' within groups (Goleman *et al.* 2002, p. 7). They propose that due to a leader's authoritative position, he or she becomes the role model from which subordinates model their behaviour because they look to their leader for stimulus.

**199**

In the second scenario, after conceding the goal the coach remains in his dugout, deciding instead to let the players regroup and regain their tactical formation. When the game restarts, he waits for the ball to go out of play before calmly emerging from the dugout. In a measured tone, he offers encouragement to the whole team, reminding them of the key messages they had focused on prior to the game and highlighting the importance of patience as there are 85 minutes left to play. Before walking back to the dugout, he gives the striker who lost possession originally a 'thumbs up' and commends him on an earlier piece of play.

In both scenarios the coach's positive or negative behaviour, moods and emotions will have a significant impact on the performance of athletes and subordinate staff. However, not all coaches are emotionally intelligent. In these cases, the role of emotional leader may fall to another member of the group who provides the emotional support for a group (Goleman *et al.* 2002). For example, in the first scenario the team captain on the pitch will play a vital role in setting the emotional tone of the group after conceding such a goal.

## DEVELOPING OUTSTANDING SPORT COACHES

Although EI has been conceptualised as a skill that can be learned and developed, there is a dearth of empirical research, both within sport and other performance domains, testing how to enhance EI through deliberate training (McEnrue, Groves and Shen 2010). There are, however, a number of studies that are worthy of attention. Of course, it is important to address not only whether EI increased through training but also whether emotional training led to increases in characteristics associated with improved performance.

Central to this discussion is the question as to whether EI can be increased through deliberate development. This question has been of interest to researchers and practitioners in various performance fields. Goleman (1998b) describes EI as a wide array of competencies and skills that drive leadership performance and consist of five areas. EI competencies are learned capabilities that must be worked on and developed to achieve outstanding performance. For example, Groves and colleagues (Groves, McEnrue and Shen 2008) found that an 11-week training program that presented information on EI resulted in significantly higher emotional intelligence for the intervention group compared to a control group. In a university setting, Schutte and Malouff (2002) provided university students with information and skills training related to emotional intelligence as part of an introductory class. Results of this study are interesting, with the intervention group scoring significantly higher on typical emotional intelligence following the semester-long course. The intervention group also displayed higher retention rates compared to students in the control group. As such an increase in EI and, importantly, performance was evident. Unfortunately, there are a limited number of studies in sport examining the effectiveness of deliberate training on EI. In one example, Crombie, Lombard and Noakes (2011) found that athletes randomly assigned to interactive EI training scored significantly higher on a performance test measure of emotional intelligence compared to athletes randomly assigned to a control group.

Although there are relatively few studies examining the role of deliberate preparation on EI in sport, there is growing recognition of the value of EI for sport coaching (Chan and Mallett 2011). Clearly, further intervention studies are needed to establish the extent to which EI training is effective and specifically the impact of training on specific EI competencies, the nature of EI training and the benefits of EI training in sport. However, given the importance of EI and emotions in sport it seems unwise to presume that coaches will develop these competencies in an *ad hoc* manner. Haime suggests that 'educating coaches in emotional intelligence and soft skills is the next frontier for high performance coaching' (2011, cited in Chan and Mallett 2011, p. 252). Reflecting this, coach education should consider incorporating EI training into course design and training experiences. The skilful handling of social situations, building relationships and managing emotions is an important attribute of effective coaches and should be given the same attention as the more traditional, technically-focused elements of coaching. If these 'softer skills' are recognised as important for facilitating and developing relationships, coach education programmes should ensure that EI, and other related skills, are not marginalised but instead given a central place within development programmes.

## CONCLUSION

Although EI is an important attribute for coaches, it must co-exist with other strengths and weaknesses in the coach's armoury. Given that sports endeavour to produce athletes who are emotionally and socially skilled, it is logical that coaching behaviour acts as an influential learning source in this regard (Chan and Mallett 2011). As such, coach education programmes should consider the importance of EI and recognize that rather than developing EI through trial and error, there is a need to purposefully include EI training as part of coach's professional development. Coaching in sport requires more than technical and tactical knowledge; coaches should be encouraged and facilitated to develop the competencies associated with EI to ensure that they effectively interact with, inspire and enhance the experiences of athletes. Technically and tactically competent coaches with the skills and ability to interact effectively with others, manage their own and others' emotions and develop quality relationships, are likely to be effective in sport environments.

## REFERENCES

Afkhami, E., Mokhtari, P., Tojjari, F., Bashiri, M. and Salehian, M.H. (2011). Relationship between emotional intelligence and coaching efficacy in coaches. *Annals of Biological Research* 2 (4): pp. 469–475.

April, K., Lifson, D. and Noakes, T. (2012). Emotional intelligence of elite sports leaders and elite business leaders. *International Journal of Business and Commerce* 1 (5): pp. 82–115.

Barbuto, J.J.E. and Burbach, M.E. (2006). The emotional intelligence of transformational leaders: A field study of elected officials. *Journal of Social Psychology* 146 (1): pp. 51–64.

Bar-On, R. (1997). *The emotional quotient inventory (EQ-i): Technical manual*. (Toronto: Multi-Health Systems).

Botterill, C. and Brown, M. (2002). Emotion and perspective in sport. *International Journal of Sport Psychology* 33: pp. 38–60.

Boyatzis, R., Goleman, D. and Rhee, K. (2000). Clustering competence in emotional intelligence: Insights from the emotional competence inventory. In *Handbook of Emotional Intelligence: Theory,*

*Development, Assessment, and Application at Home, School, and in the Workplace*. R. Bar-On and J.D.A. Parker (eds.) (San Francisco: Jossey-Bass).

Brody, N. (2004). What cognitive intelligence is and what emotional intelligence is not. *Psychological Inquiry* 15: pp. 234–238.

Butler, R.J. (1996). *Sports psychology in action*. (Oxford, UK: Butterworth-Heinemann).

Caruso, D.R., Mayer, J.D. and Salovey, P. (2002). Emotional intelligence and emotional leadership. In *Multiple Intelligences and Leadership*. R.E. Riggio and S. Murphy (eds.) (Mahwah, NJ: Lawrence Erlbaum).

Chan, J.T. and Mallett, C.J. (2011). The value of emotional intelligence for high performance coaching. *International Journal of Sport Science and Coaching* 6 (3): pp. 315–328.

Cherniss, C. and Adler, M. (2001). *Promoting emotional intelligence in organizations*. (Alexandria, VA: American Society for Training and Development).

Conte, J.M. (2005). A review and critique of emotional intelligence measures. *Journal of Organizational Behavior* 26: pp. 433–440.

Crombie, D.T., Lombard, C. and Noakes, T.D. (2011). Increasing emotional intelligence in cricketers: An intervention study. *International Journal of Sports Science and Coaching* 6: pp. 69–86.

Darwin, C. (1872). *The expression of the emotions in man and animals*. (London: John Murray).

Daus, C.S. and Ashkanasy, N.M. (2005). The case for an ability-based model of emotional intelligence in organizational behavior. *Journal of Organizational Behavior* 26: pp. 453–466.

Davies, M., Stankov, L. and Roberts, R.D. (1998). Emotional intelligence: In search of an elusive construct. *Journal of Personality and Social Psychology* 75: pp. 989–1015.

Druskat, V.U. and Wolff, S.B. (2001). Building the emotional intelligence of groups. *Harvard Business Review* 79 (3): pp. 81–90.

Gardner, H. (1983). *Frames of mind: The theory of multiple intelligences*. (New York: Basic Books).

George, J.M. (2000). Emotions and leadership: The role of emotional intelligence. *Human Relations* 53: pp. 1027–1055.

Goleman, D. (1995). *Emotional intelligence*. (New York: Bantam Books).

Goleman, D. (1998a). *Working with emotional intelligence*. (London: Bloomsbury Publishing).

Goleman, D. (1998b). What makes a leader? *Harvard Business Review* 76: pp. 93–102.

Goleman, D. (2001). Emotional intelligence: Issues in paradigm building. In *The Emotionally Intelligent Workplace*. C. Cherniss and D. Goleman (eds.) (San Francisco: Jossey-Bass): pp. 13–26.

Goleman, D., Boyatzis, R. and McKee, A. (2002). *The new leaders: Transforming the art of leadership*. (Little Brown: Great Britain).

Groves, K., McEnrue, M.P. and Shen, W. (2008). Measuring and developing the emotional intelligence of leaders. *Journal of Management Development* 27 (2): pp. 225–244.

Jones, G. (2002). Performance excellence: A personal perspective on the link between sport and business. *Journal of Applied Sport Psychology* 14: pp. 268–281.

Jones, M.V. (2003). Controlling emotions in sport. *The Sport Psychologist* 17: pp. 471–486.

Jordan, P.J., Ashkanasy, N.M. and Charmine, E.J. (2002). Emotional intelligence as a moderator of emotional and behavioural reactions to job insecurity. *Academy of Management Review* 27: pp. 361–372.

Jordan, P.J., Ashkanasy, N.M., Härtel, C.E.J. and Hooper, G.S. (2002). Workgroup emotional intelligence: Scale development and relationship to team process effectiveness and goal focus. *Human Resource Management Review* 12: pp. 195–214.

Jordan, P.J. and Troth, A.C. (2002). Emotional intelligence and conflict resolution: Implications for human resource development. *Advances in Developing Human Resources* 4: pp. 62–79.

Kellett, J.B., Humphrey, R.H. and Sleeth, R. (2006). Empathy and the emergence of task and relations leaders. *The Leadership Quarterly* 17 (2): pp. 146–162.

Landy, F.J. (2005). Some historical and scientific issues related to research on emotional intelligence. *Journal of Organizational Behavior* 26: pp. 411–424.

Lane, A. M., Thelwell, R., Lowther, J. and Devonport, T. (2009). Relationships between emotional intelligence and psychological skills among athletes. *Social Behaviour and Personality: An International Journal* 37: pp. 195–202.

Lazarus, R.S. (2000). How emotions influence performance in competitive sports. *The Sport Psychologist* 14: pp. 229–252.

Locke, E.A. (2005). Why emotional intelligence is an invalid concept. *Journal of Organizational Behaviour* 26: pp. 425–431.

Matthews, G., Zeidner, M. and Roberts, R.D. (2004). *Emotional intelligence: Science and myth.* (Cambridge, MA: MIT Press).

Mayer, J.D. (1999). Emotional intelligence: Popular or scientific psychology? *APA Monitor* 30: p. 50.

Mayer, J.D. (2001). A field guide to emotional intelligence. In *Emotional Intelligence in Everyday Life: A Scientific Inquiry.* J. Ciarrochi, J. Forgas and J.D. Mayer (eds.) (Philadelphia: Psychology Press).

Mayer, J.D., Caruso, D.R. and Salovey, P. (1999). Emotional intelligence meets traditional standards for an intelligence. *Intelligence* 27 (4): pp. 267–298.

Mayer, J.D. and Salovey, P. (1997). What is emotional intelligence? In *Emotional Development and Emotional Intelligence: Implications for Educators.* P. Salovey and D. Sluyter (eds.) (New York: Basic Books): pp. 3–31.

Mayer, J.D., Salovey, P. and Caruso, D.R. (2000). Models of emotional intelligence. In *The Handbook of Intelligence.* R.J. Sternberg (ed.) (New York: Cambridge University Press).

Mayer J.D., Salovey, P. and Caruso, D.R. (2002). *Mayer-Salovey-Caruso emotional intelligence test (MSCEIT): User's manual.* (Toronto: Multi-Health Systems).

McEnrue, M.P., Groves, K. and Shen, W. (2010). Emotional intelligence training: Evidence regarding its efficacy for developing leaders. *Leadership Review* 10 (Winter): pp. 3–26.

McFarland, L.A. and Ryan, A .M. (2000). Variance in faking across noncognitive measures. *Journal of Applied Psychology* 85 (5): pp. 812–821.

Megerian, L.E. and Sosik, J.J. (1996). An affair of the heart: Emotional intelligence and transformational leadership. *Journal of Leadership Studies* 3 (3): pp. 31–48.

Meyer, B.B. and Fletcher, T.B. (2007). Emotional intelligence: A theoretical overview and implications for research and professional practice in sport psychology. *Journal of Applied Sport Psychology* 19: pp. 1–15.

Meyer, B.B. and Zizzi, S. (2007). Emotional intelligence in sport: Conceptual, methodological, and applied issues. In *Mood and Human Performance: Conceptual, Measurement, and Applied Issues.* A. M. Lane (ed.) (Hauppauge, NY: Nova Science).

Mills, L.B. (2009). A meta-analysis of the relationship between emotional intelligence and effective leadership. *Journal of Curriculum and Instruction* 3 (2): pp. 22–38.

Palmer, B.R. and Stough, C. (2001). The measurement of emotional intelligence. *Australian Journal of Psychology* 53: pp. 85.

Parker, J.D.A., Hogan, M.J., Eastabrook, J.M., Oke, A. and Wood, L.M. (2006). Emotional intelligence and student retention: Predicting the successful transition from high school to university. *Personality and Individual Differences* 41: pp. 1329–1336.

Parker, J.D.A., Summerfeldt, L.J., Hogan, M.J. and Majeski, S.A. (2004). Emotional intelligence and academic success: Examining the transition from high school to university. *Personality and Individual Differences* 36: pp. 163–172.

Pau, A.K.H. and Crocker, R. (2003). Emotional intelligence and perceived stress in dental undergraduates. *Journal of Dental Education* 67: pp. 1023–1028.

Paulhus, D. L. (2002). Socially desirable responding: The evolution of a construct. In *The Role of Constructs in Psychological and Educational Measurement*. H. Braun, D.N. Jackson and D.E. Wiley (eds.) (Hillsdale, NJ: Erlbaum).

Paulhus D. L. and Reid, D.B. (1991). Enhancement and denial in socially desirable responding. *Journal of Personality and Social Psychology* 60 (2): pp. 307–317.

Pescosolido, A.T. (2002). Emergent leaders as managers of group emotion. *Leadership Quarterly* 13: pp. 583–599.

Petrides, K.V. and Furnham, A. (2001). Trait emotional intelligence: Psychometric investigation with reference to established trait taxonomies. *European Journal of Personality* 15: pp. 425–448.

Petrides, K.V., Furnham, A. and Frederickson, N. (2004). Emotional intelligence. *The Psychologist* 17: pp. 574–577.

Petrides, K.V., Pita, R. and Kokkinaki, F. (2007). The location of trait emotional intelligence in personality factor space. *British Journal of Psychology* 98: pp. 273–289.

Ravizza, K. (1998). Increasing awareness for sport performance. In *Applied Sport Psychology: Personal Growth to Peak Performance*. J.M. Williams (ed.) (Mountain View, CA: Mayfield Publishing).

Riggio, R.E. and Reichard, R.J. (2008). The emotional and social intelligences of effective leadership: An emotional and social skill approach. *Journal of Managerial Psychology* 23 (2): pp. 169–185.

Roberts, R.D., Zeidner, M. and Matthews, G. (2001). Does emotional intelligence meet traditional standards for intelligence? Some new data and conclusions. *Emotions* 1: pp. 196–231.

Salovey, P. and Mayer, J.D. (1990). Emotional intelligence. *Imagination, Cognition and Personality* 9: pp. 185–211.

Schulte, M.J. (2002). Emotional intelligence: A predictive or descriptive construct in ascertaining leadership style or a new name for old knowledge? *Dissertation Abstracts International* 59: pp. 7-B.

Schutte, N.S. and Malouff, J.M. (2002). Incorporating emotional skills in a college transition course enhances student retention. *Journal of the First-Year Experience and Students in Transition* 14: pp. 7–21.

Schutte, N.S., Malouff, J. M., Hall, L. E., Haggerty, D. J., Cooper, J. T., Golden, C. J. and Dornheim, L. (1998). Development and validation of a measure of emotional intelligence. *Personality and Individual Differences* 25: pp. 167–177.

Schutte, N.S., Malouff, J. M, Simunek, M., McKenley, J. and Hollander, S. (2002). Characteristic emotional intelligence and emotional well-being. *Cognition and Emotion* 16: pp. 769–785.

Slaski, M. and Cartwright, S. (2002). Health performance and emotional intelligence: An exploratory study of retail managers. *Stress and Health* 18: pp. 63–68.

Sternberg, R.J., Forsythe, G.B., Hedlund, J., Horvath, J.A., Wagner, R.K., Williams, W.M., Snook, S.A. and Grigorenko, E.L. (2000). *Practical intelligence in everyday life*. (New York: Cambridge).

Tett, R.P., Fox, K.E. and Wang, A. (2005). Development and validation of a self-report measure of emotional intelligence as a multidimensional trait domain. *Personality and Social Psychology Bulletin* 31: pp. 859–888.

Thelwell, R., Lane, A. M., Weston, N.J.V. and Greenlees, I. A. (2008). Examining relationships between emotional intelligence and coaching efficacy. *International Journal of Sport and Exercise Psychology* 6: pp. 224–235.

Thorndike, E.L. (1920). Intelligence and its use. *Harper's Magazine* 140: pp. 227–235.

Vallerand, R.J. and Blanchard, C.M. (2000). The study of emotion in sport: Historical, definitional, and conceptual perspectives. In *Emotions in Sport*. Y.L. Hanin (ed.) (Champaign, IL: Human Kinetics).

Zeidner, M., Matthews, G. and Roberts, R.D. (2001). Slow down, you move too fast: Emotional intelligence remains an elusive construct. *Emotion* 1: pp. 265–275.

Zeidner, M., Matthews, G. and Roberts, R.D. (2004). Emotional intelligence in the workplace: A critical review. *Applied Psychology: An International Review* 53: pp. 371–399.

Zerbe, W. and Paulhus, D. (1987). Socially desirable responding in organizational behavior: A reconception. *Academy of Management Review* 12: pp. 250–264.

Zizzi, S.J., Deaner, H.R. and Hirschhorn, D.K. (2003). The relationship between emotional intelligence and performance among college baseball players. *Journal of Applied Sport Psychology* 15: pp. 262–269.

# Chapter 11

# Mentoring as a coach development tool

*Christine Nash and Sarah McQuade*

Jim, a national level basketball coach, described his thoughts on mentoring as follows: 'I have never had a mentor – not directly – not assigned in I think the way is being mooted at the moment. You tend to have critical friends, people that you go to and I think that's quite important. So if that can be conveniently formalised in some way, I guess it could be a good thing. But if it's just from the point of view of the assessment of a coach, then I think that might have some difficulties to it then because there are only a few mentors around probably that could do the job.' He went on to say:

> So if mentoring is something to do with being advised, you might say it's good for someone to come along and say 'look Jim, you're going to have to stop this high pressure defence, or attempts at it because your kids aren't fit enough – don't you see it? Look they're really dragging. Unless you do a, b and c, you're going to get beaten using this pressure defence system.' Somebody told me something like that once and I thought 'oh right' and I'd been plugging away with it in the hope it might work. You need somebody like that sometimes to kind of advise you in the 'here and now' of your coaching – the sort of immediate 'oh we're playing the league leaders next week' but you also need the longer term thing. Mentoring, I think is a really solid idea, in the sense that coaches need to think beyond themselves and if they get someone to look at their practice but how it can be set up formally is an issue.

Even though mentoring has been a buzzword in sport coaching for some years, many coaches remain reluctant to adopt mentoring within their coaching practice or even, in some cases, understand what mentoring is and what it involves. This chapter will examine both the theory and practice of mentoring, highlighting the roles and responsibilities of all involved parties, some methods of incorporating mentoring into organisations, key issues and practical examples. Coaches, such as Jim, should find the answers to all their concerns for mentoring at the national level, but the chapter also offers advice to coaches at all levels of their coaching careers.

## WHAT IS MENTORING?

Mentoring is widely accepted as being a dynamic, reciprocal process that occurs within a working environment, generally involving an individual with more experience in a specific field (the mentor) and a less experienced individual, often a beginner in that field (the mentee)

(Weaver and Chelladurai 1999; Wright and Smith 2000). Within sport, mentoring is being positioned to support coach learning as a valuable tool for the coach to use. The mentor can be instrumental in helping to develop the necessary skills for both personal growth and professional development, for example, decision making, information processing, self-reflection and critical thinking (see Chapters 9 and 12). The mentor can facilitate coach learning by contextualising abstract theory into actual coaching environments (Crisfield 1998). Coaches can work in very different environments, for example within the Football Association (FA) there are different activities, ages and contexts, such as futsal, coaching youth footballers, coaching disabled performers and coaching deaf performers (FA 2013). The Professional Golfers' Association (PGA) highlight the variety of different environments ranging from the volunteer participation coach working with weekend recreational players to the highly qualified coach working with top professionals, referring to this as the 'Right Coach; Right Place; Right Time' (PGA 2013). Some of these environments are more controlled than others, depending on a number of factors including the type of sport, level of participants, age of participants and numbers in session, which makes the role of the mentor both important and complicated. In many cases, there are few suitably qualified mentors available to provide the relevant guidance. However, successful mentoring relationships can lead to benefits such as career development, job satisfaction, socialisation, organisational commitment and career advancement.

## The mentor

Research has determined there is a real need for mentors to have their role clearly defined. To ensure the maximum benefit is gained from the mentoring process, mentors are most effective when they understand the ramifications of the role that they are being asked to fulfil. Perhaps more importantly, for this relationship to be effective the mentee has to understand and endorse this role (Nash 2003). This should also be extended to clearly delineate the boundaries and parameters that the mentors are working within. The mentor's principal function is to guide and support the mentee throughout the relationship, offering a sounding board and encouraging the mentee to reflect upon behaviour by asking the difficult questions. Mentors can also add value by introducing mentees into the wider community of coaching, enabling social interaction and networking opportunities. Gladwell (2006) expands these benefits by referring to the 'connector' role of the mentor, with the caveat that mentors must be well connected themselves. Valuable learning experiences can therefore be facilitated by the mentor without direct intervention. However, allowing the mentor to act as a 'gatekeeper' to coaching networks may afford the mentor a degree of power or control over the mentee and his or her potential social interactions.

It would be wrong to suggest that a mentoring relationship is only successful between a novice coach (mentee) and a more experienced coach (mentor), although this is often the norm within sport coaching. Mentoring could be effective between coaches with more advanced levels of experience; it could be that one particular aspect of coaching practice needs improvement. For example, an early career soccer coach explained how mentoring had helped him, saying 'yes, when I was starting out – it was actually quite good, I got really good advice about organisation. That helped me spend more time actually coaching'. In this case, the mentor could be carefully selected, not merely on the basis of mentoring skills, but also on his or her proficiency in the aspects of coaching that were lacking. In this example, the more general organisational assistance does not need to be given by another soccer coach, as it is not an issue specific to the technical aspects of soccer. This mentor may not coach the same sport as the mentee; again same-sport mentoring tends to be the norm within sport coaching, perhaps because it is administratively less complicated. Given the roles attributed to the mentor, it could be suggested that in this situation the mentor is the coach's coach as coaching is about improving performance through structured practice and feedback.

In summary, the mentor may:

- provide learning opportunities to the mentee;
- be available and approachable;
- offer support and advice for improvement of practice;
- stimulate critical thinking and reflection;
- question methods and aspects of practice;
- suggest different ways of implementing plans and strategies;
- facilitate 'entry' into coaching communities.

Often, a mentor can be viewed as a role model, someone who inspires coaches to develop and achieve. Surely no coach can be more inspirational than Pat Summitt, coach emeritus of the Lady Vols basketball team, coach of the USA Olympic gold medal winning basketball team and the most acclaimed coach in her sport. Unfortunately, Coach Summitt recently had to resign her head coaching role as a result of the diagnosis of early-onset dementia. During her 38 years at the University of Tennessee, she posted a 1,098–208 record and led Tennessee to eight national titles and 18 Final Four appearances. Rather than lose the experience and expertise of Coach Summitt, the University of Tennessee are to be commended on her appointment as coach emeritus. In this role Summitt acts as a mentor to coaches and athletes, attending practices and competitions and interacting with coaching staff, athletes and recruiters. As a result of her coaching and mentoring successes, she was awarded the Arthur Ashe Award, given to those individuals whose achievements transcend sport.

## The mentee/protégé

Research has shown that non-formal and informal learning plays an important role in the development of sports coaches, relying on a supportive coaching network outside the formal learning environment (Werthner and Trudel 2006). Traditionally in coaching contexts, time is in short supply and professional skills are learned 'on the job' using a 'trial-and-error' process that can lead to difficulties (Nash and Sproule 2011; Willem and Van den Broeck 2007). This means that the mentoring programme must be perceived to be worthwhile and of benefit, otherwise sport coaches will not allocate the necessary time to engage with the process. Much of this will depend upon how the organisation sells their mentoring programme to those involved. The links to long-term coach learning and development should be highlighted, as an increase in knowledge alone is rarely sufficient to induce behaviour change. Testimonies of coaches who have been involved in positive mentoring experiences could support this type of learning as these coaches, such as Jim, could be ambassadors and/or champions of this type of coach learning and development. As this process is ultimately about learning and developing as a coach, there are certain attributes that the mentee must display to maximise the effectiveness of the mentoring process. For example, mentees must actively participate in the process and be able to speak freely to their mentor (Clutterbuck 2004). Self-disclosure to another individual improves self-understanding by allowing new practices more suited to current commitments and environments to be considered (Audet and Couteret 2005). High levels of self-disclosure in mentees can increase the amount and quality of mentoring incidents as well as improve the mentoring relationship (Wanberg et al. 2006).

Coaches at all levels of coaching ability must want to improve their coaching practice, which assumes they must be open to change. Werthner and Trudel (2006) argue that to take advantage of informal learning, learners need to have sufficiently evolved independent learning skills and motivation for the process to be successful. There are considered to be three stages in this process of change:

1 the mentee and mentor should identify a change in coaching behaviour as a result of discussion, observation and analysis;
2 the mentee must then decide how important he or she perceives the change to be and identify a level of commitment to that change;
3 after an agreed period of time the behaviour is reviewed by both mentee and mentor.

This demonstrates that from the mentee's point of view, mentoring is constructed as either a deliberate choice – something that stems from a curiosity – or as a result of the acceptance of the mentor as someone whom the professional can trust (Paquette 2012).

## Models of mentoring

As mentoring is considered to be a highly significant development tool used extensively in other professions such as teaching, medicine and business, there are a number of different models, or frameworks, which can be and are used in different organisations. These models are framed around different outcome requirements, for example, teaching or organisational structure, and often reflect the end product of the mentoring environment. For example, within teaching, mentoring of new staff has been limited to knowledge of school policies and procedures rather than the development of teaching practice (Gordon and Brobeck 2010). Organisational and management researchers have identified mentoring as an exchange relationship whereby both mentor and mentee gain some benefit from each other and the relationship (Young and Perrewé 2004). Paul (2004) considers that mentoring is different from coaching or a buddy system, because the intended outcomes are more than merely skill building.

Haggard et al. (2011) suggest that a mentoring relationship must consist of three distinct dimensions:

1 the relationship must be reciprocal;
2 there must be development benefits for mentor and mentee;
3 there must be regular and substantial interactions over an extended time period.

**209**

According to social exchange theory, individuals' beliefs about the support they receive from their employing organisations play an important role in affecting their behaviours and attitudes towards their organisations. Also, individuals' personal values, as well as their perceptions of the interpersonal relationships that they experience with their line managers, or supervisors, play an important role in affecting these beliefs. As research has not yet systematically explored the roles of these interpersonal variables in mentoring relationships, there is much more to be discovered. The three dimensions identified by Haggard *et al.* (2011) set clear guidelines for the success or otherwise of mentoring relationships and programmes.

Within sport coaching the most common models, the apprenticeship model, the competence model and the reflective practitioner model, have their origins within educational literature (Jones *et al.* 2009). Mentoring has become a 'hot topic' within sport coaching, but there are few instances of formalised mentoring schemes that have been specifically designed to meet the needs of sport coaches at all levels and contexts of coaching. Table 11.1 illustrates the various models that are currently used, and could be used, within the context of sport coaching. Recently, some sports have advocated the use of coach developers to support the individual needs of coaches, attempting to encourage a more 'coach and participant centred' approach. The emphasis of this approach would promote pedagogical and critical thinking skills and learning through practice at the expense of the more traditional skills and drills approach (Lyle 2007).

Mentoring continues to be popular as a professional learning strategy with sport coaches and with coaching organisations, although much of the effectiveness of mentoring is predicated upon the implementation and subsequent support of both the mentor and mentee. Coaches have identified that mentoring could be important to their development and would encourage coaching organisations to provide more opportunities for mentoring (Nelson, Cushion and Potrac 2013). Coaches are likely to seek advice from a variety of sources of information to help them solve their own coaching problems, and in some workplaces there may be someone available to offer guidance. However, coaching organisations should ensure that this becomes more readily available. No matter how good the intentions, not everyone is suitable as a mentor, as this is a position that requires knowledge of coaching and knowledge of teaching and learning principles as well as excellent communication and interpersonal skills. If mentors are to support coaches, then they must also be supported by the sport or organisation that they represent and initially that would require some form of mentor learning and development. Weaver and Chelladurai (1999) present a framework that demonstrates the complexity of the mentoring relationship but also highlights key principles that need to be considered by organisations seeking to implement a mentoring scheme.

By following this model, Weaver and Chelladurai (1999) assert that there will be learning and development benefits for all concerned – the mentee, the mentor and the organisation. However, these advantages will occur only if the mentoring relationship follows all the previous steps, starting with the compatibility of the mentor and mentee, and allows the necessary time to cultivate the different phases of the relationship. This framework represents one end of the continuum, the structured, mentored experience, characterised by direction, feedback and a measure of evaluation. At the other end of the continuum is the unmediated or informal arrangement from which constructive information may be gained, but which

*Table 11.1* Models of mentoring

| Model | Overview | Uses | Advantages/ disadvantages | Further information |
|---|---|---|---|---|
| Apprenticeship | Mentor is 'Master Coach' setting standards and values to be copied | Often used in sport coaching with new/ novice coaches 'apprenticed' to more experienced coaches | Practical environment/ Lack of appropriate 'Master Coach' | Butler (2005) |
| Competency | There is an explicit set of skills and techniques to be learned; mentor as trainer | Used in sport coaching where proficiency has to be demonstrated | Supports coach learning and development/ Mentors are not always 'coach educators' | Santos *et al.* (2010) |
| Reflective practitioner | Encourages learner to be self-critical; mentor questions and does not offer 'right' answer | Used extensively in teaching, becoming more common in sport coaching | Encourages practice of reflection/ Where are coaches taught skills of self-reflection? | Vella *et al.* (2013) |
| Role model | Mentor as inspiration as a consequence of previous results | Can be used to inspire and attract people into coaching | Raises profile of sport coaching/ Downside of inspirational models | Norman (2012) |
| Network | Mentor acts as 'sponsor' introducing coach to other coaches; mentor retains power | Used in sports coaching but mostly with informal mentoring situations | Mentors with extensive networks/ One way flow of information and connections | Occhino *et al.* (2013) |
| Educator | Mentor listens and creates appropriate opportunities for the mentee's professional learning | Could be used in sport coaching with more experienced coaches; mentors encourage problem solving and decision making as coaching tools | Very useful developmental environment/ Mentor has to be highly developed in learning strategies | Nash and Sproule (2009) |

lacks the structure and organisation highlighted in Figure 11.1. In some coaching environments, the more formal methods may not be possible and, equally, some coaches may prefer the absence of a formal structure. Mentoring can be related to career advancement, coach development and job satisfaction, although different kinds of mentoring may be required at different stages.

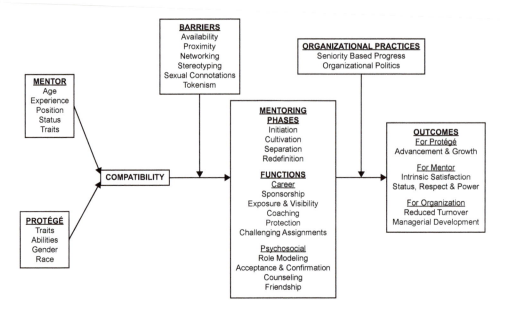

*Figure 11.1* Weaver and Chelladurai (1999) Framework for mentoring.

## Mentor/mentee training and support

For many, the mentoring relationship is conceptualised as an expert based, hierarchical and one-directional model (Kilty 2006). This is generally true at an initial level, for example, when a novice coach enters the coaching profession and is paired with a more qualified and experienced mentor. Whatever the type of mentoring relationship, the effectiveness is predicated upon the training and support offered to both mentors and mentees prior to and during the mentoring programme. Major issues identified by both mentors and mentees were time constraints (Ponte and Twomey 2014), personal qualities (Nash *et al.* 2009), communication skills (Levine *et al.* 2013), frequency of meetings (Ponte and Twomey 2014) and cultural issues (Orland-Barak *et al.* 2013), as well as problems around understanding and managing the process (Nash 2003). Issues of recruitment, training and retention of coaching personnel are part of the ongoing sport strategy in many countries. Structured mentoring programmes can be implemented to develop and maintain relationships between the new and the more experienced coaches, however the specific roles and responsibilities of each are key. The more involvement with the mentor during the relationship initiation phase, the greater the benefits the mentee may receive (Scandura and Williams 2001).

Mentor learning and development is a vital component of any effective mentoring programme, therefore the investment made in initial and ongoing support of mentors will contribute to the success of the programme. Mentors need to be carefully selected, trained and monitored (Ehrich *et al.* 2004), as effective mentoring has been related to high self-esteem, job engagement and importantly within sport coaching, low turnover of coaches (Eby and Allen 2002). There are a number of different mentor and mentee training programmes offered by various organisations in a variety of occupations. These training programmes generally include three different elements:

- pre-programme orientation – to allow participants an overview of proposed programme and expectations;
- programme training – to define and discuss role expectations and obligations for both mentors and mentees;
- ongoing support – to allow additional opportunities for collaboration and further information and training.

These training programmes often include skills and attitudes for both mentors and mentees, pairing mentors with mentees, lines of communication, managing mentor meetings and relationships and forward planning. Other coaches and club/organisational personnel can be used as valuable resources within mentoring programmes to enhance diversity in skill and knowledge development. Tracking forms, planning calendars and feedback mechanisms can be valuable in monitoring mentoring programmes over extended periods of time (Greene and Puetzer 2002).

## Case study

The following extended case study is an example of an ongoing mentoring programme, initiated at the highest levels of sport and coaching (McQuade 2013). The International Coaching Enrichment Certification Programme (ICECP) is an example of a formalised mentoring programme, evidenced through the recruitment and deployment of mentors allocated to support coaches. Although mentoring is potentially the most significant support mechanism offered to coaches by the programme, the manner in which ICECP mentor-coach relationships are initiated and managed is unclear. Equally, how effective the ICECP mentoring programme is or independent mentor-coach relationships are in supporting coach learning and practice is also unclear. Therefore an evaluation of the effectiveness of this programme was undertaken to inform coach education research as to the impact of a mentoring intervention.

## *ICECP*

The International Coaching Enrichment Certification Programme (ICECP) is a jointly delivered coach education programme between The University of Delaware (UD) and the United States Olympic Committee (USOC) and is funded by Olympic Solidarity. The ICECP provides high performing coaches from developing nations with access to theory-based learning and supports them in the practical application through the delivery of a project in their home country designed to promote further growth of the sport and the Olympic ideals. A range of coaching projects, participation initiatives and athlete development programmes around the world have been supported; examples include the development of a national judo coaching education system in Japan and a basketball coach education programme for secondary school coaches in Malawi. The ICECP, now in its sixth year, has been well received by National Olympic Committees (NOC) and the 139 coaches who have represented five continents and developing nations representing 23 sports.

**213**

The ICECP delivers four modules annually over a seven-month time from October to May, with Modules 1, 2 and 3 being delivered in the USA during October. The use of a blended approach allows coaches access to formal (lectures, workshops and seminars) and informal (apprenticeships) learning. Module 4 occurs in May of the following year and coaches who have delivered a successful project are invited back to present on the impact of their work.

The six-month time lag between Modules 3 and 4 is to allow a mentoring programme to act as the bridge between theoretical learning and the practical application of that learning in the field. Coaches are elite, high performing coaches from participation and performance domains, nominated by their NOC. Mentors from Europe and the USA have been recruited to the programme based on their technical expertise in the fields of coaching, coach education and sports science. Inevitably the relationships have a cross-cultural base. The Programme Director seeks to match the mentor's technical expertise with the technical focus of the coach's project in dyadic pairs. Coaches have the opportunity to meet their mentors at the end of Module 3 to build the relationship and explore and refine their project plans before the relationship migrates from a face-to-face to a remote or long-arm basis. The majority of the ongoing relationship then occurs remotely through electronic forums, with mentors tasked to support learning and undertake assessment functions. Coaches meet with their mentors again at Module 4 in Lausanne to prepare for their final presentation. The evaluation was undertaken by a mentor on the ICECP, and the key driver for this study was the need to develop an understanding of what constitutes effective mentoring practice in the eyes of the ICECP participants (mentors and coaches) and to critically reflect on and develop personal professional mentoring skills and practice.

Semi-structured interviews and focus groups were used with seven mentors and 20 coaches during Module 4 in Lausanne. The initial focus of the study was to explore the effectiveness of the ICECP mentoring programme and independent mentor-coach relationships. The interviews provided considerable depth of information, and this conceptualisation marked a significant step forward given the research in this context was unique. It provides the ICECP mentoring programme and independent mentor-coach relationships with a more defined, somewhat tangible shape; it could be perceived to be a job specification with associated career options for Programme Directors, mentors and coaches. Six key areas emerged from the findings.

1    In the absence of facilitating culturally based mentor-coach relationships, the significance of the relationship building phases is critical. A detailed understanding of the coach's cultural identity and an awareness of the environment in which the coach operates are critical if the project plan is to effectively underpin the relationship, the coach's personal development and the delivery, management and evaluation of the project.

2    Supporting coaches to bring their projects to fruition is marked by an extended period of what this study has referred to as 'long-arm mentoring'. The concept of the long-arm mentor, which originates in nursing, resonates well with the ICECP mentor as the majority of the relationship is conducted remotely and does have a support and supervisory function. How appropriate the terminology is could be questioned, but where time zones and continents divide mentor-coach relationships, the metaphor of the long-arm is useful. Mentors have to be able to extend their reach to perform various roles and

functions, the majority of which are conducted electronically. Familiarity with Internet technologies such as e-mail and call/instant messaging services such as Skype are taken for granted, yet there is unexplored potential in the use of other social media applications such as blogs, Facebook, YouTube and LinkedIn to replicate the presence of the mentor in the field.

3   Innovative thinking about how to use the various new and emerging technologies will be crucial in supporting and sustaining future relationships. Regardless of which communication options are used, a key message was that the mentoring dyad, specifically the coach, must commit to communicating frequently, even if it is to report that no progress has been made.

4   Mentors recognise the ICECP places an overt focus on the completion of the coaching project, and the relationship from their perception is outcome-driven. Coaches recognise this role is important but do value the psychosocial functions assumed, suggesting it develops their confidence and competence to manage the delivery of a coaching project that inevitably involves infrequently used skills such as management, planning, budgeting, stakeholder meetings and presentations. Given the overt outcome-driven focus, there is an inherent danger the relationship could be mentor-led and micro-managed; this must be pre-empted by ensuring the psychosocial functions are emphasised.

5   If the relationship is to be effective, both mentor and coach must assume responsibility for the process and outcome, with the ultimate responsibility being assumed by the mentee.

6   The ICECP is a unique coach education programme, which emphasises the delivery of a coaching project designed to grow the sport in the coach's home country. Whilst the ICECP mentoring role does resemble aspects of mentoring roles assumed across various domains, holistically it is unique and the impact across the whole field of mentoring difficult to quantify.

The findings of this study can be used as a benchmark to evaluate mentoring effectiveness within the ICECP mentoring programme and independent mentor-coach relationships. These findings can provide a comparative foundation for other mentoring programmes and relationships that have a support and supervisory function and are conducted remotely or on a long-arm basis using electronic technologies.

The case study described here highlights key considerations in mentoring within sport coaching:

■   Evaluations demonstrating the impact of mentoring programmes from the perspective of the mentor and the mentee are lacking within sport coaching.
■   This programme is designed to support elite high performing sport coaches across performance and participation pathways.
■   Aspects of long-arm mentoring need to be explored including, specifically, how electronic communication mediums allow the mentoring relationship to flourish regardless of location and distance.
■   Mentoring expertise is not necessarily sport-specific.
■   Other skills – innovation, creativity and cultural awareness – can be developed within mentoring programmes given the appropriate mentor experiences.

**215**

## e-Mentoring

The ICECP mentoring programme evaluated in the case study is an example of a mentoring programme carried out using some form of electronic medium. The more traditional methods of mentoring are carried out on a face-to-face basis, however e-mentoring, through the use of both synchronous and asynchronous communication methods, is creating virtual mentoring relationships (Rowland 2012). Some of these e-mentoring examples have evolved from e-learning or online courses, while others have developed as a result of more practical reasons, such as location and available time. E-mentoring can be explained as a developing concept with some characteristics that differ from face-to-face mentoring and which evolve through various means of practice and application (Mullen 2009; Risquez 2008). Some programmes are also known as cybermentoring, telementoring or virtual mentoring, all of which involve some form of remote access.

The available literature has referred to various benefits from the e-mentoring experience, including technological skills, professional assessment, social and psychological benefits (Williams *et al.* 2012; Eby and Lockwood 2005). These are further explained:

- Technological skills refer to online communication skills learned by mentors and mentees (Homitz and Berge 2008).
- Social e-mentor benefits refer to the opportunity to network (Shrestha *et al.* 2009).
- Psychological e-mentor benefits refer to personal satisfaction from offering support and advice to others (Murphy and Ensher 2008; Shrestha *et al.* 2009; Yaw 2007).

Many of these, more obviously social and psychological benefits, are also attributable to more traditional forms of mentoring.

Coaching is a term that has been used more recently outside the sporting context, for example in both business and life coaching. Mentoring, especially e-mentoring, has also become more mainstream. According to Zey (2011), e-mentoring is emerging as a business mechanism for several economic, organisational, technological and sociological reasons. Virtual mentoring is evolving in business as a result of factors such as the growth of multinational corporations and the subsequent remote location of workers. Although no comparable multinational corporations currently exist in sport coaching, many national coaching organisations subscribe to global coaching organisations, for example, the International Council for Coaching Excellence (ICCE). There are many disparate and commercial organisations offering sport coaching, and the provision of organised and structured coaching programmes is now more geographically dispersed. As can be seen from the examples described here, some face-to-face mentoring is occurring with mentors from external organisations and outside specific sports. This could be adopted further within sport coaching following the ICECP example.

## Mentoring evaluations – does mentoring work?

Relatively few studies in sport have been established with the specific aim of understanding and evaluating formal mentoring relationships, and little systematic attention has been paid to the specific mentor–mentee factors affecting the quality of the mentoring provided (Fagenson-Eland *et al.* 1997). However, there are still only a few studies related to formal mentoring and the links to learning in domains other than sport (Hezlett and Gibson 2005;

**216**

Lankau and Scandura 2007). Some studies have been conducted in relation to the factors that affect learning, but no studies have been conducted of how this may change throughout the stages of the mentoring process (Hale 2000; Hezlett and Gibson 2005; Kilcullen 2007).

The following issues within mentoring programmes have been identified:

- Match between mentor and mentee: Both mentor and mentee behaviours have been perceived as critical factors contributing to either a positive or negative mentoring experience for the mentee and the mentor (Hamlin and Sage 2011). Many studies identify this as a make or break factor in mentoring relationships.
- Distancing behaviour: This is an example of a mentor's negative behaviour by keeping the mentee at a distance within the relationship. For example, if the mentee asks difficult questions or challenges the mentor, then distancing behaviour can be displayed (Ghosh *et al.* 2011).
- Manipulative behaviour: This is a further example of a mentor's negative behaviour by manipulating the mentee to meet the needs or expectations of the mentor. Much of this research is based upon the personality traits of the mentor (Kim and Choi 2011).
- Lack of mentor expertise: The recruitment of expert coaches and subsequent training as mentors within the area was identified as an issue within mentoring programmes (Reid *et al.* 2013).
- General issues: Many of these issues cover aspects of communication and feedback, for example, the mentor displaying a non-threatening manner and being a good listener and role model. The mentees also need to be able to recognise the value of life-long learning, have capacity for self-appraisal, be amenable to personal and professional development and have a willingness to reflect (Wilson *et al.* 2013).

Many mentoring schemes do not acknowledge some of the recognised difficulties within programmes – the schemes are only as good as the personnel involved in the implementation of these programmes. Compared to formal mentoring, informal mentoring is spontaneously initiated and can last for extended periods of time. Bloom *et al.* (1998) work suggests that most coaches have been informally mentored by more experienced coaches during both their athletic and early coaching careers. The introductory statement from the basketball coach Jim supports this finding, leading to the conclusion that coaches in this situation gained valuable knowledge and insights that helped shape their coaching philosophies and enhanced their practice. As a result of their own experiences, they may have, inadvertently, become informal mentors themselves, although this has not always been recognised in the initial stages of coaching.

While some problems relating to mentoring programmes have been identified, many organisations still initiate and require their personnel to be part of them, whether as a mentor or mentee. UK Sport has developed a formal mentoring programme for their elite sport coaches, utilising expertise from both sport and business and acknowledging the transferability from different domains into the process of mentoring a sport coach. The programme has evolved based on three principles:

1    educating and developing identified mentors engaged in formal roles within all UK Sport Coaching Development Programmes;
2    creating a diverse group of individuals with a range of expertise to best support the development of high performance coaches;

3 raising the standards of coaching skills and expertise throughout the high performance system.

(UK Sport, n.d.)

While this appears to be a valuable and laudable programme, the extent of the impact upon coaches and, ultimately coaching practice, has not yet been determined. The effectiveness of any formal mentoring scheme may depend on the characteristics of the individual mentors who participate in the programme, as identified as a 'diverse group of individuals' above. The quality of the mentor-mentee relationship is a key factor to successful mentoring, but few programmes or research studies have explored the dynamics of this interpersonal relationship (Nash 2003). Hezlett and Gibson (2005) argue that more research into the process is required to gain a better understanding of the specific mentor and mentee behaviours that create the particular conditions under which mentoring relationships are effective.

Another coach education programme that uses mentoring as an integral part of the coach learning process is the Advanced Coaching Diploma (ACD) from the Coaching Association of Canada. The ACD is the highest possible qualification in the National Coaching Certification Program (NCCP), and the coaches who are enrolled in the program are those seeking NCCP Level 4 and 5 certification, with endorsement from their own sports organisation. The mentor coach is often called the Master Coach in this situation and is attached to a National Coaching Institute (CAC 2013). These Master Coaches are sport-specific experts and work alongside the trainee coach, or mentee, for the duration of the course, normally two years. These Masters Coaches work with the coaches during the practical delivery of their sport and offer guidance and support to enable the trainee coaches to achieve the program requirements. In Canada, under the NCCP process, coaches are described in one of three contexts:

1 In Training – coaches have completed some of the required training for a context;
2 Trained – coaches have completed all required training for a context;
3 Certified – coaches have completed all evaluation requirements for a context.

(CAC, n.d.)

Interestingly, all of the examples, UK Sport, Coaching Association of Canada and the ICECP case study, are targeting elite performing coaches across both participation and performance pathways. A recent research study identified that coaches felt mentoring was more useful in the early stage of coach development, but the examples highlighted appear to contradict the coaches' views (Nash, Sproule and Horton, in press). Learning from other people's experience is important in various workplaces, for example, to better understand the job task or to gain experience from other people's mistakes (Collins 2004).

Much of the success, or effectiveness, of mentoring programmes can be dependent upon the length of the programme, whether short, medium or long term. Allen (2011) suggests that:

- Short term programmes lead to changes in learning, for example, new knowledge, self-esteem and reciprocal learning.
- Medium term programmes lead to changes in action, for example, modified practice, changed decision-making and altered management strategies.

■ Long term programmes lead to changes in coaching conditions, for example, establishment of communities of practice (see Chapter 13), stability of coaching and coaching personnel and enhanced cooperation.

In conclusion, before deciding on the effectiveness of a mentoring programme key questions need to be addressed.

■ What is the point of the mentoring programme?
■ What specifically is the role of the mentor?
■ How will success be measured on an individual and a programme basis?
■ Were there clear aims and objectives established prior to the start of the programme?

These aims should be incorporated within the framework of a wider coach education and development strategy specific to the country, sport or level of coach. There are still questions to be answered around resourcing of these programmes. In the ICECP case study described earlier, remote support was used. However if funding was available, would supported practice in the field be more beneficial to the coaches in this instance?

## Future of mentoring in sport coaching

Mentoring may give the sport coach greater flexibility in a context where they do not have the time for formal training, and delivers 'training' in a manner that allows them to control the manner in which they learn, an important element of personal learning (Fisher *et al.* 2010). Mentoring may also help the sport coach make sense of critical events experienced in competition and training contexts (Cope and Watts 2000). Mentoring may therefore emphasize learning through experience by making it possible to develop deeper learning, as a result of the reflexivity triggered by the mentoring relationship (Carver *et al.* 2009) (see Chapter 12).

The mentor acts as the coach's coach, as coaching is about improving performance through structured practice and feedback. Throughout this chapter many examples of mentoring have been provided from various countries, sports and coaching organisations. While this is very laudable, and sport coaches attribute much of their development to influential mentors, does the research back up these claims?

## REFERENCES

Allen, T. (2011). Who Is a Mentor? A Review of Evolving Definitions and Implications for Research. *Journal of Management* 37: pp. 280–304.

Audet, J. and Couteret, P. (2005). Le coaching entrepreneurial: spécificités et facteurs de succès. *Journal of Small Business and Entrepreneurship* 18(3): pp. 471–490.

Bloom, G., Durand-Bush, N., Schinke, R. and Salmela, J. (1998). The Importance of Mentoring in the Development of Coaches and Athletes./Importance du 'mentoring' dans le developpement des entraineurs et des athletes. *International Journal of Sport Psychology* 29(3): pp. 267–281.

Butler, J. (2005). TGfU pet-agogy: old dogs, new tricks and puppy school. *Physical Education & Sport Pedagogy* 10, 3, pp. 225–240.

Carver, C., & Feiman-Nemser, S. (2009). Using Policy to Improve Teacher Induction: Critical Elements and Missing Pieces, *Educational Policy*, 23, 2, pp. 295–328.

Clutterbuck, D. (2004). Making the Most of Informal Mentoring, *Development and Learning in Organizations* 18(4): pp. 16–17.

Coaching Association of Canada (CAC). (n.d.). Trained vs. Certified. Retrieved: 20 August 2014. www.coach.ca/trained-vs-certified-s16468

Coaching Association of Canada (CAC). (2013). Advanced Coaching Diploma: The Pinnacle of NCCP Coach Training. CAC, August. Retrieved: 30 November 2013. www.coach.ca/advanced-coaching-diploma-s13778

Cope, J. and Watts, G. (2000). Learning by Doing: An Exploration of Experience, Critical Incidents and Reflection in Entrepreneurial Learning. *International Journal of Entrepreneurial Behaviour & Research* 6(3): pp. 104–124.

Cothran, D., McCaughtry, N., Faust, R., Garn, A., Kulinna, P. and Martin, J. (2009). E-Mentoring in Physical Education: Promises and Pitfalls. *Research Quarterly For Exercise and Sport* 80(3): pp. 552–562.

Crisfield, P. (1998). *Analysing Your Coaching: The Start of Your Journey Towards Coaching Excellence.* (Leeds: The National Coaching Foundation).

Eby, L.T. and Allen, T.D. (2002). Further Investigation of Protégés' Negative Mentoring Experiences. *Group & Organization Management* 27: pp. 456–479.

Eby, L.T. and Lockwood, A. (2005). Protégés and Mentors' Reactions to Participating in Formal Mentoring Programs: A Qualitative Investigation. *Journal of Vocational Behavior* 67: pp. 441–458.

Ehrich, L. S., Hansford, B. and Tennent, L. (2004). Formal Mentoring Programmes in Education and Other Professions: A Review of the Literature. *Educational Administration Quarterly* 40(4): pp. 518–540.

Fagenson-Eland, E. A., Marks, M. A. and Amendola, K. L. (1997). Perceptions of Mentoring Relationships. *Journal of Vocational Behavior* 51: pp. 29–42.

Fisher, S. L., Wasserman, M. E. and Orvis, K. A. (2010). Trainee Reactions to Learner Control: An Important Link in the e-Learning Equation. *International Journal of Training and Development* 14: pp. 198–208.

Football Association (FA). (2013). The Coaching Pathway. Retrieved: 28 November 2013. www.thefa.com/my-football/footballvolunteers/coachingvolunteering/get%20into%20coaching/~/media/4B30C67CB4AA49DA9CB58EF341D024FA.ashx/CoachingPathway0811.pdf

Ghosh, R., Dierkes, S. and Falletta, S. (2011). Incivility Spiral in Mentoring Relationships: Reconceptualizing Negative Mentoring as Deviant Workplace Behavior. *Advances In Developing Human Resources* 13(1): pp. 22–39.

Gladwell, M. (2006). *The Tipping Point: How Little Things Can Make a Big Difference.* (New York: Little, Brown and Company).

Gordon, S. P. and Brobeck, S. R. (2010). Coaching the Mentor: Facilitating Reflection and Change. *Mentoring & Tutoring: Partnership in Learning* 18(4): pp. 427–447.

Greene, M. T. and Puetzer, M. (2002). The Value of Mentoring: A Strategic Approach to Recruitment and Retention. *Journal of Nursing Care Quality* 17(1): pp. 63–70.

Haggard, D. L., Dougherty, T.W., Turban, D.B. and Wilbanks, J.E. (2011). Who Is a Mentor? A Review of Evolving Definitions, *Journal of Management*, 1, p. 280–304.

Hale, R. (2000). To Match or Mis-match? The Dynamics of Mentoring as a Route to Personal and Organisational Learning. *Career Development International* 5(4/5): pp. 223–234.

Hamlin, R. and Sage, L. (2011). Behavioural Criteria of Perceived Mentoring Effectiveness: An Empirical Study of Effective and Ineffective Mentor and Mentee Behaviour within Formal Mentoring Relationships. *Journal of European Industrial Training* 35(8): pp. 752–778.

Hezlett, S.A. and Gibson, S.K. (2005). Mentoring and Human Resource Development: Where We Are and Where We Need to Go. *Advances in Developing Human Resources* 7(4): pp. 446–469.

Homitz, D.J. and Berge, Z.L. (2008). Using e-Mentoring to Sustain Distance Training and Education. *The Learning Organization* 15(4): pp. 326–335.

Jones, R. L., Harris, R. A. and Miles, A. (2009). Mentoring in Sports Coaching: A Review of the Literature. *Physical Education and Sport Pedagogy* 14(3): 267–284.

Kilcullen, N. M. (2007). Said Another Way: The Impact of Mentoring on Clinical Learning. *Nursing Forum* 42(2): pp. 95–104.

Kilty, K. (2006). Women in Coaching. *Sport Psychologist* 20(2): pp. 222–234.

Kim, M. and Choi, K. (2011). Mentors' Negative Behaviors in Formal Mentoring (Their Relationship with Personality Traits, Protégé Attitudes, and Program Characteristics). 대한경영학회지: pp. 137, DBPIA.

Lankau, M. J. and Scandura, T. A. (2007). Mentoring as a Forum for Personal Learning. In *The Handbook of Mentoring at Work: Theory, Research, and Practice*. B. R. Ragins and K. E. Kram (Eds.) (Thousand Oaks, CA: Sage): pp. 95–122.

Levine, W., Braman, J., Gelberman, R. and Black, K. (2013). Mentorship in Orthopaedic Surgery – Road Map to Success for the Mentor and the Mentee: AOA Critical Issues. *Journal of Bone and Joint Surgery* 95(9): pp. e591–595.

Lyle, J. (2007) UKCC impact study: Definitional, conceptual and methodological review. Research Review for Sport Coach UK.

McQuade, S. (2013). An Investigation Into the Effectiveness of a Long-Arm Mentoring Program: Links to the International Coach Enrichment Certification Program (ICECP). Unpublished MSc dissertation, Northumbria University.

Mullen, C.A. (2009). Re-imagining the Human Dimension of Mentoring: A Framework for Research Administration and the Academy. *Journal of Research Administration* 40(1): pp. 10–33.

Murphy, S. E. and Ensher, E.A. (2008). A Qualitative Analysis of Charismatic Leadership in Creative Teams: The Case of Television Directors. *The Leadership Quarterly* 19(3): pp. 335–352.

Nash, C. (2003). Development of a Mentoring System Within Coaching Practice. *Journal of Hospitality, Leisure, Sport & Tourism Education* (Oxford Brookes University) 2(2): p. 39.

Nash, C. and Sproule J. (2011). Insights into Experiences: Reflections of Expert and Novice Coaches. *International Journal of Sports Science & Coaching* 6(1): pp. 149–161.

Nash, C., Sproule, J., Callan, M., McDonald, K. and Cassidy, T. (2009). Career Development of Expert Coaches. *International Journal of Sports Science & Coaching* 4(1): pp. 121–138.

Nelson, L., Cushion, C. and Potrac, P. (2013). Enhancing the Provision of Coach Education: The Recommendations of UK Coaching Practitioners. *Physical Education and Sport Pedagogy* 18(2): pp. 204–218.

Norman, L. (2012). Developing Female Coaches: Strategies from Women Themselves. *Asia-Pacific Journal Of Health, Sport And Physical Education* 3, 3, pp. 227–238.

Occhino, J., Mallett, C., & Rynne, S. (2013). Dynamic social networks in high performance football coaching. *Physical Education & Sport Pedagogy* 18, 1, pp. 90–102.

Orland-Barak, L., Kheir-Farraj, R. and Becher, A. (2013). Mentoring in Contexts of Cultural and Political Friction: Moral Dilemmas of Mentors and Their Management in Practice. *Mentoring & Tutoring: Partnership in Learning* 21(1): pp. 76–95.

Paquette, J. (2012). Mentoring and Change in Cultural Organizations: The Experience of Directors in British National Museums. *Journal of Arts Management, Law & Society* 42(4): pp. 205–216.

Paul, M. (2004). *L'accompagnement : une posture professionnelle spécifique*. (Paris: L'Harmattan).

**221**

PGA. (2013). Retrieved: 29 November 2013. www.pga.info/about-us/growing-the-game/right-coach-right-place-right-time.aspx

Ponte, E. and Twomey, S. (2014). Veteran Teachers Mentoring in Training: Negotiating Issues of Power, Vulnerability and Professional Development. *Journal of Education for Teaching* 40(1): pp. 20–33.

Reid, T., Hinderer, K., Jarosinski, J., Mister, B. and Seldomridge, L. (2013). Expert Clinician to Clinical Teacher: Developing a Faculty Academy and Mentoring Initiative. *Nurse Education in Practice* 13(4): pp. 288–293.

Risquez, A. (2008). E-mentoring: An Extended Practice, an Emerging Discipline. In *Advances in E-Learning: Experiences and Methodologies*. F. J. Garcia-Penalvo (Ed.) (Hershey, PA: Information Science Publishing): pp. 61–82.

Rowland, K. (2012). E-Mentoring: An Innovative Twist to Traditional Mentoring. *Journal of Technology Management and Innovation* 7(1): pp. 228–237.

Santos, S., Mesquita, I., Graça, A., & Rosado, A. (2010). Coaches' perceptions of competence and acknowledgement of training needs related to professional competences. *Journal Of Sports Science & Medicine* 9, 1, pp. 62–70.

Scandura, T.A. and Williams, E.A. (2001). An Investigation of the Moderating Effects of Gender on the Relationships Between Mentorship Initiation and Protégé Perceptions of Mentoring Functions. *Journal of Vocational Behavior* 59: pp. 342–363.

Shrestha, C. H., May, S., Edirisingha, P., Burke, L. and Linsey, T. (2009). From face-to-Face to e-Mentoring: Does the ''e'' Add Any Value for Mentors? *International Journal of Teaching and Learning in Higher Education* 20(2): pp. 116–124.

UK Sport. (n.d.). Retrieved: 28th November 2013. www.uksport.gov.uk/pages/mentoring/

Vella, S., Crowe, T., & Oades, L. (2013). Increasing the Effectiveness of Formal Coach Education: Evidence of a Parallel Process. *International Journal Of Sports Science & Coaching* 8, 2, pp. 417–430.

Wanberg, C.R., Kammeyer-Mueller, J.D. and Marchese, M. (2006). Mentor and Protégé Predictors and Outcomes of Mentoring in a Formal Mentoring Program. *Journal of Vocational Behavior* 69(3): pp. 410–423.

Weaver, M.A. and Chelladurai, P. (1999). A Mentoring Model for Management in Sport and Physical Education. *Quest* 51: pp. 24–38.

Werthner, P. and Trudel, P. (2006). A New Theoretical Perspective for Understanding How Coaches Learn to Coach. *The Sport Psychologist* 20(2): pp. 198–212.

Willem, A. and Van den Broeck, H. (2007). *Learning Mode of Small Business Owners*. Retrieved from Vlerick Leuvin Gent Management School website: 29 November 2013. www.FEB.UGent.be/nl/Ondz/wp/Papers/wp_07_453.pdf

Williams, S., Sunderman, J. and Kim, J. (2012). E-mentoring in an Online Course: Benefits and Challenges to E-mentors. *International Journal of Evidence Based Coaching and Mentoring* 10(1): pp. 109–123.

Wilson, M., Jacques, R., Fiddes, P. and Palermo, C. (2013). Mentoring of Medical Students: A Cross-Sectional Study. *Focus On Health Professional Education: A Multi-Disciplinary Journal* 14(3): p. 44.

Wright, S. C. and Smith, D. E. (2000). A Case for Formalised Mentoring. *Quest* 52: pp. 200–213.

Yaw, D. C. (2007). *E-mentoring in Virtual Education*. Paper presented at the Academy of Human Resource Development International Conference in the Americas (Indianapolis, IN, Feb. 28–Mar. 4).

Young, A. M. and Perrewé, P. L. (2004). The Role of Expectations in the Mentoring Exchange: An Analysis of Mentor and Protégé Expectations in Relation to Perceived Support. *Journal of Managerial Issues* 16(1): pp. 103–126.

Zey, M.G. (2011). Virtual Mentoring: The Challenges and Opportunities of Electronically-Mediated Formal Mentor Programs. *Review of Business Research* 11(4): pp. 141–152.

# Chapter 12

# Reflective practice

*Amanda Martindale and Dave Collins*

## INTRODUCING REFLECTIVE PRACTICE

### What is reflective practice?

Fiona is the coach of a U16 girls football team; she has completed her coaching awards and considers herself to be knowledgeable about football coaching at the level at which she is operating. Certainly her coaching behaviours appear to be spontaneous and she carries out her actions in a fluid and intuitive way. Yet, when asked 'why' she is carrying out certain behaviours or actions, she struggles with the explanation. Often she can't say what it is that she knows and finds herself at a loss when trying to describe why she's doing what she's doing.

Jeremy is a professional coach of a high performance judo squad and is a highly knowledgeable and competent practitioner. He can easily recognise inefficiencies in technique and form, but wishes he could give more accurate or complete descriptions of these. In his day-to-day practice he makes a huge number of judgements about the 'quality' of what he sees, for which he struggles to accurately state the criteria. Often, when pressed, he has difficulty elaborating on the rules and procedures related to the coaching skills he displays.

Dave is a rugby union coach whose approach is a mishmash of techniques. Dave seems often to be influenced by the last course he completed or coach he has watched. In fact, his athletes often joke about 'what course did you do this weekend?'

Helen is very much a 'recipe' coach. She has a tried and trusted technique, which she follows with all her track athletes. Indeed, it would be possible to set a watch by her sessions, which are almost identical in content, comment and tone.

Both Fiona and Jeremy often think about what they are doing, sometimes while they are doing it. Usually there is some puzzling, troubling or interesting pattern that they are trying to understand and make sense of, for example, 'What are the players' positions when possession breaks down? What criteria am I using when I am judging their technique? What procedures am I using when I provide feedback to my players? How am I framing the problem that I am trying to solve?' Most importantly Fiona and Jeremy are 'aware' of the strengths and weaknesses apparent in their coaching practice and so can reflect on this and take steps to do something about the areas that require improvement. By contrast, Dave and Helen seem all at sea, with apparently little thought about why they do what they do. Crucially, Fiona and Jeremy are also aware of their thinking and are able to 'think about their thinking' (known as metacognition); unfortunately, Dave and Helen are not.

The contrast between these two pairs can be assigned to the capacity for critical reflection. Fiona and Jeremy are both aware of the need for it and seem to work hard to develop their skills. By contrast, Dave and Helen are 'coaching by numbers', using what they may well describe as 'tried and trusted' methods but with little or no awareness of the need to individualise or even develop their methods. It is this entire process of reflection that Schön (1991) describes as being central to the ways in which practitioners can deal well with situations of uncertainty, instability, uniqueness and conflict that are so apparent in sports coaching practice.

Key point: reflection tends to focus interactively on the outcomes of the action, the action itself and the intuitive knowing implicit in the action (Schön 1991).

## Why is reflective practice important?

Reflective practice has become a central pillar of modern day professional practice in many fields and in particular in the 'helping professions' (for example, in teaching and nursing). One of the characteristics of expert practitioners is to be able to take their own strengths and limitations into account (Klein and Militello 2005), and it is widely accepted that the process of reflective practice can enable practitioners to do this on a regular basis. If carried out effectively, reflective practice can help sports coaches develop a better understanding of their own coaching practice and to chart the progress of their professional development. This is the case no matter what the level of coach – novice, intermediate or expert; all will benefit from the unique and personalised process of reflection on their coaching. Without this, as in the examples above, coaches can get 'stuck in a rut', trotting out the same old sessions time and again, or appearing to jump randomly from one idea to another. In either case, athlete frustration and less than optimum progress are the likely outcomes.

Of course, reflective practice is not just important for coaches themselves, but also for the performers with whom they are working. To ensure that the coaching provided is quality, a number of evaluations of effectiveness should take place. These may include evaluations of the 'process' and 'outcome' of coaching as gauged by the performers and significant others (for example, parents, employers, national governing bodies). A comprehensive assessment should also include self-evaluation made on behalf of the coach; reflective practice can offer a systematic, tangible and recordable means of self-evaluation and analysis. Apart from the obvious and necessary benefits this brings to performers and significant others in terms of justifying quality and sometimes 'cost-effectiveness', it also brings enormous benefit to the coaches themselves. For example, a chart or map (see Chapter 15) of the development of their practice (along with numerous associated examples and illustrations) can be shared with peers and/or mentors for the purpose of professional development. Significantly, the process can also provide the scaffolding for the development of professional competence and confidence, so that the coaches can see their own progress (in justifying the rationale for their general and specific practice, for example).

Crucially, however, these evaluations must take place against some realistic and rationalised standard. For example, parents will often ask why their son or daughter is failing to make progress towards the expected champion status. In such cases, setting and managing expectation (where should you expect to be) is important. In parallel, coaches assessing the process or outcome of their coaching need to have some 'standards and systems' against which they can evaluate.

**224**

## What does reflective practice mean for me?

If you are not already doing so, you should consider the use of reflective practice in your own coaching. This chapter will develop your understanding of reflective practice and take you through the necessary steps to incorporate it into your coaching practice. If you are already operating as a 'reflective practitioner', then this chapter should give you some ideas about how you can develop and extend your practice to ensure you (and your performers) are getting as much out of the process as possible. Despite its increasing use as (yet) another competency on the accreditation/qualification checklist (Collins, Burke, Martindale and Cruickshank, in press), reflective practice should not be a 'tick box' or 'paper exercise'. It has the potential to significantly influence the effectiveness of your coaching practice and, as such, is worthy of due care and consideration in the set-up, conduct and evaluation of your coaching. Nor does reflective practice have to place a heavy demand on your time. The excessive amounts of writing that coaches sometimes imagine to be a necessary feature of a 'reflective journal' are not required. The old adage of quality over quantity is especially true here; a few insightful reflections noted against clearly expressed and logical criteria and in a carefully planned and structured recording system can offer greater clarity and action summary than many paragraphs of writing without direction or purpose. The key is to organise a coherent and comprehensive approach to reflective practice that you can engage with on a regular and ongoing basis and that works for you.

## CHAPTER OUTLINE

The chapter will begin by exploring current understanding of reflective practice in coaching. The central questions of Who? What? Where? and How? will be explored to provide a comprehensive picture of how reflective practice operates within a sports coaching context. Attention will then turn to 'reflection-on-action' and the process of reflection 'after' coaching, including practical examples of how this may look and a template for recording your own reflections in this way. A further level of practice is explored by considering 'reflection-in-action', where the coach is able to utilise reflection 'during' coaching practice. A greater understanding of 'how professionals think in action' will be developed here before the practical illustration of examples to demonstrate these points. Again, a template will be included for your own use in recording and monitoring your reflection-in-action. The final section of the chapter will consider the role of reflective practice in your professional development, including how to continue developing your reflective practice and where you go from here. A summary will be provided at the end of the chapter to highlight key points and provide an action summary of messages for you to take away.

## REFLECTIVE PRACTICE IN SPORTS COACHING

### Who should reflect?

Coaches of any level can engage in reflective practice; it's not just for novice coaches developing their skills, nor is it reserved for elite performance coaches. Most importantly, it is not just a good idea for other coaches! It's all too easy to claim that we undertake reflective practice in an *ad hoc* undocumented way – that it's 'all up there' so to speak. But could you show a record of your reflective practice if asked to justify the rationale for your coaching decisions and actions? Similarly, it's best not to consider it something that might be incorporated into your coaching next season or next year, but to start now, whether that's reflecting formally for the first time or updating your use of reflection methods and mechanisms.

Reflective practice is not something that needs to be carried out in isolation. Indeed, some would argue that its true value comes from sharing and learning from peers and mentors (see Chapters 11 and 13). 'Checking your thinking' in this way is, in itself, a developmental opportunity because just as when you teach a skill to someone else, you are required to think about, verbalise and restore your concepts in an almost inevitably better and automatically more accessible fashion. Peer supervision is a process that has long been carried out in helping professions such as counselling and psychotherapy, where practitioners can check their thinking with a peer and discuss the alternatives and best course of action. This process is not just for reassurance, but is supported by the philosophy that 'two heads are better than one' and that another coach's perspective can sometimes bring new insight or a different perspective which can be beneficial in resolving an issue or concern. Notably, such 'peer supervision' is actually a requirement in some professions, as it is considered crucial for effective performance.

Additionally, many coaching programmes offer a mentorship pathway whereby a developing coach is mentored by a more experienced practitioner. A record of reflective practice can be a useful mechanism for sharing and receiving feedback on coaching practice, especially if regular observation is not logistically possible. This need not be a one-way process, as supervisors or mentors can share their thinking with tutees to 'make their thinking visible' and thereby offering a degree of 'cognitive apprenticeship' to the developing coach (Collins, Brown and Holum 1991). Unfortunately, however, the expert mentor coach often quite literally 'trains' the mentee to think, work and act according to his or her authorised version (Collins, Abraham and Collins 2012). Young coaches should avoid this sort of mentoring; effective, open and mutually beneficial two-way learning is a key characteristic of effective mentoring if only because, for the mentor, consciously reconsidering actions which may have become tacit (automatic) is bound to be useful.

## What should I reflect on?

This is perhaps the most intriguing of questions in relation to reflective practice – what should we reflect on? Consideration of the sports coaching process reveals a vast amount of possible content and a complex and evolving process that can be difficult to capture. However, the inherent difficulty of reflecting on such a complex process should not deter those involved from trying. Fortunately, the existing literature in this and other professions can offer some direction. It is certainly worth clarifying 'what' we should reflect on, as this will almost certainly have extensive ramifications for the quality of the process and indeed whether or not it is worthwhile. After all, reflective practice is not an end in itself but an integral part of effective professional practice.

As a simple breakdown, Abraham, Collins and Martindale (2006) suggested three essential areas of knowledge: sport/activity specific (know the game); 'ology' (know the individual

Table 12.1 Possible objects of reflection in sports coaching

| Possible objects of reflection (Schön, 1991) | Possible objects of reflection in sports coaching |
|---|---|
| Tacit norms and appreciations which underlie a judgement | Intuitive judgement – how you know what you know is right |
| Strategies and theories implicit in a pattern of behaviour | Knowledge which you use to understand and explain what you see |
| Feeling for a situation which has led to the adoption of a particular course of action | Blending of systematic analysis and intuitive judgement to arrive at a decision |
| Way in which the problem trying to be solved has been framed | Coaching philosophy and organisational framework |
| Role constructed within a larger institutional context | Role of the coach within the context of the sport environment |

through, for example, physiology and psychology) and pedagogy (know how to coach). Interestingly, they suggested that the third area was a common weakness and that most benefit may be gleaned, at least in the short term, from concentrated reflection (against a clear, knowledge based standard) on this factor.

Schön (1991) offers a more general perspective, stating that 'the possible objects of reflection are as varied as the kind of phenomena before him and the systems of knowing-in-practice which he brings to them' (p. 62). The content that he suggests a practitioner may reflect on are presented in Table 12.1 along with some suggestions for how these may look within a sports coaching context.

Each of these concepts will be explored more closely in turn and so that we can operationalise what they mean within a sports coaching context. It will also be useful to outline what behaviours we may expect to see in each of these areas as a coach moves from being a novice to an expert practitioner. Following each section, exemplar questions for reflection will be offered as a starting point; you may be able to think of others and develop your own.

## Intuitive judgment – how you know what you know is right

As the examples provided at the start of this chapter demonstrated, some coaches frequently seem to 'know' what the right things are to do in any given situation (for example, give feedback, stop the practice to make a coaching point, provide instruction to develop technique or summarise the learning that has taken place during a practice session or competitive event). However, when pressed to explain 'why' these decisions and actions were taken or 'how' the coach knew these were the best decisions and actions, the answers may appear elusive. This is not to say that coaches are 'pulling ideas from thin air' or acting purely on 'gut instinct', but there does seem to be some intuitive or tacit element to knowing that is accessed very quickly and without a great deal of mental effort. Of course, from a 'quality practice' perspective an intriguing question is how good these intuitive judgements may be and, from a 'professional development' perspective, how coaches can get better at making these quick on-the-spot decisions to act.

It can be easier to think of these intuitive judgements as 'skilled intuition', which Simon (1992) describes in the following way: 'The situation has provided a cue: This cue has given the expert access to information stored in memory, and the information provides the answer. Intuition is nothing more and nothing less than recognition' (p. 155). So, skilled intuition can be thought of as 'recognition' of something within the situation that enables the coach to access previously acquired information that provides the answer about what to do. For example, a badminton coach spots the presence or absence of certain athlete behaviour (for example, full arm movement rather than wrist flick) that he or she knows represents inefficient technique; coaching can be provided to develop the correct technique. An experienced coach has seen many previous examples of efficient and inefficient technique and can quickly recognise poor technique, compare this to the information stored in memory about how the technique should look and construct coaching practice to develop the individual's performance.

There is a key variable in understanding intuitive judgements in this way and that is the 'level' or expertise of the coach. Simon's (1992) description of skilled intuition refers to the 'expert', and there is a direct link between the 'expertise' of the coach and the extent to which the coach's intuition may be considered to be 'skilled'. For example, a more experienced coach will have many more examples of previous situations stored in memory from which to draw on during the process of recognition and decision making than a novice coach, who will have relatively fewer. This is not to say that 'experience' necessarily leads to 'expertise', because it is what the coach does with this experience that is all important (that is, accumulating more hours of coaching does not necessarily lead to more expertise in coaching, otherwise everyone would eventually reach expert coach status and we know that isn't the case). Indeed, professional learning is a key ingredient for developing expertise of which reflective practice is a significant part (see the last section of this chapter). Recall the initial examples of poor practice (Dave and Helen) for examples of action without learning, or even perhaps much knowledge.

The level of coaching expertise (again not just time on the job) influences the process of intuitive judgement in several crucial ways. For example, Klein and Militello (2005) suggest that expertise brings: a greater level of procedural and declarative knowledge (discussed further in the following section), greater perceptual skills to recognise important cues, more elaborate 'mental models' of what good performance should look like and a more refined sense of 'typicality' in terms of what might be expected. One might expect that with all this processing of extra information that is acquired through gaining expertise, the time taken to generate intuitive judgements may be longer; yet paradoxically as expertise develops, so the processing becomes more efficient, and expert coaches typically arrive at their decisions much more quickly than novices. The difference in time and effort it takes for novice and expert coaches to make decisions is greatly influenced by the processes involved. For example, novice coaches may move through the range of possible options considering the pros and cons for each before weighing up through a cost-benefit analysis which is the best course of action, whilst expert coaches can access previous situations quickly and arrive at the best course of action without necessarily weighing up a range of possible alternatives – they seem to be able to make decisions more efficiently.

**Box 12.1 Questions to reflect on *intuitive judgement (or skilled intuition)* might include:**

1   What cues did I notice in the coaching situation?
2   What previous coaching situations/experiences was I able to access and use?
3   How did these previous coaching situations/experiences influence my practice?
4   How does this coaching situation compare with my previous experiences?
5   What might I expect the next time I encounter this type of coaching situation?

## Knowledge which you use to understand and explain what you see

One of the objectives of many aspiring coaches is to acquire knowledge that will enable them to become a better coach. This can seem like daunting task when the breadth and depth of knowledge that is relevant for sports coaching is considered (for example, sports sciences, sport-specific knowledge and motor learning to name a few areas). Indeed, as this confirms the notion that coaching is complex and multi-faceted, where should a coach start to get to grips with reflecting on the knowledge base that is necessary for effective coaching? A useful distinction is that of procedural and declarative knowledge, terms often used in the relevant literature (Anderson 1983). Procedural knowledge refers to 'how' knowledge or 'how to do something' (for example, how to implement a team goal setting session), whereas declarative knowledge represents 'why' knowledge or 'why something works' (for example, understanding why this is likely to benefit team motivation, goals and norms).

Abraham *et al.* (2006) extend this distinction further through the development of 'the coaching schematic', which illustrates the coaching process at a conceptual level. This model suggests that knowledge sources (concepts and declarative) can be acquired in three main areas: the 'ologies' (for example, sport psychology, organisational psychology, sociology, biomechanics, nutrition, exercise physiology and motor control), sport-specific knowledge (for example, the techniques and tactics of a particular sport), and pedagogy (for example, coach behaviour, motor and cognitive learning and critical thinking). In addition, these knowledge sources inform the procedures and concepts that a coach puts into place (for example, mental skills training, fitness training, lifestyle skills development, planning of drills and practices and communication). These variables influence the performance environment directly through the organisation of training and preparation for competition and ultimately represent the overall 'goal' of the coaching process (for example, enjoyment, achievement, education, medals, personal development, fun and so on).

This coaching schematic provides a window into the range of knowledge sources that a coach could use to understand and explain what he or she sees in any given coaching situation or scenario. Of course the extent to which a coach draws on such knowledge bases will depend on the extent to which they are available (through prior education, for example) and/or on the extent to which the coach is prepared to learn and develop (by reading about goal setting interventions, for example). An important point to note, however, is that it is very difficult for coaches to develop an area of knowledge that they are not 'aware' of as being important/ relevant for their coaching. So, in the process of reflecting on knowledge, the sports coach should consider as a bare minimum which areas within the coaching schematic may be ripe for further development.

---

**Box 12.2  Questions to reflect on knowledge might include:**

1   To what extent was I aware of drawing on knowledge from 'ologies', sport-specific *knowledge* or pedagogy in my coaching practice?
2   How did these knowledge sources inform the concepts or procedures that I attempted to put into place? (use specific examples)
3   How did these knowledge sources influence the training session and/or preparation for competition?
4   How did these knowledge sources assist me in addressing the overall goal for coaching?
5   Are there any areas of knowledge development that I have become aware of that would benefit my coaching practice?

---

## Blending of systematic analysis and intuitive judgement to arrive at a decision

As well as using their intuitive judgement, sports coaches can also use a process of systematic analysis to inform their practice. That is, coaching practice does not only involve a series of on-the-spot decisions, actions and behaviours; the coach has time before, during, and after training and competitive events to systematically analyse the individual or team performance. This analysis can be of great benefit to the coach as it allows for this additional 'data' (for example, match/performance analysis statistics, GPS data, heart rate data and so on) to be incorporated into the processes of decision making and adopting a particular course of action (see Chapters 14 and 15).

So, what sort of concepts can we use to reflect on systematic analysis within a coaching context? Again, we can turn our attention to literature on the development of cognitive expertise to understand how professionals make decisions. Klein and Militello (2005) suggest that as expertise develops, so does our ability to 'do' certain things, such as the ability to run mental simulations, spot anomalies and detect problems, find leverage points, manage uncertainty, plan and re-plan, assess complex situations, manage attention and take our own strengths and limitations into account.

Consequently, sports coaches are able to consider how a particular tactical formation may work depending on the players at their disposal by running a mental simulation of various 'plays' or set pieces. They may be able to identify an anomaly or issue with a particular technique that is limiting the performer and work out a way to communicate what is necessary to adjust or adapt this in a way which is meaningful to that individual. Sports coaches can attempt to manage the uncertainty inherent in the performance environment by developing alternative courses of action depending on what situations arise at any given time (for example, race/fight/match/competition planning). They are likely to develop plans for training and competition and to constantly update and refine these as the needs of the performers or team change and evolve. As coaching practice typically involves the assessment of complex situations involving numerous individuals with differing needs, abilities and desires, sports coaches are required to manage their attention by deciding where this is best focused at any given time. Additionally, coaches have to take their own and their performers' strengths and limitations into account when planning and preparing for training and competitive events.

The systematic analysis of such features of coaching practice can be 'blended' with the coaches' intuitive judgements about any given situation to develop and refine their 'skilled intuition'. The 'feeling' a coach has for what is the best course of action in a particular situation can be driven by this blending of systematic analysis and intuitive judgement to arrive at a decision. In short, and paraphrasing Kahneman (2011), coaches need to be able to think fast and slow, using each approach in tandem or in parallel depending on the needs of the situation. Really good coaches will have both – analysis and intuition – together with a strong sense of which one is needed and when.

---

**Box 12.3 Questions to reflect on decision making might include:**

1   What 'data' or 'analysis' have I used to inform my decision making?
2   How has the identification of a performance-limiting issue influenced my decision making?
3   How has my performers'/team's needs influenced my decision making about planning for training and competition?
4   How have I decided where to place my attention during this session/practice/game/match?
5   How have my own and/or my performers' strengths and weaknesses influenced my decision making?

---

## Coaching philosophy and organisational framework

Schön's (1991) description of working with the way in which the 'problem trying to be solved' has been framed can be related to 'coaching philosophy'. For example, what is the coach attempting to achieve, using what methods, and for what purpose? Chapter 3 provides in depth coverage of the importance of a coaching philosophy.

**Box 12.4 Questions to reflect on coaching philosophy might include:**

1 How are my beliefs about sports coaching reflected in my coaching behaviours?
2 How do I put my values and principles into action in my coaching?
3 How have I created an ethical sports coaching culture?
4 How does my leadership style reflect my values and coaching philosophy?
5 How do my beliefs and philosophy inform my coaching practice?

## Role of the coach within the context of the sport environment

The role of the professional within a larger context is the final object of reflection suggested by Schön (1991). Here, this refers to the role of the coach within the context of the sport in which he or she works (for example, within the support team, organisation, institution, governing body, etc.). It also refers to the level of performer/s the coach is working with (for example, novice, developmental, elite) and context (for example, athlete-centred). Chapter 1 discusses the role of the coach in more detail.

**Box 12.5 Questions to reflect on the *role of the coach* might include:**

1 How are the roles of leader, teacher, and organiser reflected in my coaching practice?
2 How does my role as coach impact on and influence my players/athletes?
3 How do I manage the responsibilities that my coaching role brings?
4 How does my coaching role fit with our wider sporting organisation and stakeholders?
5 How does my understanding of the context I am operating in shape my coaching practice?

## Where can I reflect?

Reflective practice doesn't have to happen in the comfort of your own home or office. Indeed, you don't necessarily have to make a special effort to sit down and 'reflect'. Reflections on different aspects of your practice may come to you before, during, or after a training session or game/match, and these can be scribbled down on a notepad on the side lines, in the changing rooms, or in your car afterwards. It is important to put these reflections into a meaningful framework, but initially making some rough notes so you don't forget is a good idea – otherwise they may be gone forever. This is especially true for circumstances which are immediately obvious to you (perhaps something that either worked better or worse than you thought it might). Reflections may also come sometime after the event or just 'pop' into your head when you are least expecting it (in the shower for example). These can be incorporated with your initial reflections along with a slower, more analytical type of reflection (on some of the questions listed above, for example), which would ensure you are incorporating both the intuitive and the analytic aspects of reflective practice. In some contexts, for example Adventure Sports Coaching, it is essential the coach makes time for reflection during the event itself (for example, regarding levels of risk, potential benefits and possible consequences) (Collins and Collins 2013).

## How can I reflect?

Now that we have established why reflective practice is a good idea, who should engage with it, what can be reflected on, and where this can happen, it is time to turn to the more practical steps involved in 'how' to actually do it. We can have the best of intentions, but without the appropriate methods and techniques, the behaviour itself is unlikely to happen. Commitment to reflective practice and professional development requires coaches to seek out and use the frameworks that will best meet their needs for monitoring and recording in an effective and efficient way. Some suggestions and recommendations for 'how' to reflect are made in the sections to follow on reflection-on-action and reflection-in-action.

## REFLECTION-ON-ACTION: AFTER COACHING

The type of reflection most commonly associated with reflective practice is 'reflection-on-action' (that is, reflection which takes place after the event). This may take place following a training session, game/match or any form of interaction with players or other support professionals. The sections below offer some practical examples of how this may look in sports coaching, along with some suggested templates for your own use. It is worth comparing and contrasting these templates with others in circulation; many structured reflective pro-formas are limited in what they can provide the coach beyond a recording mechanism. Thus, many coaches anecdotally report that they write down what they already know and, perhaps consequently, find the whole process to be limited in terms of what they get out of it (Cropley, Miles and Peel 2012). The 'content' of reflective practice (or 'what' to reflect on) is all important here. Descriptions and evaluations of practice are important, but do not necessarily provide the insights or agency necessary for change that are suggested by Schön's (1991) original direction on the possible objects for reflection (see Table 12.1). The templates suggested here allow coaches to identify the 'object' of their reflection (based on their own development needs) and therefore the reflective questions that will best support this individual process. Finally, as mentioned above, it helps if the criteria against which the reflection will be made are stated up front. These can be a combination of planned for/predicted outcomes, theoretically informed methods (e.g. on pedagogy) or sport-relevant developmental pathways. The important thing, however, is that these exist up front. Otherwise, it is like setting out for a journey without a planned destination.

**233**

## Case example

The example below shows the reflections of Jeremy, the high performance judo coach mentioned at the start of this chapter. Jeremy is reflecting on coaching an injured athlete and he has identified that one of his own developmental needs as part of his Coaching Certificate was

*Table 12.2* Reflective practice entry (knowledge exemplar)

| | |
|---|---|
| **Date:** 28th November 2013<br>**Scenario:**<br>(Who, where, when, what) | **Reflections:**<br>High performance judo squad training; National training centre. Coaching an injured athlete 'Corrin' – early stage of rehabilitation following ACL reconstruction. |
| **Area of developmental need:**<br>**Object of reflection:** | Increase use of sport science disciplines in my coaching knowledge (Sport Psychology). |
| 1 To what extent was I aware of drawing on knowledge from 'ologies', sport-specific knowledge or pedagogy in my coaching practice? | Set up a performance simulation training programme for Corrin with my newly acquired knowledge of using imagery with injured athletes. I think she will find this helpful for keeping in touch with the sport whilst injured as she can still attend all training sessions. Also could help limit decay in her techniques while she is unable to train fully. |
| 2 How did these knowledge sources inform the concepts or procedures that I attempted to put into place? (use specific examples) | I used the PETTLEP model for imagery (Holmes and Collins, 2004). Each of the elements: Physical, Environment, Task, Timing, Learning, Emotion and Perspective allowed me to tailor the performance simulation to judo. Corrin was in full kit and stood on the side of the mat to simulate the training session. |
| 3 How did these knowledge sources influence the training session and/or preparation for competition? | I briefed the rest of the group on what Corrin was doing (performance simulation) and ran part of the session working in 3's with 2 in randori fighting and 1 using simulation. This allowed me to introduce them all to the concepts I was using with Corrin and made her feel part of the session. |
| 4 How did these knowledge sources assist me in addressing the overall goal for coaching? | Use of imagery could be a useful skill for all the athletes to develop further as we work toward performance enhancement. As injuries are frequent it will also provide them with a useful skill should they be unable to take part. I would like to encourage active participation in training even if injured. |
| 5 Are there any areas of knowledge development that I have become aware of that would benefit my coaching practice? | I have become aware of how individual imagery ability is. Some seemed to find it much more difficult than others. I would like to get to know more about individuals' experience of using imagery so that I can incorporate this into my guidance of the PETTLEP elements within a coaching session. |
| **Summary:**<br>(Learning and actions related to area of developmental need) | Learning: Don't be afraid to use psychology. Set it up well – clearly explain why we are doing it and what the benefits may be. Athletes are up for trying new things . . . Open communication allows them to make some great suggestions! Actions: Keep going with this to fully integrate the skill as part of our training. Review impact at individual, group and policy level (encourage injured players to attend training). Consider what other sport psychology skills may be useful for us to develop as part of training and competition preparation. |

to increase his use of the sport science disciplines in his coaching. In this example, the 'object' of his reflection is his knowledge of sport psychology and, in particular, his newly acquired knowledge of using imagery with injured athletes. This example of reflective practice shows how Jeremy has used the reflective questions related to 'knowledge' suggested above to structure his reflections, learning and actions.

## Your turn . . .

Using the template in Table 12.3, identify a recent coaching scenario, an area of your own developmental need (including appropriate criteria to reflect against, e.g. coaching certificate criteria) and an object of reflection (for example, Intuitive Judgement, Knowledge, Decision Making, Coaching Philosophy, Role of the Coach). Refer to the questions in the relevant section above and insert them into your template. Finish by considering the learning and action points. This individualised approach to reflective practice allows for 'personalised learning' which is missing from standardised approaches to reflective practice (Knowles, Tyler, Gilbourne and Eubank 2006).

*Table 12.3* Reflective practice entry (blank template)

| | Reflections: |
|---|---|
| Date: | |
| Scenario: | |
| (Who, where, when, what) | |
| Area of developmental need: | |
| Object of reflection: | |
| (Intuitive Judgement, Knowledge, Decision Making, Coaching Philosophy, Role of the Coach) | |
| Q1 | |
| (Insert) | |
| Q2 | |
| (Insert) | |
| Q3 | |
| (Insert) | |
| Q4 | |
| (Insert) | |
| Q5 | |
| (Insert) | |
| Summary: | |
| (Learning and actions related to area of developmental need) | |

## REFLECTION-IN-ACTION: DURING COACHING

A less well established type of reflection is that of 'reflection-in-action', or as Schön (1991) originally termed it, 'how professionals think in action'. This is a fascinating aspect of professional practice that has received much less attention in the reflective practice literature and can perhaps best be understood and explained through the concepts of professional judgement and decision making (PJDM), which are becoming increasingly recognised in sports literature following on the lead from parallel helping professions such as nursing and teaching.

Applied practice can be considered as an on-going series of decisions regarding a vast array of items and possibilities. For example, in sports coaching, coaches are required to make some big picture decisions regarding their coaching philosophy, values, intentions and goals. These lead to subsequent decisions about the types of characteristics or behaviours they may display to athletes (depending on their preferred leadership style, for example). On an everyday level, the coach is required to make decisions relating to the content of training sessions, tactics for the upcoming game, and selection against the next opposition. A huge number of variables are taken into consideration, weighed up against each other, and judgements are made regarding which decisions are likely to be the most effective. On an individual level, the coach is required to make decisions regarding the timing of feedback to players, optimum methods of communication, and how best to make technical adjustments. At all levels of coaching the PJDM of the coach has a huge impact on the coaching process, and at the highest level of sport, coaches are ultimately held accountable for their ability to make effective judgements and decisions when it matters the most.

In addition to this conceptualisation of coaching as a series of decisions, it is worth emphasising that in good coaching practice there are lots of things going on. In other words, coaching is a complex process as demonstrated well in chapters throughout this book. Thus, a certain amount of complexity can be regarded as a core feature of good coaching; there are just too many factors and considerations for it to be reduced to a simplistic recipe-like process. Due to the complex nature of coaching, it is important that we have ways of trying to understand it and break it down; not to simplify it as tends to be the case with many coaching process models, but so that we can navigate through the complexities using shared language and vocabulary. A focus on PJDM allows us to do this by exploring the judgements and decisions made by different levels of coaches and carefully unpacking the implications these have on coaching practice. For example, considering a sports coach's 'intentions for impact' (i.e. what the coach hopes to do, for what reasons, how the coach intends to carry this out and evaluate its effectiveness) is one way to do this (Martindale and Collins 2005).

Another feature of effective coaching is the use of 'nested thinking' to maintain both a top-down and a bottom-up perspective. For example, a performance coach will have clear goals and objectives for the season (let's call these programme level intentions) and will give a great deal of thought as to what needs to happen across the weeks of the season for this to take place (intervention level intentions). Subsequently, these intentions influence the coach's thinking on a week by week, game by game or match by match basis (session level intentions). In this sense we can say the coach has a top-down perspective on the process. However, we know that a bottom-up perspective is also apparent in sports coaching. For example, a result during one week/event/match can influence the coach's decision making about what needs to happen in order to stay on track with the season targets and objectives so adjustments can be made accordingly (see Abraham and Collins 2011).

Schön (1991) notes that professional practice has at least as much to do with 'finding the problem' as with 'solving' the problem found. He also declared that in real-world practice problems do not present themselves as 'givens'; they must be constructed by the professional. The sports coach is required to go through a process of 'framing' the problematic scenario (for example, a situation that is puzzling, troubling or uncertain, such as how to overcome strong opposition). In a way the coach becomes like a researcher or an investigator testing out different hypotheses until it becomes clear which will yield the best way forward. Of course there is artistry to this process too, especially as the coach develops expertise and begins to utilise skilled intuition as mentioned earlier. As part of an effective 'framing' process, the coach will formulate a coherent plan for change which may be based on past experience, adaptation of a previous situation to this one and the creation of a virtual world or mental model. Thus, reflection-in-action may be like a 'sketchpad' for the sports coach to try out various solutions to difficult problems (Schön 1991).

Further implications for the PJDM of sports coaches are that decision making takes place at multiple levels (programme, intervention and session as outlined previously), and that due to the complexity of the coaching process they are likely to be seeking multi-faceted impact (in other words to carry out one intervention for more than one purpose). The following case example illustrates some of these concepts and applications.

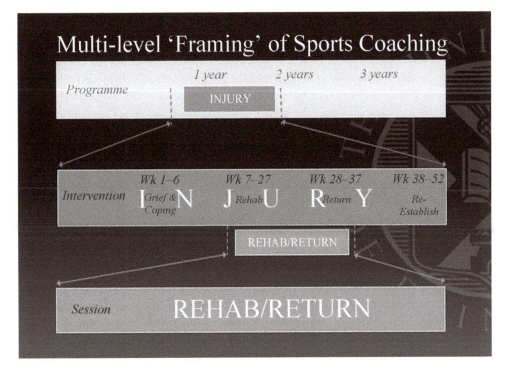

*Figure 12.1* Illustration of multi-level 'framing' of a sports coaching scenario.

## Case example

Figure 12.1 provides an illustration of multi-level 'framing' that can take place during a sports coaching scenario. Schön (1991) states that 'it is through the process of framing the problematic situation that we may organise and clarify both the ends to be achieved and the possible means of achieving them' (p. 41). So, the process of framing allows sports coaches to organise and clarify what their objectives are and how they intend to go about achieving these. This is an extremely valuable process given the complexities of sports coaching mentioned earlier.

Figure 12.1 illustrates how Jeremy is framing the coaching scenario related to his injured judo athlete, Corrin. In this example, Corrin's injury represents one 'phase' within the overall coaching programme. Whilst it is a significant injury (with rehabilitation expected to last up to 12 months) Jeremy expects that Corrin will then resume competing as part of the on-going judo high performance programme. Within the injury phase, Jeremy has identified several sub-phases that Corrin is likely to experience (he consulted with the medical team, physiotherapist and sports psychologist for input here), including grief and coping, rehabilitation, return and re-establishment as an athlete. As her coach, Jeremy hopes to oversee Corrin's transition through these phases and provide her with the necessary support as she works toward re-establishment. This is demonstrated by looking at the 'session-level' framing; in any given individual session with Corrin, Jeremy will consider which injury phase she is in and what her needs are likely to be as she works towards a full recovery.

Jeremy's framing of this coaching scenario allows him to maintain coherence in his practice and offers him a useful tool to use for reflection-in-action. It can help guide him in his coaching judgements and decisions about what may be the most appropriate action for Corrin at any given time. Jeremy feels that his framing of the scenario provides him with a 'roadmap' to stay on track with what he is trying to achieve in the complex process of coaching Corrin back to full fitness. He can form 'intentions for impact' that he thinks will benefit Corrin during each of the sub-phases and incorporate these within his coaching preparation and practice. Finally, Jeremy feels confident that his coaching interactions with Corrin session by session are feeding into an overall plan for her successful recovery from this serious injury. Importantly, Corrin is re-assured that Jeremy has communicated this phased approach to re-establishment and she has not been eliminated from his future plans.

## Your turn . . .

Using the template illustrated in Figure 12.2, identify a recent or current coaching scenario and attempt to carry out the process of 'framing' outlined above. Begin by identifying whether the overall coaching programme contains any distinct phases either for an individual athlete or for your team. Next, try to identify whether a specific phase contains any sub-phases within it and the likely timescales involved for each of these. Consider how individual coaching sessions may feed into each of the sub-phases and into the overall coaching programme. Finally, consider how this framing of your coaching scenario may help to maintain coherence in your practice and guide your reflection-in-action.

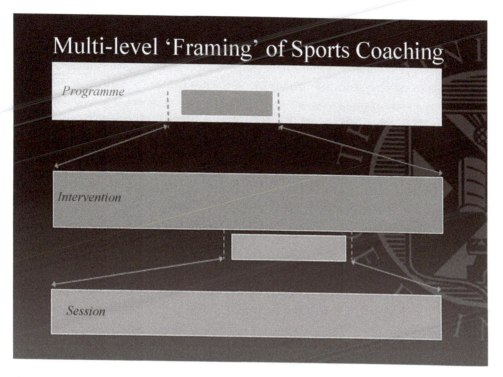

*Figure 12.2* Template for multi-level 'framing' of a sports coaching scenario.

## REFLECTIVE PRACTICE FOR PROFESSIONAL DEVELOPMENT

### Developing your reflective practice and professional learning

Hopefully this chapter has extended your knowledge and awareness of how reflective practice can be a useful part of your sports coaching toolbox. The examples and templates offered for reflection-on-action and reflection-in-action can be used to support and develop your existing reflective practice procedures. It is certainly worth reviewing your current reflective practice techniques to ensure you are getting as much as possible from the process (for example, by considering the content of your reflection or 'what' you are reflecting on and how much you get out of this). Reflective practice is one way of contributing to your continued professional learning as a sports coach, but it is not for the faint hearted. Conducted effectively, using the elements of challenge and agency suggested by Schön (1991), the reflective coach is one of the characteristics of those seeking to accelerate their coaching expertise as the following quote suggests: 'Many practitioners, locked into a view of themselves as technical experts, find nothing in the world of practice to occasion reflection. . . . For them, uncertainty is a threat; its admission is a sign of weakness. Others, more inclined toward and adept at reflection-in-action, nevertheless feel profoundly uneasy because they cannot say what they know how to do, cannot justify its quality or rigor. For these reasons, the study of reflection-in-action is critically important' (Schön 1991, p. 69).

## Where do I go from here?

Further support for your reflective practice is available from mentors, peers and communities of practice. Each of these avenues offers opportunities to discuss the methods, content and outcomes of your reflective practice. It is worth establishing trusting relationships with colleagues whom you can contact to 'check your thinking' or act as a 'sounding board' for your framing, intentions and actions. This can be a two-way process as they will likely be very grateful for the same opportunity. It is also possible to develop the skill of self-reflective awareness (e.g. using mindfulness training), and it may be that additional practice such as this can provide the scaffolding to support the further development of this skill within a coaching context. Further reading on reflective practice is suggested at the end of this chapter. For further discussion of mentoring see Chapter 11 and for communities of practice see Chapter 13.

## REFERENCES

Abraham, A. and Collins, D. (2011). Taking the next step: Ways forward for coaching science. *Quest* 63: pp. 366–384.

Abraham, A., Collins, D. and Martindale, R.J.J. (2006). The coaching schematic: Validation through expert coach consensus. *Journal of Sports Sciences* 24: pp. 549–564.

Anderson, J. R. (1983). *The architecture of cognition.* (Cambridge, MA: Harvard University Press).

Collins, A., Brown, S. J. and Holum, A. (1991). Cognitive apprenticeship: Making thinking visible. *American Education* 3: pp. 1–18.

Collins, D., Abraham, A., & Collins, R. (2012). On Vampires and Wolves - exposing and exploring reasons for the differential impact of coach education', *International Journal Of Sport Psychology*, 43, 3, pp. 255–272.

Collins, D., Burke, V., Martindale, A., & Cruickshank, A. (2014). *The Illusion of Competency Versus the Desirability of Expertise: Seeking a Common Standard for Support Professions in Sport.* (Auckland, NZ: Sports Medicine).

Collins, L. and Collins, D. (2013). Decision making and risk management in adventure sports coaching. *Quest* 65: pp. 72–82.

Cropley, B., Miles, A. and Peel, J. (2012). Reflective practice: Value of, issues, and developments within sports coaching. (Research project for Sports Coach UK).

Holmes, P., & Collins, D. (2001). The PETTLEP approach to motor imagery: a functional equivalence model for sport psychologists. *Journal Of Applied Sport Psychology* 13, 1, pp. 60–83.

Kahneman, D. (2011). *Thinking, fast and slow.* (New York: Farrar, Straus and Giroux).

Klein, G. and Militello, L. (2005). The knowledge audit as a method for cognitive task analysis. In *How professionals make decisions.* Montgomery, H., Lipshitz, R. and Brehmer, B. (Eds.). (London: LEA).

Knowles, Z., Tyler, G., Gilbourne, D. and Eubank, M. (2006). Reflecting on reflection: Exploring the practice of sports coaching graduates. *Reflective Practice* 7: pp. 163–179.

Martindale, A. and Collins, D. (2005). Professional judgment and decision making: The role of intention for impact. *The Sport Psychologist* 19: pp. 303–317.

Martindale, A. and Collins, D. (2012). A professional judgment and decision making case study: Reflection-in-action research. *The Sport Psychologist* 26: pp. 500–518.

Schön, D. (1991). *The reflective practitioner: How professionals think in action.* (Aldershot: Ashgate).

Simon, H. A. (1992). What is an explanation of behavior? *Psychological Science* 3: pp. 150–161.

## Further reading

Knowles, Z., Borrie, A. and Telfer, H. (2005). Towards the reflective sports coach: Issues of context, education and application. *Ergonomics* 48: pp. 1711–1720.

Tarrant P. (2013). *Reflective practice and professional development.* (London: Sage).

## Web links

European Mentoring and Coaching Council: www.emccouncil.org/uk
Sports Coach UK: www.sportscoachuk.org/

# Chapter 13

# Learning through communities of practice in sport coaching

*Christine Nash and Cedric English*

Exponents of situated learning argue that through social interaction, authentic activity and participation within communities of practice, learners are better able to construct meaning in practical ways so that knowledge can be applied outside of formal learning settings (Kirshner and Whitson 1997; Lave and Wenger 1992). King (1990) suggests that the process of constructing new knowledge or the process of transforming previous knowledge into new formats is actually enhanced through peer interaction. Additionally, Bleed (2001) reports on the importance of socialisation in the learning process. So, promoting learning partnerships through many of the social media outlets now available could enable sports coaches to network. This process of networking can be very beneficial within the coach learning and development process and the translation of theory into the actual practice of coaching.

A kayaking coach, Steve, stated: I want ideas, I want to be inspired, to be given ideas about the best ways of coaching, ways of engaging with different athletes so that I've got a really good toolbox that I'm able to actually draw upon and encouragement to be creative and imaginative and not too prescriptive. I like the idea that coaching should be about discussion and the sharing of ideas. The kind of coaches that I talk with have got a lot of experience, a real breadth of experience. I would think that one of the main things is actually to share their experience with the people around them – not just listen to somebody so there should be room for that kind of discussion. Networking is very, very important and discussion about the current issues within the sport which relates to things like health and safety, codes of practices, how people manage the legal aspects in terms of risk management, aspects about coaches supporting each other, having some kind of forum for expressing our views and opinions on these issues. A lot of the issues within coaching have been constrained by the political-legal framework outside the organisation, for example, Health and Safety. The Health and Safety Executive may not have a good understanding of the issues relating to risk or risk management within the activities but the coaches actually do so are probably better able to manage risk within the coaching context.

Many of the issues identified by Steve relate to the coaches' ability to interact with one another – in other words, to form communities of practice. How this helps coaches, enables them to develop their practice and, most importantly, allows them to relate their learning to authentic coaching practice is covered within this chapter. An evaluation of the informal learning practices of coaches, and the place and various forms of communities of practice within this process, is presented.

## WHAT IS A COMMUNITY OF PRACTICE?

A community of practice (CoP) is defined by Wenger, McDermott and Snyder (2002) as 'a group of people who share a common concern, set of problems, or a passion about a topic, and who deepen their knowledge and expertise in this area by interaction on an on-going basis' (p. 4). Central to a CoP is a situated perspective on learning, which focuses attention on the integrated relationship between individual, activity and environment; hence knowledge construction is inseparable from relevant contexts and activities. The activities of sport coaching are framed by the culture, both locally and globally. The meaning and purpose of coaching within the CoP are socially constructed through negotiations among current and past members of that community. Therefore, the activities within the sport coaching CoP are the ordinary practices of coaching. The learning that takes place within the sport coaching community can therefore be construed as acts of membership within the sport coaching CoP.

According to Lave and Wenger (1992), this premise is based on the following assumptions:

- *Learning is fundamentally a social phenomenon.* People organize their learning around the social communities to which they belong. Therefore, coaching environments are only powerful learning environments for performers whose social communities coincide with that coaching environment.
- *Knowledge is integrated in the life of communities that share values, beliefs, languages and ways of doing things.* These are called communities of practice. Authentic knowledge is integrated in the experiences, social relations and expertise of these communities. Therefore to be able to learn as a sport coach, coaches must engage within the sport coaching community to develop social and professional relationships to enhance the learning environment.
- *The processes of learning and membership in a community of practice are inseparable.* Because in this situation learning is bound up with community membership, coaches find that their engagement and status within the community can be constantly changing. As learning develops, identities and relationships to the group change.
- *Knowledge is inseparable from practice.* Within sport coaching it is the authentic coaching practice that determines effectiveness and, ultimately, success. Coaches learning must be related to doing – actively coaching. And by actively coaching, coaches learn.

Much of the traditional thinking around learning has focussed upon the learner as an individual; however CoPs promote and encourage learning as a shared activity. The conceptualisation of a coaching community of practice (CCoP) has been used within the sport coaching context to further refine those activities (Culver and Trudel 2006). Studies have been carried out to examine the effects of a CoP within various sports and coaching contexts, for example, football, ice hockey, swimming and BMX biking (Occhino, Mallett and Rynne 2013; Trudel and Gilbert 2004; Nash and Sproule 2011; Farrell 2001).

## DEVELOPMENT OF COPs

Sports coaching is largely a social activity where engagement with athletes, support staff, other coaches and experienced others can enhance insight into the activity for all involved. This CoP, or collaborative circle, is defined by Farrell (2001, p. 13) as 'a primary group consisting of peers who share similar occupational goals and who, through long periods of dialogue and collaboration, negotiate a common vision that guides their work'. Bourdieu (1993) suggests that the individuals in this CoP are roughly of equal status, are often close in age and enter these communities with similar amounts of social capital. As the community develops, the group cultivates a common vision or goal, a shared group language or communication style and membership rituals.

According to Corte (2013), these collaborations or CoPs typically develop through seven stages:

1   formation
2   rebellion
3   quest
4   creative work stage
5   collective action
6   separation
7   reunion.

Within sport coaching, formation occurs when coaches belonging to the same sport or discipline meet through a social network of acquaintances, usually other coaches or involved individuals. These sports coaches can feel isolated in their practice or unable to advance. A gatekeeper plays the crucial role of either attracting or explicitly recruiting other members into the circle. Because of this filtering, members tend to already have much in common when they start working together, which facilitates successful cooperation early on (Farrell 2001). After evolving through the various stages, separation occurs when the group disintegrates, as tensions that emerged among members in the previous stages reach their peak. Quite often these CoPs can be reunited after a period of time.

Wenger proposed another model of CoP development (Figure 13.1). Although learning is a complex process, often the role of the learner has been passive. As a result, Wenger's concept of CoP is framed by the social theory of learning. According to Culver and Trudel (2008), the following assumptions are integral within sport coaching:

1   humans are social;
2   knowledge is competence in a valued enterprise;
3   knowing is active participation in that enterprise;
4   meaning is the ultimate product of learning.

The phases identified in Figure 13.1 identify stages of development within a CoP, from the initial stage of Potential to the last stage of Memorable. This differs from the model proposed by Corte (2013) in terms of the number of stages as well as the types of activities.

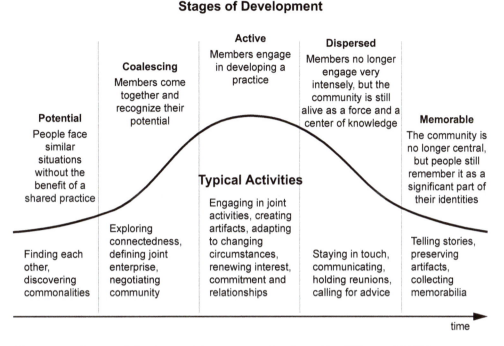

**Stages of Development**

Figure 13.1 Stages of development in a community of practice (Wenger 1998b).

The five stages suggested by Wenger are possibly more easily applicable to the context of sport coaching, given both the stages of development and the examples of typical activities highlighted.

## COPs AND ORGANISATIONS

Organisational culture can be defined as the behaviour of people who are part of an organisation and the meanings that these people attach to their actions. The culture can include organisational values, visions, norms, working language, processes, symbols, artefacts, beliefs and habits. New members to an organisation can be inducted into organisational culture, collective behaviours and assumptions, as well as how the organisation can be viewed from both an internal and external perspective.

Communities of practice can be seen as self-organising systems and have many of the benefits and characteristics associated with Putnam's concept of social capital (Putnam 2002). According to Field (2003), social relationships are essential and, furthermore, interaction allows people to build communities, to commit themselves to each other and to develop the social fabric that enhances a sense of belonging and the concrete experience of social networks. In the high performance sports environment, the development of a high performing culture within the organisation is crucial to long-term success (Cruikshank, Collins and

Minten 2013). There are a number of factors that can impact upon the success or effectiveness of a sporting organisation, as highlighted below:

- Power dynamic – the interpersonal dynamics at play in sport are complex. Bloom, Schinke and Salmela (1998) investigated the power relationships between players and coach. According to Kellett (2002), the coach as an authoritarian dominant enforcer of discipline, using threats to discipline players to achieve improvements in performance, is a perception well established in coaching literature and evidently still pervasive in modern sport. However, given the more recent club situation, the coach could be accountable to a director or a board. This alters the original power dynamic and should be considered at the start of a coaching appointment.
- Trust – the role of the individual is paramount to the establishment and maintenance of a CoP. Many authors (Wenger 1998a; Kramer and Tyler 1996, p. 128; Lave and Wenger 1992, p. 39) agree that trust is a pivotal and essential element in long-term social relationships. Individuals will often refrain from any interaction with others whom they do not trust. Trust is the confidence an individual has that another person or persons will behave only as they are expected to and will do so in a socially acceptable and ethical manner.
- Belonging – Skinner, Zakus and Cowell (2008) maintained that a sense of community arises out of the fundamental human need to create and maintain social bonds, to develop a sense of belonging and to further develop a self-identity. Membership of a community provides a sense that individuals have invested a piece of themselves to become members. This sense of community identity and community belonging are non-tangible benefits of participation in sport (Collins and Kay 2003).
- Talent development – Christensen, Laursen and Sorensen (2011) used social learning theory to identify how talented footballers learn through participation in specific social practices. They determined that the footballers' ability not just to reach the top level of their sport but also to have a long-term career will be influenced by the social construction of these social practices.

It is important to remember that within high performance sports, teams are often part of a business enterprise and as such it is hard to examine the performance of the coach and players in isolation. For example, finance can have significant influence on the efficient and effective functioning of a team. This may be highlighted in more professional organisations as the amount of money that is made available to the coach or manager to buy players, but it could also be manifest in less full time organisations as the ability to pay for facilities and equipment. Coaches need to manage the coaching culture and also be aware of the dynamic present within organisations and teams (McKenna 2013). Research into organisational culture within sporting organisations is still relatively new, however as Kaiser, Engel and Keiner (2009) point out, sport has a high degree of symbolism as well as espoused values and artefacts.

Many examples of CoPs in sport and sport coaching have been highlighted in previous texts. The following case study exemplifies CoPs in sport coaching but within the context of the routes to high performance coaching within the sport of cricket. South African cricket is a sport at top level within the world competition framework and as such the examination of CoPs within this sporting context adds value.

## COMMUNITIES OF PRACTICE: A SOUTH AFRICAN STUDY

In writing this chapter on CoP it became apparent, considering the increased research in the area of coach learning, what was required was something new to the realm of coach development. The purpose therefore was not only to add to increasing research into the work associated with CoP, by bringing together previous research in this area, but at the same time to introduce a 'new' area for consideration.

Whilst interviewing South African (SA) cricket coaches during two separate studies, evidence began to emerge surrounding the polarising effect the administrative function had on the development environment of both athlete and coach. In this context, the effect may be described as ubiquitous, so much so that its importance could not be discounted as a factor in both coach learning and athlete development. Before delving headlong into the evidence, it is necessary to understand the context for this evidence and to describe how this thought process came about.

*Before continuing, it must be noted that at no stage during these investigations into talent development pathway structures, organisational cultures and coach learning were racial issues, such as quota systems, included in any of the evidence. Many observations were noted; however, the purpose of the investigation was to investigate and focus solely on a successful talent development environment, structural change and the associated effects on that environment.*

## THE ENVIRONMENT

International sport officially re-opened to South Africa in 1991, with immediate success on a number of levels. In 1992 the South African cricket team progressed to the World Cup semi-final. This success was soon followed in 1994 with the football team winning the African Nations Cup, and in 1995 with the SA rugby team winning the Rugby World Cup. Political ideologies aside, the immediate results of the early 1990s suggested that the talent development pathways South Africa had in place prior to and during the apartheid era were such that they produced cricketers of an internationally competitive standard. Since SA's re-entry to international cricket, the structure of the domestic game has undergone two major changes. One was based on political ideologies shaped by the past, the other was structural, based on increased competitiveness, efficiencies and logistics.

Before the 2004 adoption of the franchise system, the domestic cricket structure in SA consisted of eleven provinces and approximately 160 professional cricketers. At the time, the structural change reduced the 'professional' game to six franchises and approximately 100 professional cricketers, and was summed up by an interviewed Administrator:

> The challenge at the moment is there are 11 provinces and 6 franchises. This means 160 professional players has now reduced to 100. This means a huge number of opportunities are gone.

**247**

At the beginning of the 2004/05 cricket season, South Africa adopted a franchise approach based on the Australian system as a template and is confirmed by another Administrator interviewed:

> They tried to model 'it' (the franchise system) on the Australian system, but by the nature of the beast they (Australia) have only got 6 states, so each state has got a team. We (SA) have a hell of a diverse culture here; our goal should be to afford the opportunity for as many people as possible to play for South Africa.

The principle surrounding this structural change was to lead to a more competitive environment at franchise level cricket (domestic elite) and is summed up by the following extract from the official Cricket South Africa (CSA) website:

> The franchise system has become the bedrock on which Cricket South Africa's (CSA) strategy to become a leading player in the world is based. It has produced strength versus strength contests that compare favourably with the domestic competitions in Australia which are generally regarded as having the highest standard of play in the world.
>
> (www.cricket.co.za)

Until the inception of the franchise system each province had a provincial team, each with its own respective development pathway. One interviewed coach confirms the progressive nature of the development pathway and its closely related competitive nature, allowing for more realistic and achievable transition between levels:

> Before the franchise structure there was the 'A' and 'B' section divided between 11 provinces and approximately 160 cricketers, all of them professional; this has now reduced to 6 professional teams of 100 players. Early adaptation in the 1990's was easier because you had a competitive 'B' section below and an only marginally stronger 'A' section and then international cricket.

Importantly, what the pre-2004 system seemed to provide was not only numerous pathways, but numerous pathways for both early and late developers to have the opportunity to play 1st Class cricket and go on to represent their country. There seemed a unified strategy in not only identifying and providing diversified pathways, but also providing competitive environments, or 'excellence at every level' (www.cricket.co.za).

This first study involved interviewing 16 players, coaches and administrators involved at all levels of SA cricket. Evidence suggests that the structural changes made to SA cricket in 2004 of reducing the number of professional teams and professional playing contracts not only highlighted the sensitivity and interrelated nature of a successful development pathway, but also highlighted the unique nature of that pathway. As one interviewed coach stated:

> There are not enough cricket teams in South Africa, too many cricketers are not playing the game and leaving a vacuum from the ages of 24 onwards as there are no opportunities. The current franchise system was to mirror the Australian system, but it's not right

for SA because SA has a far larger population to consider. More opportunities need to be created which would be better for development of players of colour and increase opportunities.

This structural change has led to a number of 'snowball' effects down the development pathway. An example of such effects, due to a reduction in the number of professional playing opportunities, has in turn lead to a reduction in the average age of amateur, semi-professional and professional players. One interviewed coach said:

> South African cricket is losing a lot of cricketers, especially around the 26, 27, 28 year old range, just when they are mentally/physically able – this will hurt the system.

This, in turn, has not only affected the positive cultural effects that experienced players bring to the developmental learning environment, but has also reduced the perceived competitiveness of the amateur game. As observed by one interviewed coach:

> The lack of a solid club structure means there is no avenue for young amateur cricketers. It also means that there is a big gap with not many cricketers being of 23 to 28 years of age. If young players have not been contracted to one of the six franchises then there is a greater possibility they will leave the system all together. The system needs more teams as a large number of players, who are good enough, are not getting an opportunity.

This perceived 'drop' in competitiveness of the amateur game has led to Provincial Governing Bodies taking more responsibility for the development process, which, in turn, has had a ripple effect on the overall age of individuals taking part in cricket at the amateur, semi-professional and professional level. The 'taking control' of the development process, brought about by the reduction in natural pathways, has not only led to earlier specialisation but has also made it increasingly difficult for individuals who find themselves developing later and unable to gain an opportunity to play top flight cricket as they are not part of the official pathway. Individuals who are in this position similarly have no way of proving themselves worthy of selection or contract, since the reality is a solid club structure that is held in high regard by administrators and selectors is no longer in place. It is these individuals, between 23 to 28 years of age, who may then be lost to the game. What the coaches described as a void, in both an age-related and cultural sense, has the potential to affect the CSA's strategy of 'excellence at every level'.

This brief description of a study inadvertently highlights the casual effect of administrative decisions, based on finance and logistics, on athletic development and the environments in which athletes compete. The second study involved interviewing only cricket coaches. Of the 14 coaches identified, all had at least five years of experience operating at the professional (franchise), semi-professional (1st class) and amateur (school, club and university) development environments. A significant number of the coaches gained experience coaching at all of the developmental levels, while 13 of the 14 had first class playing experience. Only a small number had gained international experience, however, out with the SA development environment.

**249**

All of the coaches had their own story of how they developed their coaching and how their career progressed, however, central to their learning was the considerable impact informal mentorship and past playing experience had on their individual learning experiences. Nevertheless, the coaching environment within which the coaches operated seemed to prescribe a very different experience. Coaches coaching at the elite end of the continuum benefitted from contact and discussion with lead coaches, with information concerning what was to be expected and information of player profiles being disseminated from the top. Information seemed to create a clear picture as to the 'type' of cricketers that were required and the necessary game strategies for the professional level. Further down the age-related development continuum, coaches who operated within the system still had the benefit of this type of coherent, top-down information transfer.

Coaches at the development end of the continuum, but 'out with the system', felt their learning and development was more *ad hoc* and their method or approach was based more on their own experiences of the game, rather than feeling part of the bigger picture of South African cricket. A common reason given was that the administrators of the game did not seem to give enough cognisance to the importance of coaches and coaching practice within this environment. As one of the interviewed coaches highlights the need to educate the administrators as to the role to the coach and the importance of the coach's position in the development pathway:

> The coach is ultimately not in control of his own destiny. He never feels that he can decide where his career is going to go. I feel in my role I am now in a position to, not only be educating the coaches, but I need to be educating the administrators as well.

Coaches involved in schools and in clubs, important elements of the development pathway, felt isolated due to not being part of the age-related development pathway of the Provincial Governing Body. From an administrative perspective, focus seemed to be on performance and success of the cricketers 'in the system' and under administrative control.

These experiences described here may be compared to those in the first study, involving the development environment of SA cricketers. Changes to the structure of the competitive game at the professional level have had a contributory effect, not only on opportunities for the cricketer, irrespective of colour, but also on opportunities for coaches to progress and develop at semi-professional and professional level. For example, before the change from a provincial structure to a franchise structure, there were 11 provinces each with an A and B team, together with each of those provinces having their own age-related development programmes. In addition to this, there was a competitive club structure, adding to an environment that had a number of opportunities for a division and natural movement of labour in the coaching environment.

Those same decisions that have had an implicit effect on the competiveness at amateur level have also had the perceived effect of increasing the learning gap between those coaches who operate out with the system and those who are considered to be in the system. In essence, the decisions made at administrative and macro-level, and affecting the overall structure of development pathways, have the ability to affect what occurs on a micro-level. These administrative effects are not localised to that of macro-level decision making, they may be seen at a meso-level (professional and semi-professional) and micro-level (amateur) too. For example, at semi-professional and professional level, budgetary discussions concerning athlete contracts will, more often than not, not involve the coach. Discussions concerning the remit of the coach will initially not involve the coach.

At amateur level, similar challenges occur. At university level club cricket, budgets, league structure and decisions whether students will play and practice during exam time will be made by the Committee, and in most instances without input or control of the coach or the participants. From the two research studies described here, it is evident that the stages associated with athletic development are similar to those associated with the learning and development of a coach, and that decisions made at an administrative level affect both the athlete and coach. Within this context, evidence suggests that a community of practice exists that shares 'joint enterprise' (Culver *et al.* 2009, p. 366), and has a 'collective union' by sharing 'a common set of problems or concerns' (Wenger *et al.* 2002). Within a development pathway, it may be deemed separate from that of the communities formed by coaches and athletes, but is equally important due to their role and decision-making powers.

The objective of this vignette was to begin further investigation into the effects of this administrative community of practice (AnCoP), not only from a negative perspective, but to illustrate how a better understanding of the role of the AnCoP will aid a more coherent and strategic coach development structure. In addition, a better understanding of this function may also begin further study in the areas of organisational culture and the communities' impact on a development pathway.

The above case study emphasises the 'relational dynamics' between the coach, athlete and organisation; for successful coach learning to be effective there should be distinct focus on the coaching relationship and its 'systematic interface' with development environment (Kahn 2011, p. 194). Many business coaching authors such as Brunning (2006); Cavanagh and Palmer (2009); Kemp (2008); Passmore (2007) and Kahn (2011) establish that the success of a coaching intervention is based on the quality of the coaching relationship and highlight the importance of 'engagement of relatedness rather than one particular method or skill' (Kahn 2011, p. 194; Kemp 2008, p. 32; Passmore 2007, p. 69). It is this 'relatedness' that ought to be embedded throughout the culture of the organisation.

Jones (2007, p. 107) refers to a 'culture of practice', and it is this culture of practice that Galipeau and Trudel (2005) note as the difference between an athletes community of practice (ACoP) and a coaches community of practice (CCoP). Within both a playing and a coaching environment there will exist a natural hierarchy, much of which is based on experience. Within a performance or participation environment, inclusive of the experienced members, there usually exists a leader who is formally in charge of the team. It is this relationship with the experienced team members, and especially the captain or leader, the coach needs to acknowledge and nurture.

Furthermore, coaches will also have their own natural hierarchy, based on the same power relationship (their knowledge base) and built up through their experiences playing the sport or through the more formal and informal learning environment. Galipeau and Trudel (2005) noted that the power differential was a major factor between the ACoP and CCoP and made reference to two 'types' of power, that of 'expert power and legitimate or positional power'. Expert power they refer to as the knowledge base of the coach, while positional power refers to the coach's social standing, with a correlation between coaches trying to increase positional

**251**

power through the increase of their expert power. They additionally highlight that coaches operating in a performance-based sporting environment, no matter how athlete-focussed they may be, will still exert their power over the athlete due to the nature of coaching and job protection.

However, do coaches always have this level of 'absolute power'?

As Slack and Parent (2006) explain, much discussion centring on organisational culture assumes that sports organisations would be driven by one single culture, making it somewhat utopian to think all members of a sports organisation would have a collective thought process. There are a number of factors that dictate a single organisational culture will be difficult to achieve. Natural subcultures arise throughout the levels of development, associated to different cultures of practice. As explained in the associated case study, the CCoP for those coaches operating 'within the system' will create a very different culture of practice than for those operating 'out with' the system'. Recent findings have highlighted that many coaches consciously opt 'out of the system' as a result of their dislike of this power differential (Nash et al. 2013).

The very nature associated with the stages of sports development (Bloom 1985) dictates that, even though everyone within the sports organisation may not be thinking alike, there must be a dominant culture. The rationale behind this is that for organisational culture to be applied within any organisation, there must be a shared understanding and common value. Nonetheless, it is this shared understanding (Sathe 1983) and common value that must permeate through and assist in providing a stable base to offer commonality through the organisation.

Schein (1996) provided one of the more inclusive descriptions that may be identifiable to that of systems theory and the importance of understanding the environment and the individual's role within it. He viewed organisational culture as a 'pattern of basic assumptions – invented, discovered or developed by a given group as it learns to cope with its problems of external adaptation and internal integration – that has worked well enough to be considered valid and therefore, to be taught to new members as the correct way to perceive, think and feel in relation to those problems' (p. 9). The relationship between any sporting governing body and the environment in which it operates may be recognised as a source of complexity and interdependence. With this in mind, it is of the utmost importance for the governing body to fully understand the environmental mechanisms and how all elements involved within this complex, interrelated relationship function.

At the beginning of the chapter, Steve the kayaking coach alluded to the lack of alignment surrounding elements imposed on the coaching environment from administrative bodies that do not necessarily understand the coaching process and its requirements. As highlighted by Cruikshank, Collins and Minten (2013), organisational effectiveness requires a number of factors. Each of these factors raised earlier, power dynamic, trust, belonging and talent development, may be related to the four interrelated elements that emerged from the SA study. The four elements that emerged were *relationships, learning and development, environment and structure* and *control*. Each of these four elements is wholly influenced by the central function, administration. These effects lead to increasing complexity within the coach and athlete development environment, no matter the development level of practice.

In the development of team cohesiveness and a positive team culture, coaches may wish to demonstrate 'real' power, however in terms of the coaches' identity and relationship compared to the AnCoP, it is 'perceived' power, as the 'real' power remains with the AnCoP. It is this 'real' power that the AnCoP holds, through the negotiated meanings and identity formed, due to its remit to formally administer and control the environment within which the sport takes place. The tools developed and boundaries drawn are formalised, leading to marginalisation by 'rules' set by the AnCoP, which affect, directly and indirectly, the environment within which the CCoP and ACoP develop.

The resultant effect is a 'cultural dislocation' to learning and development, not only between the negotiated meaning established between the AnCoP and the CCoP, but also between those coaches who are 'in the system' and those seen to be 'out with the system'.

For consistent and continuous development for the athlete, it is important that there is a systematic and strategic alignment to coach development between the AnCoP and the CCoP, since an organisation that does not marginalise, and functions in a coordinated fashion, 'thrives on an intensive negotiation of meaning and is thus more likely to be more dynamic and more pervasively creative' (Wenger 1998a, p. 261). To promote an effective and cohesive coaching structure, one centred on coach learning and progression, cognisance needs to be given by the AnCoP on the importance of this domain. In context, this approach is crucial, particularly for the development and learning experiences of coaches involved at the early stages of the development continuum. The self-perceived role of the coach, within a structural context, will influence the way the coaches learn. This rationale stems from an organisational culture context, with not only an emphasis on motivation and a desire to be a part of the 'bigger picture', but also a collective organisational vision of cross functional learning, rather than one of protectionist functional parochialism.

The work of Rynne (2013) and Rynne and Mallett (2012) supports the studies highlighted above and suggests that culture change occurs when all involved parties 'buy into' the process. Further, Rynne and Mallett (2012) contend that in the high performance, or elite, coaching environment there are issues that interfere with coach learning, such as political, institutional and personal power concerns. For example, within one of the Australian Academies of Sport, coaches, ostensibly working towards the same outcome, refused to share information and ideas with other coaches and performers.

The CoP approach to learning can benefit both coaches and organisations by allowing coaches to situate their learning in their own coaching environment. For learning to occur it is essential that sport coaches engage in joint activities and discussions, help each other and share information. Coaches can then build trusting relationships that enable them to learn from each other, allowing coaches to create opportunities for others to solve real problems within authentic challenge environments; in other words in real learning situations. Coaches who belong to a CoP are practitioners who share a repertoire of resources – experiences, stories, tools, ways of addressing recurring problems; in other words, a shared practice. This takes time and sustained interaction.

## REFERENCES

Bleed, R. (2001). A Hybrid Campus for the New Millennium. *Educause Review* 36(1): pp. 16–24.

Bloom, B. (Ed.) (1985). *Developing Talent in Young People*. (New York: Ballantine Books).

Bloom, G. A., Schinke, R. J. and Salmela, J. H. (1998). Assessing the Development of Perceived Communication Skills by Elite Basketball Coaches. *Coaching and Sport Science Journal* 2(3): pp. 3–10.

Bourdieu, P. (1993). *The Field of Cultural Production* (edited by R. Johnson). (New York: Columbia University Press).

Brunning, H. (2006). *Executive Coaching: Systems Psychodynamic Perspective.* (London: Karnac Books).

Cavanagh, M. and Palmer, S. (2009). Editorial Leadership Coaching in a Challenging World: Growing with Our Clients. *International Coaching Psychology Review* 4(1): pp. 4–5.

Christensen, M., Laursen, D. and Sorensen, J. (2011). Situated Learning in Youth Elite Football: A Danish Case Study Among Talented Male Under-18 Football Players. *Physical Education and Sport Pedagogy* 16(2): pp. 163–178.

Collins, M. F. and Kay, T. (2003). *Sport and Social Exclusion.* (London: Routledge).

Corte, U. (2013). A Refinement of Collaborative Circles Theory: Resource Mobilization and Innovation in an Emerging Sport. *Social Psychology Quarterly* 76(1): pp. 25–51.

Cruickshank, A., Collins, D. and Minten, S. (2013). Culture Change in a Professional Sports Team: Shaping Environmental Contexts and Regulating Power. *International Journal of Sports Science and Coaching* 8(2): pp. 271–290.

Culver, D. and Trudel, P. (2006). Cultivating Coaches' Communities of Practice: Developing the Potential for Learning Through Interactions. In *The Sports Coach as Educator: Re-conceptualising Sports Coaching.* R. Jones (Ed.) (London: Routledge): pp. 97–112.

Culver, D. and Trudel, P. (2008). Clarifying the Concept of Communities of Practice in Sport. *International Journal of Sports Science and Coaching* 3(1): pp. 1–10.

Farrell, M. P. (2001). *Collaborative Circles: Friendship Dynamics and Creative Work.* (Chicago: University of Chicago Press).

Field, J. (2003). *Social Capital.* (London: Routledge).

Galipeau, J. and Trudel, P. (2005). The Role of the Athletic, Academic, and Social Development of Student-Athletes in Two Varsity Sport Teams. *Applied Research In Coaching & Athletics Annual* 20: pp. 27–49.

Jones, R. (2007). Coaching Redefined: An Everyday Pedagogical Endeavour. *Sport Education and Society* 12(2): pp. 159–173.

Kahn, M. (2011). Coaching on the Axis: An Integrative and Systemic Approach to Business Coaching. *International Coaching Psychology Review* 6(2): pp. 194–210.

Kaiser, S., Engel, F. and Keiner, R. (2009). Structure-Dimensional Analysis: An Experimental Approach to Culture in Sport Organisations. *European Sport Management Quarterly* 9(3): pp. 295–310.

Kellett, P. (2002). Football-as-War, Coach-as-General: Analogy, Metaphor and Management Implications. *Football Studies* 5(1): pp. 60–76.

Kemp, T. J. (2008). Searching for the Elusive Model of Coaching: Could the 'Holy Grail' Be Right in Front of Us? *International Coaching Psychology Review* 3(3): pp. 219–226.

King, A. (1990). Enhancing Peer Interaction and Learning in the Classroom through Reciprocal Questioning. *American Educational Research Journal* 27: pp. 664–687.

Kirshner, D. and Whitson, J. A. (1997). *Situated Cognition: Social, Semiotic, and Psychological Perspectives.* (Mahwah, NJ: Erlbaum).

Kramer, R.M. and Tyler, T.R. (1996). *Trust in Organizations: Frontiers of Theory and Research.* (California: Sage).

Lave, J. and Wenger, E. (1992). *Situated Learning: Legitimate Peripheral Participation.* (Cambridge: Cambridge University Press).

McKenna, J. (2013). Culture Change in a Professional Sports Team: Shaping Environmental Contexts and Regulating Power. *International Journal of Sports Science & Coaching* 8(2): pp. 309–314.

Nash, C. and Sproule, J. (2011). Insights into Experiences: Reflections of Expert and Novice Coaches. *International Journal of Sports Science & Coaching* 6(1): pp. 149–161.

Nash, C., Sproule, J., Hall, E. and English, C. (2013). *Coaches Outside the System.* Research Report for Sports Coach UK.

Occhino, J., Mallett, C. and Rynne, S. (2013). Dynamic Social Networks in High Performance Football Coaching. *Physical Education and Sport Pedagogy* 18(1): pp. 90–102.

Passmore, J. (2007). Leading in Partnership: Using a Competency Approach for Public Service Leaders. *International Journal of Leadership in Public Services* 3(4): pp. 38–43.

Putnam, R.D. (Ed.). (2002). *Democracies in Flux: The Evolution of Social Capital in Contemporary Society.* (New York: Oxford University Press).

Rynne, S. (2013). Culture Change in a Professional Sports Team: Shaping Environmental Contexts and Regulating Power. *International Journal of Sports Science & Coaching* 8(2): pp. 301–304.

Rynne, S. and Mallett, C. (2012). Understanding the Work and Learning of High Performance Coaches. *Physical Education and Sport Pedagogy* 17(5): pp. 507–523.

Sathe, V. (1983). Implications of Corporate Culture: A Manager's Guide to Action. *Organizational Dynamics* 12(2): pp. 4–23.

Schein, E.H. (1996). Culture: The Missing Concept in Organization Studies. *Administrative Science Quarterly* 41(2): pp. 229–240.

Skinner, J., Zakus, D. and Cowell, J. (2008). Development Through Sport: Building Social Capital in Disadvantaged Communities. *Sport Management Review (Sport Management Association of Australia and New Zealand)* 11(3): pp. 253–275.

Slack, T. and Parent, M. (2006). *Understanding Sport Organizations: The Application of Organization Theory.* (Champaign, Illinois; Leeds: Human Kinetics).

Trudel, P. and Gilbert, W. (2004). Communities of Practice as an Approach to Foster Ice Hockey Coach Development. *Safety in Ice Hockey* 4: pp. 167–179.

Wenger, E. (1998a). *Communities of Practice: Learning, Meaning and Identity.* (Cambridge: Cambridge University Press).

Wenger, E. (1998b). Communities of Practice: Learning as a Social System. In: *Systems Thinker.* Retrieved: 27 November 2013. www.co-i-l.com/coil/knowledge-garden/cop/lss.shtml

Wenger, E., McDermott, R. and Snyder, W.M. (2002). *Cultivating Communities of Practice.* (Cambridge, MA: Harvard Business Press).

# Section 4

Technology, in particular digital technology, is evolving quickly, and for many has become a well established part of everyday life. Although much of this technology is now becoming available to coaches at all levels, many do not know what is available or how or when to incorporate these aids into their coaching practice.

- Chapter 14 considers some of the uses of technology within sport coaching. These technologies can be broken down into three key areas of optical technologies, data and coach education. It is not the purpose of this chapter to list a number of applications useful for coaches, but more to give an overview of those that could assist the coach in the various aspects of coaching practice.
- Chapter 15 reviews the use of geotechnologies in sport coaching. Geotechnologies, or geospatial technologies, encompass a variety of tools and methodologies for collecting, managing, analysing and presenting spatial data (data which includes a reference to a geographic location). As sports are inherently spatial in nature and by necessity confined to a specific location such as a tennis court, football pitch or cross country track, geography has a significant influence on the spread and development of sport. Geotechnologies may be used in sport coaching for analysing individual sports activities, collecting data and interpreting and presenting the results.

# Chapter 14

# Technology in sports coaching

*Jill Clark and Christine Nash*

This chapter will investigate the use of technology, specifically digital and information technology, in sport coaching and discuss some of the recent innovations that are changing how coaches analyse performance and provide feedback to their athletes; in other words how technology is changing the coaching process. As it would be impossible to cover all types and uses of such technology in sport, this chapter will focus on a few areas of interest with some practical examples to illustrate the use of digital technologies in current and emerging coaching practices.

In his review of the top technologies that have a significant impact on the development of sport in the modern era, Professor Steve Haake noted that the use and adaptation of technology in sport is nothing new (Engineering Sport 2013), and he provided an interesting perspective on the influence of some of the more unlikely innovations such as the invention of the lawn mower paving the way for the development of croquet and tennis courts. Technical innovations have also come in the form of the material used for equipment and clothing, for example, rubber for tennis and soccer balls and the switch from wood to carbon fibre for tennis rackets, to innovation in design such as the shape of skis, the design on an indoor cycling track or the addition of dimples to golf balls to improve the distance travelled (Scientific American 2005).

Although many of these technologies have been developed to help both the participants in sport and the spectators of sport, sport coaching has also benefitted from many innovations and been able to adopt and adapt technology to deconstruct activity, analyse action and reconstruct improved performance. Before considering what and how digital technology can help sport coaches, it is useful to review what coaching entails. As discussed in Chapter 1, a sport coach needs to fulfil a variety of roles, encompassing a wide range of skills. This includes the ability to:

- observe
- record
- analyse
- compare
- provide feedback
- develop tactics
- plan
- learn.

From analog recording systems, such as the ubiquitous training room whiteboard and the chalk-and-talk approach, to the latest digital technologies – tablets, sensors, video, location tracking, presentation media, web based applications and social media – sport coaching has looked to exploit available technology to help analyse performance and provide feedback. Although many coaches and coaching organisations may not have the resources to invest in the latest technology, there are options available for all levels of coaching and at minimal cost. The following sections will review some of the technologies and their application in coaching and discuss some of the issues involved in their use.

## OPTICAL TECHNOLOGIES

### Video

Two of the primary tasks for any coach, whether at the amateur or elite level, are to observe performance and provide feedback to athletes. Hynes, O'Grady and O'Hare (2013) consider being able to record performance a key requirement for coaches. Raupach (2012) discusses the use of video analysis in helping athletes fine tune their technique and some of the applications, including Dartfish and Ubersense®, which are available to help analyse those video recordings. Although more advanced, and by implication expensive, technologies are available, Raupach offers some practical suggestions for using more commonplace technology such as an iPad® and the YouTube™ platform for sharing video content. He argues that having access to expensive hardware and software isn't necessary to record and analyse performance and that coaches can make good use of generic technologies to assist them; with access to instant playback, a coach has an opportunity to provide instant feedback. In a subsequent article Raupach (2013) looks specifically at the use of video for analysing the performance of a number of elite runners. He describes how video recordings of running styles, in combination with an understanding of kinesiology, helps a coach identify similarities and differences in style and what, if any, specific aspect of that style that may require modification. Different distances and different terrains – long distance versus sprinting, track versus cross country – all require different functional movements and, as a number of team games rely upon running, it makes sense for the coach to concentrate on an efficient and effective running style to suit the context of the sport or activity.

Similarly Elliott and Reid (2008) discuss the application of video technology in a study of tennis, noting that the technology can assist by helping to capture and describe movement, which in combination with other assessment factors such as fitness and flexibility, can play a part in performance enhancement. They provide a useful summary of what they categorize as descriptive and objective technologies – the former including picture and video technologies for capturing movement and comparing the performance of different players, and the latter including more advanced capabilities of 3D and opto-reflective motion analysis for quantifying various aspects of movement like shoulder rotation and wrist flexion. The visual nature of the analysis, from both groups of technology, also provides valuable player feedback. Although the complexity and time-consuming nature of 3D analysis means the analysis is often undertaken by video analysts and not sport coaches, sports coaches do need to understand the results and provide feedback to the performers.

Although the use of video technology to assist performance development is becoming increasingly mainstream, its application is not limited to improving athlete performance; it has also proven successful in helping coaches develop their own reflective practice (see Chapter 12). In a study into the benefits of integrating video reflection to facilitate a coach education programme for inexperienced sports coaches, Carson (2008) argues that using video helps coaches develop a more holistic, and accurate, assessment of performance and reduces the chances of missing vital pieces of information. A number of coaches taking part in the study, many of whom had never had the opportunity to analyse their personal performance before, agreed using video helped them improve: 'It was a way of identifying my personal needs, to look back at the session and identify ways to improve'; 'It allowed me to gain more knowledge of the subject' (p. 384). This point of view was reinforced by an experienced kayaking coach who considered that 'video technology is very useful on the river but more useful as a reflective tool afterwards. It enhanced my knowledge to some extent – yeah, in terms of making me think about coaching.'

Carson (2008) considers the benefit of video reflection lies in highlighting strengths and weaknesses of practice and allowing for a better cognitive understanding of the coaching process. The initial video reflection allowed the coaches to identify areas they need to improve on, and subsequent reviews of improved performance allowed them to consider professional standards and recognised coaching practice. A major advantage of using video for assessing coach performance was a reduced reliance on memory, allowing for a more accurate and reliable analysis of coaching behaviour. It has been suggested that not only do coaches not accurately remember what they see in competition or training, but they are also unaware of the impact this lack of awareness has upon performers (Millar, Oldham and Donovan 2011). As a result of using video, there was less chance of inappropriate or inaccurate interpretations of the recorded sessions. As one coach commented, 'I thought that I'd performed this demonstration really well until I saw it on the video. I'd actually got my foot positioning wrong, which confused the player' (p. 386). Another coach highlighted the benefits of being able to see a coaching session from the athlete's perspective.

Some practical issues were also raised during the course of the study, such as having the necessary skills to operate the recording equipment, often at locations outside where wind interference could be a problem, and finding the optimum recording positions. The study recommended that some guidance and best practice documentation on using such technology for an application like sport coaching would be useful.

Another example of video technology in sport coaching is the Hawk-Eye ball tracking system, which is based on a number of court- or pitch-side high-speed cameras linked to a video processing and analysing system. The video from each camera is combined to produce an accurate 3D representation of the path of the ball (Top End Sports 2013). Perhaps better known for its line-calling and adjudication role in Masters and Grand Slam tennis matches, the technology has also been used in cricket and, to a lesser extent, in snooker as a visual aid for spectators. In addition to providing feedback, the technology has also developed into a comprehensive coaching and training system. In tennis, Elliott and Reid (2008) noted that the ball-tracking data collected by Hawk-Eye during major tournaments provided a unique opportunity for coaches to analyse many aspects of stroke production. The data included information on the height of the ball at the time of impact, the speed the ball was travelling, the length of each rally and the location of the ball (and by implication, the player) when the ball was struck. (Chapter 15 will discuss the importance of location in sport coaching in further detail.) Sanz and Terroba (2012) also discuss the use of technology in tennis, including the use of Dartfish video analysis and analytical software, and the impact this has had on the tactical analysis of tennis.

Singh Bal and Dureja (2012) considered the application of Hawk-Eye technology in cricket and the use of the video recordings to analyse bowling patterns, the posture and positioning of the batsmen and the placement and movement of fielders during play. Having access to such comprehensive and detailed video recordings provides coaches with insights into performance that were previously unavailable. It also means that coaches are able to view not only the tactics of their performers and teams but also those of their opponents. These systems can also analyse how players or teams react in specific situations, for example, free kicks, corners and serves, and allow coaches to advise their players as to what the opposition are likely to do in certain scenarios. Jordet and colleagues (2012) have examined video footage of penalty kicks within soccer over a number of years and consider there are certain coachable behaviours that would ensure greater success for penalty-taker, team and coach.

Sport coaching has often been able to take advantage of innovations developed for other applications. For example, the coaching of elite swimming has benefitted from some work previously undertaken by mechanical engineers. By applying the principles of mechanics and stream lining to the analysis of elite swimmers, new software has been developed to analyse video recordings and help assess swimming techniques (Engineering and Physical Sciences Research Council 2008). The software, Glide Coach, allows coaches to focus on one particular aspect of swimming, the glide phase, which has previously not received much attention due the inherent difficulties of a coach being able to see what's going on under the water (Thow, Naemi and Sanders 2012).

All of these examples demonstrate that with the additional observational capabilities provided by video systems, from the basic recoding facilities on a tablet device to the sophisticated multi-recorder Hawk-Eye setup, video analysis has changed the way in which coaches and athletes can monitor and track performance. With access to increasingly detailed information, often in real-time and in three dimensions, coaches can review and develop not only the performance of their athletes but also their own performance as a coach.

## Lasers

Other optical technologies have also been adopted within sports coaching to great effect. The introduction of laser-timing technology at the Manchester Velodrome provided a revolutionary new approach to monitoring training sessions and performance improvements. The system, adapted from an existing military application, uses a network of lasers installed around a cycle track that read a personalised code embedded in a tag attached to each cycle. This makes it possible to track up to 30 individual cyclists training simultaneously, something that was previously impossible using the old break-beam system (UK Sport 2009). According to Sir David Brailsford, a former performance director of British Cycling:

> This technology was a major step forward in training for us and helped to provide more accurate data to hone our performance ahead of the Olympics. Cycling is a sport that relies a lot on technology. The bikes are part of it, but the day-to-day training is just as technical, and it is therefore important that it can be analysed and measured objectively.
>
> (BAE Systems Newsroom 2012)

The sport of archery has also benefited from the adoption of laser technology. Using a laser pointer device attached to her head, South African archer Karen Hultzer used the technology to improve posture and accuracy during training sessions (CSIR 2012). Increasing numbers of golfers are using laser-based rangefinders to improve their appreciation of distance, slope angles and height differences across golf courses (Robertson and Burnett 2013), and the discipline of modern pentathlon has benefited from the adoption of laser guns in preference to the more traditional pistols.

## Sensors

With increasing sophistication, miniaturisation and portability, mobile sensors are now a feature of many sports, from personal fitness monitors to the latest in tracking and wearable technology like Google Glass and smart watches. Added to that, the next stage in the evolution of the Internet, the Internet of Things or the Internet of Everything (Cisco 2013), will see the integration of many of these sensors in a global network of devices. Information such as heart rate, activity levels and performance metrics can be collected, processed and published online, increasingly in real time (Novatchkov *et al.* 2011), providing an invaluable resource of analytical data for coaches and athletes alike.

Robinson *et al.* (2011) describe the use of sensors within the discipline of Olympic sprint kayaking. Their study focused on an analysis of both K1 and K4 events, matching equipment and athletes and the optimum placement of crew members within each kayak. Through the use of an accelerometer and data logger (PadLog), they measured the dynamics of each craft during sprint racing. Based on the observations of the coaches (using video recordings and race performance timings) and the accelerometer data, coordinated stroke rhythm emerged as a crucial element for peak performance; effective forward prolusion would be produced through the symmetrical application of force to the left and right blades. For the K1 athlete, the accelerometer data highlighted a low acceleration phase in the middle of the stroke that hadn't been picked up by the coaches. For the K4 crew, data collected by the PadLog sensor, in conjunction with video analysis, helped to identify differences in acceleration generated by different members of the team. With a clearer understanding of crew and stroke dynamics, coaches were able to better match equipment (paddles) with athletes and work to address imbalances in the stroke phases.

Perkins *et al.* (2011) describe the use of Inertial Measurement Units (IMU), a combination of accelerometers and gyros that detect motion in three dimensions and transmit data wirelessly. IMUs have been embedded in a variety of sports equipment, including golf clubs and baseball bats, with the aim of developing new training systems and improving performance. With respect to the baseball case study, the IMU was used to analyse the three phases of swing – start (acceleration), hitting zone and the follow through (deceleration). The metrics derived from the sensor data included the bat head speed and maximum acceleration, and the amount of time from initiating the swing to ball impact. By comparing the metrics collected from players of all abilities, coaches were able to identify any problem areas within each swing and develop the necessary training programmes to correct the defects. Although the swing is equally important in golf, coaches must also consider the range of clubs used during the course of play. By embedding an IMU in a golf club, small deviations in club head orientation

**263**

that affect the angle of the clubface in relation to the target line may be detected (Perkins *et al.* 2011). By tracking the swing, coaches can correct any misalignments to ensure the optimal clubface angle.

There are many other examples of the use of sensor technology to achieve better performance in sport, such as dynamometers for measuring muscle torque and electromyography for evaluating muscle activation (Elliott and Reid 2008) – too many to review within the scope of this chapter. One area that does merit further consideration is wearable technology; the 'new wave of smart sports equipment' that 'aims to put a digital coach in your pocket' (New York Times 2014). With wearable devices now available for a range of sport activities, including swimming, snowboarding, soccer and rugby, Hynes *et al.* (2013) consider the use of wearable technologies as a means for aiding coaches to plan, monitor and compare training sessions.

Marsland *et al.* (2012) describe the identification of cross-country ski movement patterns using micro-sensors worn by skiers. With the device positioned in the centre of the upper back of the skiers, traces of gyroscope and accelerometer movement plotted versus body position were collected to illustrate the various components of cross-country ski technique – the stride, kick double pole and offset skating. When comparing the profiles of different skiers, the observations highlighted that although there were certain characteristics common to techniques and individual athletes, there were also slight differences in technique between different athletes, something that could be potentially useful for correcting issues related to asymmetry. Similar devices, such as the Catapult system, have been worn by rugby, ice and field hockey, American football and basketball players, enabling coaches to track and compare practice session data with the aim of improving performance.

Although still to be made available on general release (at the time of writing), Google Glass™ technology promises to provide a unique opportunity for coaches to both capture the perspective of their athletes during practice and provide real-time feedback through the heads-up display. Described as no more obtrusive than a pair of sunglasses, the devices include a miniature screen and video recorder and can incorporate the latest developments in augmented reality (the integration of sound, graphics, video or other digital content with a live view of a physical location). Pro tennis player Bethanie Mattek-Sands trialled the technology at the Wimbledon championships during 2013 (VentureBeat News 2013), and early results have been encouraging. The head coaches of a number of National Basketball Association (NBA) teams have also been investigating the use of Google Glass™ technology to develop new coaching strategies and improve team performance (Sport techie 2014).

Taking these individual solutions to the next level, Novatchkov *et al.* (2011) discuss the development of a mobile coaching framework based on what they refer to as ubiquitous technologies (p. 48). They describe how recent developments in computer science – networked and miniature devices, wearable technology and integrated body sensors – have resulted in many new ways to collect, transfer, process and analyse sports-specific data. As a result of these innovations, new coaching and training systems have been developed that have produced better techniques, resulted in fewer injuries and provided instant feedback for athletes. The next step is to build on the progress made so far and develop a mobile coaching framework based on:

- mobility
- low power consumption

- minimal interference with an athlete's training
- integration facilities
- ease of use
- clear presentation.

The new sensor network should also include devices that measure force and weight displacement, resistance training and other biomechanical or physiological attributes. The network must also be robust and secure, supporting reliable data transfer with integrated web applications, and provide better algorithms to analyse the often complex data captured during training and competition. This will improve both the speed of processing the data and the interpretation of the results to provide instant, or near instant, feedback, something Hynes *et al.* (2013) also consider as an essential requirement for both coach and athlete. Nadkarni (2014) emphasises that point, advising that 'Only with real time instruction can an athlete truly see real time results'.

Novatchkov *et al.* (2011) recognise that although such systems are not universally available at present due to a number of reasons (including unreliable data connections and some resistance to implementation, a point also made by Sawicki (2009)), they will provide a 'future-oriented basis for athletes and experts in means of assistance, mentoring, support and prevention' (p. 48).

Hynes *et al.* (2013) also discuss the development of an integrated system that combines wearable sensing components with web technologies. The prototype system, CoachViz, incorporates sensing components (including vests worn by athletes), processing components for collecting and storing the data and a visualisation component for presenting the results of the analysis in an intuitive and easily understood format.

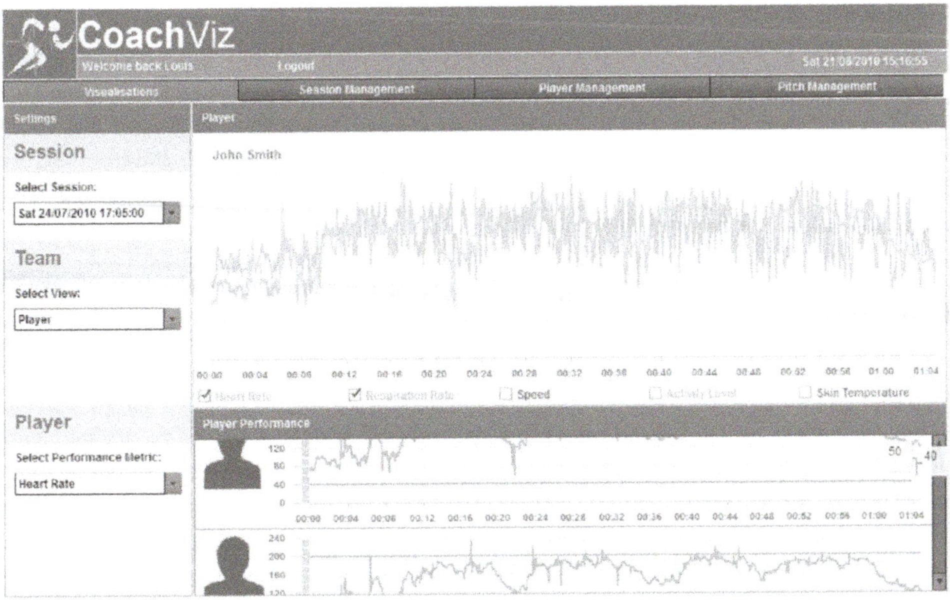

*Figure 14.1* CoachViz – Integrated data collection, analysis and presentation.

The authors argue that there is a significant amount of what they describe as 'technology-enhanced sports equipment' (p. 113) that could be harnessed to revolutionise coaching, but how best to incorporate these technologies to present a holistic view of performance remains to be seen.

Although the technologies described here may provide coaches with many new tools and techniques to record and analyse performance, relying on such technology alone will not transform a bad coach into a successful or effective coach. There is also a danger of needlessly investing time and resources trying to find an application for the latest must-have gadget. In a recent experiment that involved attaching a video camera to a curling stone (Business Insider SPORTS 2014), the end result seem to offer little as to a better understanding of the performance of the curlers or the behaviour of the curling stone. There are other resources available to support coaches, especially at the elite level, including physiological testing and biomechanical analysis, that could also be considered. The art and skill of the coaches is understanding how, when and perhaps most importantly, why they should use these technologies in their coaching.

## DATA

Sports generate a lot of data, whether in the form of individual player or team performance metrics, coaching or managerial decisions or game strategies (Schumaker, Solieman and Chen 2013). With the number and type of sport-specific data-collecting devices that participate in sensor networks, mobile frameworks and the Internet of Everything set to increase dramatically in the coming years, this will have a significant impact on the type and volume of data that are available. Although improved access to detailed and accurate performance metrics has the potential to benefit both coaches and athletes alike, making the most of this resource will pose some additional challenges. The issue is not so much how to collect the data, but rather knowing what data should be collected and how to make the best use of it (Schumaker et al. 2013).

In a review of the use of wearable technology and helmet cameras in American football, Chris Kluwe, a retired professional player, argues that the next big change in the game will be the widespread adoption of this technology by coaches to improve tactics and ultimately win games. With real-time streaming of information from players to players and from players to coaches, the focus will switch from the field of play to the IT department (Wohlsen 2014). Kluwe notes that the successful teams will be the ones that make the data available to players in a way that they can use it effectively, while the others will be left dealing with information overload. In this article, former NFL player Kluwe added, 'Now your IT department is just as important as your scouting department. Data mining is not for nerds anymore. It's also for jocks.'

Data mining is generally described as the analytical process of discovering patterns and relationships and a 'search for new, valuable, and nontrivial information in large volumes of data' (Kantardzic 2011, p. 2). Although the term 'data mining' is relatively new, the technologies and techniques used have been available for some time. However, recent innovations in computer processing capabilities and data storage (both local and cloud-based) and improved algorithms for analysing the data are producing faster and more accurate results. Although beyond the scope of this chapter to discuss the processes in detail, this is an area of sports research that has received more attention recently, for example, Ofoghi, Zeleznikow, MacMahon and Raab (2013) and Schumaker et al. (2013).

Hynes *et al.* (2013) describe how a team coach may be receiving physiological and positional data on, for example, 11 players every two seconds during training or competition, and that coach will be required to interpret this complex and detailed data over extended periods, not just an individual event. Analysing that data will require data mining techniques to provide useful insights into, and predict future, athlete behaviour (Sanz and Terroba 2012). As Elliott and Reid (2008) point out, having access to the latest technologies and access to all the data is one thing, but if coaches are to take advantage of recent innovations, they must have the necessary skills to collect, manage and incorporate disparate sources of data into their coaching regimes. Sanz and Terroba (2012) agree that the skill of the coach will be in assessing, interpreting and learning from the data to make better decisions and develop better coaching strategies. Hynes *et al.* (2013) also add that coaches who develop this expertise in the interpretation and analysis of the data will be at a distinct advantage and their services much sought after.

With increasing access to so many technologies, it is all the more important for coaches to consider what they want to achieve first. If there's a specific area of coaching practice or athlete development that requires attention, that should drive the search for a solution – rather than a particular technology looking for an application. The best solution may rely on a more traditional approach, take advantage of new technologies, or be a successful combination of both; it's up to the coaches to decide what is the most appropriate for their particular requirements.

Two other aspects of data to consider are metadata and the presentation of the data. Although often not captured with the data for the sake of expediency, metadata – information that describes the data – is an invaluable additional resource for coaches and athletes. Ideally, when data is collected, metadata should also be recorded and should include information such as:

- how the data were collected
- the purpose of the data
- the time and date of data collection
- the content and quality of the data
- the creator or author of the data
- any subsequent updates to the data
- any standards the data complies with.

This will provide an indication of the provenance, quality and accuracy of the data, and although it may seem to be an unnecessary overhead, as more and more data are captured and used in coaching, it is important to be able to track and archive performance metrics for future comparisons. Knowing who collected the data and how, when and why it was collected will provide coaches with a context for the revaluation of that data. A well managed and documented data archive is not only useful for reviewing the performance of individual athletes over time, but also for reviewing the performance of the coach. This review process may be undertaken by coaches on their own, but perhaps more effectively, it could also benefit from the input of a mentor or network of like-minded coaches (see Chapters 11 and 13).

The other aspect of data to consider is presentation. Once the data has been analysed, the next step is to make that information available to other coaches and athletes alike in easy to use and easily understood formats, which could include diagrams, charts, graphs, videos and maps (Chapter 15 will discuss the presentation of spatial data in more detail). From team tactics sketched on a whiteboard to the latest interactive iPad app, coaches have often relied on some form of graphical interpretation of an event or activity to provide feedback to athletes. Such representations of the data are not only more accessible and easier to understand and use, but also presenting the data visually is perhaps the most effective way to communicate the results due to the volume of raw sports data. Without effective communication, the results of the analysis will be lost. David Gourlay, Head Coach of Bowls Scotland, reported the successful use of video technology and notational analysis in providing what he described as 'objective and validated' feedback to individual and team members of the Scottish Lawn Bowls Elite Squad. He added:

> The technology enables us to monitor and analyse every aspect of game playing and overall performance and the ability to replay certain events for further analysis and discussion with the individual or team. It also provides invaluable information about opponents' strengths and strategies and will form a huge part of our player development and therefore I cannot overstate its importance within the programme.
>
> (Bowls Scotland 2012)

Many TV and Internet sports programmes use the latest data display techniques to help describe and explain sports events and activities. Techniques such as video analysis of unstoppable free kicks (BBC SPORT Football 2013) and SimulCam, a technology that allows the movement of one athlete to be superimposed over another for a comparison of posture, style and technique, provide insights into performance that were previously unavailable. Although such technology may be beyond the budget of many coaches and coaching organisations, the adoption of digital presentation aids as part of the coach's toolkit is becoming increasing prevalent. There are some free, open source solutions available, such as Kinovea, which allow coaches to compare and contrast performances.

However, as before, simply having access to the latest presentation tools doesn't guarantee they will be of benefit to coaches; what works for one coach, individual athlete or team may not work in another context. Khacharem, Zoudji, Kalyuga and Ripoll (2012) investigated the use of what they referred to as 'instructional visualizations' in the game of soccer, 'external representations or visual-spatial displays printed on paper or shown on a computer screen that can be perceived by a person' (p. 326). The effectiveness of these visualisations, presented in dynamic (for example, video animations) or static (for example, diagrams) forms, was investigated to better understand their role in developing player tactical learning and what, if any, differences may exist between the various levels of performance. The study highlighted the positive effects of static presentations compared with dynamic presentations for non-expert players. This group of learners attained higher recall performance with a lower number of repetitions and less effort when using static as opposed to dynamic presentations that 'provided these players with more time for processing, organising and integrating required information, facilitating the understanding of the playing system' (p. 336). Conversely, dynamic presentations were seen as more beneficial for expert players; their already developed sense of dynamic perception and detailed knowledge base allowed them to cope with the transient nature of the information in a dynamic presentation. Khacharem *et al.* (2012) concluded that instructional strategies designed 'to reduce extraneous cognitive load' (p. 337) are better for non-expert learners, but as those learners gain more expertise such a strategy becomes redundant. The study recommended that coaches and educators working with soccer players consider the level and individual 'cognitive characteristics' of their players when using different presentation formats to develop coaching strategies; a single presentation style is unlikely to yield the best results for all levels of players.

In a study into how athletes develop movement skills, Nishiyama and Suwa (2010) investigated the use of software to represent and visualise changes in an athlete's body posture. By representing the discrete phases of movement with different colours, and providing that feedback in a graphical form, a baseball player was able to review his own posture and swing and significantly improve his batting average in a relatively short space of time. Nishiyama and Suwa (2010) argue the main benefits for athletes using the visualisation software included being able to see for themselves how their body moved, and having the opportunity to compare performance on any given day and over a number of days. This enabled the baseball player in the study to understand his own body movements and how they influenced his batting swing.

While such techniques are revolutionising the presentation of sports data and the manner in which feedback is given to athletes, it's important for coaches to be aware of the potential for cognitive overload through providing too much or too many sources of information at one time. As with most things, simplicity is key and less is often more. Again the skill for the coach will be finding the right balance between different communication and presentation techniques that work best for them and their athletes.

## COACH EDUCATION

The increasing adoption and use of digital technologies in coaching has not only benefited athletes and players but has also resulted in considerable changes to the way coaches themselves learn and progress professionally. Social media, online learning, smartphones, tablets and other recent innovations have all influenced how coaches access and use sports related resources.

### Using social media

Social media applications such as Twitter, Facebook, Google+, YouTube, Flickr, Instagram, Pinterest, blog sites and so on, have revolutionised how information is collected and shared online. Many sports organisations and professional bodies have been incorporating these new technologies to promote and support their particular sport. Examples include the sportscoachUKTV channel on YouTube and a number of Twitter accounts, such as the Coaching Family, @CoachingFamily; sources of funding available to coaches in the UK, @scUKCoachFund; national coaching information and resources, @CAC_ACE and @SportNZ; and national agencies such as @Ausport and @CoachingEd.

However, with so many applications to choose from, trying to keep track of multiple social media feeds and maintaining an effective balance between online and face-to-face communication can create other issues. A review of who you want to communicate with, and how, before signing up for too many accounts can help develop a more focused strategy for creating an online presence. Abbott (2010) described how such a strategy, which included the selective use of certain social media sites, was developed by CanoeKayak BC, a provincial sport organisation supporting and promoting paddle sports. The organisation serves over 5,000 members, including competitive and developing athletes, coaches and officials. To address some of the issues of providing timely and effective communication with access to limited resources, CanoeKayak BC developed links between their main organisation website, their Facebook page, Twitter account and blog site. This enabled them to provide information for affiliated clubs and members, develop a volunteer official sign-up facility and offer technology training. By using the analytical tools provided by many of the sites, CanoeKayak BC was able to profile who was using their sites and how, and develop future communication strategies accordingly. Based on their experiences of using social media, CanoeKayak BC recommended the following strategy (Abbott 2010):

- decide on a social network by focusing on a small number of applications
- decide how much/little you wish to control
- send periodic 'scatter messages' to increase contacts
- be 'flashy' if that's appropriate for your organisation and the message you want to convey
- be prepared to spend time 'maintaining' and 'engaging'
- do your research and make sure you are reaching your target audience
- activate your followers and get them involved
- make the most of free or low cost applications.

It's also worth considering the following when using social media as a channel of communication:

- Aim to provide updates on a regular basis but avoid excessive posting – inform but don't overwhelm.
- Be mindful of where your target audience is located and the time zone – for example, if the people you wish to communicate with are in the USA, consider what's the best time of day to post an update (early afternoon or evening).
- It isn't necessary to follow numerous individual accounts; for example on Twitter and Google+ relevant posts can be tracked using hashtags (#) – use #sportcoaching to follow posts referencing sport coaching. (Be aware that using #coaching on its own will highlight posts on life coaching and business coaching as well as sport coaching, although some of that information may also be useful.) There are also a number of cross-platform search options such as #tagboard that allow users to search for hashtags across a number of social media outlets.

## Digital literacy skills

Digital literacy skills – the skills for finding, assessing and creating information using digital technologies – are as relevant to sport coaches as they are for all users of digital resources.

The following list summarises some of the digital skills coaches may find useful within their coaching practice and as they develop online profiles:

- **Get involved:** Sign up, register, join, follow, like, +1.
- **Share:** Effective communication and learning involves give and take.
- **Take advantage of free or low-cost resources:** The Internet provides access to a wealth of resources, much of which is freely available, in the form of short courses, education resources such as templates for content delivery, webinars, training, podcasts and so on.
- **Keep it brief:** The Internet is drowning in content, so to capture and retain your audience's attention, learn to write clearly and concisely.
- **Personal information management:** Find an approach that works for you to keep track of the resources that you've consulted and/or found useful.
- **Data management and analytical skills:** Data are just facts and figures unless you do something useful with them. Learn to work with a variety of data sources and develop the necessary skills to process that data into a form that adds value for you and your athletes. Take advantage of free cloud-based data storage options for storing and sharing your resources.
- **Learn to discriminate:** Don't settle on the first resource you find – there will be others. No one individual or organisation has all the answers, so keep looking. Learn to evaluate different resources.
- **Be critical:** Critical thinking is a combination of skills and techniques that start with asking questions and acquiring and reviewing evidence, and lead to deducing substantiated conclusions.
- **Assess:** Assess what you've learnt so far and where you need to improve. Provide feedback on resources you've used.
- **Licensing:** Understand digital publishing rights and usage – what's involved in making content available online and the implications of using content created by others.

Chapter 9 discussed the many challenges faced by coaches, including being habitually short of time and often in need of a 'quick fix' for a particular issue. Time spent creating a short list of useful and trusted online resources would be time well spent, given the increasing amount of information coaches have to access to.

## Online learning

Online learning is an established and effective method of course delivery and very much in demand within coach education. Sports Coach UK (2013) found 'coaches perceive online resources to offer them greater flexibility to learn in their own time and to access information that would otherwise be hard to find'. The UK sport coaching landscape is notably different to other countries and regions, such as Europe, North America and Australia. The sport coaching workforce in the UK tends to participate on a volunteer or part-time basis, although coaches can also be working within ancillary professions, such as PE teaching, sport development or coaching support. In the USA, the greatest challenge within coach education has been the voracious appetite for online learning. Australian sources comment that in the past two years the demand for digital learning has grown by 56%.

In a review of access to and the use of technology in sports coaching, Nash and Sproule (2011) noted that many coaches have been encouraged to consider integrating new technologies into their coaching sessions. There is a perception of coaches working with preliminary level athletes that such technologies were the preserve of elite performance coaches. However, many experienced coaches consider the use of such technology, in the form of online training resources and easily accessible coaching-related content, as a potential substitute to attending some coach education courses. Moss (2010) provided a review of technology used to evaluate and develop coaches as part of the Canadian National Coaching Certification Program (NCCP). He described the use of a number of technologies to help coaches prepare for training sessions (including Formstack, YouTube and Scribd), engage in interactive coach development sessions (including Fuze Meeting) and develop tools for online coaching portfolios.

With the increasing availability and choice of content, such as free MOOCs (Massive Open Online Courses), training videos, podcasts and session planners, a wide range of coaching resources for all levels of coaching ability is now readily available. A junior coach of a current top ten tennis player recently remarked when interviewed:

> I learn from the internet – tennis1 website especially which has got 2 things – it's got a library of various things – how you would coach a forehand, how would you coach young children sort of games – so you've got a library but what they've got is little video clips of about every top player – forehands from the side, forehands from the back, forehands from the forehand side . . . they've got hundreds so if ever I'm in any doubt when I see a player I might go back to tennis 1 just to reinforce it. It doesn't matter what player – the style may be different but the technique is the same. The other thing is Silicon Coach which helps me learn a lot visually. I also get a lot of up to date stuff from the net – more recent and relevant than the information from the NGB.

In a review of online coach education, Sports Coach UK (2013) reported that coaches are using online resources to help develop their skills and knowledge on a weekly basis and are increasingly taking advantage of the greater flexibility to learn in their own time and to access information that would otherwise be hard to find. Although there are some age/employment variations in the pattern of use, the findings of the review were consistent across the coaching profession. Coaches report that the most useful digital resources included videos, generic sport/coaching websites, NGB websites and the Sports Coach UK website. The most useful online experiences for coaches were those that supported the exchange of ideas, networking and being able to watch video footage/YouTube clips to learn techniques and develop ideas for their own coaching practice.

However, the Sports Coach UK report concluded that there comes a point when the remote and often asynchronous nature of online resources is at odds with the interactive and practical nature of coaching. Although accessing coach education resources online provides a flexible additional option, there are limits to what a coach can expect to achieve using these resources alone. Such resources should be considered a complement to more traditional resources, rather than a wholesale replacement. Digital and online does not always mean better. There may be issues concerning the reliability and sheer volume of some of the information that's available; perhaps there are not enough practical examples available at present. The challenge for coaches and the wider coaching profession is to get the right balance between online and offline coach education resources and to take advantage of what both environments have to offer.

## LOOKING AHEAD

The last few years have seen the development of many new innovative technologies that have had a significant impact on sport coaching. As never before coaches can record, analyse and assess performance and provide detailed, instant feedback to their athletes. As digital technologies continue to evolve, sport coaches will continue to adapt these innovations to their own requirements in the quest for better performance and the 'perfect' technique.

With the Internet of Everything and the network of sensors and recording devices developing to provide a platform of real-time integration, virtual sport coaches are set to have an increasingly influential role in the development of coaching practice. Nadkarni (2014) considers the next step for golf coaches will be a world in which any player can capture his or her golf swing digitally and submit it to a coach who will review it immediately. The coach will provide instant feedback on how to improve the swing or give advice on what type of shot to play given the location on the course. Such interactive and remote coaching not only benefits the aspiring golfer; Nadkarni also sees this as a way for coaches and golf academies to significantly increase their revenue. Coaches no longer have to be physically present with one golfer, but can be virtually present with a number of golfers. Babolat, a leading manufacturer of tennis rackets, recently announced the release of a smart tennis racket, the Babolat Play Pure Drive (BBC NEWS Business 2014). Hailed as a virtual tennis coach, the racket comes equipped with sensors recording movement and string vibrations and the ability to connect to a smartphone or computer. During play the racket counts forehands and backhands, serves and smashes and compares the results with data collected in previous sessions.

In a drive to improve the content and delivery of coach education programs for team handball, Lopes *et al.* (2009) describe the development of a new system based on Second Life, a 3D virtual world. Using shared 3D simulations and avatars (a figure representing a person in a virtual environment or online game), the system focused on improving the understanding of the dynamics between defensive and offensive players, and allowing trainee coaches to interact with automated avatar players and visualise their tactics in a shared environment. As technology such as this develops and matures, other coaching programmes will undoubtedly benefit from similar simulated practice environments.

Taking advantage of avatar-based and robotics technologies, the world's first Cybathlon, a championship for what are described as robot-assisted parathletes (known as pilots), is due to be held in 2016. The competition will include a number of disciplines that 'apply the most modern powered knee prostheses, wearable arm prostheses, powered exoskeletons, powered wheelchairs, electrically stimulated muscles and novel brain-computer interfaces' (Cybathlon 2014). What skills will a coach need to support such disciplines, and what coach education programmes will be required to teach those skills?

The increased use of technology and technological aids may also present some ethical issues, a subject that is discussed further in Chapter 3, and the ongoing requirements for

**273**

coaches to learn and develop (see Chapter 9) must also be considered. Access to the Internet and an ever increasing choice of digital technologies and applications have revolutionised how, and when, that learning and developing will take place. The principles of learning and development remain the same, but the contexts for learning and the amounts of information available to support that learning have been transformed. Coaches and coaching organisations must adapt to these changes in terms of how they collect, organise and deliver that information, the pace of change, their own changing requirements and perhaps most importantly, the requirements of their athletes.

## REFERENCES

Abbott, M. J. (2010). *Leveraging Technology and Social Media to Enhance Operations, Member Engagement, and Community Visibility.* Paper presented at Sport Leadership Ottawa 18–21 November.

BAE Systems Newsroom (2012). *Military Precision Helps British Cyclists in Competition.* Retrieved: 28 February 2014. www.baesystems.com/article/BAES_069044/military-precision-helps-british-cyclists-in-competition

NEWS Business (2014). *Smart Racquet on Hand to Transform Tennis Coaching.* Retrieved: 2 April 2014. www.bbc.co.uk/news/business-25857296

BBC SPORT Football (2013). *Gareth Bale's 'Unstoppable' Free-Kicks – Pat Nevin Analysis.* Retrieved: 26 March 2013. www.bbc.co.uk/sport/0/football/21686619

Bowls Scotland (2012). *New Beginnings – The Launch of the Elite Programme for Lawn Bowls 2012.* Retrieved: 27 March 2014. www.bowlsscotland.com/component/content/article/4-latest-news/160-new-beginnings-the-launch-of-the-elite-programme-for-lawn-bowls-2012

Business Insider SPORTS (2014). *We Put a GoPro on a Curling Stone.* Retrieved: 8 April 2014. www.businessinsider.com/gopro-on-a-curling-stone-2014–2

Carson, F. (2008). Utilizing Video to Facilitate Reflective Practice: Developing Sports Coaches. *International Journal of Sports Science and Coaching* 3(3): pp. 381–390.

Cisco (2013). *Internet of Everything.* Retrieved: 21 March 2014. www.cisco.com/web/about/ac79/docs/IoE/IoE-AAG.pdf

CSIR (2012). *CSIR Laser Technologist Makes SA 2012 London Olympics Team as Archery Coach.* Retrieved: 21 March 2014. ntww1.csir.co.za/plsql/ptl0002/PTL0002_PGE157_MEDIA_REL?MEDIA_RELEASE_NO = 7525183

Cybathlon (2014). *Championship for Robot-Assisted Parathletes.* Retrieved: 2 April 12014. www.cybathlon.ethz.ch/

Elliott, B. and Reid, M. (2008). The Use of Technology in Tennis Biomechanics. *ITF Coaching and Sport Science Review* 15(45): pp. 2–4.

Engineering and Physical Sciences Research Council (2008). *Gliding to Gold: World-Beating Software Could Boost British Swimming.* Retrieved: 28 February 2014. www.epsrc.ac.uk/newsevents/news/2008/Pages/glidingtogold.aspx

Engineering Sport (2013). *Top Technologies in Sport.* Retrieved: 27 February 2014. engineeringsport.co.uk/2013/10/02/top-technologies-in-sport-number-1/

Hynes, G., O'Grady, M. and O'Hare, G. (2013). Towards Accessible Technologies for Coaching. *International Journal of Sports Science & Coaching* 8(1): pp. 105–114.

Jordet, G., Hartman, E. and Jelle Vuijk, P. (2012). Team History and Choking Under Pressure in Major Soccer Penalty Shootouts. *British Journal of Psychology* 103(2): pp. 268–283.

Kantardzic, M. (2011). (2nd ed.). Data-Mining Concepts. In *Data Mining: Concepts, Models, Methods, and Algorithms* (Hoboken, NJ, USA: John Wiley and Sons, Inc.): pp. 1–24.

Khacharem, A., Zoudji, B., Kalyuga, S. and Ripoll, H. (2012). Developing Tactical Skills Through the Use of Static and Dynamic Soccer Visualizations: An Expert–Nonexpert Differences Investigation. *Journal of Applied Sport Psychology* 25(3): pp. 326–340.

Lopes, A., Bruno Pires, M. C., Santos, A., Sequeira, P., Morgado, L. and Camerino, O. (2009). Pedagogy, Education and Innovation in 3-D Virtual Worlds: Use of a Virtual World System in Sports Coach Education for Reproducing Team Handball Movements. *Journal of Virtual Worlds Research* 2(1): pp. 3–16.

Marsland, F., Lyons, K., Anson, J., Waddington, G., Macintosh, C. and Chapman, D. (2012). Identification of Cross-Country Skiing Movement Patterns Using Micro-Sensors. *Sensors* 12: pp. 5046–5066.

Millar, S., Oldham, A. and Donovan, M. (2011). Coaches' Self-Awareness of Timing, Nature and Intent of Verbal Instructions to Athletes. *International Journal of Sports Science and Coaching* 6(4): pp. 503–513.

Moss, A. (2010). *Using Technology to Evaluate and Develop Coaches in the NCCP*. Paper presented at Sport Leadership Ottawa 18–21 November.

Nadkarni, V. (2014). Mobile Interactive Coaching Technology. *SiliconIndia* p. 38.

Nash, C. and Sproule, J. (2011). Coaches Perceptions of Their Coach Education Experiences. *International Journal of Sport Psychology* 42: pp. 1–20.

New York Times (2014). *Digital Coach Perched Right in Your Pocket*. Retrieved: 22 March 2014. www.nytimes.com/2014/01/16/technology/personaltech/a-digital-coach-for-your-pocket.html?smid=tw-share&_r=0

Nishiyama, T. and Suwa, M. (2010). Visualisation of Posture Changes for Encouraging Meta-Cognitive Exploration of Sports Skill. *International Journal of Computer Science in Sport* 9(3): pp. 42–52.

Novatchkov, H., Bichler, S., Tampier, M. and Kornfeind, P. (2011). Real-Time Training and Coaching Methods Based on Ubiquitous Technologies: An Illustration of a Mobile Coaching Framework. *International Journal of Computer Science in Sport* 10(1): pp. 36–50.

Ofoghi, B., Zeleznikow, J., MacMahon, C. and Raab, M. (2013). Data Mining in Elite Sports: A Review and a Framework. *Measurement in Physical Education and Exercise Science* 17: pp. 71–186.

Perkins, N. C., King, K., McGinnis, R. and Hough, J. (2011). Coaches and Athletes Can Use Data from Wireless Sensors to Improve Sports Training. *Mechanical Engineering* 133(7): pp. 40–45.

Raupach, K. (2012). Technology Can Help You Unlock Your Coaching Potential. *Modern Athlete and Coach* 50(4): pp. 25–28.

Raupach, K. (2013). Technology Can Help You Unlock Your Coaching Potential III. *Modern Athlete and Coach* 51(2): pp. 37–41.

Robertson, S. J. and Burnett, A. F. (2013). An Evaluation of High-Level Player-Reported Measurement of Approach-Iron Shot Distances in Golf. *International Journal of Sports Science and Coaching* 8(4): pp. 789–800.

Robinson, M. G., Holt, L. E., Pelham, T. W. and Funneaux, K. (2011). Accelerometry Measurements of Sprint Kayaks: The Coaches' New Tool. *International Journal of Coaching Science* 5(1): pp. 45–56.

Sanz, D. and Terroba, A. (2012). New Technologies Applied to Tactical Analysis in Tennis. *ITF Coaching and Sport Science Review* 56(20): pp. 22–24.

Sawicki, O. (2009). The Interaction of Sport and Technology: The Broad Versus Detailed Perspective. *Coaches Plan* 16(2) pp. 15–16.

Schumaker, R. P., Solieman, O. K. and Chen, H. (2013). *Sports Data Mining*. Integrated Series in Information Systems 26. (New York: Springer).

Scientific American. (2005). *How do Dimples in Golf Balls Affect Their Flight?* Retrieved: 3 April 2014. www.scientificamerican.com/article/how-do-dimples-in-golf-ba/

Singh Bal, B. and Dureja, G. (2012). Hawk Eye: A Logical Innovative Technology Use in Sports for Effective Decision Making. *Sports Science Review* 21(1–2): pp. 107–119.

Sports Coach UK (2013). *The Appetite for Online Coach Education: Now and the Future.* Retrieved: 26 March 2014. www.sportscoachuk.org/resource/appetite-online-coach-education-now-and-future

Sporttechie (2014). *Three Ways Google Glass Could Be Utilized by the NBA.* Retrieved: 4 April 2014. www.sporttechie.com/2014/03/13/three-ways-google-glass-could-be-utilized-by-the-nba/

Thow, J., Naemi, R. and Sanders, R. (2012). Comparison of Modes of Feedback on Glide Performance in Swimming. *Journal of Sports Sciences* 30(1): pp. 43–52.

Top End Sports (2013). *Hawk-Eye Line-Calling System.* Retrieved: 4 April 2014. www.topendsports.com/sport/tennis/hawkeye.htm

UK Sport (2009). *Military Precision Keeps British Cyclists on Track for Success.* Retrieved: 21 March 2014.www.uksport.gov.uk/news/military_precision_keeps_british_cyclists_on_track_for_success/

VentureBeat News (2013). *Pro Sports First: Tennis Player to Wear Google Glass at Wimbledon This Week.* Retrieved: 4 April 2014. venturebeat.com/2013/06/20/pro-sports-first-tennis-player-to-wear-google-glass-at-wimbledon-this-week/

Wohlsen, M. (2014). *Augmented Reality Is About to Turn Football Into a Real-Life Videogame.* Retrieved: 25 March 2014. www.wired.com/business/2014/03/future-winning-super-bowl-department/?mbid=social_twitter

# Chapter 15

# Using geotechnology tools in sports coaching

*Jill Clark and Joseph Kerski*

Sports are inherently spatial – the *position* of the ski slalom gates, the *distance* covered by an endurance runner, the *length* of the pitch, the *height* of the dive board and so on. Sports are also by necessity confined to a specific location, or place, such as a tennis court, football pitch or cross country track. These two elements, space and place (Bale 2003), are fundamental to the study of sports for both the participant and the coach.

Hughes (2008) notes that 'Coaching is about enhancing player or athlete performance. A principal means by which that is achieved is through feedback' (p. 101). This feedback comes from monitoring and assessing past performances, a process which Hughes notes has relied on a variety of measuring tools over the years. From pen-and-paper based recording systems to the more advanced software applications and video technology that are in use today, capturing and analysing accurate and reliable data provides an invaluable source of performance information for coaches. Hughes describes some of the notational techniques that have been used, the development of performance databases and the work being undertaken by others to find better ways of recognising and representing patterns in data. Many of these patterns develop from the location where a particular activity takes place – where a squash player was when a shot was played, what action a rugby player took at a certain position, where a football (soccer) player was when the team gained, or lost, possession of the ball and so on. This locational aspect of sport can be analysed using geotechnologies.

## GEOTECHNOLOGIES

Geotechnologies, or geospatial technologies as they are also referred to, encompass a variety of devices, software tools and methodologies for collecting, managing, analysing and querying spatial data – data that includes a reference to a geographic location and a description of the space and place. These technologies include GNSS (Global Navigation Satellite Systems) receivers that are capable of receiving data from the Global Positioning System (GPS, American), the GLONASS (Russian), Galileo (European), IRNSS (Indian) or the Beidou (Chinese) satellite navigation systems, remote sensors (including aircraft, satellites and webcams) and Geographic Information Systems (GIS) application software. A GIS provides the tools to integrate and analyse spatial data. The 'G' can be thought of as the geography, or map component. The map can show topography or imagery, or drink stops planned along a route, a 3-D terrain profile and much more.

The 'I' component of GIS can be thought of as the information, or data, behind the map. If the map shows the drink stops along a marathon route, this information could indicate who is staffing that stop, what type of drinks are available and which athletes get which drinks. The 'S', or systems, component of GIS brings together the map and the database with application software that allows users to query the data seamlessly and simultaneously. The spatial data typically used in conjunction with geotechnologies include satellite imagery, aerial photography, topographic, street and trail maps and so on. In addition, geotechnologies can also be used to analyse an almost infinite variety of thematic data – data representing particular phenomena or events associated with specific geographic areas. This could include the location of swimming pools selected to host a series of swim meets, the trail routes for a mountain biking tournament or the different venues for an Australia vs. England Ashes test cricket series. Using these technologies to map and analyse sports-related spatial data is not only an invaluable resource for those participating in sports – analysing individual performances and assessing the results – but they also offer considerable potential for those who coach sports, by providing a better understanding of both the locational context in which sport takes place and the locational factors that influence sport.

In recent years there has also been a proliferation of location tracking applications such as Endomondo, RunKeeper, MapMyTracks and MapMyRun, which have proven very popular with sports and exercise enthusiasts. Many of these web-based tools offer a free service for tracking outdoor and sports activities, providing feedback on average pace and speed, course gradients, calories burned, progress towards goals and targets achieved. With a GPS-enabled smartphone and a downloaded application (or app), participants can track their activities, often in real-time, receive in-session information from their personal 'virtual' coach and sign up for training plans based on their choice of activity and level of participation. The tracked activities can then be posted online and performance monitored over time. Although primarily geared towards recreational sports and outdoor enthusiasts, applications like these provide tools for comparing performances and collaborating with others. However, it should be noted that most GPS-enabled smartphones and low-cost GPS receivers come under the category of recreational or civilian grade GPS, which means they are usually only accurate to within 5–10 meters (16–32 ft.). An informal survey of running/tracking applications on two popular makes of GPS-enabled smartphones was conducted recently by a Swedish consumer affairs program SVT Plus (2012). The results indicated wide discrepancies in both the performance of the applications and locational accuracy between the two smartphone models. Such discrepancies may have implications for both recreational and elite athletes and their coaches alike.

## Box 15.1

Useful summaries of GPS devices and positional accuracy are provided on the Open-StreetMap, ArcGIS Resources and Ordnance Survey websites.

For outdoor activities in areas free from interference, for example away from tree canopies or buildings, the accuracy of civilian grade GPS receivers will probably meet the requirements of most recreational sports enthusiasts but may not suffice for a more rigorous analysis of performance. Training programmes rely on accurate data, especially when attempting to maximize the training effect, with minimum outlay of time and resources from coach and athlete. However, for non-professional clubs and associations with limited funding, these less accurate devices may be the only option; as a relative measure of location and performance, they can still be useful.

Within the discipline of sports coaching, GPS and other tracking technologies are being increasingly adopted as coaches and athletes alike seek to identify and maximise every advantage in their quest for better performance. A number of recent studies have investigated the use of such devices for measuring movement in a sports context, for example the use of GPS in cricket, tennis and field-based team sports by Vickery, Dascombe, Baker, Higham, Spartford and Duffield (2014). Increasingly accurate tracking devices are being developed to provide the level of monitoring that is required for professional sports, such as the Catapult System used in a variety of sports disciplines all over the world.

Macutkiewicz and Sunderland (2011) describe the use of GPS to assess the activity levels of elite women field hockey players. The speed of movement of individual players was monitored using GPS to identify the total number of sprints in a session. The results indicated clear differences in activity levels at different positions. 'Forwards spent a greater percentage of their playing time at high intensity and covered a greater percentage of total distance sprinting than the other outfield positions' (p. 972). The study quickly established that a generic approach to training was no longer appropriate and that more tailored training and conditioning were required. In a similar investigation using GPS to assess the relative performances of Australian football players in elite and sub-elite leagues, the Australian Football League (AFL) and West Australian Football League (WAFL) identified that movement patterns were closely tied to positional roles and players in the elite league, and demonstrated a significantly higher intensity of performance compared to sub-elite players (Brewer, Dawson, Heasman, Stewart and Cormack 2010). The study concluded that 'specific knowledge of positional requirements and movement patterns necessary to match game demands is important for designing training programs for individual players to assist the transition between different positional roles and levels of competition' (p. 622). The use of GPS monitoring to compare the movements of sub-elite players with elite players, in combination with specific training drills, has been a significant step forward in improving the performance of the sub-elite players. With the ready availability of GPS and other methods of assessing athletes, these technologies are extremely useful for the coach; the effectiveness of training programmes and coaching input are made easier with objective and quantifiable measurements. For longer term monitoring, coaches would be able to examine fitness levels, positional play and, perhaps more importantly, evidence of overtraining or burnout.

Macquet, Eccles and Barraux (2012) describe a research project into the use of head-mounted videotaping devices in orienteering to capture 'behavioural and contextual' (p. 93) data and as a post-race review aid. Although the video wasn't geotagged (a process which involves storing geographical reference metadata with the source imagery describing the location where the video was collected), it did provide invaluable insights as to the behaviour of the orienteer at certain locations on the course. In particular, the study highlighted the challenges of handling a map and navigating the course at the same time. As the participant in the study noted, 'I'm trying hard to run uphill, so I'm looking at the map less often' (p. 94). A key skill for elite orienteers is to quickly and accurately interpret the course map they have been given, and focus their effort on the most appropriate task given the terrain they are covering at any given time, whether that is an increase in physical endeavour to improve competition times or more time spent on studying the map and the surroundings. Having a recording of the session provides both the orienteer and coach with an opportunity to review performance and consider what, if any, changes are necessary. Playback of training sessions is already used in some sports and is of value to the coach and athlete for both individual and team effectiveness. Geotagging would be a useful addition to data available for some sports if this process becomes more widespread and readily available to both coaches and athletes.

These studies have successfully identified improvements in tactics and coaching strategies; however, opportunities for further visual analysis and reporting of the data and the results, and combining the study data with other datasets are often not pursued. Whether this is a result of a lack of awareness of the tools and technologies that are available to assist with this, a lack of funding or a lack of appreciation as to how these technologies could apply to sports coaching remains unclear. For example, few of the study reports included any visual representations of the data and the analysis to help illustrate their findings. The orienteering example could be enhanced if the video captured during the study was encoded with spatial reference information. This would in turn allow the video to be shown against a backdrop of 2-D, or even 3-D, mapping of the course, allowing the orienteer and coach to visualise the chosen route and analyse performance at each stage. Many sports use visualisation as a competitive aid (see Chapter 4). For example, at the start gate, downhill skiers can be seen visualising the terrain and the gates prior to racing. This information is often augmented by coaches, watching competitors on various sections of the race course and then relaying this information to their skiers still waiting to race. Think of how effective this information would be if it was set in the context of terrain maps and previous race performances. Although automatic geographic encoding of videos is still relatively new, there are some devices on the market, such as ContourGPS, that allow the user to capture a continuous trace of location, speed and elevation. The project 'Orienteering and TV in the Future' is currently investigating ways to improve TV broadcasts from orienteering races. Part of the project is looking into new opportunities in tracking competitors using GPS encoded video, and simulating runs over virtual 3-D courses. Some videos demonstrating the potential in orienteering and ski-orienteering have been posted on the project's website. Although developed for broadcast purposes, this does illustrate the potential for comparing GPS encoded video footage for a number of competitors to see how different athletes tackled the same course. This technique has been used successfully in other TV broadcasts such as Ski Sunday (BBC), with simultaneous re-plays of the routes followed by different downhill skiers. This allows coaches, other competitors and spectators alike to see what the conditions are like along the route and where time was lost or gained. It also provides an opportunity for coaches to relay information about the course back to competitors waiting at the start line.

The following sections describe some of the benefits of using other geotechnologies in conjunction with GPS devices to analyse and report on the data, and suggest some applications within sports coaching.

## Data integration

One of the most powerful features of geotechnologies such as GIS is the ability to combine and analyse data, both spatial and non-spatial (attribute) data, from a variety of sources to provide a better understanding of events and activities at a given location. Those data sources could include location data (GPX files) from a GPS device or a GPS-enabled smartphone; athlete or player information, such as position, height, weight, body fat and blood pressure and historical records for a particular sport. They could also include data in the form of photographs, videos, scanned documents, and a variety of formats including shapefiles (vector data format for GIS software), KML files, image files (PNG, JPG, BMP and so on), and text, spreadsheet and database formats such as CSV, XLS and MDB. Together, these disparate data sources can be queried and analysed to add context, identify relationships and understand influences that may have been previously undetected or unquantified.

An increasing number of applications and web-based map display and analysis tools, such as QuickRoute, RouteGadget and GPS Visualizer, are available for tracking and analysing many outdoor sports – running, orienteering, skiing and so on. QuickRoute is a Windows based application for mapping GPS data from a variety of GPS devices and provides integration with Google Earth™ to visualise the data. RouteGadget provides utilities for mapping and comparing

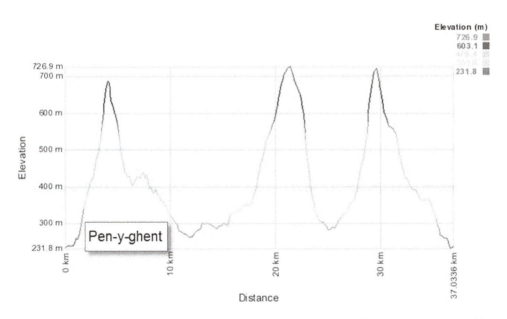

*Figure 15.1* An orienteering route in the Yorkshire Dales plotted as an elevation profile. Image reproduced courtesy of GPS Visualizer (www.gpsvisualizer.com).

*Figure 15.2* Mapping a training route with elevation and pace profiles. Image produced courtesy of Runkeeper (www.runkeeper.com).

orienteering routes, and GPS Visualizer provides facilities for analysing GPS data and creating maps. Some tools, such as GPS Visualizer, also provide options for creating elevation profiles based on GPS tracks (see Figure 15.1).

The elevation profile provides additional detailed information about the nature of the terrain and the different challenges faced by competitors at various locations along the route. The next step is to measure actual performance against the elevation profile. Using a free tracking application, the route taken on a training run is shown plotted against both an elevation and a pace profile (see Figure 15.2).

Both coaches and athletes can now see for themselves where performance varied over the course of the training or event route, and compare this with past performance over the same route. The coach can use this information, in conjunction with the athlete, to aid preparation. For example, coaches want some form of objective confirmation that a training programme is effective, and if this is not the case, they need to know where to make adjustments. Some

*Figure 15.3* Map and Coach – tracking orienteers near Tibro, Sweden. Image reproduced courtesy of MapandCoach™ (www.mapandcoach.se).

athletes experience difficulties running uphill, running downhill or moving laterally, and these difficulties may be due to lack of fitness. Coaches may also need to examine the GPS trace to ensure that there are no technical or tactical issues that require further, and more detailed, input from the coach.

Although GPS tracks provide a more detailed picture of the locational context for sport, from a coaching perspective they do not tell the whole story. To integrate other data sources – additional or alternate background mapping, photos, training schedules, physiological data such as heart rate and so on – requires other geotechnologies such as GIS application software that provides the tools to integrate and analyse spatial data. One such example is the Swedish MapandCoach™ service for orienteers. Designed to support the analysis of orienteering training and competition data, the live system provides real-time tracking of GPS, heart rate and inter-beat interval data, as well as data from other wireless sensors. In the first example, the GPS traces from four different competitors in a recent orienteering event in Sweden are plotted against a background of aerial photography (see Figure 15.3). The data can also be plotted over a terrain or an orienteering map, as in Figure 15.4.

Saupe *et al.* (2007 cited in Netek and Burian 2012, p. 204) investigated the role of elevation during performance and the impact on heart rate. Using a combination of data from heart rate, speed/cadence monitors and a GPS device, researchers were able to plot the variations in heart rate values over the course of a 50 km cycle training ride.

**283**

*Figure 15.4* Plotting competitor heart rate variations during the course of an orienteering event. Image reproduced courtesy of MapandCoach™ (www.mapandcoach.se).

## Analysis

For some applications, plotting a location against a backdrop of topographic data or satellite imagery may be all that is required to convey the necessary information and context for an event or activity. However, GIS tools provide the capabilities to do much more with the data, with techniques and methodologies to support spatial analysis, an investigative technique that 'concerns *what* happens *where,* and makes use of geographic information that links features and phenomena on the Earth's surface to their locations' (de Smith, Goodchild and Longley 2013, p. 52). It is often not just the location itself that is important, but also what is nearby, what the location is connected to, or is within a distance from and so on. This broad area of study also covers network analysis, the study of routing and travel times between connected locations.

### Box 15.2

The topic of spatial analysis is one that has received a great deal of consideration over the last 50 years, and numerous references are available for anyone wishing to learn more about the technologies and tools. A good place to start for further reading is the book 'Geospatial Analysis – A comprehensive guide' at www.spatialanalysisonline.com.

*Figure 15.5* Video footage of the Federer vs. Murray match, London Olympics, 2012. Image reproduced courtesy of Damien Demaj, Esri.

In the context of sports coaching, analysing the locational context of an event or activity helps coaches to derive additional information that may help improve performances or gain a tactical advantage. For example, Damien Demaj, cartographer with Esri (a GIS software supplier), recently described how he used ArcGIS software to analyse the London Olympics Gold Medal tennis match between Roger Federer and Andy Murray (Demaj 2012a).

The patterns of play, match tactics and sequences of winning shots were tracked using location information derived from video footage of the match. The information recorded included what type of stroke was played at what location, who played the stroke at that location and the coordinates of each point. By tracking the coordinates of these events, it was possible to identify stroke lines and player movements (see Figures 15.5–15.7).

Demaj (2012b) subsequently developed this project to assess the spatio-temporal variation in important service points during the match to produce maps of serve clusters. The direction of the serve was used to group similar serve locations, to identify where each player was hitting serves and the relationship between location and the success of the serve (see Figures 15.6 and 15.7).

Just as shot-tracking is important in analysing tennis matches, identifying the preference of spot kick takers in many ball games, such as soccer and rugby, is a vital piece of information for the coach. The former All Blacks rugby coach Graham Henry once noted, 'A successful coach is one who prepares his team to deal with all eventualities. Not only must your players be fully briefed on the game plan and understand their individual requirements but you must also familiarise them with the particular strength and weaknesses of the opposition' (Hughes 2008, p. 101). A variety

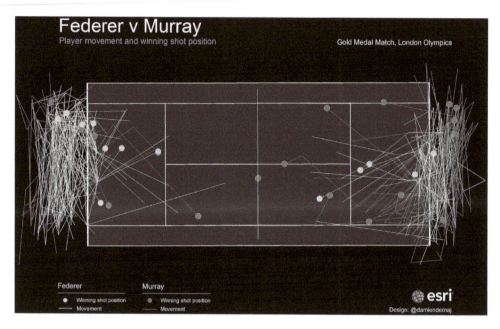

Figure 15.6 Match analysis of the Federer vs. Murray match, London Olympics, 2012. Images reproduced courtesy of Damien Demaj, Esri.

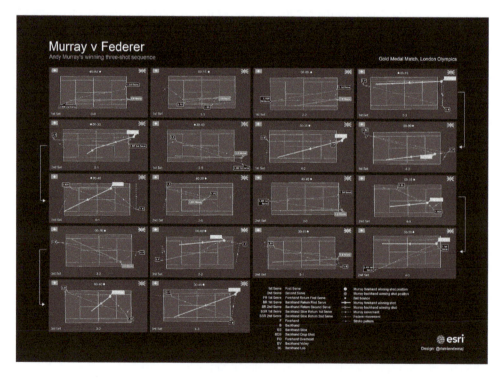

Figure 15.7 Match analysis of the Federer vs. Murray match, London Olympics, 2012. Images reproduced courtesy of Damien Demaj, Esri.

of techniques are emerging to assist in the analysis of this location-specific data. Reich, Hodges, Carling and Reich (2006) describe the use of shot charts by basketball coaches, not just to provide descriptive summaries of shot locations but also to determine how better to defend against certain players given their specific preferences and abilities for taking shots. As a result of related research, Goldsberry (2012) introduced CourtVision, a collection of analytical and visualisation techniques to 'quantify, visualize and communicate' spatial aspects of US National Basketball Association (NBA) performance. This research project aimed to identify critical space-based variations in player and team performance, quantify the relationship between space on the court and a player's performance and develop predictive models for effective offensive and defensive strategies. Over the course of five years, Goldsberry compiled a database of shot location, shooting range and shot outcome information for over 700,000 goal attempts during every NBA game. From this database of information for individual players and attempts on goal over the 1,300 square foot 'shooting area', a set of case studies was mapped, including the statistics for Miami Heat basketball player LeBron James. The results revealed that although James' scoring percentage was 36% above the league average, a weak spot for James was at the top of the key (free throw lane). Additional metrics were also derived from the shot analyses including the 'Spread' – a count of the location from which a player has attempted at least one goal shot and an indication of a player's shooting territory – and the 'Range', the spatial influences on shooting effectiveness. Although currently limited to the analysis of shooting performance, Goldsberry sees applications of the CourtVision metrics to the development of team tactics and analysis of other 'where' related questions in basketball such as, 'Where do the most intercepts occur?' or 'Where does Team A block their shots?' and so on.

In addition to these analytical techniques discussed here, the Table 15.1 provides a brief summary of some of the available geospatial techniques and their potential applications in sports coaching.

*Table 15.1* Summary of available geospatial techniques

| Spatial analysis technique | Sports coaching application |
| --- | --- |
| **Point-in-polygon** <br> Determines if a given location lies within a particular area. <br><br> | Field positions – identify which player is in which tactical zone. <br> Flag positions on a golf green – how does the position of the flag on the green influence the type of approach play required? |
| **Line or area intersections** <br> Intersecting two or more sets of data involves comparing their spatial footprints to determine if they overlap at any point. <br><br> | Comparing routes chosen by novices and elite athletes over an event course. Did the terrain have an impact on their choice of route? <br> Midfield and defensive players – where and how much do their positional zones overlap? |

*(Continued)*

*Table 15.1* (Continued)

| Spatial analysis technique | Sports coaching application |
| --- | --- |

**Nearest neighbour (or proximity) searches**
Given a particular feature at a location, identifying what other features are nearby. Useful for identifying cluster patterns in data.

Identifying the best strategies for a rowing team given the location of the nearest rival rowing team at specific points along a river. A hockey coach may have noticed that players drift out of position during a match and cluster around the puck/ball instead of maintaining a defensive or attack structure. Using proximity analysis, the coach can illustrate the behaviour of the players during the post-match analysis. Identify the number of backhand shots played at a given location on a tennis court.

**Select by location**
Identify which features are present or events occur at a particular location.

Identify the number of control gates along a particular section of a ski slalom course.

**Buffer**
Identify an area or zone of a specified size around an existing feature.

Identifying the appropriate fielding configuration in a baseball match for a hitter who regularly hits the ball a certain distance in a general direction.
Identifying the area around golf holes from which there is a probability over x percent that a player of a certain ability can putt the ball into the hole.

**Union**
Merge two or more sets of areal features (polygons) into one dataset.

Comparing the general length and direction of golf shots hit by elite and novice players from one tee over the course of a competition.

Analysing the optimal zones around a hockey goal where shots can be made depending on the location of team members and the goalie.

**Distance matrix**
Summary of distances from a given location.

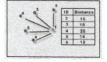

In planning a marathon, determining the distance between checkpoint A and checkpoint C, or checkpoint A to checkpoint D.
Identifying the nearest player in relation to the current position of the ball at a given point in time during a match.

## Terrain modeling

The ability to map features on the surface of the earth in the form of a 3-D terrain model can also provide additional information for coaches and athletes by creating a virtual landscape against which to visualise events and activities. The terms Digital Terrain Model (DTM) and Digital Elevation Model (DEM) are often used interchangeably to describe such a model of the earth's surface. DTMs or DEMs are derived from a particular type of spatial data known as raster data. Raster data structures are made up of a 2-D array of grid cells, with each cell referenced by a row and a column number, encoded with additional attribute information such as elevation, forest cover, land use and so on. The smaller the grid cell size, the more detailed the map will be (see Figure 15.8).

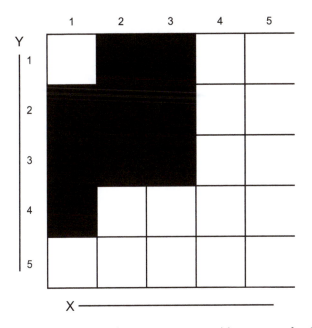

*Figure 15.8* Areas on the earth's surface are represented by groups of neighbouring cells that share the same attribute value, such as the type of land cover.

There are a number of web-based applications that provide access to terrain models such as Earth View in Google Maps™, ArcGIS Explorer® and the Google Earth™ desktop application. Terrain models like these are finding increasing application in sports and sports coaching, particularly in sports such as skiing, running, mountain biking and so on. For example, when reviewing the performance of an athlete who has just completed a training run, a coach can assess the impact of variations in terrain on the athlete's performance by plotting the training course on top of a topographic base map draped over a terrain model and studying the physical profile of the route.

Alternate routes may also be identified based on an analysis of the terrain – for example, a route that avoids particularly steep sections (a gradient greater than four) or detours significant barriers to movement such as wetlands (see Figure 15.9).

**289**

*Map and separate route line object. Trondheim, Norway.*

*Figure 15.9* Displaying route information over a terrain model in Google Earth™ – Trondheim, Norway. Reproduced courtesy of QuickRoute (www.matstroeng.se/quickroute).

## Tracking

When TV cameras can no longer follow the action or when an event is taking place in an area that is inaccessible, sports enthusiasts and coaches alike have turned to Internet-based tracking services to follow the action or monitor performance. Longer distance and endurance events, such as the Sydney to Hobart yacht race, the Triathlon world cup, the annual Tour de France road cycle race and Ironman competitions, have led the way in adopting and promoting real-time, or near real-time, tracking for spectators, support teams and coaches. The Brisbane to Gladstone yacht race online tracking site, Yacht Tracker, attracted 15 million hits in 2011. Viewers could not only track individual yachts and their progress, but also they had access to more sophisticated analysis of average speed and race handicap for a continually updated assessment of the race.

Tracking events like this not only improves spectator access to the live action and involvement with the sport, but also provides competitors and coaches alike with the ability to replay the sailing routes for post-race analysis, re-assessing coaching strategies and improving performances. It provides an invaluable instructional aide for coaching both novices and advanced sailors alike. In 2004 the RiverRat project, an MIT iCampus initiative, investigated the use of GPS as a means of improving those two aspects of sailing, spectator interest and coaching. On the coaching front, the researchers noted that sailing posed two particular problems – the length of time the sailor was out on the water making instant, or

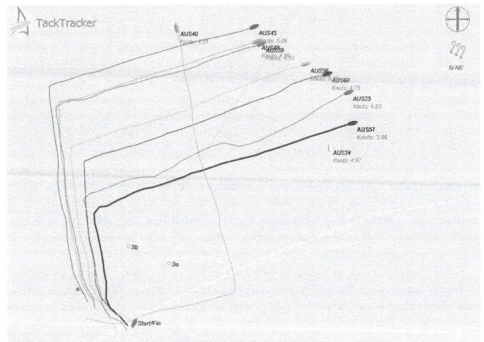

Leg01 Beat

| Trackee | Distance(m) | Time(h:m:s) | VMG | Knots | Min Knots | Max Knots | Port Dev.(deg) | Stbd Dev.(deg) |
|---|---|---|---|---|---|---|---|---|
| AUS60-Miss Pibb | 1833 | 00:11:53 | 3.66 | 4.73 | 3.29 | 5.44 | -36 | 40 |
| AUS59-Evie | 1828 | 00:12:03 | 3.65 | 4.92 | 3.16 | 5.81 | -37 | 45 |
| AUS57-Soria | 1853 | 00:12:16 | 3.53 | 4.89 | 2.81 | 5.68 | -41 | 45 |
| AUS56-Black Adder | 1789 | 00:12:19 | 3.59 | 4.71 | 3.23 | 5.64 | -35 | 44 |
| AUS48-Shining Star | 1901 | 00:12:01 | 3.65 | 5.12 | 2.86 | 18.15 | -37 | 46 |
| AUS40-Debacle | 2225 | 00:15:45 | 2.89 | 4.58 | 2.39 | 8.88 | -41 | 53 |
| AUS34-Yertle | 1986 | 00:13:37 | 3.24 | 4.73 | 1.64 | 6.06 | -44 | 47 |
| AUS45-Karma | 1780 | 00:11:46 | 3.71 | 4.90 | 3.39 | 5.59 | -37 | 43 |
| AUS25-Street Hassle | 2688 | 00:17:34 | 2.48 | 4.96 | 2.78 | 7.21 | -35 | 75 |

*Figure 15.10* Tracking the 2014 Jan 11 Yngling Mini Regatta, Sydney Harbour. Image reproduced courtesy of TackTracker www.tacktracker.com Basemap: OpenStreetMap – © OpenStreetMap and contributors, Creative Commons-Share Alike License (CC-BY-SA). www.openstreetmap.org/copyright. Map tiles courtesy of MapQuest (www.mapquest.com).

near-instant, feedback from the coach almost impossible, and the difficulty for novice sailors in trying to emulate the choice of course and tactics of the more advanced sailors. The RiverRat team developed a prototype real-time tracking solution for use in the instruction of sailing, as well as an aid for spectators and as a means of improving boating safety. The use of similar technology to record sailing events is now widespread, helping to improve race starts, general boat handling and race tactics. For example, TackTracker provides tracking solutions for competitors and coaches to track, record and analyse individual sessions and competitive events (see Figure 15.10).

In the majority of these examples, the tracking information has been recorded using a GPS device. Although GPS devices have been widely adopted within sport, they are not without limitation. Despite marked improvements in location accuracy, battery life and general robustness, the signals they receive remain subject to interference from high rise buildings, heavy precipitation and tree cover. GPS devices also traditionally haven't worked well indoors, as the penetration of satellite signals through buildings is unreliable. Even if signals are detected, they can be deflected by walls, floors, ceilings, windows and so on, resulting in false and inaccurate readings (Batty 2012). However, indoor tracking has been receiving a lot of attention recently with a number of large technology companies, for example, Apple, Google, Microsoft and Nokia, all investing in indoor tracking solutions. Although many of the early adopters of this technology have been retailers and marketing companies, other applications will almost inevitably appear as the technology matures. The use of similar tracking techniques for indoor sports, such as football tournaments or tennis matches, will soon become commonplace in match and performance analysis.

One alternative, or supplement, to GPS for tracking sports events is radio technology. Events and activities can also be tracked using RFID (Radio Frequency Identification). RFID technology comprises an embedded transponder, or ID tag, a transceiver (decoder) and an antenna. The antenna transmits a radio signal to the transponder, reading and writing information to the tag as required. The radio waves can be transmitted up to a distance of 100 meters, depending on the frequencies used and the power of the transmitting device. This technology is now widely used in many long distance events, such as marathons, for tracking the progress of competitors along the route and ensuring compliance with race rules. Also referred to as chip timing technology, the tags or sensors are encoded with an athlete's ID and are usually attached to the running shoes or worn as an ankle bracelet. The exact timing of the event start and finish, and the time when a competitor reached certain locations along the course, is recorded as competitors pass over a special mat.

RFID technology is also finding application in activities that are not so remote, in events that take place within the confines of various sporting arenas. Wyld (2006) describes the increasing use of RFID within sports, both for those participating in and those administering sport. He cites an example of a system developed by the Fraunhofer Institute for Integrated Circuits in Germany, which involved embedding RFID tags in soccer balls and the shin-pads of players on both teams and placing transceivers around the pitch to read the transmitted signals. The technology made it possible to track the position of both players and ball throughout the course of a match and the resulting metrics were used to measure and quantify the performance of the players, and the officials, during the game.

Other recent developments that are likely to be of interest to sports coaches are geo-fencing and geo-triggers. A geo-fence is a virtual geographic boundary that may be based on the location of existing features, such as the perimeter of a town, or generated dynamically based on a prescribed distance from a specific location. GPS or RFID technologies are then used to monitor activity across that boundary. A geo-fence could define an area of interest such as a school playing field, sports stadium or outdoor pursuit course. Any device that is configured to work with geo-fences, such as a mobile phone, can also be configured with a series of geo-triggers – a specific action or message that is activated once the device crosses the geo-fence boundary. Although many current examples of the use of geo-fencing are again found in retail, marketing and telecommunications, there are opportunities to apply this technology within sports coaching. For example, a geo-fence could be established around a section of a cross-country ski, orienteering or triathlon course, providing coaches with real-time monitoring of an event as an athlete enters/exists certain sections of the course.

## Reporting and communication

Effective communication is an essential skill for coaches, for both providing feedback for athletes and articulating coaching strategies. However, developing the necessary skills and having access to the appropriate tools to facilitate that communication haven't always been a priority in sports coaching. Goldsberry (2012) in his NBA study noted that in the past, much of the advanced analytical information that has been collected in basketball in particular, and sports in general, hasn't been communicated effectively to those directly involved in the sport. As a result, much of the potential of the information has been lost. An often repeated, and perhaps rather hackneyed, expression is 'a picture is worth a thousand words' – mapping and visualising the results can be a much more effective way to get the message across. Goldsberry (2012) comments on how the ability to generate what he describes as 'reasoning artefacts' that are easily understood by players, coaches and analysts 'will in turn improve personnel transactions, practice regimens, and game plans' (p. 6); he adds that almost everyone can understand a well-designed map or chart. Hughes (2008) noted, 'Needless to say, the more accessible and understandable the data, providing the complexity is not lost, the better for the coach in the quest to improve athlete performance' (p. 112).

Geotechnologies provide the tools and techniques to output the results of data analysis in the form of maps, charts, overlays and so on; formats that are potentially a much more effective aid for communicating results than the ubiquitous bullet point slide show, tabular information or spreadsheets. For example, for the analysis of the tennis match between Federer and Murray, compare the source table of results with the results of the spatial analysis of the data (see Figure 15.11). Which do you think is the more successful format for presenting the results?

The influence of location during the course of play, such as the number of winning shots hit from the back of the court, is difficult to discern in tabular format, but with the various data points plotted on a map of the court and relative movements of the players, the relationship between location and a particular action is highlighted.

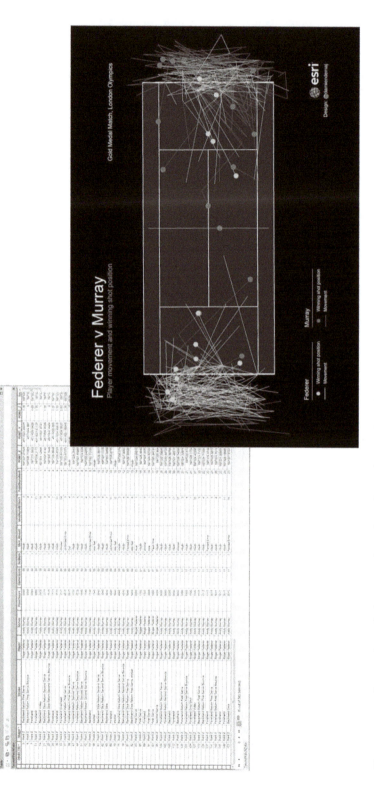

*Figure 15.11* Comparing tabular reporting of results with map-based reporting. Data and image reproduced courtesy of Damien Demaj, Esri.

## GEOTECHNOLOGIES IN SPORTS COACHING MANAGEMENT AND ADMINISTRATION

### A cautionary tale ...

A football coach reported the following problems:

> I was taking a team to compete in a competition in Paris and the problems started when we left Scotland. The bus broke down in Cumbria so we did not arrive in time for our first scheduled stop. The players were meant to be getting out of the bus, having a short training session, eating and then getting back on the bus. We were meant to be arriving for the ferry, and to pick up more people, in Dover at 8pm. Because of the issues with the coach, we did not make any of our scheduled stops, did not get the appropriate nutrition or perhaps more importantly, sleep. We did not arrive for the ferry until 5am and had to wait until 8am until we could board the ferry. Due to the time change, we did not get to Paris until 1pm. We had planned to arrive in Paris the previous evening, go to the training venue, eat, sleep and then be ready to compete the following day at 3pm – 2 hours after we actually arrived! We did not use any type of GPS [as a navigational aide] which added to the difficulties – we were trying to find locations, training, eating and sleeping, as well as the competition venue, without any local knowledge. We had a good team but they did not perform well – I would definitely be more informed in the future.

### Geotechnologies in sport logistics

Geotechnologies are also finding application in the planning, management and administration of sports coaching (see Chapter 2). Lyle (2010) notes that 'There can be little doubt that planning should be a central feature of the coaching process and of coaches' practice' (p. 85). In considering all the factors that contribute to the development of a successful coaching plan, he notes that the coach may have control over many aspects of the plan, such as training session content and game preparation, but there are a number of what he describes as *confounding factors* that coaches typically have less control over, such as player re-location and facilities availability. Solving these logistical issues requires a different set of skills and resources. Geotechnology tools have a role to play in assisting coaches to address these issues and contributing to the overall development of their coaching plans.

### Scheduling coaching sessions

'At the strategic level, there is system management, scheduling, and getting people and resources to the right place and the right time' (Lyle 2010, p. 97).

Before any coaching session can begin, all participants and resources must be assembled at the most appropriate location. That may seem a rather obvious statement, but until recently the locational aspect of that requirement was not always the easiest to evaluate. Locations have not always delivered what they have promised in terms of the available facilities. However, with the development of geotechnologies and the increasingly easy to use and readily available mapping tools, finding the optimum location for participants and resources should be less of an oner-ous task for coaches. Opsahl (2008) describes the implementation of a GIS-based solution to help resolve some practical issues that had arisen when a policy of assigning sport practice sites on a rotational, rather than locational, basis met with disapproval from parents. Although the rotational policy implemented by the Parks, Recreation, and Cultural Resources departments in Cary, North Carolina, USA ensured children (in the 6–10 age group) could take it in turn to practice their particular sport closer to home, parents were increasingly unhappy about lengthy travel times and associated costs for the sessions that were arranged at more remote locations. To address some of these concerns, the technology department investigated the potential for location-based practice assignment policy by using GIS software to collate and analyse a variety of spatial data sets including postal code boundaries, travel routes, practice site location, coach and player location and player preferences (for a particular location, team or coach). The new coaching session assignment process involved a number of steps:

- assign coaches to the nearest practice facility;
- identify the location of the players;
- identify which players wanted to be on the same team as other players or with a particular coach.

The analysis revealed clusters of children living near the designated practice locations. By combining this information with their particular preferences, children were assigned to the most suitable team, at the most suitable location. The assignments were then emailed to the coaches so they knew who to expect at each session. The new location-based assignment policy has seen an improvement in attendance levels, fewer complaints from parents, and bet-ter use of carpooling with larger groups of players travelling to the same location together.

## Box 15.3

This particular study provides a good example of the nearest neighbour analysis tech-nique discussed earlier – identifying cluster patterns in data. Some other tools and applications that have been developed for team management and event scheduling include Sportsvite (sportsvite.com/teams/manage), TeamSnap (www.teamsnap.com) and Arrange My Game (www.arrangemygame.com).

## Identifying locations and allocating resources

Aside from the logistical issues of getting everyone to the optimum location on time, there's also the associated problem of identifying the most appropriate location to develop sporting facilities in the first place. Whether it is a matter of finding the most suitable physical location, for example to host a marathon, kayaking or outdoor swimming event, determining the trans-port access arrangements or identifying existing facilities, geotechnologies can again assist.

As part of their Sport England funding submission for 2009–2013, Canoe England (CE), part of the British Canoe Union, used GIS technology to support their application. The remit of the CE includes the development of the UK coaching framework and the coaching awards. CE support and promote a variety of canoe disciplines, including canoe slalom and sprint racing, and list among their objectives the provision of better coaches for the various disciplines. CE also wishes to increase the number of participants of all ages, in all disciplines. As part of the Places to Paddle initiative, CE recognised the need to provide improved facilities to 'enhance and create a sustainable range of inclusive performance environments that meet the discipline needs of the 21st century and secure access to existing sites' (Canoe England, p. 26). Using geotechnologies and working with partner organisations (including various coaching bodies such as Sports Coach UK and Plas y Brenin (Sport England's national centre for mountain activities and paddle sports), CE have identified a major site in each region to promote and develop canoe trails close to centres of population. The graphical representation of the analysis (Figure 15.12) provides a useful overview of the proposals, strengthening the case for development of the new facilities (see Figure 15.12).

In Australia, the Government commissioned an Independent Sport Panel Report (the Crawford Report) to investigate 'reforms required to ensure the Australian sporting system remains prepared for future challenges at both the community and elite levels' (The Future of Sport in Australia 2009 – letter to Minister of Sport, Australian Government). As part of a wide-ranging remit, the report also looked at the role of sports coaches and restated the goal to have the best coaches available to develop the best athletes and to encourage a wider participation in sport at the grassroots. To achieve this goal, the report acknowledged the need to develop and expand the pool of available coaches. This would require the provision of world class training facilities and the necessary sporting infrastructure to support coaches and the wider adoption of sport in local communities. Recent audits indicated many of the current facilities were either underused; for example, club facilities closed over the weekends, or failed to meet current requirements. However, the facilities data and other supporting information, such as the level of participation in sport at the grassroots, were also often difficult to access and of variable quality. As a result, inconsistencies in the data made it difficult to make regional comparisons and draw national conclusions. Before the specific issues of providing better facilities for coaches could be addressed, the Crawford Report recognised the need to have access to better sport and facilities data – data that are correct, current and easily accessible by all the relevant bodies in Australian sport. The data also had to be owned by local communities, who would be more likely to take responsibility for the information and keep it up to date. These local communities would be best placed to quantify their own requirements, cross-border issues and regional priorities, such as ensuring coaches have access to the best facilities, whatever their location.

To achieve all of these goals, the Crawford Report recommended the further investigation into web-based GIS tools, which the Panel considered, would provide the following advantages:

- Web-based data would be easily accessible by many individuals and organisations.
- It would provide the necessary data collections tools, allowing the designated local communities to capture, maintain and promote their own data.
- Web-based GIS tools could also integrate and analyse data in a variety of formats, making it easier for individual communities and organisations to share their data without having to standardise on a particular format.

**297**

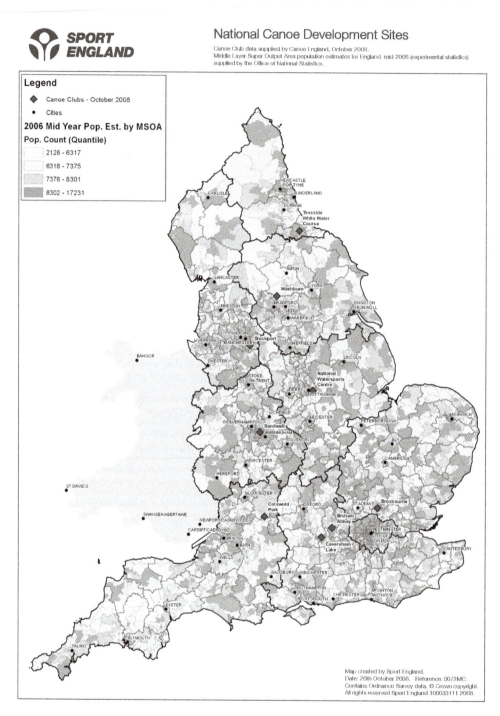

*Figure 15.12* National canoe development sites in England. Image reproduced courtesy of Sport England.

The Panel saw an opportunity to quickly, and effectively, connect existing and new databases through a web-based mapping application, to provide the type of detailed assessment that was previously missing. This would provide coaches and sports administrators alike with access to sport facilities data, transport information, data on individual sports and the changing demographics of local populations, with a shift away from more traditional Australian sports to those sports played by increasing numbers of Asian immigrants living in Australia, such as badminton and table tennis – sports for which there were currently few facilities. Being able to collect, analyse and share this level of information would make a significant contribution to the development of plans for the provision of sports facilities, helping to identify what facilities should be built where. Money would be made available if the problems were well understood and documented (that is they had the data to back up the claims).

In the UK, Taylor, Higgins, Francis and Francis (2012) also investigated the siting of new or improved sports facilities through a study looking into the potential barriers to sports participation and the development of new policies to address those barriers. Some of the factors listed as contributing to the problems of non-participation in sport included:

- the proximity of existing sports facilities;
- the location of concentrations of socio-economic groups with low sports participation rates;
- access to public transport;
- access to cycle path networks;
- amount and location of land available to develop for sports facilities.

All of these factors have one thing in common – **WHERE** – where are the sports facilities, the transport links, the cycle paths and the land available for development? As soon as 'where' is being considered, geotechnologies have a role to play in helping to collate and analyse the data and report the results. The Taylor study made use of GIS tools and techniques to structure and integrate diverse data sets and then query the data based on the factors listed above. For example, how close were existing sports facilities to transport links, and did the target socio-economic groups have easy access to sports facilities? The GIS-based analysis added an invaluable visual dimension to the reporting of the results to help those tasked with planning, developing and operating any new or improved sports facilities to see what facilities were required to meet national and local objectives for sports participation and where these facilities were required.

## The role of location in the identification of elite athletes

There have been a number of studies recently that have investigated the role of birthplace and the proximity to sports facilities in the development of professional athletes and elite performers. Does where you were born and raised have a bearing on your chances of becoming an elite athlete and, if yes, what are the determining factors about your location?

One of the first studies to consider the importance of location was undertaken by Côté, MacDonald, Baker and Abernethy (2006), who investigated if where athletes were born had a significant influence on their chances of playing professional sport. The study was based on birthplace information for all American players gathered from the major sports association websites in the USA (the National Hockey League (NHL), National Basketball Association

(NBA), Major League Baseball (MLB), Professional Golfers' Association (PGA) and Canadian players in the National Hockey League (NHL)). Using statistical analysis techniques, the study revealed a geographic bias in the results, indicating professional athletes generally tended to come from cities with a population less than 500,000 and that contextual factors – access to facilities, safe play areas, early exposure to a number of sports and opportunities for young players to experience success in sport – are influential in achieving elite status in sports performance. However, smaller towns with populations less than 1,000 produced significantly fewer professional sports players, primarily due to the lack of facilities, sports infrastructure and a quorum of playing partners to develop sports skills.

MacDonald, King, Côté and Abernethy (2009) followed up with a similar study of the influence of location in the identification and development of female golf and soccer professionals in the USA. Again using birthplace information for the study group of athletes gathered from official websites, and population data from a demographics website for each birthplace, the distribution of athletes was compared to general non-athlete population statistics using similar statistical analysis techniques. As with the earlier study, the results indicated an over-representation of Ladies Professional Golf Association (LPGA) golf players born in cities with a population of less than 250,000 – approximately 46% of girls in the USA were born in cities and towns of less than 250,000, yet these same locations accounted for 75% of the LPGA players. For female soccer players, cities and towns with a population of less than 1 million were over-represented, accounting for almost 99% of the professional soccer players but only 69% of the general female population. The results reinforced the findings of the earlier study in that smaller towns and cities provided female athletes with improved opportunities for developing expertise in their chosen sport with abundant safe play space in smaller, less urbanised communities, better engagement of families, schools and communities and the likelihood of a more supportive relationship between coaches and athletes. For both studies, understanding the link between environment and expertise to identify the factors influencing the development of professional athletes will help design the systems and coaching strategies to develop sports talent regardless of location.

However, both these studies investigated the influence of geography and location without using any of the geotechnologies discussed earlier, with a spatial statistical analysis and a tabular reporting format used to analyse the data and communicate the results of the investigation. The use of geotechnologies for sports research is an area that has received little attention until relatively recently, perhaps because of a lack of recognition of what geotechnologies can offer and what tools are available. The same datasets could also be analysed with geotechnologies to identify the patterns, and quantify the relationships, between athlete development and location (Figure 15.13). By reporting the results of the analysis in this graphical format, the strong correlation between city size in Ohio and the number of NBA players born in those cities is clearly visible (see Figure 15.13).

## Promoting active lifestyles

Hardly a week goes by without news of the latest health study and exhortations from various sources to exercise more and lead healthier, more active, lifestyles. Providing information on available resources, in terms of sports facilities and coaches for both recreational participants and elite athletes alike, is an important part of promoting these policies. There are a number

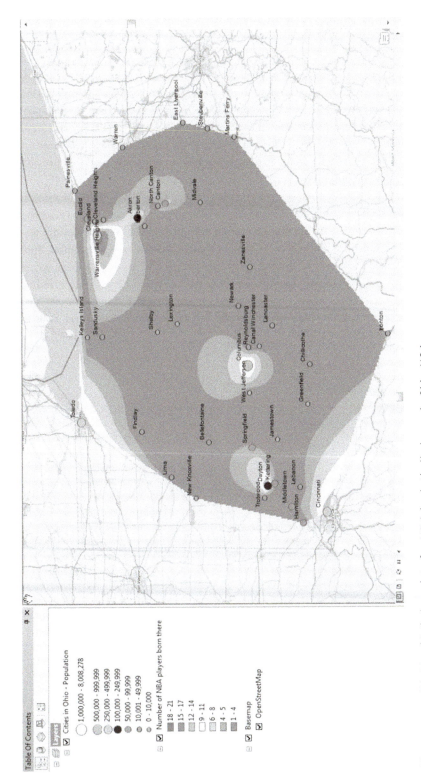

*Figure 15.13* Plotting birthplace data for NBA basketball players in Ohio, USA.

Source: Birthplace data: www.basketball-reference.com/friv/birthplaces.cgi

Basemap: OpenStreetMap – © OpenStreetMap and contributors, Creative Commons-Share Alike License (CC-BY-SA). www.openstreetmap.org/copyright

Software: ArcGIS® 10.1

of government and national sports organisations in the United Kingdom providing basic map-based sports facility search tools, such as the Take Life On and Active Places initiatives in Scotland and Wales respectively. Visitors to these sites simply enter either their location or choose one or more sports and the location of relevant nearby sports facilities in their area are displayed on a map. The BookACoach scheme in the United States adopts a slightly different approach, providing options for those interested in developing skills in their chosen sports to search for coaches based on a user-defined location (city or zip code). (See Figure 15.14.)

Options to search for resources by location are increasingly prevalent today, with access to easy-to-use geospatial technologies and map data; this is now a commonly used tool provided by many businesses and organisations.

As part of a stated objective to develop a coaching strategy for 2010–2016, focusing on recruiting, training, deploying and retaining sports coaches, Sport Wales has also recognised the importance of knowing where activities currently take place to help them identify what coaching resources are needed and where. Using a technique known as segmentation, Sport Wales (2011) produced a series of 12 distinct sports market profiles, or groups sharing common characteristics and aspirations. Each profile describes a typical person in a given age group, with similar preferences when it comes to participating in sport. A map was produced to accompany each profile, illustrating where people sharing the same characteristics as the

*Figure 15.14* Using geotechnologies to locate sports coaches. Image reproduced courtesy of BookACoach (www.bookacoach.com).

segment profile are likely to be located in Wales. For example, the profile 'Lisa' (Figure 15.15) describes an 18–35 year old female with at least one child, working in service industries and on a low income. 'Lisa' prefers indoor activities and personal fitness classes. 'Lisa' is generally found in south east of Wales, in or near the major cities.

With detailed analysis and spatial profiling, Sport Wales are developing strategies to provide targeted sports resources for each profile.

Applications like these could also benefit from the data integration and analytical capabilities of geotechnologies. Among the reasons cited for 'Lisa' not currently participating regularly in sport was a perceptions that there weren't enough sports facilities nearby, and it took too long and cost too much to travel to facilities farther away. To extend the basic location tools offered, options for calculating distances and cost to and from the sports facilities (relevant for those on a low income such as 'Lisa'), the different transport options for getting there and other facilities nearby, for example child care services, could be added to the search tools. A simple query in Google Maps™, specifying bus as the preferred method of transport, identifies the best route and the bus stops closest to a sports centre. Using some of the other spatial analysis techniques discussed earlier, such as buffer analysis, it would be possible to compile a map of facilities that occur within prescribed distances from a specified location – for example, to show all the facilities that are within one mile, two miles or five miles from my current location.

## Health and safety

Geotechnologies also have a role to play in helping coaches comply with health and safety policies. Two areas of health and safety in particular could benefit from the data integration and analytical tools:

- Risk assessments – Where and what are the hazards?
  - Travel to and from events?
  - At the event location?
- Emergency evacuation procedures
  - Where are the evacuation routes/rendezvous points?
  - How do coaches, athletes and others present get to those exits in an emergency?

EventScotland, part of the Scotland's national tourism organisation, has provided a practical guide to hosting and managing events. The guide recommends always having site plans – floor plans for indoor venues and base topographic maps for outdoor events, which include information such as access roads, paths, the local terrain and so on. Event organisers are encouraged to add their own information to the site plans, such as the location of medical facilities, car parking arrangements, emergency routes and rendezvous points and so on. The Guide to Safety at Sports Grounds (the Green Guide 2008) published by the Department of Culture, Media and Sport provided some suggestions as to what should be included in the plan, such as:

- a reference grid;
- a north arrow;
- the scale of the plan;
- the principal points of ingress and egress – specifically all emergency exits and escape routes, disabled access, and so on;
- pathways, routes and roads;
- the location of high risk areas (for example, fuel stores);
- location of safe areas and first aid facilities.

The city of San Diego in California included the following in their site plan technical specification for any sports events:

- The primary site plan or route map should be computer-generated using scaled drawings and measurements to depict the components of the event to ensure appropriate review of the event plans.
- Site plans, route maps and supporting drawings/diagrams should be submitted in PDF format and in an 8 1/2" x 11" or 11" x 17" standard format.
- There are many online mapping sites that provide basic mapping capabilities. If one of these mapping sites is used, the 'plain', 'road', or 'parcel' view must be used as the base for the map so that the reviewing authorities can clearly see the scaled dimensions, locations and activities proposed on the map.
- Aerial or ortho-type photomaps should not be used as the base mapping for the site plan although such maps may be submitted to provide supplemental information. (Source: www.sandiego.gov/specialevents/pdf/planningguide.pdf)

Many of these online mapping sites referred to in the specification, such as Yahoo, Bing, ArcGIS Online, OpenStreetMap, Google Maps™ and other mapping sites allow users to save their maps with a free personal public account and share the map compilations with other users. The information required for site plans is easy to collate, prepare and present using geotechnologies – integrating many different sources of spatial data and communicating the information in an accessible format (for example, a .pdf file or a URL to an online map) that can be shared with other interested organisations.

## Communication

Geotechnologies can also be used to help promote coaching activities and events and assist in showcasing coaching initiatives. The use of digital story maps is becoming an increasingly popular format for illustration and reporting. Sites such as MapStory (http://mapstory.org/) and Esri's Story Maps (http://storymaps.arcgis.com) provide templates for combining a variety of data sources (text files, spatial data, multimedia, tabular data and so on) to produce a map-based context for reporting events and activities.

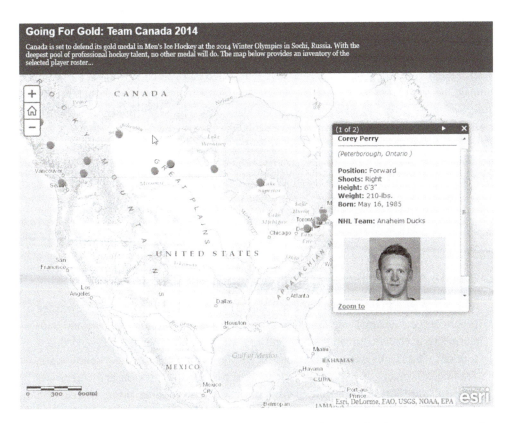

*Figure 15.16* Using a story map to illustrate the Canadian ice hockey player roster for the 2014 Winter Olympics. Image courtesy of EntertainMaps.com, January 2014.

**305**

## CONCLUSION

Geotechnologies can provide additional tools and techniques to record, analyse and report on the spatial element of sport at all levels of participation. To date the application of geotechnologies in coaching has mostly been limited to the use of GPS devices to track athletes and activities. Some of the examples discussed in this chapter also highlight some of the areas in the wider context of sports coaching where geotechnologies could be of use. Anytime **where**, **who** and **what** are important – where are the best sports facilities, who uses these facilities or could be using these facilities, what is available to coach at these locations – there may be an opportunity to use geotechnologies to help answer those questions.

Geotechnologies should be just one of a number of tools at the disposal of the coach and coaching organisations to assess athletes, provide feedback, develop coaching strategies and promote activities. Sports Coach UK currently provides a list of suggestions, *Technology to Use in Your Coaching,* for coaches to consider using. This list includes a number of tools discussed earlier, such as RunKeeper and Sports Session Planner, but at the time of writing didn't include any geotechnology tools for investigating the spatial relationships in the performance data. The coach resource list would also benefit from a list of data resources, such as base mapping, transport information or sports-related local services. Where would a coach or coaching organisation currently go to get this information?

There are many easy-to-use, and increasingly web-based, geotechnology applications available and a great deal of sports-related digital spatial data, much of which is in the public domain, to support research, analysis, policy development and planning for sports coaches and coaching organisations. The next stage is to take advantage of the full analytical capabilities these tools offer, and make the most of data that is already being collected. As the sports coaching community continues to adopt geotechnology tools for a variety of coaching tasks, geotechnology applications and services developed to meet the specific requirements of sports coaches will soon become an indispensible part of the coaching toolkit.

### Box 15.4 Geotechnology resources

The choice of GIS and mapping-based applications range from the more advanced proprietary commercial software, such as ArcGIS, GE Smallworld, MapInfo and Cad-Corp, free open source mapping applications, including MapWindow GIS and Quantum GIS (QGIS), to basic applications for displaying and interrogating spatial data. Traditionally, many of these applications were available as desktop and enterprise-wide software installations, but there is an increasingly diverse range of web- and smartphone-based geotechnology services available now that provide mapping and analytical capabilities without the need to install software locally.

## Free GIS software
### Online
ArcGIS Online: http://www.arcgis.com
MangoMap: http://mangomap.com/
Mapbox: http://www.mapbox.com
Cartodb: http://cartodb.com/

### Desktop
ArcGIS Explorer Desktop: www.esri.com/software/arcgis/explorer
ArcGIS for Desktop: http://www.esri.com/software/arcgis/arcgis-for-desktop
Quantum GIS: www.qgis.org
MapWindow: www.mapwindow.org
GRASS: http://grass.osgeo.org
gvSIG: www.gvsig.org
Opticks: http://opticks.org (image display and analysis)
Google Earth: www.google.com/earth/index.html

# REFERENCES

Bale, J. (2003). *Sports geography*. (London: Routledge).

Batty, P. (2012). *Geospatial technology in 5 to 10 years*. Geothought blog. Retrieved: 25 November 2013. http://geothought.blogspot.co.uk/.

Brewer, C., Dawson, B., Heasman, J., Stewart, G. and Cormack, S. (2010). Movement pattern comparisons in elite (AFL) and sub-elite (WAFL) Australian football games using GPS. *Journal of Science and Medicine in Sport* 13: pp. 618–623.

Canoe England (British Canoe Union). Sport England Funding Submission 2009–2013. Retrieved: 7 December 2013. www.bcu.org.uk/files/BCU%2009–13%20Plan%20-%20%20Final%20 submission%20for%20circulation.pdf.

Côté, J., MacDonald, D.J., Baker, J. and Abernethy, B. (2006). When 'where' is more important than 'when': Birthplace and birthdate effects on the achievement of sporting expertise. *Journal of Sports Sciences* 24(10): pp. 1065–1073.

Demaj, D. (2012a). *Using ArcGIS for sports analytics*. Retrieved: 10 December 2013. http://blogs. esri.com/esri/arcgis/2012/09/05/using-arcgis-for-sports-analytics/.

Demaj, D. (2012b). *Using spatial analytics to study spatio-temporal patterns in sport*. Retrieved: 10 December 2013. http://blogs.esri.com/esri/arcgis/2013/02/19/using-spatial-analytics-to-study-spatio-temporal-patterns-in-sport/.

de Smith, M.J., Goodchild, M. F. and Longley, P.A. (2013). (4th Ed.). *Geospatial analysis*. (The Winchelsea Press: Winchelsea, UK).

Goldsberry, K. (2012). Court vision: New visual and spatial analytics for the NBA. Paper presented at the MIT Sloan Sports Analytics Conference 2012. Boston, USA, March 2–3. Retrieved: 30 November 2013. www.sloansportsconference.com/wp-content/uploads/2012/02/Goldsberry_Sloan_Submission.pdf.

Hughes, M. (2008). Notational analysis for coaches. In *An introduction to sports coaching*. Jones, R.L., Hughes, M. and Kingston, K. (Eds.) (Oxford: Routledge): pp. 101–113.

Lyle, J. (2010). Planning for team sports. In *Sports coaching: Professionalisation and Practice*. Lyle, J. and Cushion, C. (Eds.) (London: Elsevier Ltd): pp. 85–90, 97.

MacDonald, D.J., King, J., Côté, J. and Abernethy, B. (2009). Birthplace effects on the development of female athletic talent. *Journal of Science and Medicine in Sport* 12: pp. 234–237.

Macquet, A-C., Eccles, D. and Barraux, E. (2012). What makes an orienteer an expert? A case study of a highly elite orienteer's concerns in the course of competition. *Journal of Sports Sciences* 30(1): pp. 91–99.

Macutkiewicz, D. and Sunderland, C. (2011). The use of GPS to evaluate activity profiles of elite women hockey players during match-play. *Journal of Sports Sciences* 29(9): pp. 967–973.

Netek, R. and Burian, J. (2012). Analysis of elevation data with time aspect for athletes. *Proceedings from the GIS Ostrava 2012 – Surface Models for Geosciences Conference,* Ostrava, Czech Republic, pp. 201–213. Retrieved: 11 January 2014. http://gis.vsb.cz/GIS_Ostrava/GIS_Ova_2012/sbornik/papers/netek.pdf.

Opsahl, A. (2008). GIS eases scheduling of sports practices for parks department. Digital Communities. www.digitalcommunities.com.

Reich, B. J., Hodges, J.S., Carlin, B.P. and Reich. A. M. (2006). A spatial analysis of basketball shot chart data. *The American statistician* 60(1): pp. 3–12.

Saupe, D., Lüchtenberg, D., Röder, M. and Federolf, C. M. (2007). *Analysis and visualization of space-time variant parameters in endurance sports training.* (Bibliothek der Universität Konstanz).

Sport Wales (2011). People segmentation. Retrieved: 10 January 2014. www.sportwales.org.uk/media/937443/02lisa.pdf.

SVT Plus (2012). Run rappers are not good enough. Retrieved: 22 January 2014. www.svt.se/plus/artiklar/loparapparna-haller-inte-mattet.

Taylor, M.J., Higgins, E., Francis, M. and Francis, H. (2012). A multiparadigm approach to developing policy for the location of recreational facilities. *Systems Research and Behavioral Science* 29: pp. 240–252.

The RiverRat Project. Retrieved: 15 January 2014. http://web.mit.edu/riverrat/index.html.

Vickery, W. M., Dascombe, B. J., Baker, J. D., Higham, D. G., Spratford, W. A. and Duffield, R. (2014). Accuracy and reliability of GPS devices for measurement of sports-specific movement patterns related to cricket, tennis and field-based team sports. *Journal of Strength And Conditioning Research/National Strength & Conditioning Association* 28(6): 1697–16705.

Wyld, D. C. (2006). A look at the future of sports in the context of RFID's 'weird new media revolution'. *The Sports Journal* 9(4).

# Section 5

Within this short concluding chapter, 'Putting It All Together' offers coaches some suggestions on how to integrate the various chapters in this book to become the most effective coach possible. It also looks at the concept of the expert sport coach – the culmination of structured learning and development within sport coaching.

# Chapter 16

# Putting it all together

*Christine Nash*

High performance in sport has been attributed to innovations in sport science, technological advances, training systems and nutritional analysis. However, little attention has been given to the place of the coach in the furtherance of sporting achievement, as there is a tendency to concentrate on scientific aspects that are perceived as easier to control (Williams and Hodges 2005). Although the coach has a crucial role to play, the support systems available are generally in place for the athlete. Many countries have an infrastructure in place for coach education, continuing professional development and sport science support. This is usually organised under the auspices of a governmental agency, a national governing body of sport and, depending on the country, an autonomous national coach education organisation. As with many frameworks that involve a number of different organisations, the manner in which the organisations interact to provide the best experience for coaches, through identification, selection, education, employment and deployment, and support coaches to allow them to offer the best service possible to athletes, is not often as successful in practice as was originally envisaged.

The coach has to become the orchestrator of the coaching process, the one who understands the athlete/s, the team, the support staff and the objectives of the coaching programme. This is a daunting and complex task, and perhaps the more the coach understands the process and all the ramifications, the more overwhelming it becomes. There are, however, some tools available for coaches to facilitate the process. But first, before focusing on the tools, there are some assumptions about coaching that need to be challenged.

Coaching needs to be considered as a cyclical process that involves long term engagement with athletes and teams as well as support staff; it does not involve luck, but is based upon a scientific mix of planning, monitoring and evaluation. To achieve effective coaching programmes the coach needs to understand how to integrate all necessary components to get the best performances. However, regardless of how skilled coaches are, they are only able to develop the talent they have. Following a planned and reflective coaching process will improve both individual and team performance, but only within the limits of the talent available.

Although the use of a coaching and support team is also essential, many coaches are not able to coordinate the provision of expert services and support for their athletes. Sports science support is generally one of the key areas to be considered part of that support, and while sport science can have a significant and positive impact on coaches and athletes, there is still a general consensus that the transfer of sport science knowledge to coaching is poor (Martindale and Nash 2013). Coaches have mainly viewed sport science, and by association, sports scientists, as inaccessible, too technical and too research driven – in many cases non-applicable to the actual sports or coaching setting. This leads to the question originally posed by Williams and Kendall (2007), does sports science research influence or inform coaching practice?

High level sport is developing multidisciplinary support teams to meet the needs of athletes at this level of performance. It is becoming more typical for 'professional' teams to have a number of assistant coaches and a medical network consisting of doctors, physiotherapists, physiologists, strength and conditioning specialists, rehabilitation consultants, psychologists and, more recently in some sports in the UK, clinical psychiatrists. While there are obvious advantages from this type of input, care must be taken to ensure that the support team is actually working together as a team to support the performers. Much has been written about the success and longevity of Sir Alex Ferguson with Manchester United Football Club, but how many coaches understand and can implement his methods? The Ferguson Formula has been highlighted for business, life and sport coaching as comprising eight principles:

1 starting with the foundation
2 daring to rebuild your team
3 setting high standards and holding everyone to them
4 never relinquishing control
5 matching the message to the situation
6 preparing to win
7 relying on observation
8 never stop adapting.

(Elberse and Ferguson 2013)

Although these eight principles may not work for everyone in every context, there are some key messages that coaches involved in any type of coaching domain can modify to suit their own particular circumstances.

As most sport coaches provide services, the management of people, problems and performance and associated resources is therefore a critical concern for sport coaches who have a management brief, for example football managers in the illustration above. This is particularly true in professional sport coaching, in which production and consumption takes place as an interface between clients and employees who are the human resources of the organisation (Surujlal and Mafini 2012). As the sport coach is among paid professional employees in sport organisations, there is a responsibility to ensure that the professional sport coach is able to perform his or her multiple roles in an effective manner. As O'Boyle (2014, p. 233) stated, 'The role of the coach is central to the overall performance of any team or athlete and how this performance is managed and evaluated may have significant impacts on overall sporting success'.

The different sections of this book have highlighted the main areas that coaches are required to manage to be both effective and successful, whatever that means in their particular coaching environment. The ability to plan (Chapter 2) is taken as read by many involved within sport coaching, but how many coaches have the ability to plan in the necessary detail and also manage the planning process for a team of, in many cases, disparate individuals? The planning process, as with the coaching process, is irrevocably linked to the role of the coach, (Chapter 1) but coaches need to understand their function and responsibilities, and this generally relates to an understanding and appreciation of their coaching philosophy (Chapter 3). The impact of a well considered and ethical coaching philosophy cannot be overstated, and coaches need to recognise the connection between philosophy and practice.

The competition environment (Chapter 4) is generally considered to be the most important context for coaches to demonstrate effectiveness. However, Section 2 illustrates the number of different situations that a coach must take into account and manage before considering the competitive arena. Coaches must plan to create environments for skill learning (Chapter 5), talent development (Chapter 7) and tactical awareness (Chapter 8). If this was not onerous enough, they must also maintain the motivation levels and achievement incentives for their performers (Chapter 6). Of course developing skill, talent and tactical awareness are long term processes, but sport coaches need to be aware of their place within this process to maximise success. John Wooden, an acknowledged expert basketball coach, defined success as 'a direct result of self-satisfaction in knowing you did your best to become the best you are capable of becoming' (Wooden and Carty 2005, p. 23). So how do you become the best you can?

## WHAT DOES IT TAKE TO BECOME AN EXPERT COACH?

The complex relationship between knowledge, expertise and experience is one that has raised many questions. In some situations, the words 'knowledge', 'expertise' and 'experience' are used interchangeably, but often incorrectly. It is an observed fact that people can coach for many years without appearing to learn from their experience (Rutt Leas and Chi 1993). In this case the idea of expertise arising from experience would appear to be flawed. Many coaches wish to develop knowledge and choose to do so in a variety of manners, including attending coach education courses, using the Internet, networking, observing other coaches and mentoring (Griffiths and Armour 2013). Does the knowledge learned through these mediums necessarily translate into expertise or even competence? With this in mind, it has become essential that the underpinning concepts that contribute towards the acquisition of expertise in sports coaching are understood. In a series of three articles, Gilbert and Trudel examine the major factors influencing the development of coaching expertise, including the stages that coaches pass through on the journey (Gilbert and Trudel 2012, 2013; Trudel and Gilbert 2013).

A pivotal question in expert research is how do we distinguish between **effective** coaching practice and **expert** coaching practice? Recently, a review of expert sport coaching research identified 27 differing explanations or criteria to identify the expert coaches (Nash, Martindale, Collins and Martindale 2012). If it is so difficult to recognise expertise in sport coaching, surely it would be more complicated to recognise expert coaching practice, given all the different dimensions and contexts covered within this book.

A key outcome of coaching practice is to establish which methods of practice organisation and delivery are most effective for enhancing participant development. However, consider how this would change depending on whether it was a team or individual being coached, a child beginner or adult elite participant, or what phase of the coaching cycle was being observed? Although coaching behaviour has been determined to be the 'hallmark' of expert coaches, namely demonstrating how they actually put their knowledge and experience into practice, Gilbert and Trudel (2004) established that there were few coaches whose practice was worthy of simulation. The competence of the best coaches is mostly studied by using expertise models, although it must be noted that competence and expertise are two very

**313**

different entities. Coaches who demonstrate high levels of knowledge, enthusiasm and commitment are often labeled experts; however, expertise is more than this. According to Nash and Collins (2006) expert coaches have been shown to possess the following:

1 Expertise is domain specific and developed over a prolonged period of time.
2 Experts recognise patterns faster than novices.
3 Expert knowledge is structured to allow easier recall.
4 Experts sort problems into categories according to features of their solutions.
5 Experts initially are slower to solve problems than non-experts but are faster overall.
6 Experts are more flexible and are more able to adapt to situations.
7 Experts develop routines to allow processing capacity to be focused on ongoing environments.
8 Experts take deeper meanings from cues than novices.

These attributes are often difficult to distinguish given the unpredictable nature of coaching, especially within the contexts of practice and competition (Jones 2007). Kahneman and Klein (2009) have suggested that expert coaches should be selected by their peers, but given the attributes under discussion, how many peer coaches would have the necessary background to both understand these eight criteria and then recognise them in a multitude of coaching contexts?

## COACH DEVELOPMENT TO EXPERTISE

Vygotsky (1978) found that new abilities in a novice are first developed during collaboration with an educator or more competent peers and then internalised to become part of the individual's mental model of the world. He described the gap between what an individual can accomplish independently and what he or she can accomplish with the help of someone who is more competent as the zone of proximal development. He believed the role of education is to provide learners with experiences that are within their zone of proximal development. In the context of coach education, this would suggest that a more knowledgeable coach provide scaffolding or support to facilitate the learner's development.

Schinke, Bloom and Salmela (1995) examined the career structure of expert coaches and identified a potential seven stages within their career. Stages one through three reflected the development of a coaching philosophy, as a result of their involvement in sport as a performer. The final four stages follow coaching development from voluntary positions to international elite coaching level, and although the study recognises that all coaches do not progress through all stages, there is no discussion as to what factors limit the development of coaches. Saury and Durand (1998) concluded that early exposure and prolonged experience were important factors in the development of expertise. They also noted that motivation and social climate as well as the commitment to long term practice were essential.

Ericsson carried out a number of subsequent studies into the development of expertise, initially in music, but latterly in sport (Ericsson, Krampe and Tesch-Römer 1993). These studies identified the notion of deliberate practice of which, 'The most cited condition concerns the subjects' motivation to attend to the task and exert effort to improve their performance.

In addition, the design of the task should take into account the preexisting knowledge of the learners so that the task can be correctly understood after a brief period of instruction. The subjects should receive immediate informative feedback and knowledge of results of their performance. The subjects should repeatedly perform the same or similar tasks' (Ericsson, Krampe and Tesch-Römer 1993, p. 367). This has evolved into the notion of deliberate practice, often called the 10,000 hours or 10-year rule of expertise (Starkes and Ericsson 2003).

Weiss considered that understanding changes in perceptions, physical competencies, emotions, social influences and achievement behaviours is critical in terms of developing a knowledge base of transitions (Weiss 2003). This holistic approach to the development of the athlete must also be considered for the long term development of the coach. 'Although considerable research exists on sport coaching, our understanding of coach development is limited. To better understand the development of coaches, it is useful to adopt a life span perspective that focuses on developmental paths and activities. According to Brofenbrenner's ecological systems theory, coaching development occurs when coaches engage regularly in social interactions and domain related activities that become increasingly more complex over time' (Gilbert, Côté and Mallett 2006, p. 70).

More recently, the premise of psychological characteristics in developing expertise has been examined in music and sport, as well the effectiveness in the transition process between school and university life (MacNamara and Collins 2009 and 2010). This stresses the difficulties associated with transitions to excellence, acknowledging that the road to excellence is both complex and dynamic; often, learning to cope with difficulties and setbacks while developing can build resilience (Collins and MacNamara 2012). The use of this inclusive approach would be beneficial when applied to the transitions to expertise within sport coaching.

## Creativity and innovation

The diverse topics covered in this book all agree that sport, and therefore coaching, is evolving at a rapid rate. Many of the available opportunities for coaches to be both effective and successful depend upon their awareness of their values, feelings, motives and cognitions. This can also be construed as awareness of inherent contradictory self-aspects, which can influence thoughts, feelings, actions and behaviours (Ilies, Morgeson and Nahrgang 2005). Coaches are often completely immersed in practice or competition, a state considered as 'flow – the state in which people are so involved in an activity that nothing else seems to matter' (Csikszentmihályi 1991, p. 4). Perhaps the state of flow and the state of self-awareness can be mutually exclusive, although coaches have solved many coaching problems by combining these two states. Consider the elite swimming coach who reflected 'I often find that while I am completely caught up in coaching, immersed in the actual activity that I have that "eureka moment" – the answer to the situation that has been bugging me. The problem then becomes, how do I remember the answer? I solved that by using the voice recorder on my mobile phone. I think that being in "the zone" allows you to be incredibly aware of your surroundings – I remember that as a swimmer but I never really considered that coaches would have similar experiences.' Elite coaches' life stories and developmental journeys are described as 'messy, fragmented and endlessly fascinating' and 'they demonstrate a need to understand the interconnections between coaches' lives and their professional practice' (Jones *et al.* 2004, p. 1).

**315**

Innovation is one factor in maintaining and acquiring the competitive advantages so vital in sport that goes far beyond traditional thinking – treating innovation, technology, information, globalisation and competitiveness as the drivers of growth (Sternberg and Lubart 1999). How to enhance coach's searching, saving, sharing, delivery, acquisition, creation, use and trading of 'knowledge' is one the most important issues of knowledge management and continual development (Sheikh 2008). For example, Hoffman, Ward, Feltovich, DiBello, Fiore and Andrews (2014) advocate the concept of 'accelerated expertise', which they developed for the military context. There are clear applications to the sport coaching environment in, for example, tactical awareness, training for resilience, cross training and strategic development. However, for coaches to accelerate their learning and innovation within coaching, they need to embrace learning from other domains that are possibly more advanced in terms of research and application.

Christensen (2014) discussed the various learning styles in coaching within the context of soccer and advocates an 'approach that favours the coaches' biographical learning and development of expertise as personal journeys in authentic learning situations, an encouragement to create breathing spaces in the coach's professional life and assistance in learning from them' (p. 220).

The effects of two opposing coaching styles, one learner-centred and the other coach-centred, can be seen in Figure 16.1, The coaching dance. Although based within business coaching, this model aspires to the same aims of improving and enhancing performance

Figure 16.1 The coaching dance (Thompson 2012).

(Thompson 2012). The coach-centred side of the diagram is a directive model where the coaches actively evaluate their learners, make comments on their performance, set specific goals for them and advise the correct way to find 'the answer'. In contrast, the learner-centred approach encourages a more problem-solving or facilitative approach where coaches improve performance by listening, questioning, challenging and reframing ideas without providing any concrete answers. Hui, Sue-Chan and Wood (2013) determined that in rote tasks coach-centred, or directive, coaching was sufficient, whereas in more challenging and dynamic environments the problem-solving or facilitative coaching approach produced the best results.

Much of this concluding chapter, and the primary focus of this book, has been to support sport coaches to make the correct decisions within a number of contexts, both practice and competition, to develop their coaching knowledge and practice. Sport coaches are generally motivated, hard-working and in many countries volunteers who support their own development through time, commitment and effort.

Sport coaches need to experience coaching by reflecting on their experiences and constructing their own understanding and knowledge of both the coaching process and coaching practice. To accomplish this they must be encouraged to ask questions and explore and evaluate what they know. This necessitates the use of active techniques, for example, authentic problem solving and experimentation, to create further knowledge and then to reflect on and discuss what they are doing and how their understanding is changing – a process that is both an iterative and lifelong.

## REFERENCES

Christensen, M. (2014). Exploring biographical learning in elite soccer coaching. *Sport, Education and Society* 19(2): pp. 204–222.

Collins, D. and MacNamara, Á. (2012). The rocky road to the top. *Sports Medicine* 42(11): pp. 907–914.

Csikszentmihályi, M. (1991). *Flow: The psychology of optimal experience.* (New York: Harper Perennial).

Elberse, A. and Ferguson, A. (2013). Ferguson's formula. *Harvard Business Review* 91(10): pp. 116–125.

Ericsson, K. A., Krampe, R. T. and Tesch-Römer, C. (1993). The role of deliberate practice in the development of expertise. *Psychology Review* 100: pp. 363–406.

Gilbert, W., Côté, J. and Mallett, C. (2006). Developmental paths and activities of successful sport coaches. *International Journal of Sports Science and Coaching* 1(1): 69–76.

Gilbert, W. and Trudel, P. (2004). Analysis of coaching science research published from 1970–2001. *Research Quarterly for Exercise and Sport* 75: pp. 388–399.

Gilbert, W. and Trudel, P. (2012). The role of deliberate practice in becoming an expert coach: Part 1 – defining coaching expertise. *Olympic Coach* 23(3): pp. 19–27.

Gilbert, W. and Trudel, P. (2013). The role of deliberate practice in becoming an expert coach: Part 2 – reflection. *Olympic Coach* 24(1): pp. 35–44.

Griffiths, M. and Armour, K. (2013). Volunteer coaches and their learning dispositions in coach education. *International Journal of Sports Science and Coaching* 8(4): pp. 677–688.

Hoffman, R. R., Ward, P., Feltovich, P. J., DiBello, L., Fiore, S. M. and Andrews, D. H. (2014). *Accelerated expertise: Training for high proficiency in a complex world*. (London: Psychology Press, Taylor and Francis Group).

Hui, R., Sue-Chan, C. and Wood, R. (2013). The contrasting effects of coaching style on task performance: The mediating roles of subjective task complexity and self-set goal. *Human Resource Development Quarterly* 24(4): pp. 429–458.

Ilies, R., Morgeson, F. P. and Nahrgang, J. D. (2005). Authentic leadership and eudaemonic well-being: Understanding leader–follower outcomes. *The Leadership Quarterly* 16(3): pp. 373–394.

Jones, R. (2007). Coaching redefined: An everyday pedagogical endeavour. *Sport Education and Society* 12(2): pp. 159–173.

Jones, R. L., Armour, K. M. and Potrac, P. (2004). *Sports coaching cultures*. (London: Routledge).

Kahneman, D. and Klein, G. (2009). Conditions for intuitive expertise: A failure to disagree. *The American Psychologist* 6: p. 515.

MacNamara, Á. and Collins, D. (2009). More than the 'X' factor! A longitudinal investigation of the psychological characteristics of developing excellence in musical development. *Music Education Research* 11(3): pp. 377–392.

MacNamara, Á. and Collins, D. (2010). The role of psychological characteristics in managing the transition to university. *Psychology of Sport and Exercise* 11(5): pp. 353–362.

Martindale, R. and Nash, C. (2013). Sport science relevance and application: Perceptions of UK coaches. *Journal of Sports Sciences* 31(8): pp. 807–819.

Nash, C. and Collins, D. (2006). Tacit knowledge in expert coaching: Science or art? *Quest* 58: 464–476.

Nash, C., Martindale, R., Collins, D. and Martindale, A. (2012). Parameterising expertise in coaching: Past, present and future. *Journal of Sports Sciences* 30(10): pp. 985–994.

O'Boyle, I. (2014). Determining best practice in performance monitoring and evaluation of sport coaches: Lessons from the traditional business environment. *International Journal of Sports Science and Coaching* 9(1): pp. 233–246.

Rendell, M., Farrow, D., Masters, R. and Plummer, N. (2011). Implicit practice for technique adaptation in expert performers. *International Journal of Sports Science and Coaching* 6(4): pp. 553–566.

Rutt Leas, R. and Chi, M.T.H. (1993). Analyzing diagnostic expertise of competitive swimming coaches. In *Cognitive Issues in Motor Expertise*. J. L. Starkes and F. Allard (Eds.) (Amsterdam: Elsevier Science Publishers B.V.): pp. 75–94.

Saury, J. and Durand, M. (1998). Practical knowledge in expert coaches: On-site study of coaching in sailing. *Research Quarterly for Exercise and Sport* 69(3): pp. 254–266.

Schinke, R. J., Bloom, G. and Salmela, J. H. (1995). The career stages of elite Canadian basketball coaches. *Avante* 1(1): pp. 48–62.

Sheikh, S. A. (2008). Use of new knowledge and knowledge management to gain competitive advantage. *Communications of the IBIMA* 1(4): pp. 34–41.

Starkes, J. L. and Ericsson, K. A. (2003). (Eds.) *Expert performance in sport: Advances in research on sport expertise*. (Champaign, IL: Human Kinetics).

Sternberg, R. J. and Lubart, T. I. (1999). The concept of creativity: Prospects and paradigms. In *Handbook of Creativity*. R. J. Sternberg (Ed.) (New York: Cambridge University Press): pp. 3–15.

Surujlal, J. and Mafini, C. (2012). Coaches' perceptions of the management of professional sport coaches in South Africa. *African Journal for Physical, Health Education, Recreation and Dance* 18(1): pp. 122–138.

Thomson, B. (2012). *The coaching dance: A tale of coaching and management.* (Winchester: Docuracy Ltd.).

Trudel, P. and Gilbert, W. (2013). The role of deliberate practice in becoming an expert coach: Part 3 – creating optimal settings. *Olympic Coach* 24(2): pp. 15–28.

Vygotsky, L.S. (1978). *Mind in society: The development of the higher psychological processes.* (Cambridge, MA: MIT Press).

Weiss, M. (2003). *Developmental sport and exercise psychology: A lifespan perspective.* (Morgantown: Fitness Information Technology).

Williams, A. M. and Hodges, N. J. (2005). Practice, instruction, and skill acquisition in soccer: Challenging tradition. *Journal of Sports Sciences* 23: pp. 637–650.

Williams, S.J. and Kendall, L. (2007). Perceptions of elite coaches and sports scientists of the research needs for elite coaching practice. *Journal of Sports Sciences* 25(14): pp. 1577–1586.

Wooden, J. and Carty, J. (2005). *Coach Wooden's pyramid of success: Building blocks for a better life.* (Ventura, California: Regal Books).

Wu, C., Lee, C. and Tsai, L. (2012). Influence of creativity and knowledge sharing on performance. *Journal of Technology Management in China* 7(1): pp. 64–77.

# Index

Note: Page numbers in *italics* indicate boxes, figures, tables and templates.

# Index

Carson, F. 261

CCoP (coaches community of practice) 251–3; *see also* communities of practice

central net and wall games 152

*Ceteris paribus* 56

cheating 61–2

Chelladurai, P. 210–11, *212*

coach behaviours in talent development 143–4, *144–5*

coach-centred approach to coaching 162–3, 316–17

coach developers: defined xxvi; mediated and unmediated education and xxvii; as mentors 210; role of xxviii

coach development 314–17; *see also* coach developers; coach education; communities of practice; emotional intelligence; mentoring; reflective practice; tactical knowledge

coach education: in creativity and innovation 187; in critical thinking skills 183–4; in decision making 184–5; in linking critical thinking and decision making 185–6; operationalisation of 177–8; *see also* coach education courses/programmes

coach education courses/programmes: categories of 178; coaching philosophy and 58; dogma 4–7; emotional intelligence and 200–1; knowledge development and 151; limitations of 179; mentoring and 217–18; online learning 271–3; reasons for participation in *180*; subject matter for 178–9; views of 179–80, 181

coach educators, role of 181–3

coaches: gender of 4; key to success of 9–10; learning of 179–81; levels of 12–14; minorities as 13; personal qualities of 8; role of 3–7, 10–12, *232*, 311, 312–13; skills of 8, 259; values of 55, 59, 60–1; as volunteers 3, 271; *see also* coach development; coach education; coaching expertise; coaching philosophy; feedback from coach

coaches community of practice (CCoP) 251–3; *see also* communities of practice (CoPs)

coaching *see* sport coaching

Coaching Association of Canada 69, 181, 218

coaching effectiveness, defined 180–1

coaching expertise: characteristics of 148–9, 313–14; defined xxv; development of xxvii–xxviii, 314–17

coaching philosophy: cheating, Olympism, humanism, and 61–3; development of 57–8, 65–6; espoused theory and theory-in-use 65–6; overview of 54–6; practice and 58–61; professional development and 56–7; reflective practice and *231, 232*; stories as 63–4; talent development and 137–8

coaching schematic 229–30

coaching style 58–9, *316*, 316–17

coach system in talent development 143–4, *144–5*

CoachViz *265*, 265–6

Cohen, Martin 55

Collins, D. 20–1, 25, 26, 31, 314

commitment: context specific nature of 139; to practice 104–8

communication: competition and 79; geotechnology and 293, 305

communities of practice (CoPs): case study of 247–53; development of 244–5, *245*; organisations and 245–7; overview of 242–3

competence model 210, *211*

competency theory of emotional intelligence 195

competition: context of 71–2; debriefing and revisions 81; decision making 82–3; at event 79–80; planning for 39–40; in practice 82; preparation for 72–6, *74*; role of 19; using last weeks before 76–9

competition phase 18

conditioned games 99, 165–6

constructive alignment 21–4, *22, 23*, 42

constructivism 150, 169

context of coaching 7, 14

**322**

Lightning Source UK Ltd.
Milton Keynes UK
UKHW032159161020
371545UK00019B/368